To Mark,
with gratitude
and thanks for your
mentorship and support.

May Ky

Voluntary Regulation of NGOs and Nonprofits

How can nonprofit organizations and NGOs demonstrate accountability to stakeholders and show that they are using funds appropriately and delivering on their promises? Many nonprofit stakeholders, including funders and regulators, have few opportunities to observe nonprofit internal management and policies. Such information deficits make it difficult for "principals" to differentiate credible nonprofits from less credible ones. This volume examines a key instrument employed by nonprofits to respond to these challenges: voluntary accountability clubs. These clubs are voluntary, rule-based governance systems created and sponsored by nongovernmental actors. By participating in accountability clubs, nonprofits agree to abide by certain rules regarding internal governance in order to send a signal of quality to key principals. Nonprofit voluntary programs are relatively new but are spreading rapidly across the globe. This book investigates how the emergence, design, and success of such initiatives vary across a range of sectors and institutional contexts in the United States, the Netherlands, Africa, and Central Europe.

MARY KAY GUGERTY is Associate Professor in the Daniel J. Evans School of Public Affairs at the University of Washington, Seattle.

ASEEM PRAKASH is Professor of Political Science and the Walker Family Professor for the Arts and Sciences at the University of Washington, Seattle.

Voluntary Regulation of NGOs and Nonprofits

An Accountability Club Framework

Edited by

Mary Kay Gugerty

and

Aseem Prakash

CAMBRIDGE UNIVERSITY PRESS

CAMBRIDGE UNIVERSITY PRESS
Cambridge, New York, Melbourne, Madrid, Cape Town, Singapore,
São Paulo, Delhi, Dubai, Tokyo, Mexico City

Cambridge University Press
The Edinburgh Building, Cambridge CB2 8RU, UK

Published in the United States of America by Cambridge University Press,
New York

www.cambridge.org
Information on this title: www.cambridge.org/9780521763141

First published 2010

Printed in the United Kingdom at the University Press, Cambridge

A catalogue record for this publication is available from the British Library

ISBN 978-0-521-76314-1 Hardback

For Dan and Aidan
M. K. G.

For Nives and Alexander
A. P.

Contents

Figures

Tables

Contributors

RENÉ BEKKERS is Associate Professor and Head of Research at the Department of Philanthropic Studies at the Vrije Universiteit Amsterdam. He received his PhD in 2004 with a dissertation on giving and volunteering in the Netherlands, which was awarded the Gabriel Rudney memorial award by the Association for Research on Nonprofit Organizations and Voluntary Action (ARNOVA) in November 2005. Bekkers has been a co-designer of the Giving in the Netherlands Panel Survey since 2001. In his current research, funded by a grant from the Netherlands Organization for Scientific Research (NWO), he is studying the impact of education on giving and volunteering.

ANGELA BIES is Assistant Professor at the Bush School of Government at Texas A&M University. Her research interests include nonprofit accountability, capacity-building, and evaluation. Her current research focuses on a national accountability reform in Poland's nongovernmental sector, as well as a comparative study of nonprofit capacity-building in Pennsylvania, Minnesota, and Texas. She served as lead qualitative analyst on a longitudinal study concerned with accountability and US secondary school reform, sponsored by the National Science Foundation. She is a former nonprofit executive and served in several public service settings including the US Peace Corps, the United Way of the Greater Minneapolis Area Council of Agency Executives, the National Endowment for the Arts, the Council on Standards for International Education and Travel, and the National Charities Information Bureau/ Rockefeller Brothers Fund national panel on nonprofit accountability.

WOODS BOWMAN is Professor of Public Services Management at DePaul University. Before joining the DePaul faculty he served as Chief Financial Officer of Cook County, 1990–1994 and interim Executive Director of Goodwill Industries of Metropolitan Chicago, 1995. He edits ARNOVA Abstracts and writes the Nonprofit Ethicist column for the *Nonprofit Quarterly*.

DANA BRAKMAN REISER is Professor of Law at the Brooklyn Law School. An expert in the emerging field of the law of nonprofit organizations, she has been at the forefront of research in this area. Her writing focuses on two distinct, but related concerns in nonprofit law: nonprofit accountability and governance, and the role of members and other nonfiduciary constituencies in nonprofit organizations. She is a member of the Government Relations Committee of the Nonprofit Coordinating Committee of New York. Before joining the faculty, Professor Brakman Reiser was a Legal Fellow in the Office of the General Counsel of Partners HealthCare System, Inc. and served as a Law Clerk to Judge Bruce Selya of the United States Court of Appeals for the First Circuit. She also was a Note Editor of the *Harvard Law Review*.

PETER FRUMKIN is Professor of Public Affairs and Director of the RGK Center for Philanthropy and Community Service at the Lyndon B. Johnson School of Public Affairs at the University of Texas at Austin. He is the author of *On Being Nonprofit: A Conceptual and Policy Primer* (2002) and *Strategic Giving: The Art and Science of Philanthropy* (2006), and co-editor (with Jonathan Imber) of *In Search of the Nonprofit Sector* (2004), and he has written articles on topics related to nonprofit management, philanthropy, cross-sector partnerships, and service contracting. Prior to coming to the LBJ School in 2005, he was an Associate Professor of Public Policy at Harvard University's John F. Kennedy School of Government, where he was affiliated with the Hauser Center for Nonprofit Organizations. Professor Frumkin has also been a Senior Fellow of the New America Foundation, and has worked as a foundation program officer, a nonprofit manager, and program evaluator for both nonprofit and public agencies.

MARY KAY GUGERTY is Associate Professor at the Daniel J. Evans School of Public Affairs at the University of Washington, Seattle. Her research interests focus on the emergence and design of collective action institutions among individuals and organizations, particularly in developing countries. Her research has been published in the *American Journal of Political Science, Economic Development and Cultural Change, Journal of Public Economics*, and *Public Administration and Development*, among others. She currently serves as the program director of African Studies at the University of Washington and on the editorial board of the *Journal of Public Administration Research and Theory*. Professor Gugerty earned her PhD in Political Economy and Government at Harvard University and holds a Masters in Public Administration from the John F. Kennedy School of Government at Harvard.

ANDREAS ORTMANN is Professor of Economics at the Australian School of Business at the University of New South Wales. He is also a visiting professor at CIFREM (Interdepartmental Center for Research Training in Economics and Management), University of Trento, Italy. In 2006–2007 he was a visiting scholar at Harvard Business School in Cambridge, MA. He has published in *Journal of Economic Theory*, *International Journal of Game Theory*, *Journal of Economic Behavior and Organization*, *Economics Letters*, *Behavioral and Brain Sciences*, *Experimental Economics*, *History of Political Economy*, and *Rationality & Society*. He is interested in the origin and emergence of languages, moral sentiments, and other conventions, as well as experimental methodology.

ASEEM PRAKASH is Professor of Political Science and the Walker Family Professor for the Arts and Sciences at the University of Washington, Seattle. He is the founding, General Editor of the Cambridge University Press Series on Business and Public Policy and the co-editor of *Journal of Policy Analysis and Management*. He is the author of *Greening the Firm: The Politics of Corporate Environmentalism* (2000), co-author (with Matthew Potoski) of *The Voluntary Environmentalists: Green Clubs, ISO 14001, and Voluntary Environmental Regulations* (2006), co-editor (with Matthew Potoski) of *Voluntary Programs: A Club Theory Perspective* (2009), and co-editor (with Jeffrey Hart) of *Globalization and Governance* (1999), *Coping with Globalization* (2000), and *Responding to Globalization* (2000).

KATARINA SVÍTKOVÁ is Dean of the School of Business Administration at the Anglo-American University in the Czech Republic. She is an Affiliate Researcher at the Center for Economic Research and Graduate Education–Economic Institute (CERGE-EI) of Charles University and the Academy of Sciences of the Czech Republic. She holds a PhD in Economics from CERGE-EI. Her research focuses on issues of nonprofit certification, philanthropy in transition economies, and the development of pension and social welfare systems.

MARY TSCHIRHART is Professor and Director of the Institute for Nonprofits at North Carolina State University and Professor of Public Administration. Before arriving at NC State, she was a faculty member at Syracuse University's Maxwell School and Indiana University's School of Public and Environmental Affairs. She earned a doctorate in organizational behavior and human resource management from the University of Michigan. Professor Tschirhart serves on the board of the Association for Research on Nonprofit Organizations and Voluntary

Action (ARNOVA), as the Vice President for North America of the International Research Society for Public Management, and as Chair of the Nonprofit Management Education Section of the National Association of Schools of Public Affairs and Administration. She is the past Division Chair of the Public and Nonprofit Division of the Academy of Management.

DENNIS R. YOUNG is Bernard B. and Eugenia A. Ramsey Professor of Private Enterprise in the Andrew Young School of Policy Studies, Georgia State University, and serves as the Director of the Nonprofit Studies Program and Professor of Public Administration and Urban Studies (Joint with Economics). He is also President and founding CEO of the National Center on Nonprofit Enterprise and has written many articles and several books, including *The Music of Management: Applying Organizational Theory* (2004) and (with Richard Steinberg) *Economics for Nonprofit Managers* (1995). He is co-editor (with Dwight Burlingame) of *Corporate Philanthropy at the Crossroads* (1996). He is founding editor of the journal *Nonprofit Management & Leadership*, which he edited from 1990 through 2000, and was named in the *NonProfit Times* "Power and Influence Top 50" list. A former President of the Association for Research on Nonprofit Organizations and Voluntary Action (ARNOVA), Dr. Young recently received this organization's Award for Distinguished Achievement and Leadership in Nonprofit and Voluntary Action Research.

MARYAM ZARNEGAR DELOFFRE is a PhD candidate in political science at George Washington University in Washington, DC. Her dissertation examines the emergence and design of NGO accountability institutions in the humanitarian and development sector. Her research interests include the evolution of humanitarianism, the agenda-setting of humanitarian NGOs, and the policy effects of NGO accountability. She is recipient of the Association for Research on Nonprofit Organizations and Voluntary Action (ARNOVA) Emerging Scholar Award and the Columbian College of Arts and Sciences Graduate Student Research Grant among others. She holds an MA in international organization from the Institut d'Etudes Politiques de Paris-Sciences Po and a BA in political science and French from the University of Illinois Urbana-Champaign.

Preface

The growth in the scale and scope of the nonprofit sector has been accompanied by numerous accountability challenges. Nonprofits have responded to these demands for increased accountability in a variety of ways. This volume focuses on a key accountability instrument employed by nonprofits: voluntary programs or codes, or voluntary clubs as we term them. Voluntary clubs seek to create institutional incentives for participating actors to adopt specific codes of conduct and practices beyond what is legally required of them. If accountability issues can be viewed as "agency problems," voluntary clubs provide an opportunity for nonprofits (as agents) to signal to their resource providers and authorizers (as principals) that they are governing as agreed and delivering as promised. By virtue of their membership in such accountability clubs, nonprofits expect that the resource providers will reward them with more resources and less onerous governance costs.

Voluntary clubs are complex institutional structures. To explore their institutional design issues, we draw on the club approach which is well established in political economy. We bring in the principal–agent perspective to explore agents' motivations for establishing and joining voluntary clubs, and the principals' responses to them. The empirical chapters explore three core themes: (1) the emergence of voluntary accountability clubs, (2) club sponsorship, and (3) club design and effectiveness.

This volume makes two key contributions. Theoretically, it outlines an accessible yet robust framework for studying voluntary programs in the nonprofit sector. The book expands on club theory to account for variations in the emergence, recruitment, and efficacy of voluntary programs. Empirically, this book provides careful application of the club perspective across a range of voluntary programs and contexts. These programs vary by sector type, sponsor type, and target participant type. This is the first book we know of that examines a wide range of voluntary programs in the nonprofit sector by employing a single theoretical perspective.

We began working on this project in the summer of 2007. We developed an introductory concept chapter and carefully identified scholars doing interesting work on nonprofit accountability. Thanks to generous financial support from the Office of the Dean, Daniel J. Evans School of Public Affairs and the Marc Lindenberg Center, both at the University of Washington, we organized a workshop for the authors at University of Washington in April 2008. At this workshop, the contributors presented the first drafts of their chapters. They received valuable feedback from one another and from University of Washington graduate students and faculty who served as discussants. After the workshop, we provided detailed feedback on every chapter; our feedback also reflected the comments offered by Cambridge University Press reviewers. The chapters were revised in summer 2008 and again in spring 2009. The result is a series of very strong, coherent chapters that respond to the theoretical framework outlined in the introductory chapter. Our theoretical framework also draws on our article "Trust but Verify? Voluntary Regulation Programs in the Nonprofit Sector" published in *Regulation and Goverance* 4(1) (2010): 22–47.

This project has received valuable support, input, and feedback from the following individuals: Leigh Anderson, Sandra Archibald, Sara Curran, Stephan Hamberg, Christopher Heurlin, Sanjeev Khagram, Andrea Lairson, Stephen Page, and Christi Siver. Our sincere gratitude goes to John Haslam, the Commissioning Editor, for his support and encouragement. Most of all, we want to thank our families, who supported us and tolerated the long hours we put in to bring this project to fruition. We dedicate this volume to them.

The club framework

1 Voluntary regulation of NGOs and nonprofits: an introduction to the club framework

Mary Kay Gugerty and Aseem Prakash

The global nonprofit and nongovernmental (NGO) sector has expanded substantially during the past two decades.[1] As a result of this "global associational revolution" – marked by massive infusion of funds from governments, international organizations, foundations, and individuals – the nonprofit sector became a major component of the social service delivery system in most countries (Salamon *et al.*, 2003; Salamon, 1994). This growth also thrust nonprofits and NGOs into the middle of contemporary policy debates over the appropriate role for governments and markets in the provision of public services (Giddens, 1998; Anheier and Salamon, 2006). With this expansion, the nonprofit sector also became a target for increased scrutiny, in part because it appeared to attract "bad apples" along with well-intentioned, principled organizations. Scandals and charges of nonprofit mismanagement and misappropriation have been extensively covered by the media (Fremont-Smith and Kosaras, 2003; Gibelman and Gelman, 2004; Greenlee *et al.*, 2007).[2] As a result, nonprofits face growing demands for accountability from resource providers as well as from the constituents they claim to serve (Edward and Hulme, 1996; Spiro, 2002; Brody, 2002; Ebrahim, 2003).

While scandals tend to impose costs on the specific wrongdoers, they can muddy the reputation of all actors with similar sectoral scope or organizational characteristics. Indeed, high-profile cases of governance failure have tended to impose negative reputational externalities on all

---

[1] Since both nonprofit and nongovernmental organizations (NGOs) are subjected to the nondistribution constraint – they cannot distribute profits to their principals or owners – we use the term nonprofit for both types of organizations. This chapter draws on Prakash and Gugerty (2010).

[2] Nonprofits are also criticized for accentuating "democracy deficits" by providing public goods and advocating on behalf of constituents without publicly elected leadership, especially if they appear to be substituting for democratically elected governments. This volume does not examine this issue. We focus on voluntary programs which have emerged in this sector in response to perceived governance failures.

nonprofits. A recent global opinion survey found that in a number of countries worldwide, the nonprofit sector is now less trusted than government or business (Edelman Trust, 2007). Public scandals may undermine the credibility of nonprofits as a category of actors, thereby reducing the ability of credible nonprofits to raise funds and to function with a reasonable degree of autonomy. Scandals can also attract the interest of regulators, who come under increased pressure to "do something" about the problem. In the United States, corruption and governance scandals in the for-profit and nonprofit sectors led to increased Congressional scrutiny of the regulatory framework governing the nonprofit sector (Independent Sector, 2005, 2007). In many developing countries, rapid growth in the nonprofit sector combined with weak regulatory institutions have spurred government initiatives to increase regulatory authority over nonprofits, often with the intent of controlling or curtailing what is viewed as political activity (Gugerty, 2008). Thus, credible nonprofits – the good apples – can be expected to seek ways to differentiate themselves from the bad apples and credibly to signal their commitment towards good governance to their funders, authorizers, and supporters. This volume examines how voluntary accountability clubs might be employed, successfully as well as unsuccessfully, as institutional vehicles for this task.

We begin this volume with the premise that the accountability challenges nonprofits face can be viewed as agency problems between nonprofits and their stakeholders, or principals. Given the widespread perceptions of such agency conflicts, the challenge for "good" or "credible" nonprofits is to demonstrate to their resource providers and authorizers that they are governing as agreed and delivering as promised. Multiple principals, legal as well as constructed, make accountability claims on nonprofits and these claims may not always cohere, thereby accentuating agency problems (Mahon, 1993).[3] Thus, nonprofits need to decide which of these claims to address and through what mechanisms.

Scholars, policymakers, and nonprofits themselves have invested considerable effort in identifying appropriate and effective oversight and governance mechanisms to mitigate agency conflicts and make nonprofits more accountable. Potential policy options include increased government regulation (including more stringent operating and reporting requirements), self-regulation through industry associations, and the use of

---

[3] Agency relationships can be formal and legal. Here, the principals have legal course to shape the activities of their agents. In some other cases, a given set of actors may construct themselves as principals of some other actors. While such constructed principals might not be able to make legal claims on their agents, they may still be able to shape agents' behaviors by imposing costs and bestowing benefits.

private accreditation or certification mechanisms. This volume examines the role that voluntary programs, defined as rule-based systems created and sponsored by nongovernmental actors, can play in mitigating agency conflict and resolving agency dilemmas between nonprofits and their principals. We conceptualize these programs as "clubs," in the political economy sense of the term (Prakash and Potoski, 2006). While the club framework has been employed to study voluntary programs among for-profit firms (Potoski and Prakash, 2009b), this is the first book to apply the framework systematically in the context of the nonprofit sector. In doing so, we also extend the club perspective and build on previous studies of nonprofit voluntary programs (Gugerty, 2009) by bringing in agency theory to explore how principal–agent dynamics influence club emergence, design, participation, and efficacy.

Nonprofit accountability clubs are rule-based institutions that create standards for behavior, regulate membership, and enforce compliance among members. In some cases, they offer certification or formal accreditation. The number of these programs is on the rise (Bothwell, 2001; Sidel, 2003; Lloyd, 2005; Lloyd and de las Casas, 2005). According to One World Trust, more than three hundred nonprofit codes of conduct and standard-setting programs exist globally (Warren and Lloyd, 2009). Gugerty (2009) examines thirty-two programs in operation globally; Sidel (2003) documents seventeen programs in Asia alone. Voluntary programs can take a number of different forms including self-regulatory collectives, third-party accreditation programs, or industry association-sponsored programs. We argue that underlying this apparent institutional diversity is a set of common collective action challenges, and that these voluntary programs constitute a common institutional response to these challenges. Below we outline how a deductive, theoretical perspective derived from agency and club theory can add to the study of voluntary programs among nonprofits. Our objective is to develop a generalized approach that can help accumulate knowledge about nonprofit accountability programs across a range of settings.

Accountability and agency in nonprofit organizations

In this volume we argue that agency dilemmas are at the heart of challenges to nonprofit accountability. An agent is an actor who is expected to act on behalf of a principal (Mitnick, 1982). Agency conflicts arise when agents do not act according to the wishes of the principals. Instead, they act in response to their own preferences, which may not align with those of the principals (Berle and Means, 1932; Ross, 1973; Mitnick, 1982; Fama and Jensen, 1983; Moe, 1984; Wood, 1988; McCubbins *et al.*, 1989; Waterman and Meier, 1998; Shapiro, 2005). An agency view of accountability implies that some actors possess the right to hold other actors to a set of given standards, to judge their performance in meeting those standards, and to take action if standards are not met (Edwards and Hulme, 1996; Grant and Keohane, 2005). Thus accountability relationships involve three components: agreement or recognition of standards for behavior, information about actual behavior, and the ability to judge performance and hold actors to account (Rubenstein, 2007). We view accountability as a set of relationships and this differentiates our view from other definitions that focus on accountability as a process, as, for example, the process by which public agencies manage diverse stakeholder expectations (Romzek and Dubnick, 1987). This also makes accountability relationships, which are judged after the fact, distinct from the institutional structures or "checks and balances" that are designed to prevent malfeasance in the first place (Grant and Keohane, 2005). Of course, such institutional structures are a response to accountability relationships, and, in a dynamic setting, actors are likely to anticipate accountability demands and engage in institutional design to address the concerns of principals – indeed such behavior is the subject of this volume.

In the agency model of accountability, agents are empowered to undertake tasks on behalf of principals and are expected to fulfill the wishes of principals. These wishes can be specified through a specific contract or set of standards agreed upon between the agent and the principals or can be based on commonly accepted standards for professional behavior.[4]

Our perspective on accountability can be distinguished from several other approaches, including organizational ecology, resource dependence, stakeholder theories, and semiotic approaches. From an organizational ecology perspective, accountability is a narrative process. It is the way in which organizations account rationally for their actions: how they document their use of resources and construct logical sequences of decisions, rules, and actions – whether truthful or not (Hannan and Freeman, 1989). The demand for these "accounts" arises from norms of procedural rationality in which legitimacy (defined as the probability that external actors will endorse an organization's actions) depends on the appearance of

---

[4] Some strands of the accountability literature distinguish between delegation and trusteeship as distinct forms of accountability (Grant and Keohane, 2005) or highlight distinctions between hierarchical, electoral, legal, and professional forms of accountability (Romzek and Dubnick, 1987). We retain the focus on the core characteristics of all forms of accountability in our definition: standards, information, and sanctions. While specific accountability relationships such as trusteeship or electoral accountability may give rise to different institutional mechanisms for setting standards, delivering information, or undertaking sanctions, the need for each of the three mechanisms is common to all accountability relationships.

conformity to these norms. Accounts reassure investors and supporters that they are not wasting their time, effort, or resources. Since organizations are in a competition for survival, those organizations that can repeatedly produce credible accounts will be more likely to survive. From this perspective, the key attributes of accountability valued by principals are predictability and reliability.

Resource dependency approaches highlight the social control that resource-holding organizations can exert over others (Pfeffer and Salancik, 1978). When the resource is critical to the consuming organization and few substitutes are available, the resource-holding organization may be able to exert strong influence over the resource-consuming organization. Consequently, the consuming organization will be willing to spend a great deal of time and effort complying with the demands of the resource provider. Of course organizations that are dependent on a large number of external organizations may face conflicts in this regard. Resource dependency suggests that key resource providers will be important principals for any organization, but resource-based relationships comprise only one set of potential accountability demands. Stakeholder perspectives on for-profit firms (Freeman, 1984) expanded the list of potential principals who could make claims on an organization by extending beyond those principals who have ownership authority over an organization. Stakeholder approaches suggest that nonowner actors may construe themselves as principals of organizations (although they may make these claims with varying success; Mitchell *et al.*, 1997). When such actors have the ability to exert influence by withholding or granting legitimacy or reputation, organizations have every incentive to heed their claims. While both resource dependency and stakeholder approaches highlight the potential for multiple principal problems, neither approach privileges the role of information problems in creating the potential for agency abuse. This is the unique contribution of agency theory.

Finally, our agency perspective on accountability should be distinguished from semiotic approaches that view accountability as a symbol and a sign, a form of "political theater" that is pluralistic, constantly renegotiated, and not amenable to systematic definition (Ebrahim and Weisband, 2007). We find the theater analogy interesting, because to assess the complexity of accountability one needs to identify the key actors (who is accountable to whom, why, and through what mechanisms). While we favor clearly defining accountability in terms of standards, information, and sanctions, we recognize that accountability involves relationships of power. As a result, accountability is not normatively "good" in and of itself, that is, more "accountability" (or more rules and procedures) is not necessarily better for all actors. Indeed, as we point out later in this introductory chapter, an important motivation for the emergence of accountability clubs is the desire to preempt more intrusive demands from resource providers for information on how nonprofits are deploying resources.

The advantage of an agency perspective as a starting point for thinking about accountability lies in the parsimonious framing of the relationships among nonprofits and those that entrust them with authority and resources. Accountability is a contested concept and nonprofits, like other organizations, are often engaged in strategic efforts to manage their accountability relationships with others (Kearns, 1994). Indeed, we argue that participation in accountability clubs is a strategy on the part of nonprofits to manage, and even shape, their accountability relationships. We conceptualize nonprofits as agents charged with undertaking specific activities on behalf of various principals, particularly donors and governments. Agency dilemmas among nonprofits, as with other kinds of actors, may arise when the preferences of nonprofits (more specifically, preferences of the key individuals who manage them) diverge from those of donors or other principals, when the preferences of principals are not clearly defined, or when the preferences of multiple principals are in conflict.

Preference substitution is perhaps the most common agency dilemma among nonprofits. Governments are increasingly charging nonprofits to provide a variety of public services, but many governments possess very weak regulatory and oversight mechanisms with which to ensure that their mandates are fulfilled. Private donors often provide funding to nonprofits to undertake specific activities in areas such as education, public health, environment, women's empowerment, and economic development. While they expect nonprofits to spend these resources judiciously and effectively to deliver services to the target populations, they often do not have the capacities to monitor nonprofits' operations adequately. Citizens provide resources to advocacy nonprofits with the expectation that they will effectively advocate issues which the citizens care about. Again, they do not have the resources or the willingness to monitor how their funds have been spent. In sum, inadequate monitoring creates opportunities for nonprofits to engage in preference substitution. Nonprofits may also engage in preference substitution when the goals of various principals conflict, a point we return to below.

Principals may be inclined to provide resources to nonprofits to undertake desired services for two reasons. First, principals may favor the pursuit of specific objectives (often the amelioration of specific government and market failures) but may not have the competencies to undertake this activity themselves. They recognize that with their field-level knowledge, nonprofits are better positioned to serve such objectives. Second, in relation to for-profit firms and governments, principals may view non-profits as more "trustworthy" actors, where trust is understood as the belief that agents will undertake activities as promised and will not engage in deliberate strategic behavior that undermines the interests of principals. The literature suggests that nonprofits may be viewed as trustworthy because they are constrained from distributing profits to owners – the assumption being that the generation and appropriation of profits makes actors do "bad things" such as cutting back on quality in order to increase profits (Hansmann, 1980; Rose-Ackerman, 1996). Thus, nonprofits are deemed trustworthy not necessarily because of what they do but because of their institutional design. The absence of the profit motive may be particularly important when organizations produce "credence" goods whose quality is difficult to observe even after purchasing. Of course, governments do not generate or distribute profits and yet trust in governments is highly variable across countries. Indeed, the literature recognizes that trust may not be a sufficiently robust basis for contracting (Ortmann and Schlesinger, 2003), particularly when principals – such as institutional donors and governments – are themselves accountable to others for demonstrating results. Moreover, the nondistribution constraint will tend to constrain only one form of opportunism: strategic behavior designed to increase profits (Ben-Ner and Gui, 2003). Other forms of opportunism may remain. Even in the absence of outright fraud, nonprofits may suffer from "goal displacement" or "mission drift" in which nonprofits operate according to the preferences of managers and boards (themselves unelected), while disregarding the preferences of funders, beneficiaries, or government authorizers (Steinberg and Gray, 1993; Ortmann and Schlesinger, 2003).

Agency concerns are not only the purview of principals – strategic preference substitution on the part of some nonprofits may harm other organizations operating in the same sector as well. As in any other category of collective actors, there are "good" and "bad" nonprofits. There is no evidence to believe *ex ante* that the nonprofit sector is more (or less) prone to agency failure than the public or commercial sectors. However, if there is a nontrivial percentage of "bad apples" (which could mean corrupt or merely ineffective organizations) in the pool of nonprofits, principals have an incentive to identify these bad apples to avoid supplying them with resources. If principals are unable to distinguish between "good" and "bad" nonprofits, they may begin to view all nonprofits with more caution, perhaps even suspicion. In extreme cases, they may become wary of providing any resources lest they fall into the wrong hands. The inability to differentiate nonprofits may depress the overall volume of resources principals are willing to provide to nonprofits, an issue that is extremely worrisome in the current economic climate. Some studies suggest that in the United States, the cost of this reduction in resources may be as much as $100 billion a year (Bradley *et al.*, 2003). Many nonprofits, including the good ones, may be forced to exit the market, or curtail the scale or scope of their activities, a situation that neither the principals nor the nonprofits desire. These dynamics are analogous to the market for lemons described by Akerlof (1970). When there are information asymmetries between the buyer (principal) and the seller (nonprofit), and heterogeneity in quality of the seller, bad sellers can eventually drive good sellers out of the market.

But even if every nonprofit is "good" and seeks to follow principals' preferences, goal conflict among multiple principals can give rise to similar agency dilemmas. Governments may care more about equity in the provision of nonprofit services, while institutional donors may care more about responsiveness to their particular constituency (Smith and Lipsky, 1993). When each principal has a distinct contract with the nonprofit, these contracts may differ substantially in their goals. Nonprofits might not be in a position to order these competing demands. In response, they may seek to adequately satisfy several constituencies. When principals are unable to observe whether nonprofits are adequately addressing their concerns, however, they may again be reluctant to provide resources.

Thus the presence of information asymmetries and multiple principals in the nonprofit sector may result in increased inefficiencies, as a result of agency costs or agency slippages. To combat information deficits, principals may stipulate extensive reporting requirements and oversight mechanisms. Furthermore, principals may begin to make only small, short-term grants to nonprofits as opposed to larger, long-term ones.[5] Given the difficulties in observing nonprofit quality, principals are likely to create reporting requirements that are appropriate for the "average" nonprofit. Consequently, the good nonprofits are likely to be overregulated while the bad ones are likely to be underregulated. Adverse selection problems may follow. If the heterogeneity among nonprofits is substantial, bad nonprofits might even drive good nonprofits out of the funding market. Even if this dire prediction does not come true, agents will be forced to devote an increasing share of their resources to governance and oversight rather than to program implementation. Particularly good nonprofits that attract funding

---

[5] Another option might be for principals to establish ongoing, collaborative oversight and reporting arrangements with funded organizations; this is the "venture philanthropy" model. Such relationships may help mitigate agency conflicts, but given that the number of such relationships that any one principal can undertake will be limited, it may still have the effect of depressing the overall amount of funding available to nonprofits.

from multiple sources may find themselves facing especially high administrative costs; many nonprofits argue that multiple reporting requirements
consume a great deal of organizational time and energy (Ebrahim, 2005).
Short-term funding may lead nonprofits to prioritize short-term projects,
where benefits can be demonstrated more quickly, over long-term projects,
which might have a greater impact but only in the long run (Henderson,
2002). In sum, in response to agency conflicts rooted in information
asymmetries, principals may reduce the supply of resources to nonprofits
or increase governance costs that constrain nonprofits' effectiveness.

The anticipation of "market failure" in the philanthropy market gives
"good" nonprofits the incentive to address accountability concerns proactively. Nonprofits may voluntarily establish (or join) mechanisms that
supply informational signals about their internal governance and activities
to their principals, along with providing assurances that nonprofits are
making serious efforts to conform to the objectives set by the principals.
By doing so, nonprofits hope to obtain an ongoing or increased supply of
donor funds, greater operational freedom, and decreased governance costs.
Further, their proactive voluntary regulation might dampen the demand for
new laws that restrict their activities in even less desirable ways. The next
section examines the agency dilemma faced by nonprofits and their principals in more detail and suggests some ways in which voluntary accountability programs among nonprofits may address these dilemmas.

Agency dilemmas among firms and public bureaucracies

Principal–agent theory derives originally from theories of the firm in
which principals wish to contract with agents to carry out specific tasks
(Alchian and Demsetz, 1972; Holmstrom, 1982). Problems can arise
because principals can observe only outcomes and not the full effort of
agents. If unanticipated or unwanted outcomes are observed, principals
may have difficulty distinguishing the extent to which bad luck or malfeasance contributed to the outcome. To overcome these obstacles, principals can attempt to write detailed contracts, but contracts typically cannot
cover all contingencies. Principals can engage in costly monitoring, but
will likely always face some agency losses because of asymmetric information. Principals may therefore attempt to minimize these losses using
additional mechanisms, including screening and selection of agents
prior to contracting or institutional design that includes built-in checks
and balances (Kiewert and McCubbins, 1991).

Among firms, shareholders, as providers of capital, are the principals
who attempt to exercise control over the agents (managers) through the
board of directors. While the firm is accountable to several "stakeholders"

(Freeman, 1984), in the final analysis, shareholders are the ultimate principals because they have the claim over the residual. Because agency conflict leads to a reduction in the residual, shareholders have incentives to monitor agents. The firm, therefore, devises mechanisms (with varying levels of success) to align agents' preferences with those of the principals, with the objective of maximizing the production of the residual. The most common strategy is contract design: agent compensation is tied to performance.

Where agents are unable to refuse a contract and face multiple competing principals, however, agency dilemmas can be conceptualized as a problem of delegation, analogous to the dilemmas faced by the US Congress and the President, both of whom wish to control the actions of bureaucrats. Public agencies cannot refuse to contract with Congress but may exercise substantial autonomy in the implementation of policy. In this case the competing principals tend to focus on monitoring, procedural controls, and the development of institutional checks and balances to reduce agency costs and exert influence over agents (Miller, 2005). Monitoring may take two forms. Principals can engage in expensive *ex post* monitoring and hearings, or "police patrols," or they can rely on lower-cost "fire alarms" – complaints from constituents when they are not receiving what they want from bureaucrats (McCubbins and Schwartz, 1984). Another option is to focus on procedural rules and the professionalization of agency staff with the goal of making the procedural aspect of bureaucratic action more transparent and predictable to all sets of principals (Moe, 1984). The focus is on legitimacy of procedures, rather than control of outcomes (Miller, 2005).[6] Alternatively, principals can rely on institutional design, agreeing to a set of checks and balances in the bureaucratic process that ensure that no one principal can gain undue influence over outcomes. Thus, in the context of public organizations, agency dilemmas often give rise to procedural mechanisms of control, rather than to more expensive monitoring mechanisms.

Agency dilemmas among nonprofits

We have noted how governance among private firms in market economies tends to rely on contract design between shareholder-owners and manager-agents to address problems of hidden information and hidden action. The effectiveness of contract design is supported by the institutional environment of the market. Share value is publicly available

---

[6] In the US context, this focus on procedures assumes the existence of interest groups with an interest in monitoring the activities of bureaucrats and a court system that can enforce procedural mandates (Miller, 2005).

information. In an ideal world, unhappy shareholders have mechanisms through which they can discipline managers. They can use "exit" (divestiture) as well as "voice" (voting out the board) (Hirschman, 1970) to signal their appreciation or displeasure regarding agency issues. Contract design is not perfect, of course: shareholders are collective actors who face collective action dilemmas in monitoring managers, and managers can game the system by artificially inflating share value and then selling their options (Gourevitch and Shinn, 2005). Market institutions provide additional control. An active market for corporate control provides another venue for "discipline" (Manne, 1965). Third-party "reputational intermediaries" that include stock analysts, investment banks, and bond-rating agencies provide outside information on the performance of managers.[7]

Nonprofits, on the other hand, do not have shareholders. They do not have a well-defined primary principal with claim to the residual and, therefore, with incentives to monitor and restrain agency conflict. Furthermore, nonprofits cannot distribute the residual even if they were to generate it (Hansmann, 1980). Unlike firms which seek to maximize the residual, nonprofits commonly pursue multiple goals, a condition which accentuates their agency problems since the claims of their various principals are not ordered in any clear or consistent way (Johnson and Prakash, 2007). The external institutional environment does not help nonprofits to mitigate agency issues either. For one, nonprofits are not embedded in institutions (such as the stock market) where standardized evaluations of performance help to assess agent behavior (Spar and Dail, 2002). Instead, nonprofits face multiple, sometimes conflicting, claims of accountability from a variety of actors (boards, donors, host governments, and members), each wanting nonprofits to be assessed in their own particular institutional setting and with their own preferences as benchmarks.

In this way, nonprofits are analytically similar to public bureaucracies, in that they are collective agents that face demands from multiple principals exerting varying amounts of influence and control. Unlike public agencies, however, nonprofit principals are rarely "warring" over alternative outcomes (Moe, 1984). Congress (and political parties), the President, and bureaucrats are all relatively well informed of each other's identity and interests, while nonprofit principals may not even be aware of one another's identity. Nor are principals typically concerned with controlling the overall agenda of the nonprofit. Rather, each principal has an

---

[7] Needless to say, the current economic problems suggest that stock markets are vulnerable to manipulation. Corporate boards may collude with managers instead of serving as watchdogs on behalf of shareholders. Further, the quality of information on which market actors act tends to be variable.

interest in ensuring that its own particular preferences are addressed. But nonprofit principals, unlike Congress and the President, cannot rely on judicial enforcement of procedural requirements; they cannot institute a set of institutional checks and balances nor can they rely on groups with vested interests to monitor the activity of nonprofits. Nonprofit beneficiaries can seldom vote with their dollars as can customers and shareholders, and often cannot exercise voice, as can Congressional constituents. This raises additional accountability concerns for nonprofits because their beneficiaries cannot signal their pleasure or displeasure in obvious ways.

This analysis suggests that agency dilemmas in nonprofits, while analogous to those in the public and private for-profit sectors, will exhibit substantial differences. Given the context of multiple principals with individualized agendas, weak institutionalization of public information and reporting requirements, and the lack of a constituency with either purchasing or voting power, nonprofits and their principals have every incentive to develop mechanisms for reducing agency losses. But in the context of multiple principals and multiple goals, contract design will be a limited tool. Given that the development of institutions that provide checks and balances as well as public information is a long-term process, the options in the short and medium term are likely to focus on the development of mechanisms for monitoring and reporting and institutions for screening and selection. In particular, nonprofits have incentives to develop mechanisms that provide a reputational signal to principals. This may appeal to principals who prefer to rely on a reliable signal of quality rather than engage in expensive monitoring. But nonprofits and their principals may differ on how this signaling is to be accomplished. Institutional donors may want a more specific signal that ensures that nonprofit activities are aligned with their specific funding priorities. Governments want to ensure that nonprofits are serving charitable purposes that justify their tax exemption. Individual donors want a straightforward mechanism for identifying worthy organizations for giving. Nonprofits, on the other hand, would like a signal that is credible for multiple stakeholders. In this way nonprofits might avoid having to face "police patrols," either in the form of individualized reporting requirements for multiple donors, or in the form of stricter government regulation. How can these competing interests be served? What constitutes a credible signal? What kinds of information must it contain?

Signaling as a response to agency dilemmas

The economics literature has long examined problems of signaling under conditions of asymmetric information. The classic treatment is Spence's (1973) discussion of labor market signaling. Since true information about the quality of potential employees is not fully visible to employers, job applicants have incentives to find signals of quality. A college education is one such signal. Since high-quality individuals will find it more costly to obtain a college education than low-quality individuals, a college education serves as a signal of quality, regardless of whether a college education actually improves employee productivity. Education induces a "separating equilibrium" in which "good" and "bad" types are revealed.

Where preexisting signaling institutions do not exist, however, signal-seekers, such as nonprofits, face the challenge of creating credible signaling institutions. To do so, they must ascertain what type of signal induces a separating equilibrium that distinguishes high-quality from low-quality nonprofits. In other words, what kind of signal establishes sufficient information on reputation? A second challenge has to do with who will bear the costs of constructing the signal and how the flows of information will be coordinated. The institutional design of voluntary signaling programs must solve both the external credibility problem and an internal collective action problem.

Among for-profit firms, two types of signaling institutions have arisen, both of which are responses to market failures. First, firms may join voluntary certification programs to signal their adoption of policies that internalize the negative externalities of production, such as reduced pollution or emissions, higher labor standards, or the use of environmentally friendly or sustainable cultivation and harvesting practices. Voluntary environmental programs work by encouraging "beyond compliance" behavior on the part of firms and, sometimes, by making information on compliance public. In return for participation, program participants receive the value of a positive reputation for which stakeholders can choose to reward them (Prakash and Potoski, 2006).

Second, firms may join voluntary programs in response to problems of asymmetric information between sellers and buyers, as occurs when buyers cannot fully observe supplier quality. This creates a market for certification in which sellers are willing to pay an intermediary to provide a signal of supplier quality. Voluntary certification programs such as ISO 9000 (King *et al.*, 2005; Potoski and Prakash, 2009a) and ISO 14001 (Prakash and Potoski, 2006) can help firms to communicate their adoption of particular management practices to potential buyers. The problem of asymmetric information between firms and customers is analogous to the information asymmetries faced by nonprofits and their principals. Creating a credible signal implies that the cost of program participation must be sufficiently high that low-quality organizations do not participate. Thus clubs are inherently based on exclusion – if everyone can belong, the reputational signal of the club is devalued. In addition, the institution must be able to ensure that participants do not shirk in meeting the program obligations. To return to our job market example, universities have degree requirements and grades to certify graduates. How do voluntary programs certify their members? Previous work on voluntary programs sought to strengthen the analytics of for-profit voluntary programs by employing a common, deductive framework rooted in club theory (Prakash and Potoski, 2006). Extending the club theory perspective to nonprofits raises interesting and important questions about the design of accountability institutions. In particular, how do key features of nonprofit governance, structure, and context affect the emergence, design, and participation in voluntary regulation programs? The next section turns to these questions.

Voluntary clubs among nonprofits

In economic theory, clubs are rule-based institutions that create benefits that can be shared by members, but which nonmembers are excluded from enjoying.[8] Clubs thus function to produce and allocate impure public goods, that is, goods that can only be created or enjoyed collectively. Such goods are neither fully private (in which case they could be provided by markets) nor fully public (in which case it would be impossible to exclude others from enjoying them). Club goods are excludable goods that are nonrival within the club. Excludability means that it is feasible for one actor to exclude others from appropriating the benefits of a good for which the actor has contributed resources; in the case of clubs nonmembers can be excluded. Without excludability, other actors have an incentive to "free ride," that is, to enjoy the good's benefits without contributing to its production, maintenance, or protection (Olson, 1965). Rivalry means that if one actor consumes a particular unit of a good, it is no longer available for another actor to consume: if I am eating an apple, then you cannot eat the same apple. Among club members, all participants can enjoy the benefits of club membership. Clubs can therefore be viewed as institutions that provide excludable, collective benefits for members. In the case of nonprofit clubs, the club good being produced is a reputational signal of nonprofit quality that distinguishes high-quality from low-quality nonprofits. Thus, an actor (such as an association of nonprofits) might establish an institution (a voluntary program) which produces positive reputation or signal (a club good) for its members.

Voluntary programs as clubs perform three functions (Prakash and Potoski, 2007). First, they require club members to adopt policies and

[8] The literature on clubs is large. Key contributions include Tiebout (1956), Wiseman (1959), Buchanan (1965), and Cornes and Sandler (1996).

undertake activities that go beyond what is legally or operationally required of them. These activities and policies are tied to outcomes that principals care about. Second, by requiring members to undertake these activities, clubs impose nontrivial membership costs on members; these costs create the separating equilibrium and therefore form the basis for the reputational signal created by the club. Third, to compensate members for incurring new costs, the club provides benefits. The most important benefit, the benefit of a good reputation or "brand," has characteristics of a club good because all members can benefit from it at any given time, but it is available only to members and cannot be appropriated by nonmembers.

By joining a voluntary program, nonprofits agree to incur the costs of adopting the required governance mechanisms. This signals to principals that nonprofits are serious about tackling agency conflict. Thus, voluntary club membership provides information about practices and management systems that principals cannot observe and therefore helps to mitigate information asymmetries between principals and agents. It is in this sense that clubs are accountability mechanisms – their central function is to provide information necessary for principals to make decisions about agent performance. Further, because club membership is a public declaration of the intentions of a nonprofit, reneging on club obligations imposes "audience costs" (Fearon, 1994). Thus, club membership provides assurance to principals that agents have incentives not to renege on their obligations.

Principals may welcome voluntary clubs because they serve to reduce the monitoring and enforcement costs that principals might otherwise face. Nonprofits may welcome clubs because they streamline reporting requirements to principals and move them away from individual contracts with principals and toward trustee forms of accountability. Arguably, voluntary clubs also produce positive externalities for society that flow from the effective use of funds provided by the principals. These externalities might include building social capital (Putnam, 1993), providing citizens with civic experience (Almond and Verba, 1965; Brady *et al.*, 1995), and providing goods and services that are underprovided by markets and government (Weisbrod, 1988). However, these social externalities, by their very nature, are not captured by participating nonprofits and therefore cannot serve to draw nonprofits to clubs.

For members, club membership creates two types of benefits: branding (collective) benefits and private benefits (Prakash and Potoski, 2006). Branding benefits, the central analytical feature of voluntary clubs, accrue to club members only and are a key incentive for joining the club, since nonparticipants are excluded from enjoying them. These benefits manifest as goodwill, funding, contracts, or other compensation that members receive from their principals in response to their club membership. These benefits are tied directly to the credibility and strength of the signal produced by club membership. For example, club members often receive a certification that enables them to advertise that they are different from nonmembers by virtue of their club participation. For nonprofits, there are several potential benefits tied to this reputational signal. To the extent that donors and potential members, whether individual or institutional, have difficulty distinguishing among high- and low-quality organizations, nonprofits have incentives to create credible signals about the quality of their governance and the effectiveness of their programs. There is some evidence that donors are willing to reward club participants with additional funding (Bekkers, 2006). In addition, in countries where government attitudes toward nonprofits are hostile, such a signal may also help protect an organization from unwanted government interference or scapegoating (Gugerty, 2008). In addition to the benefits created through the nonprofit "brand," nonprofit clubs might provide tangible material benefits to participants that also have the characteristics of club goods. For example, club membership or certification might be a prerequisite for tax-exempt status or for receiving government grants or contracts.

Participation in a voluntary club may create private benefits through organizational learning. Through complying with club requirements, organizations may find ways to streamline or reduce the costs of other reporting requirements. Compliance procedures may encourage more efficient or effective use of donor or government funds; to the extent that increased effectiveness can be documented, this may in turn lead to both increased funding and higher social benefit. Analytically, however, nonprofits can appropriate such benefits by establishing accountability systems but not formally joining the club. After all, the obligations imposed by such clubs are often quite straightforward. While the benefits of organizational learning might emerge as a result of participation in a club, they can also be generated and appropriated independent of club membership. Unlike branding benefits, they do not have a collective character to them. Thus analytically, private benefits do not constitute the raison d'être for nonprofits to join an accountability club.

If reputational benefits are so important, why don't nonprofits create them by unilateral action in order to boost their credibility with principals? This might be a lower-cost option. In other words, why are signals via clubs more credible than signals by an individual nonprofit? Club membership offers several advantages over unilateral actions for mitigating agency conflict and enhancing reputation with principals (Prakash and Potoski, 2007). From the principals' perspective, a unilateral declaration by a nonprofit to abide by certain standards is less credible because when individual nonprofits make and enforce their own rules, they can more easily change them. Further, there is no exit cost in terms of loss of face among peers who have decided to continue in the club.

In contrast, clubs are institutionalized systems whose rules and obligations are often sticky; club membership therefore signals a long-term commitment to curb agency conflict. Second, there are exit costs. When a nonprofit joins a club, it shares the same institutional space with other nonprofits which have taken public vows to fulfill club obligations. Hence, if a nonprofit exits, its absence is quickly noticed in the peer group, and loss of reputation follows. Furthermore, because clubs can also gain from "network effects" (Bessen and Saloner, 1988; Prakash and Potoski, 2007) in building reputations, actions taken as part of a club can do more to boost a nonprofit's standing with the principals than the same action taken unilaterally.

Mitigating collective action dilemmas in clubs

Like any other governance mechanism, clubs are vulnerable to institutional failures that bear upon collective action problems. For voluntary clubs, two collective action dilemmas are most salient (Prakash and Potoski, 2006). The first, the Olsonian dilemma, centers on a club's capacity to create excludable benefits that are sufficient to offset the cost of club membership. In response, clubs must develop brands that create a separating equilibrium. To do so, clubs must impose obligations on their participating members that are stringent enough to demonstrate their credible commitment to mitigating agency slippage, yet are reasonable enough that some minimum number of participants is willing and able to pay the costs of meeting them.

The second dilemma, the shirking dilemma, pertains to a club's ability to compel participants to adhere to its rules. This is a challenge because participants might have incentives to free ride on the club's reputation: they could join the program and enjoy the benefits of its reputation, but shirk their responsibility to adhere to its standards. Not all members might shirk. However, if a certain proportion of participants shirk, it might undermine the club's ability to send a credible signal to principals. To curb shirking, clubs need to monitor participants' behaviors and sanction noncompliance. A club that sets high standards and has a reputation for effectively policing its participants is likely to have a stronger standing among its principals. Thus, the two attributes, club standards and club monitoring and enforcement, are the key institutional dimensions of voluntary clubs.

Club standards

Club standards establish the requirements for club membership. Given that principals, including donors and governments, often specify reporting guidelines for nonprofits, club standards can be viewed as establishing the amount of "beyond guideline" behavior required by the program. The amount of beyond guideline behavior required by the club is important because it establishes the credibility of the signal of participant quality and demonstrates the seriousness with which the club seeks to reduce agency conflicts. Nonprofits that are already closer to the standards will incur lower additional costs to join. Thus, the expectation is that high-quality nonprofits will be more likely to join voluntary programs, potentially increasing the strength of the reputational signal provided by the club.

For analytical purposes, we can consider two ideal types of standards: lenient and stringent (Prakash and Potoski, 2006). Lenient club standards require marginal effort (above the legal and donor requirements) for potential participants to join the program. These tend to be low-cost clubs. They also tend to have a marginal impact on correcting agency slippages. Consequently, while nonprofits might find it easy to join a lenient voluntary club, they should also expect small reputational gains by virtue of club membership. Stringent club standards impose requirements which extend substantially beyond the legal and donor guidelines. The advantage of stringent standards is that the club brand is more credible and can serve as a robust signal of club members' commitment to reducing agency conflicts. While these are high-cost clubs, they can also be expected to create sizeable reputational benefits for their participating members.

Club design may need to take into account multiple, sometimes competing objectives. Ideally, one might want to design a low-cost club which creates significant reputational benefits. This is not possible and club sponsors need to be cognizant of this trade-off. Further, while stringent standards might enhance the club's credibility with principals, they might result in low membership levels as well. As a result, such clubs might capture only low levels of network effects and scale economies in building the club brand simply because only a few nonprofits will be able to meet the more demanding membership requirements. Thus, pitching the club standards at a level appropriate for the potential nonprofits and yet acceptable to key principals is an important institutional design issue that the designers of any club must confront (Prakash and Potoski, 2007). To have any signaling power whatsoever, clubs must clearly articulate the standards for nonprofit behavior, even if minimal, and make those standards public so that they are available to nonprofit principals to use in judging nonprofit quality. Stronger standards will typically be associated with stronger signals, but the credibility of the signal also depends on enforcement, as discussed below.

Club monitoring and enforcement

The stringency of standards represents one component of club credibility. The second component is the extent to which clubs can demonstrate that members are complying with standards. Willful shirking among club members can occur because: (1) the goals of the participants and the club sponsors diverge, and (2) participants are able to exploit information asymmetries (regarding their adherence to club standards) between themselves and club sponsors.

One perspective suggests that nonprofits may not be subject to the same collective action problems as firms because of the centrality of principled beliefs or values to their actions (Keck and Sikkink, 1998), because of normative sociological pressures for behavior (March and Olsen, 1989), or because the actions of managers are more trustworthy since they face a nondistribution constraint (Hansmann, 1980). Such normative beliefs and pressures could potentially mitigate shirking, but it is not clear whether they will be sufficiently credible to outside stakeholders. As we noted at the outset, increasing pressure on nonprofits to demonstrate "accountability" and "results" suggests that these normative tendencies are not perceived as sufficiently strong by many stakeholders. In the absence of credible normative pressures, nonprofits, like firms and bureaucracies, will need some kind of enforcement mechanism. Monitoring and reporting in clubs attempts to enhance the credibility of the club signal by providing information about adherence to standards that mitigates between club members and club sponsors as well as between club members and principals. While a reduction in such asymmetries may mitigate agency conflicts, clubs may also need to incorporate sanctioning mechanisms to further enhance the credibility of compliance.

Voluntary club theory identifies various components ("swords," in short) of effective and credible monitoring and enforcement systems (Prakash and Potoski, 2006). The first component is verification – how do clubs verify that members are complying with established standards? Clubs can use disclosure or transparency requirements that require nonprofits to provide and make public particular information. Alternatively, clubs could require that participants produce documents and certify compliance. The certification could be first-party (self-certification), second-party (peer certification), or third-party (independent agent). Once verification mechanisms have been established, clubs face the question of how to handle cases of noncompliance, the second component of credible monitoring and enforcement. Club sponsors must decide how to respond when organizations are not in compliance. First, they must decide whether to make that information public. In addition, they may need to develop penalties that are imposed on noncompliant organizations. The threat of sanction may be credible because club sponsors have a vested interest in ensuring the club's credibility. At the same time, club sponsors may not want to acquire a reputation for being harsh and adversarial. They may want to promote organizational learning, which can only happen if organizations are willing and able to report mistakes. In clubs sponsored by nonprofits themselves, there may be a fear that public sanctions will identify "bad apples" that weaken the reputation of the sector as a whole. In addition, club sponsors may arguably have a greater impact if they retain nonprofits with imperfect compliance in the club because they can retain leverage over these nonprofits' policies. Enforcement mechanisms may run the gamut from weak to strong: the weakest enforcement is asking club members to pledge their adherence to the code, without actual verification. Stronger enforcement might involve some form of self- or peer verification or certification, with the very strongest clubs relying on third-party certification. Clubs may make public the names of those organizations that do not provide required information or are found to be out of compliance, or they may be removed from the club.

The stringency of these two features determines the overall signaling power of the club, which can be seen as a continuum from very weak to quite strong, depending on the mix of standards and enforcement employed. Table 1.1 lays out an analytic typology for nonprofit clubs illustrating how standards and enforcement interact in club design and how principals are expected to view the combinations of standards and swords that give rise to weak or strong clubs. The reduction in agency loss or agency slippage is expected to be smallest in clubs with lenient standards and weak swords; such clubs are analogous to "fire alarms" since their monitoring mechanisms typically rely on potential complaints from nonprofit principals who detect deviations from club standards, rather than institutionalized reporting. These are low-cost clubs that may be able to attract larger numbers of participants owing to ease of entry, but they are likely to create only marginal branding benefits for participants since they are likely able to identify only extreme cases of malfeasance. Such clubs typically have standards that are relatively broad and aspirational in nature and include only minimal monitoring mechanisms. Agency losses will be better reduced in clubs that feature stringent standards and significant enforcement, such as third-party certification mechanisms. Such

Table 1.1 *Analytical typology of nonprofit clubs*

Club standards	Club "swords"	
	Weak monitoring and enforcement	Strong monitoring and enforcement
Lenient standards		
Costs	Low cost to join	Medium cost to join
Benefits	Marginal branding benefits	Moderate branding benefits
Principals' assessment	Marginal reduction in agency loss	Moderate reduction in agency loss
Stringent standards		
Costs	Medium cost to join	High cost to join
Benefits	Moderate branding benefits	High branding benefits
Principals' assesment	Moderate reduction in agency loss	Significant reduction in agency loss

clubs are more likely to distinguish high-quality nonprofits from lower-quality organizations since such clubs will be too costly for lower-quality organizations to join. In this way, stronger clubs help to allay principals' concerns about nonprofit governance and effectiveness. Because of their greater signaling and branding power, principals are also more likely to reward participants in these clubs with higher levels of funding or greater discretion.

So far in this chapter we have sought to develop a robust yet accessible theoretical framework that demonstrates how voluntary programs, defined as rule-based systems created and sponsored by nongovernmental actors, seek to mitigate agency conflict and resolve agency dilemmas in nonprofits. The club framework seeks to unify disparate work on nonprofit accountability initiatives by providing a useful and tractable way to analyze programs across a range of academic disciplines, empirical settings, and institutional actors. In the next section we elaborate the key research questions derived from this framework and show how the chapters in this volume address them.

Research questions and case selection

This volume examines three interrelated sets of questions about nonprofit voluntary accountability programs that provide the organizing structure for the book. The first set of questions examines the emergence and evolution of clubs, investigating who establishes clubs and the factors that drive club emergence. Second, the volume examines the relationship between club sponsorship and design. How does sponsorship affect club design, club strength, and its potential effectiveness? Voluntary clubs might be designed and sponsored by independent actors or by the participants themselves. We examine how self-regulatory clubs differ from those sponsored by independent agencies. The third set of questions pertains to club design and effectiveness. Club design is likely to affect a club's ability to recruit members, its potential to shape member behavior, and therefore the willingness of principals to reward participation. How do club principals reward nonprofits for participation? In which types of clubs are these benefits most significant?

In order to explore club emergence, design, and effectiveness systematically, case selection must be based on common criteria, including a minimum definition of what constitutes a club. At its core, an accountability club imposes certain obligations on members (no matter how lenient) and seeks to convey these obligations to outside principals (no matter how imperfectly). A set of standards or principles for behavior is considered a club if the standards are agreed upon collectively and if the sponsoring organization makes attempts, even if minimal, to communicate the existence and the content of these standards to external stakeholders and principals. If such a set of standards contains no reporting, monitoring, or enforcement mechanisms it can be considered a very minimal club, but a club none the less because it seeks to signal quality (in an imperfect way) to external principals.

Nonprofit clubs are also voluntary. Nonprofits must make a conscious choice to participate; this voluntary decision is what gives rise to the collective action dilemmas inherent in clubs. Thus, rating systems established by watchdog agencies are not clubs in the sense in which we employ the term because nonprofits do not make a conscious decision to "join." Although rating systems do have the potential to mitigate information asymmetries, they do not involve voluntary adherence or submission on the part of nonprofits. The collective action issues (the Olsonian and shirking problems) which are key elements in our theoretical approach are less relevant for these rating systems.

This volume is intended to address our research questions by examining nonprofit clubs across an array of settings and from multiple perspectives. As we elaborate below, our cases are selected to maximize variation across the critical variables that we hypothesize will affect emergence, design, and effectiveness. We include cases that confirm our theoretical predictions as well as those that do not. First, our cases vary by nonprofit setting, both geographic and industry/sector. The volume includes a number of US clubs, as well as clubs from the Netherlands, the Czech Republic, and sub-Saharan Africa, as well as clubs that are transnational in scope. Cases also vary by sponsorship. Many of the clubs examined in the volume are self-regulatory, in that they have been developed by and are run by participating nonprofits (chapters 4–10). Four chapters also include cases on independently sponsored clubs (chapters 3, 9, 10, and 11), one of which compares self-regulatory and independent clubs that operate in the same market for members (chapter 9). The clubs examined in the volume also vary in the identity of major principals: two cases examine clubs where the government is the dominant principal (chapters 3 and 6); in two cases private donors are key principals (chapters 9 and 11); and in six cases there are multiple principals making claims on nonprofits (chapters 4–5 and 7–10). Finally, cases vary in the scope of club membership. Five chapters examine clubs that are open to all nonprofits (chapters 4–5 and 9–11), while five chapters analyze clubs that are restricted to particular types of nonprofits, including humanitarian organizations (chapter 8), foundations (chapters 6 and 7), academic centers (chapter 5), and health and education organizations (chapter 3). Taken together the chapters examine club emergence and structure in 150 cases and present detailed case studies of thirteen nonprofit clubs.

In addition to showing variation on key independent variables related to our research questions, our cases also exhibit variation in the type of data and research design they employ. Three chapters (3, 4, and 10) employ cross-sectional data to explore determinants of club design at a given point of time. Five chapters exploit longitudinal data to examine the trajectory of clubs over time (chapters 3, 5, 6, 8, and 9). Finally, three chapters compare competing clubs operating in response to the same set of principals, controlling for context and environmental factors to focus in on the impacts of sponsorship and membership on club design and effectiveness (chapters 8–10). Below we lay out our research questions in more detail and describe the contributions of each chapter.

Book outline

In extending the club perspective to the study of nonprofit accountability systems, the empirical cases presented in this volume examine issues pertaining to the emergence (Part I), sponsorship and design (Part II), and design and effectiveness (Part III) of nonprofit accountability clubs. In the concluding chapter we offer comments regarding the issue of institutional efficacy and discuss how the empirical cases can inform the club approach to the study of voluntary governance.

Part I of the volume examines club emergence. The chapters in this section examine the potential for nonprofit clubs to increase accountability in relationship to current requirements, how and why voluntary initiatives arise, and how key features of their environment affect the prospects for emergence. What standards will send an appropriate signal to principals about nonprofit quality? The determination of appropriate nonprofit club standards is not clear-cut, given the diversity in the nonprofit sector and the lack of clear reporting standards across organizations. Indeed, the determination of appropriate standards is often hotly contested.[9] For example, some clubs set fundraising and other administrative ratios that measure overhead and fundraising expenditures as a percentage of revenues, in spite of the belief by some that comparisons of such ratios across organizations are meaningless (Bowman, 2006). Moreover, rewarding organizations on the basis of a narrow set of outcomes can give rise to perverse outcomes as organizations attempt to "game" the system. Given the focus on fundraising ratios, for example, nonprofits have the incentive to organize their reporting in such a way that such expenses are minimized.

In chapter 2, "Filling the gaps in nonprofit accountability: applying the club perspective in the US legal system," Dana Brakman Reiser sets the stage for the chapters that follow by illustrating the challenges inherent in the development of nonprofit standards. The chapter uses a legal perspective to examine the potential roles that voluntary clubs might play in the US context by complementing and supporting enforcement of legal and regulatory mandates. Brakman Reiser looks at three components of nonprofit accountability – financial, organizational, and mission – and examines the baseline standards for nonprofit reporting relating to each. She argues that while financial standards are the most developed, extant standards still leave substantial room for agency losses. But the observation and enforcement of governance and organizational accountability is even more problematic, she argues. While nonprofits are required upon incorporation to file documents reporting on their governance structure, subsequent enforcement opportunities are minimal. It is in the area of mission accountability that Brakman Reiser observes the weakest standards but also the largest scope for voluntary clubs to improve nonprofit accountability. Currently, baseline standards on how nonprofits report on their mission are almost nonexistent, in spite of the fact that the mission forms the rationale for nonprofit existence and provides the basis for tax-exempt status. Thus, at least in the US context, Brakman Reiser observes significant scope for "beyond compliance" standard-setting by voluntary clubs. Her chapter illustrates the potential for nonprofit clubs to improve both the performance and the information provision of nonprofits and highlights the multiple dimensions of nonprofit accountability that may form the basis for conflict or confusion among nonprofit principals.

---

[9] For the forestry case, see Sasser *et al.* (2006).

The next two chapters turn to the issue of club emergence in the US context. Given the potential for clubs to improve nonprofit reporting and performance, we might expect to see a large number of clubs emerging. Yet the emergence of clubs across areas of nonprofit activity appears uneven. As Brakman Reiser suggests, the ability of clubs to address particular features of nonprofit accountability varies, and clubs may be more likely to emerge where the accountability demands of principals are clear-cut or better articulated.

Chapter 3, "Trends and patterns in third-party accreditation clubs," is authored by Woods Bowman and examines the development of accreditation and certification clubs in the United States. Paralleling the growth of the nonprofit sector, he finds sharp increases in the number of accreditation programs since 1980. Bowman shows how the US club landscape is dominated by education and health accreditation clubs that are sponsored by independent agencies. Bowman attributes this to the role of the dominant principal in these sectors, the US federal government. A case study of one of the largest health accreditation agencies, the Joint Commission, illustrates how the increasing needs of the US federal government for regulation and standardization of the sector supported the development of the club. Bowman also shows how the standards set by clubs tend to cluster on areas that reflect the concerns of principals. Voluntary clubs in health tend to focus on standards for quality of services and outcomes, while standards in education clubs focus on governance, finances, and fundraising.

In contrast, in chapter 4, "Self-regulation at the state level: nonprofit membership associations and club emergence," Mary Tschirhart examines the emergence of voluntary clubs among state-level nonprofit associations and finds relatively little emergence and far weaker clubs. Given that the vast majority of US nonprofits are locally based, statewide associations might be expected to develop voluntary clubs that respond to state-level principals, including state attorney generals' offices that regulate nonprofit incorporation and activity. Seventy percent of states have statewide nonprofit associations; of these thirty-five states, twenty have developed collective codes of conduct that function as weak clubs for the sector but only five associations sponsor clubs that include any active screening or monitoring. Tschirhart examines the factors underlying these patterns and finds that neither nonprofit sector size, state association capacity, nor association membership in the National Council of Nonprofit Associations is associated with the emergence of these clubs. The relative weakness of state-level clubs is somewhat of a surprise in a federal system such as the USA, and given the potential discussed by Brakman Reiser for clubs to act as important complements to state regulatory activity. But as the next section of the volume explores, this may stem in part from the conflicting incentives faced by the sponsors of these associations.

Part II of the volume examines the relationship between club sponsorship and club design, with a particular focus on self-regulatory clubs. In market settings featuring asymmetric information, entrepreneurs are likely to enter the market in order to sell information about suppliers to willing buyers. The profit motive provides the incentive for intermediaries to bear the costs of information gathering and dissemination. Among nonprofits, however, most voluntary clubs are developed by entities that are themselves nonprofit (Ortmann and Svítková, 2007; Gugerty, 2009). Given the impact of public scandals on nonprofit reputation and fundraising, voluntary clubs are likely to be initiated by nonprofit industry associations with a clear stake in maintaining the reputation of the industry. For example, this is how the health accreditation club examined by Bowman began. Clubs could also emerge in response to external threats to the sector, such as the threat of increased government regulation; in this case we might again expect that nonprofit associations would be likely sponsors as they seek to protect their members from regulatory demands. Part II focuses on the design of clubs sponsored and run by nonprofit associations on behalf of their members. A common theme in this section is the tension that exists in these associations between membership recruitment and club sponsorship. When club sponsors are membership associations, sponsors may find it difficult to restrict club entry, diluting the signaling capabilities of the club.[10]

Self-regulatory collective clubs may also have weaker incentives to expose fraud or noncompliance because there is ambiguity in how stakeholders will interpret such exposure (Nunez, 2007). If exposure of wrongdoing is seen as a sign of vigilance, principals may reward members for participation, but if it is instead viewed as a sign of widespread fraud among all participants, exposure may have negative consequences for members. Self-regulating organizations may therefore choose a much more lax enforcement regime than principals would prefer (DeMarzo *et al.*, 2005). Thus the overall expectation is that self-regulatory clubs will be weaker than those sponsored by independent agencies.

Dennis Young examines club emergence and design among nonprofit "infrastructure" organizations in chapter 5, "Nonprofit infrastructure associations as reluctant clubs." His two cases, the Independent Sector and the Nonprofit Academic Centers Council (NACC), were concerned in their early years with professionalization and field development. In

---

[10] An alternative hypothesis is that self-regulatory systems have the incentive to pursue their own interest by restricting entry, leading to cartel-like behavior (Shaked and Sutton, 1981).

more recent years, however, both associations have faced demands from nonprofit principals for stronger quality certification mechanisms. In recent years, the Independent Sector has developed a weak club in which nonprofits can sign on to a code of ethics developed by the association; the code and its signatories are posted on the organization's website. As Young describes, the association's accountability initiatives over the past five years have been in large part a response to initiatives by Congress to increase the regulation of the nonprofit sector. In contrast, the NACC has resisted pressure to become an accreditation agency and continued its focus on the legitimation of the field of nonprofit studies. Young is pessimistic about the ability and the utility of such infrastructure organizations developing stronger accountability clubs since they recruit and reflect such a broad-based and diverse set of institutions. It remains to be seen whether initiatives such as that of the Independent Sector are a sufficiently credible signal to government regulators.

In chapter 6, "Foundation accountability clubs and the search for philanthropic standards," Peter Frumkin describes the development of accountability clubs among US foundations. Foundations are an interesting case, since they are not dependent on other entities for resources and do not face the same kind of conflicting demands from multiple principals faced by many service and advocacy nonprofits. Frumkin shows how accountability clubs among foundations developed as a response to proposals for increased government regulation and as a mechanism for maintaining foundation autonomy. Like the Independent Sector case discussed by Young, the Council on Foundations was motivated to develop principles for conduct only when faced with the threat of government regulation. In part, this reluctance also stemmed from the difficulty of promulgating standards covering a wide variety of organizations, and in fact, the development of standards led to a schism in the field with a number of foundations forming a competing association. While he describes and acknowledges the shift toward club sponsorship among both national and regional-level associations of foundations, Frumkin, like Young, is pessimistic about the potential and ability of foundation associations to sponsor strong accountability clubs.

Chapter 7 examines a foundation-sponsored club in a quite different context. In "Do self-regulation clubs work? Some evidence from Europe and some caveats from economic theory," Andreas Ortmann and Katarina Svítková examine the development of a voluntary club, the Czech Donors Forum. In the Czech Republic, as in many post-transition economies, the influx of foreign assistance during the transition period led to an explosion in the number of nonprofits operating in the country. At the same time government authorities had very little capacity for regulation and oversight of the burgeoning sector. The result was a public perception that many nonprofits were not public interest organizations, but instead were pursuing their own interests. In this context, the Czech Donors Forum (CDF) was established by a group of foundations with the goal of promoting philanthropy and increasing trust in the nonprofit sector. To accomplish these goals, the CDF set out to develop a self-regulatory mechanism for members. As Ortmann and Svítková argue, however, the CDF has consistently resisted pressures for transparency in its own reporting as well as resisting demands for more stringent standards and enforcement for the self-regulatory club. In contrast to the case of US foundations, Czech foundations appear less concerned with the need to preempt government regulation, and the CDF effort has yet to evolve into a full-fledged club. Ortmann and Svítková note that levels of giving to nonprofits in the Czech Republic have been stagnant and speculate that the inability or unwillingness of the CDF to develop stronger signals of credibility may be one reason why.

In chapter 8, "NGO accountability clubs in the humanitarian sector: social dimensions of club emergence and design," Maryam Zarnegar Deloffre explains the divergent paths taken by two humanitarian accountability clubs as they attempted to define accountability in the wake of post-Rwanda evaluations of humanitarian activity. Humanitarian agencies form an important test case for the club framework, since their claims to legitimacy are strongly rooted in normative principles, often described as the humanitarian "imperative." Zarnegar Deloffre describes how humanitarian agencies and key principals both agreed on the need for better accountability mechanisms for the sector after the Rwanda intervention. Many principals stressed the need for third-party certification mechanisms, while humanitarian agencies largely resisted this tendency, arguing that it would interfere with the humanitarian principle of independence. Yet even among these agencies, demands for accountability were interpreted in different ways. One set of agencies favored a strong "beyond compliance" approach focused on legal duties and obligations for humanitarian assistance as well as detailed standards for quality assistance. These agencies formed the Sphere humanitarian charter. The other set of agencies did not believe that humanitarian agencies could meet their moral duty by means of technical standards, and this group split off to form its own accountability program, Compas Qualité. Zarnegar Deloffre's chapter shows how norms and ideas can play an important role in structuring club design. The chapter also demonstrates how competing definitions of accountability among nonprofits can result in a partitioned accountability landscape in which club membership is in some sense "mutually exclusive." Zarnegar Deloffre's chapter challenges the agency perspective presented in this volume by showing how commitment to ideas and norms can limit the power of principals to place claims on nonprofits.

Part III of the volume connects issues of club design and club effectiveness across a range of settings. This final section examines how clubs sponsored by independent agencies differ from those run by nonprofits and investigates the extent to which principals reward club members for their participation. Previous chapters have shown how the presence of dominant principals, particularly government, can shape the emergence of clubs. The demand for strong signals of quality can help to raise the benefits of club participation so that nonprofits are willing to bear the cost of developing accountability clubs. The demand for signals can also create a market that encourages independent agencies to develop clubs. The demand for independent sponsorship might arise when principals, particularly donors or government, desire signals with stronger separating properties that favor third-party systems, since the reputation and survival of those intermediaries depends on the production of quality information (Ortmann and Svítková, 2007; Biglaiser, 1993).

When more than one principal makes accountability demands on nonprofits, competing demands may lead to a broadening or watering down of standards to meet the needs of these multiple principals if their accountability demands do not cohere. Alternatively, multiple clubs may emerge in the same policy domain to meet the needs of different principals, and clubs may even compete for members. In such cases it is unclear whether clubs will partition or segment the market amongst themselves, or whether nonprofits might join multiple clubs to serve the needs of multiple principals – and with what effect on club effectiveness. Several chapters in this volume take up this issue.

Angela Bies examines multiple clubs operating in a single domain in chapter 9, "The impact of sponsorship on club standards and design." She studies two clubs operating in the state of Minnesota, one sponsored by the Minnesota Council of Nonprofits (MCN), a membership association of nonprofits, and the other by the Minnesota Charities Review (MCR), a charity watchdog agency. From its inception just after World War II, the Charities Review viewed its role as monitoring charities on behalf of donors. The Council of Nonprofits was established in 1997 as a nonprofit membership association focused on improving the operations and effectiveness of its members and on advocating for the sector. The Council was the first to develop an accountability club, developing a detailed set of management and governance principles in consultation with stakeholders, but deciding explicitly against including provisions for monitoring, reporting, or enforcement. The Charities Review developed a voluntary club, the Accountability Wizard, in 2005 as a complement to its charity ratings system. Bies shows how the Charities Review's responsiveness to donors results in a program with a stronger emphasis on reporting and monitoring. The Council, on the other hand, is more concerned with raising the performance and reputation of the sector as a whole, and as a result developed a more detailed set of standards, but refrained from engaging in strong monitoring or enforcement. The Minnesota case is notable for the high degree of cooperation and coordination between the two clubs. The result is an accountability landscape in which nonprofits can choose to join one or both clubs, depending on the expected benefits.

Parallel clubs are also emerging in sub-Saharan Africa, a region that has witnessed an explosion in the number and scope of nonprofits over the past two decades. In chapter 10, "The emergence and design of NGO clubs in Africa," Mary Kay Gugerty examines the development and potential effectiveness of accountability clubs in sub-Saharan Africa, arguing that the need for signaling mechanisms in this region is critical, since rapid nonprofit growth has taken place in an environment characterized by relatively weak regulatory capacity and resource scarcity. In this environment, flows of donor funds to nonprofits tend to attract the attention of both well-intentioned and opportunistic actors, threatening the reputation of legitimate organizations.

In many African countries, the threat of new, repressive government regulations is a key factor in the development of accountability clubs. A novel feature of the African story is the tendency for clubs to emerge initially as a kind of government–nonprofit partnership in which governments outsource regulatory activities to national nonprofit associations, accompanied by some minimal regulatory authority. But these clubs tend to suffer from the same tendencies toward weak standards and lenient enforcement noted by Young, Tschirhart, and Frumkin. Most national clubs prove quite weak in terms of their regulatory power and therefore their ability to send credible signals to nonprofit principals. In response, nonprofits in many countries also initiated voluntary certification clubs that seek to establish more stringent standards, along with monitoring and enforcement intended to send more credible signals of nonprofit legitimacy and quality. Thus, as in the humanitarian sector and in Minnesota, parallel programs sometimes coexist side-by-side.

Many nonprofit clubs are relatively young and systematic evidence on the benefits gained through participation is not yet available. In chapter 11, "The benefits of accreditation clubs for fundraising nonprofits," René Bekkers takes up this question, providing some of the first systematic evidence on this question. He studies the Central Bureau of Fundraising (CBF) charity accreditation program in the Netherlands. The CBF is an example of a strong club that elaborates detailed standards that are verified by the CBF before the accreditation seal is issued. Bekkers examines whether knowledge of the CBF program motivates higher levels of donations to charities by individuals, as well as whether club participation brings benefits to participants in the form of high levels of donations. Using detailed national-level data, Bekkers shows that individuals who are aware of the CBF program give more to charity, a clear indication that voluntary clubs can increase the faith of principals in the nonprofit sector. He also shows that certified organizations increase their fundraising revenues in the years following accreditation, indicating that strong clubs can induce principals to reward nonprofits, allowing clubs to deliver important club goods to their members. Interestingly, Bekkers also finds that the CBF tends to be "leaky" – nonmembers as well as members benefit from the accreditation program, albeit not to the same extent.

The final chapter, "Conclusions: nonprofit accountability clubs," is co-authored by Aseem Prakash and Mary Kay Gugerty. This chapter returns to the research questions posed in the introductory chapter and examines them in light of the ten empirical chapters. In pulling together their theoretic and empirical findings, it highlights the strengths and weaknesses of the club approach to understanding nonprofit accountability programs. Finally, it identifies areas for future research.

REFERENCES

Akerlof, G. A. 1970. The Market for "Lemons": Quality Uncertainty and the Market Mechanism. *Quarterly Journal of Economics* 84(3): 488–500.
Alchian, Armen A. and Harold Demsetz. 1972. Production, Information Costs, and Economic Organization. *American Economic Review* 62(5): 777–795.
Almond, Gabriel and Sidney Verba. 1965. *The Civic Culture: Political Attitudes and Democracy in Five Nations*. Boston: Little, Brown.
Anheier, Helmut and Lester Salamon. 2006. The Nonprofit Sector in Comparative Perspective. In W. Powell and Richard Steinberg, eds. *The Nonprofit Sector: A Research Handbook*. New Haven: Yale University Press, pp. 89–116.
Arumi, A. M., R. Wooden, J. Johnson, S. Farkas, A. Duffett, and A. Ott. 2005. *The Charitable Impulse*. New York: Public Agenda.
Bekkers, René. 2006. The Benefits of Accreditation for Fundraising Nonprofits. Paper presented at the 2006 Conference of the Association for Research on Nonprofit Organizations and Voluntary Action (ARNOVA).
Ben-Ner, A. and B. Gui. 2003. The Theory of Nonprofit Organizations Revisited. In H. Anheier and A. Ben-Ner, eds. *The Study of Nonprofit Enterprise: Theories and Approaches*. New York: Kluwer, pp. 3–26.
Berle, A. A., and G. C. Means. 1932. *The Modern Corporation and Private Property*. New York: Harcourt, Brace and World.

Bessen, S. M. and G. Saloner. 1988. *Compatibility Standards and the Market for Telecommunication Services.* Santa Monica, CA: Rand.

Biglaiser, Gary. 1993. Middlemen as Experts. *The RAND Journal of Economics* 24(2): 212–223.

Bothwell, R. O. 2001. Trends in Self-Regulation and Transparency of Nonprofits in the U.S. *International Journal of Not-for-Profit Law* 2(3). Accessed via www. icnl.org/journal/vol2iss3/arn_bothwell.htm, November 2007.

Bowman, H. W. 2006. Should Donors Care about Overhead Costs? Do They Care? *Nonprofit and Voluntary Sector Quarterly* 25: 288–310.

Bradley, Bill, Paul Jansen, and Les Silverman. 2003. The Nonprofit Sector's $100 Billion Opportunity. *Harvard Business Review* (May): 272–294.

Brady, Henry, Kay Schlozman, and Sidney Verba. 1995. Beyond SES: A Resource Model of Political Participation. *American Political Science Review* 89(2): 271–294.

Brody, Evelyn. 2002. Accountability and Public Trust. In L. Salamon, ed. *The State of Nonprofit America.* Washington, DC: Brookings Institution and the Aspen Institute.

Buchanan, J. M. 1965. An Economic Theory of Clubs. *Economica* 32: 1–14.

Chhaochharia, Vidhi and Suman Ghosh. 2008. Do Charity Ratings Matter? Working paper, University of Miami.

Cornes, R. and T. Sandler. [1986] 1996. *The Theory of Externalities, Public Goods, and Club Goods* 2nd edn. Cambridge University Press.

DeMarzo, P., M. Fishman, and K. Hagerty. 2005. Self-Regulation and Government Oversight. *Review of Economic Studies* 72(3): 687–706.

Ebrahim, Alnoor. 2003. Accountability in Practice: Mechanisms for NGOs. *World Development* 31(5): 813–829.

2005. Accountability Myopia: Losing Sight of Organizational Learning. *Nonprofit and Voluntary Sector Quarterly* 34(1): 56–87.

Ebrahim, Alnoor and Edward Weisband, eds. 2007. *Global Accountabilities.* Cambridge University Press.

Edelman Trust. 2007. Edelman Trust Barometer 2007. Accessed via www.edelman. com/trust/2007/trust_final_1_31.pdf.

Edwards, Michael and David Hulme, eds. 1996. *Beyond the Magic Bullet: NGO Performance and Accountability in the Post-Cold War World.* West Hartford, CT: Kumarian Press.

Fama, Eugene and Michael Jensen. 1983. Separation of Ownership and Control. *Journal of Law and Economics* 26: 301–326.

Fearon, James. 1994. Domestic Political Audiences and the Escalation of International Disputes. *American Political Science Review* 88(3): 577–592.

Freeman, R. E. 1984. *Strategic Management: A Stakeholder Approach.* Boston: Pitman.

Fremont-Smith, M. and A. Kosaras. 2003. *Wrongdoing by Officers and Directors of Charities: A Survey of Press Reports, 1995–2002.* Working Paper No. 20, Hauser Center for Nonprofit Organizations, Harvard University, Cambridge, MA.

Gibelman, Margaret and Sheldon Gelman. 2004. A Loss of Credibility: Patterns of Wrongdoing among Nonprofit Organizations. *Voluntas* 15(4): 355–381.

Giddens, Anthony. 1998. *The Third Way: The Renewal of Social Democracy.* Cambridge, UK: Polity Press.

Gourevitch, Peter and James Shinn. 2005. *Political Power and Corporate Control: The New Global Politics of Corporate Governance.* Princeton University Press.

Grant, Ruth and Robert Keohane. 2005. Accountability and Abuses of Power in World Politics. *American Political Science Review* 99(1): 29–43.

Greenlee, Janet, Mary Fischer, Teresa Gordon, and Elizabeth Keating. 2007. An Investigation of Fraud in Nonprofit Organizations: Occurrences and Deterrents. *Nonprofit and Voluntary Sector Quarterly* 36: 676–694.

Gugerty, Mary Kay. 2008. The Effectiveness of NGO Self-Regulation: Theory and Evidence from Africa. *Public Administration and Development* 28 (May): 105–118.

  2009. Signaling Virtue: Voluntary Accountability Programs among Nonprofit Organizations. *Policy Sciences* 42: 243–273.

Hannan, Michael and John Freeman. 1989. Structural Inertia and Organizational Change. *American Sociological Review* 49(2): 149–164.

Hansmann, Henry B. 1980. The Role of Nonprofit Enterprise. *Yale Law Review* 89: 835–898.

Henderson, Sarah L. 2002. Selling Civil Society: Western Aid and the Nongovernmental Organization Sector in Russia. *Comparative Political Studies* 35(2): 139–167.

Hirschman, A.O. 1970. *Exit, Voice, and Loyalty.* Cambridge, MA: Harvard University Press.

Holmstrom, Bengt. 1982. Moral Hazard in Teams. *Bell Journal of Economics* 13(2): 324–340.

Iannaccone, Laurence. 1998. Introduction to the Economics of Religion. *Journal of Economic Literature.* 36 (September): 1465–1496.

Independent Sector. 2005. Strengthening Transparency Governance Accountability of Charitable Organizations: A Final Report to Congress and the Nonprofit Sector. Resource Document. Independent Sector. Accessed via http://info. ethicspoint.com/files/PDF/resources/Panel_Final_Report.pdf, November 20, 2008.

  2007. Principles for Good Governance and Ethical Practice: A Guide for Charities and Foundations. Resource Document. Panel on the Nonprofit Sector, Independent Sector. Accessed via www.nonprofitpanel.org/report/ principles/Principles_Guide.pdf, October 1, 2007.

Johnson, Erica and Aseem Prakash. 2007. NGO Research Program: A Collective Action Perspective. *Policy Sciences* 40(3): 221–240.

Kearns, Kevin. 1994. The Strategic Management of Accountability in Nonprofit Organizations: An Analytical Framework. *Public Administration Review* 54(2): 185–192.

Keck, M. and K. Sikkink. 1998. *Activists beyond Borders: Advocacy Networks in International Politics.* Ithaca: Cornell University Press.

Kiewert, D. Roderick and Mathew McCubbins. 1991. *The Logic of Delegation.* University of Chicago Press.

King, Andrew A. and Michael J. Lenox. 2000. Industry Self-Regulation without Sanctions: The Chemical Industry's Responsible Care Program. *Academy of Management Journal* 43(4): 698–716.

King, Andrew A., Michael J. Lenox, and Ann Terlaak. 2005. The Strategic Use of Decentralized Institutions: Exploring Certification with the ISO 14001 Management Standard. *Academy of Management Journal* 48(6): 1091–1106.

Lenox, Michael and Jennifer Nash. 2003. Industry Self-Regulation and Adverse Selection: A Comparison across Four Trade Association Programs. *Business Strategy and the Environment* 12: 343–356.

Light, Paul, 2004. *Fact Sheet on the Continuing Crisis in Charitable Contributions.* Accessed via http://wagner.nyu.edu/news/confidence.pdf, October 20, 2009.

Lloyd, Robert. 2005. *The Role of NGO Self-Regulation in Promoting Stakeholder Accountability.* One World Trust.

Lloyd, R. and L. de las Casas. 2005. *NGO Self-Regulation: Enforcing and Balancing Accountability.* Alliance Extra. Accessed via www.alliance magazine.org/node/2025.

McCubbins, Matthew and Thomas Schwartz. 1984. Congressional Oversight Overlooked: Police Patrols versus Fire Alarms. *American Journal of Political Science* 28: 16–79.

McCubbins, Matthew, Roger G. Noll, and Barry Weingast. 1989. Structure and Process as Solutions to the Politician's Principal Agency Problem. *Virginia Law Review* 74: 431–482.

McGuire, M. 1972. Private Good Clubs and Public Goods Club. *Swedish Journal of Economics* 74: 84–99.

Mahon, John. 1993. Shaping Issues/Manufacturing Agents. In Barry M. Mitnick, ed. *Corporate Political Agency.* Newbury Park, CA: Sage, pp. 187–212.

Manne, Henry. 1965. Mergers and the Market for Corporate Control. *Journal of Political Economy* 73(2): 110–120.

March, James and Johan Olsen. 1989. *Rediscovering Institutions: The Organizational Basis of Politics.* New York: Free Press.

Miller, Gary, 2005. The Political Evolution of Principal–Agent Models. *Annual Review of Political Science* 8: 203–225.

Mitchell, R. K., B. R. Agle and D. J. Wood. 1997. Towards a Theory of Stakeholder Identification and Salience: Defining the Principle of Who and What Really Counts. *Academy of Management Review* 22: 853–886.

Mitnick, Barry M. 1982. Regulation and the Theory of Agency. *Policy Studies Review* 1(3): 442–453.

Moe, Terry. 1984. The New Economics of Organization. *American Journal of Political Science* 28: 739–777.

Nunez, J. 2007. Can Self-Regulation Work? A Story of Corruption, Impunity and Cover-Up. *Journal of Regulatory Economics* 31: 206–233.

Olson, M. 1965. *The Logic of Collective Action.* Cambridge, MA: Harvard University Press.

Ortmann, Andreas and Mark Schlesinger. 2003. Trust, Repute and the Role of Nonprofit Enterprise. In Helmut Anheier and Avner Ben-Ner, eds. *The Study of Nonprofit Enterprise: Theories and Approaches.* New York: Kluwer.

Ortmann, Andreas and Katarina Svítková. 2007. Certification as a Viable Quality Assurance Mechanism in Transition Economies: Evidence, Theory and Open Questions. *Prague Economic Papers* 2. Accessed via www.rse.cz/pep/pdf/300. pdf, October 20, 2009.

Ostrower, F. and M. Stone. 2006. Governance: Research Trends, Gaps and Future Prospects. In W. Powell and R. Steinberg, eds. *The Nonprofit Sector Research Handbook*. New Haven: Yale University Press.

Panel on the Nonprofit Sector. 2007. *Principles for Good Governance and Ethical Practice: A Guide for Charities and Foundations: Reference Edition*. Washington, DC: Independent Sector.

Pfeffer, J. and G. Salancik. 1978. *The External Control of Organizations: A Resource Dependency Perspective*. New York: Harper and Row.

Potoski, M. and A. Prakash. 2009a. Information Asymmetries as Trade Barriers: ISO 9000 Increases International Commerce. *Journal of Policy Analysis and Management* 28(2): 221–238.

eds. 2009b. *Voluntary Programs: A Club Theory Perspective*. Cambridge, MA: MIT Press.

Prakash, A. and M. K. Gugerty. 2010. Trust but Verify? Voluntary Regulation Programs in the Nonprofit Sector. *Regulation and Governance* 4(1): 22–47.

Prakash, A. and M. Potoski. 2006. *The Voluntary Environmentalists*. Cambridge University Press.

2007. Collective Action through Voluntary Environmental Programs: A Club Theory Perspective. *Policy Studies Journal* 35(4): 773–792.

Pratt, John W. and Richard J. Zeckhauser, eds. 1985. *Principals and Agents: The Structure of Business*. Cambridge, MA: Harvard Business School Press.

Putnam, Robert, with Robert Leonardi and Raffaella Nanetti. 1993. *Making Democracy Work*. Princeton University Press.

Romzek, Barbara S. and Melvin J. Dubnick. 1987. Accountability in the Public Sector: Lessons from the Challenger Tragedy. *Public Administration Review* 47: 227–238.

Rose-Ackerman, S. 1996. Altruism, Nonprofits, and Economic Theory. *Journal of Economic Literature* 34: 701–728.

Ross, Stephen A. 1973. The Economic Theory of Agency: The Principal's Problem. *American Economic Review* 62: 134–139.

Rubenstein, Jennifer. 2007. Accountability in an Unequal World. *Journal of Politics* 69(3): 616–632.

Salamon, Lester. 1994. The Rise of the Nonprofit Sector. *Foreign Affairs* (July/August): 3–64.

Salamon, Lester, W. J. Sokolowski, and Regina List. 2003. *Global Civil Society: An Overview*. Baltimore: Center for Civil Society Studies, Johns Hopkins University.

Sasser, E., A. Prakash, B. Cashore, and G. Auld. 2006. Direct Targeting as NGO Political Strategy: Examining Private Authority Regimes in the Forestry Sector. *Business and Politics* 8(3): 1–32.

Shaked, A. and J. Sutton. 1981. The Self-Regulating Profession. *Review of Economic Studies* 48(2): 217–234.

Shapiro, S. P. 2005. Agency Theory. *Annual Review of Sociology* 31 (August): 263–284.

Sidel, Mark. 2003. Trends in Nonprofit Self-Regulation in the Asia Pacific Region: Initial Data on Initiatives, Experiments and Models in Seventeen Countries. Mimeo, University of Iowa Law School.

Smith, Steve Rathgeb and Michael Lipksy. 1993. *Nonprofits for Hire*. Cambridge, MA: Harvard University Press.

Spar, Debora and James Dail. 2002. Of Measurement and Mission: Accounting for Performance in Non-Governmental Organizations. *Chicago Journal of International Law* 3(1): 171–181.

Spence, M. 1973. Job Market Signaling. *Quarterly Journal of Economics* 88: 355–374.

Spiller, Pablo. 1990. Politicians, Interest Groups, and Regulators: A Multiple-Principals Agency Theory of Regulation, or "Let Them Be Bribed." *Journal of Law and Economics* 33(1): 65–101.

Spiro, Peter. 2002. Accounting for NGOs. *Chicago Journal of International Law* 3 (1): 161–169.

Steinberg, R. and B. Gray. 1993. The Role of Nonprofit Enterprise in 1993: Hansmann Revisited. *Nonprofit and Voluntary Sector Quarterly* 22(4): 297–316.

Terlaak, Ann and Andrew King. 2006. The Effect of Certification with the ISO 9000 Quality Management Standard: A Signaling Approach. *Journal of Economic Behavior and Organization* 60: 579–602.

Tiebout, C. M. 1956. A Pure Theory of Local Public Expenditures. *Journal of Political Economy* 64: 416–24.

Vakil, Anna C. 1997. Confronting the Classification Problem: Toward a Taxonomy of NGOs. *World Development* 25(12): 2057–2070.

Warren, Shana and Robert Lloyd. 2009. Civil Society Self-Regulation: A Global Picture. One World Trust Briefing Paper No. 119, June.

Waterman, Richard W. and Kenneth J. Meier. 1998. Principal–Agent Models: An Expansion? *Journal of Public Administration Research and Theory* 8(2): 173–202.

Weisbrod, Burton. 1988. *The Nonprofit Economy*. Cambridge, MA: Harvard University Press.

Wiseman, J. 1959. The Theory of Public Utility Pricing: An Empty Box. *Oxford Economic Papers* 11(1): 88–97.

Wood, B. Dan. 1988. Principals, Bureaucrats, and Responsiveness in Clean Air Enforcements. *American Political Science Review* 82: 213–234.

Part I

Club emergence

2   Filling the gaps in nonprofit accountability: applying the club perspective in the US legal system

Dana Brakman Reiser

Clubs hold significant promise for improving nonprofit accountability if they are consciously designed to complement principals' existing enforcement systems. Although there are legal routes for regulators, funders, and other principals to encourage and enforce financial and organizational accountability, they will be chronically insufficient to educate nonprofit leaders and to provide them with incentives for compliance. Clubs can be designed to backstop and reinforce these baseline enforcement mechanisms. The challenge for clubs, however, is to strike the right balance between imposing meaningful standards and swords in light of other enforcement activity and remaining affordable. This chapter will explore whether and how clubs can help to fill these important gaps and, thereby, improve the overall picture of nonprofit accountability.

Before one can evaluate the potential contribution of clubs to the goal of improving nonprofit accountability it is necessary to elaborate two important foundational concepts. The first is the concept of multiple principals. The club framework helpfully identifies and responds to the problem that multiple principals lay claims to the loyalty and action of nonprofit agents. For the purposes of this chapter, however, it will often be useful to divide this universe of principals into public and private categories. Public principals include state and federal regulators charged with nonprofit supervision, as well as government grantmakers who provide public money to nonprofit grantees. Private principals include a wide range of principals outside of the public sector: donors of all sizes, staff members, partner organizations, beneficiaries, and even the public at large. There are certainly important variations among principals within these two categories. Still, separating principals in this manner illuminates the ways clubs can be designed to work in concert with the baseline of nonprofit accountability enforcement. Likewise, a further and sometimes cross-cutting division of principals into funding and nonfunding principals will often be revealing.

The second concept that requires deconstruction is that of accountability itself. This volume views accountability as a set of claims made upon nonprofits by various principals, based upon agreed standards of behavior. Accountability claims are judged based on the information that nonprofits can provide to their principals. Nonprofit accountability claims are not monolithic (Brody, 2002; Fishman and Schwarz, 2006). Rather, they include at least three necessary subtypes: financial accountability, accountability as an organization, and accountability as to mission (Brakman Reiser, 2004; Brody, 2002; Brody, 1996; Swords, 1998). These strands of accountability differ in many respects. Importantly here, these include the standards articulated by public and private principals in each case and the extent to which existing enforcement mechanisms empower principals to enforce the standards they impose. Accountability clubs function by requiring members to demonstrate adherence to standards that may replicate or go beyond current mandates. In order to understand what standards clubs might set and what they require of members, we must first understand what baseline expectations are in the three realms of non-profit accountability.

The first part of this chapter takes each strand of accountability claim in turn. It develops a working understanding of the features of three types of accountability and describes the current legal landscape for their enforcement by public and private principals in the United States.[1] The second part identifies the distinct opportunities for clubs to play a complementary role in each of these important areas.

The varying accountability baselines

Public and private principals have significant power to demand and enforce financial accountability standards. They also frequently articulate organizational accountability standards and engage in some enforcement activity. However, the constraints of legal doctrine, limited resources, and practical priorities check the gains public and private principals can achieve in these areas. These constraints, paired with additional policy and constitutional limitations, significantly limit principals' engagement on issues of mission accountability. The following sections reveal the varying baselines of financial, organizational, and mission accountability standards established and enforced by principals. In order for account-ability clubs to complement existing enforcement mechanisms, these baselines should form the foundation for club design.[2]

---

[1] This chapter limits its analysis to those principals and accountability mechanisms available within the US legal system, leaving comparative analysis to future work.

[2] Club designers should fashion their standards and swords with an eye toward standards imposed and enforced by principals, including public principals. The two should not, however, work directly in tandem. Nor should club membership be made a requirement

Financial accountability

Financial accountability looks to whether a nonprofit organization safegu-ards its financial resources (Brakman Reiser, 2004; Brody, 2002; Swords, 1998). Fiduciary duties obligate a nonprofit's leaders to shield current assets, to invest prudently, and to prevent theft, destruction, or harmful neglect of funds and other property. Nonprofits also must attend to their relationships with funders and would-be funders as a route to obtaining future assets.

All principals are properly concerned with financial accountability. Public principals are charged with ensuring the safety of assets dedicated to charitable purposes. The frequency with which donors attempt to sue to enforce gift restrictions, despite severe limitations on standing to do so, attests to the outrage they feel at the prospect of misapplication, pilfering, or loss of donated funds (Brody, 2007). Nonfunding private principals – staff, beneficiaries, partner organizations, and the public at large – also have legitimate concerns about the financial accountability of their organ-izations. For example, if a nonprofit college makes foolish investments, it may need to cut salaries to faculty and other employees, raise tuition fees paid by students, or reduce its programmatic offerings to all for whom they offer advantages. Still, these concerns are somewhat more distant and abstract than those of public or funding principals. Each set of principals also experiences a somewhat different legal and practical baseline for enforcement of financial accountability, in the absence of clubs.

In the United States, public principals focus their enforcement efforts squarely on financial accountability concerns, with good reason. The mandates of state attorneys general (AGs) in the charitable area typically speak specifically in terms of safeguarding charitable assets (Ross, 1990). Their existing tools of investigation and enforcement are also amenable to use in discovering and proving financial accountability lapses. AGs are charged with enforcing fiduciaries' obligations of care and loyalty, breaches of which threaten financial resources. Public principals at state and federal levels also mandate that nonprofits submit financial disclosures to them; both types primarily request financial information. Political incentives will, at least in egregious and public cases, also align to encourage AGs to pursue remedies against thieving nonprofit fiduciaries and sham charitable solic-itations. The problem with AG enforcement, therefore, is not lack of will or expertise. Rather, it is a failure of resources. Most states' AG offices do not even contain charities bureaus, and those which do exist are understaffed and underfunded (Bograd, 1994; Crimm, 2001; Fremont-Smith, 2004).

for receiving government recognition or largesse. Clubs are valuable precisely because they are part of an independent, self-regulatory environment. Entanglement with regulators threatens to undermine this useful autonomy.

Another set of public principals provides some additional authority and resources to enforce financial accountability: federal tax authorities. Tax enforcement comes into play when failures in financial accountability are intertwined with failures to comply with the requirements to retain tax-exempt status. For example, the Internal Revenue Service (IRS) can impose penalty taxes on nonprofit insiders receiving excessive compensation as part of its effort to enforce the tax code's ban on private inurement in exempt entities (IRC § 4958). For those tax-exempt nonprofits designated as private foundations, the tax code also establishes financial accountability standards requiring appropriate investment of nonprofit assets. If a private foundation makes an investment that places its exempt functions in jeopardy or maintains excessive holdings of a single business, penalties again apply (IRC §§ 4943, 4944).

Federal tax regulators also enforce financial accountability through tax rules that prescribe requirements for deducting charitable contributions. Federal tax law expressly requires donees to inform donors of the portion of any donation that is tax deductible when a contribution is made wholly or partly *quid pro quo* (IRC §§ 170(f)(8), 6115). It also requires that donors provide substantiation in order to deduct any charitable contribution over $250. Failure to comply with these substantiation requirements can result in disallowance of the donor's deduction and penalties for the donee organization. Financial accountability certainly includes tracking and managing the donations a nonprofit receives. The practical effect of the tax law substantiation requirements is to compel nonprofits to track donations, so they can provide receipts to donors. When tax concerns are raised by the same conduct that implicates financial accountability, tax regulators therefore provide additional enforcement. Here too, though, resource constraints will be a limiting factor.

The special significance of financial accountability for funding principals, whether private or public, also suggests they might be reliable enforcers of this strand of accountability. However, legal obstacles will hamper their efforts. Donors as a class generally lack legal standing to sue, even to enforce restrictions placed on their own charitable gifts (Chisolm, 1995). Whether or not they have provided funding, private principals will generally be precluded from asserting generic claims of lax or wrongful management of a nonprofit's finances (Blasko *et al.*, 1993; Chisolm, 1995). Public principals engaged in regulation, particularly state AGs, have a virtual monopoly on this type of enforcement. Unless funding principals can secure additional remedies by negotiation, all that will be left to them will be to threaten to cut off future support or to involve public principals or the media.

Large donors could condition their contributions on enforcement rights to shore up their demands for financial accountability. Repeat donors could do likewise in return for continued funding. To secure such rights, donors would need to negotiate continuing disclosures, as many grant-makers do. Further, donors would need to secure rights to redirect resources deemed misspent. Public funding is frequently accompanied by financial disclosure obligations, and various remedies as to appropriated funds are available (Siegel, 2006). For private funding principals, however, limited access to legal enforcement remedies may remain a hindrance, leaving them to rely solely on threats of nonrenewal or public exposure. Private funding principals also will hesitate to negotiate for remedies that will return their contributions, as this possibility can endanger deductibility (Siegel, 2006). Furthermore, funding principals will be primarily concerned with the use of the funds they have contributed. Even those with the power and inclination to negotiate enforcement rights will likely not assert broader rights to enforce financial accountability. Finally, nonfunding private principals, as well as small or one-time donors, will not articulate and enforce financial accountability standards on a regular basis. Indeed, the cost of negotiating financial accountability commitments may be more than even many major and repeat funding principals are willing to absorb.

Thus, while we can expect public and private principals to engage in some enforcement of financial accountability, it will be incomplete. Public principals set standards but suffer from inadequate resources to enforce them. Some private principals will be able to obtain financial accountability commitments and enforcement rights necessary to police them, at least with respect to their donated funds. Many other private principals will not. Thus, the baseline of financial accountability enforcement by principals is significant, but hardly comprehensive.

Organizational accountability

Organizational accountability receives some attention from public and private principals, though certainly not as much as financial accountability. Organizational accountability imperatives require nonprofits to follow their own internal rules of governance (Brakman Reiser, 2004). They must adhere to the organizational structure they have selected, making decisions and engaging in transactions through transparent and legitimate processes. Organizational accountability requires nonprofits to populate their governing bodies, set operational processes by which these groups will run, and ensure that they do in fact function accordingly. A nonprofit has serious organizational accountability failures if its board is languishing with unfilled seats or the committee structure and processes outlined in its bylaws and board procedures do not bear close relation to its operating practices.

Both public and private principals should value organizational accountability. It serves the independent goal of providing order and predictability to nonprofits' operations. There are serious risks attendant on a nonprofit that is unwilling or incapable of managing its own affairs in an orderly fashion in line with its legal responsibilities. If it is difficult to follow a group's chain of command or determine when a meeting will be held, principals will find it especially hard to obtain the information and feedback they require. Moreover, organizational accountability has instrumental value in providing the mechanisms by which nonprofits pursue and measure financial and mission accountability. When a nonprofit has adequate governance structures, principals can track its financial affairs, fiduciary compliance, and progress toward achieving its mission.

Public principals have established a range of organizational accountability standards. These depend in large part on the legal form of organization a nonprofit chooses to inhabit, as well as its tax status. Most US nonprofits organize as nonprofit corporations (Phelan, 2000), a large portion of which claim exemption from federal income taxation and accept tax-deductible contributions (Fishman and Schwarz, 2006; Fremont-Smith, 2004; Weitzman *et al.*, 2002). State statutes require nonprofit corporations to document their internal governance procedures by drafting articles of incorporation and bylaws and define a set of procedures that will apply as a matter of default (RMNCA §§ 2.02–03, 2.05–06). The default rules contemplate that directors will hold meetings and establish committees (RMNCA §§ 8.20–25). When members are empowered with a role in governance, they too must be given opportunities to exercise that role (RMNCA §§ 7.01, 8.01). State law's characterization of nonprofit leaders as fiduciaries also requires them to guide their organizations using appropriate procedures. In particular instances, federal tax law backs up these state law obligations, for example, by its establishment of a safe harbor from the penalty tax on excessive compensation available if a nonprofit utilizes particular governance practices (Treas. Reg. § 53.4958–6).

Despite their articulation of organizational accountability standards, public principals do not provide adequate enforcement in this area. Nonprofits do have to file their organic governance documents with state and federal authorities in order to obtain incorporation and preferential tax treatment. Once incorporation and exemption have been obtained, however, public principals have neither the means nor the authority to track a nonprofit's everyday operations (Brody, 2004; Fremont-Smith, 2004). Failures of attention and mismanagement might attract regulatory attention, but AGs rarely prosecute lapses of organizational accountability unless they are accompanied by financial losses (Brody, 1998). Rather than engaging in expensive *ex post* enforcement actions based solely on organizational accountability failures, at least some public principals do pursue organizational accountability *ex ante* by offering or participating in training programs for nonprofit fiduciaries, their counselors, and other interested constituencies (Brakman Reiser, 2004). Many simply choose to spend their limited enforcement resources and political capital elsewhere. Thus, there is some enforcement of nonprofit organizational accountability by public principals, but certainly not as much as is needed.

Additionally, few private principals establish or enforce organizational accountability standards. Funding principals are most likely to have the resources and relationships with nonprofits necessary to do so. But small donors and even moderate or large donors of one-time gifts will hesitate to absorb the costs of enunciating and particularly policing a nonprofit's operations. These costs will not be justified to safeguard smaller or single contributions. Large and especially repeat funders may find it worthwhile to expend these resources. Additionally, repeat player status with an individual nonprofit or a larger group of grantees may allow major funding principals to gain expertise and exploit economies of scale. Even these principals, though, will face enforcement obstacles. Funding principals can condition their gifts on receiving information regarding the governance process, but again restrictions on standing will limit their remedies.

Nonfunding private principals will be even less reliable enforcers of organizational accountability. Those with a consistent and substantial stake in the operations and outcomes of a particular nonprofit might take the time and resources to articulate their expectations as to the nonprofit's governance. Perhaps a university faculty or an important partner organization would be willing and able to do so. They will be further stymied, however, by a lack of enforcement mechanisms. Exclusive standing for public principals will make litigation or its threat unavailable. Whether nonfunding private principals can acquire additional remedies by contract will depend on their bargaining power with a relevant nonprofit. Powerful staff groups or partner organizations may be able to bargain for enforcement authority over organizational accountability issues when they broker employment or affiliation agreements. Individual citizens or broad community groups are unlikely to secure these concessions. Each factual situation will be different, but nonfunding private principals seem an unlikely source of consistent organizational accountability enforcement.

As such, the picture of organizational accountability enforcement is not empty, but not terribly encouraging. Public principals establish organizational accountability standards through statutes and legal doctrine. However, their incentives and ability to enforce these standards are limited. Among private principals, significant repeat donors and others in major continuing relationships with a nonprofit may at times enunciate standards and negotiate enforcement rights. Often, however, significant obstacles and disincentives will hamper their efforts. Taken together, while organizational accountability will receive some attention from principals, ideal enforcement remains elusive.

Mission accountability

Accountability to mission forms the final strand of the nonprofit accountability web. Nonprofit organizations are formed in order to pursue some purpose – their mission. Legal standards promulgated by public principals require this mission to be stated in a nonprofit's articles of incorporation, though in rather generic form. A more detailed sense of mission is developed over time. Mission evolves explicitly when the nonprofit writes and amends its operational documents, such as articles, bylaws, and mission statements contained within them. Mission also transforms implicitly, as the nonprofit crafts fundraising and informational materials in which it describes its mission, and pursues programs and activities that give principals their idea of the goals of the organization. Illegitimately straying from its mission undermines a nonprofit's claim to favored nonprofit status and tax benefits. Furthermore, widespread failures in mission accountability endanger the place of the nonprofit sector within society, by raising questions about its ability to serve the various economic (Hansmann, 1980, 1981) and social roles (Brakman Reiser, 2003; Bucholtz, 1998; de Tocqueville, 1969) attributed it, as well as its general trustworthiness.

While accountability to mission is therefore vital, it is very difficult to measure or track. To do so, one must first define or discover a nonprofit's mission. As nonprofits are marked by multiple constituencies, arriving at a single statement of a group's mission can be quite difficult. A simplifying assumption might be made that nonprofits' missions are discernible from the words used to describe their purposes in their articles of incorporation. This assumption, however, gives only a starting point for the analysis. This form of words is often quite general, perhaps forming for "all lawful purposes under § 501(c)(3)," and little will be accomplished by simply comparing this statement with current programs and activities. Rather, some idea of the history and development of an organization's programs and activities is needed to fill out a view of its overall mission. Even then, one cannot simply decry any nonprofit whose mission has changed; evolution of nonprofit mission is permissible and, often, desirable.

Instead, the inquiry must consider whether any such transformation of mission has been achieved legitimately.

Public principals do address the most basic mission question at a non-profit's inception. An organization must articulate its purposes within some concept of charity or mutual benefit in order to obtain nonprofit incorporation (Fremont-Smith, 2004). To obtain federal tax-exempt status and eligibility to offer deductible contributions, an entity must show it is "organized and operated exclusively for religious, charitable, scientific, testing for public safety, literary, or educational purposes" (IRC §§ 501(c)(3), 170(c)). Occasionally, public principals will challenge whether this purpose has been maintained. For example, the IRS stripped a university of its exemption as a result of its racially discriminatory policies on grounds that they violated public policy and were therefore incompatible with its charitable status (*Bob Jones University* v. *United States*). The US Supreme Court clarified, however, that the decision to reject an institution's mission should be made neither frequently nor lightly. It explained, "a declaration that a given institution is not 'charitable' should be made only where there can be no doubt that the activity involved is contrary to a fundamental public policy" (*Bob Jones University* v. *United States*). Notably, this case, and any case in which the right to nonprofit incorporation or tax-benefited status is at risk, will address only the easy mission question: whether the organization has any charitable mission at all. Such cases will rarely even pose the more difficult questions of mission accountability, such as whether a nonprofit has appropriately operated in pursuit of its chosen mission, legitimately transformed that mission, or both.

Public principals can be involved in questions of mission pursuit and change at the state level. Regulators and courts occasionally will confront mission accountability issues in sales of substantial assets, mergers, or dissolutions, in those states that require attorney general or court approval for these deals (Fremont-Smith, 2004). Courts also play this role in the realm of cy pres actions. Under this venerable doctrine, if the purposes for which a charitable trust was made are no longer capable of being achieved, the trustee may appeal to a court for authority to change those purposes (Scott *et al.*, 2008). Traditionally, a court applying cy pres would permit any such changes with an eye to approaching the donor's preferred purposes as nearly as possible, though modern interpretations give courts some additional leeway. Individual restricted gifts to a nonprofit corporation are generally treated as charitable trusts subject to cy pres (Scott *et al.*, 2008; Brody, 2007). If restricted gifts with outmoded purposes form all or a substantial part of the assets of a nonprofit corporation, changing the use of these funds will be not only a change of mission, but also subject to cy pres doctrine. In addition, the doctrine or its approach has at times been applied more broadly to changes of charitable purposes of nonprofit corporations (Brody, 2007; Fremont-Smith, 2004). Thereby, public principals will sometimes have a role in overseeing mission transformation.

Yet, these opportunities for public principals to enforce mission accountability are quite rare. Many states do not require governmental approval for even major nonprofit transactions (Fremont-Smith, 2004). Cy pres is an extraordinary remedy for extraordinary situations. Further, the large run of nonprofit decisions that raise questions of fealty to mission are unreviewed and unreviewable by government actors because they do not rise to the level at which these legal regimes operate. When a nonprofit changes its activities or programs using nonrestricted funds, cy pres generally will not be triggered. The everyday and long-term decisions about which of a broad range of activities a nonprofit should pursue or cut to fulfill its charitable purposes most effectively are consigned completely to resolution through its autonomous process of governance.

As such, one can expect public principals to engage in precious little enforcement of mission accountability. This action will be limited to policing the basic nonprofit/for-profit boundary and occasional involvement in reviewing mission evolution through cy pres or transactional approvals. Limited resources will again work to curtail public enforcement. Further, the institutional competencies of these regulators are in tracking financial fraud and mismanagement, particularly when such acts lead to the waste of charitable assets or unjustified tax revenue losses. The subtle inquiries required for delineating organizational mission and evaluating the legitimacy of its transformation do not map on to these skills. Moreover, while public principals might be subject to political pressure to root out embezzlement of charitable funds or fraudulent uses of donated contributions, calls for them to track the mission accountability of nonprofits seem far less likely. Indeed, it would be undesirable and highly suspect for government regulators actively to police the substance of nonprofits' missions. There are serious free speech and associational concerns raised by the prospect of public principals informing nonprofits of what their mission is, and how they should or should not be pursuing it (Silber, 2001).

Like their public counterparts, private principals concerned with the vitality and longevity of individual nonprofits and the sector more broadly should prize mission accountability. However, the practical problems of monitoring mission and policing transformation will make it similarly difficult for them to enforce it. Additionally, private principals will have a particular problem in acting as enforcers of mission accountability-bias. By its nature, mission evolution is a process within which multiple principals spar over the proper evolution and articulation of a nonprofit's mission. Even decisions regarding how to implement mission once a vision of it is accepted by all principals will often be fraught and resolvable only by compromise. As players in this drama of mission transformation, individual principals are uniquely unsuited to play the role of objective monitor or enforcer.

Principals therefore engage in scant articulation and enforcement of mission accountability standards. On the public side, requirements of charitable purpose are mostly limited to hollow statutory exhortations and the far-off and slim potential for litigation or other regulatory involvement. Likewise, private principals have little to offer in establishing or enforcing mission accountability standards because each principal will be biased by its own role within the nonprofit. There is a critical need for additional mechanisms by which mission accountability can be pursued.

Nonprofit principals establish and enforce standards for nonprofit accountability. Public principals establish these standards through regulation. Funding principals may be able to negotiate them by contract. Other private principals may have more or less abstract expectations about nonprofit accountability, but rarely will have outlets to create enforceable standards. Public principals can use the legal system to police their accountability standards. Private principals' access to legal remedies is uncertain. When legal remedies are unavailable, private principals can enforce by removing their support – financial or otherwise – from non-compliant nonprofits. Thus far, this chapter has explained how legal and practical limitations skew principals' efforts to articulate and enforce standards toward financial accountability. Organizational accountability standards are widespread, but receive spotty enforcement by principals. Principals are unlikely to engage in either identification or enforcement of mission accountability standards at a high level. Club sponsors have the opportunity to create institutions that increase nonprofit accountability by designing accountability clubs to complement these differential baselines.

The complementary potential of accountability clubs

The extent to which an accountability club can offer net benefits to principals and nonprofit members depends on how the standards and swords it selects interact with the baseline of principal enforcement outside the club context. The standards principals establish set an appropriate floor for standards a club might adopt. Club designers must decide whether to adopt these standards or ones that are more stringent than this floor. In addition, they must select the swords they will use to enforce the standards they select. When making these decisions, club designers must also remain cognizant of costs a given standard or sword will generate.

One might assume that a club with accountability standards duplicating those articulated by principals and enforcing them with weak swords would offer little information to principals and few benefits to members. This is only true, however, if principals' standards are well understood, substantially complied with, and the level of an individual nonprofit's compliance with them is transparent to principals and enforceable by them. Duplicative standards can create benefits if nonprofits who would join the club do not understand the standards imposed by legal mandate or negotiated by other principals. A club with standards duplicating those of principals would offer private benefits by educating previously ignorant club members, even if it did not employ powerful swords. The state nonprofit associations examined by Tschirhart in chapter 4 and the early period of the Minnesota Charities Review Council described by Bies in Chapter 9 of this volume appear to be playing this constructive role.

It is also possible that while most nonprofits who would join the club do understand the standards their principals have established, many would not comply with them in the absence of the club. Principals' limited resources might lead nonprofits to the rational decision to ignore legal mandates, or even negotiated standards, and accept the slight risk of detection and penalty. Ignoring principals' standards is particularly sensible if principals are unable to distinguish compliant from noncompliant nonprofits or if principals lack effective enforcement mechanisms. In such contexts, a club with duplicative standards could offer branding benefits. If swords are strong enough to make membership a reliable signal, such a club would solve real information asymmetry problems faced by principals.

When principals' standards are generally understood and compliance is transparent and enforceable, clubs with duplicative standards will not generate net private benefits for club members. With or without club membership, those nonprofits that obtain and improve their operations as a result of compliance with the relevant requirement will reap the private benefits of doing so. The source of the mandate appears irrelevant. Even in this situation, though, clubs can be designed to offer some incremental branding benefits. Club membership could make a nonprofit's compliance with legally mandated or negotiated standards more transparent to non-funding private principals. Those public and funding principals who enunciate standards can be assumed to know their content, and the reasons why they would be useful. Knowledge of the intricacies of the law's requirements and the link between these standards and account-ability may not be known or understood by private nonfunding principals such as small donors, beneficiaries, and the general public. Clubs can correct this information asymmetry by providing private nonfunding principals with information about the standards that can secure accountability and details of which nonprofits meet them. This information is useful whether the compliance occurs in order to obtain club membership or in response to principals' demands. Clubs also can package information about a range of accountability standards together into a digestible brand for principals at various levels of involvement and experience. As described by Bies, the CRC Smart Givers program appears to exemplify this function. It provides measures of nonprofits' financial and organizational accountability, topics most likely covered by existing standards. By identifying relevant practices, linking them together, and making them widely accessible, it provides useful information to less sophisticated principals.

If principals set standards that are well understood by nonprofits, if compliance with them is transparent across a wide range of principals, and if effective enforcement is available, clubs will provide neither branding nor private benefits by duplicating this floor. In this situation, clubs should consider whether adding more stringent standards will achieve greater nonprofit accountability. This determination will require analysis of possible standards and swords to enforce them, as well as the additional costs of compliance these will generate. Designers must avoid the situation where costs of participation become so significant that the club loses its ability to recruit members and becomes irrelevant.

Principals' enforcement capacity differs widely across the three strands of nonprofit accountability. There are also significant differences with regard to the standards set by principals, the clarity of those standards to nonprofits, and the transparency of compliance. Club sponsors should react to these very different baselines of obligation and enforcement, in a conscious effort to create clubs that offer the greatest benefit to principals and members. The remainder of this chapter offers more detailed guidance on this important project of institutional design.

Limited gains in financial accountability

Principals tend to focus their efforts to establish and enforce accountability standards in the financial area. Public principals mandate that fiduciaries carefully deploy and invest nonprofit assets, without using them for personal gain. Funding principals ally with public principals to demand that nonprofits comply with the wishes of their donors and safeguard donated funds. Public principals have broad powers to investigate and prosecute lapses in financial accountability and concentrate those resources they have on these cases. They also use disclosure mandates to check and enforce compliance with financial accountability standards. Standing limitations will often prevent funding principals from using litigation to enforce financial accountability standards as a matter of default. However, those funding principals who donate substantial sums will have the power to negotiate for financial controls, can utilize other remedies, and will sometimes be able to enforce their standards in court.

Bowman in chapter 3 of this volume describes the "focus on finances" by many nonprofit watchdog groups. Accountability clubs that concentrate in this area should adopt standards and swords that will allow them to play a useful complementary role. To take one example, imagine a club considering a standard that would require club members to obtain audited financial reports. A financial audit is one mechanism for promoting financial accountability, as it provides an opportunity for outside review of an organization's financial operations and internal controls. The audit may itself turn up lapses in financial accountability, which can then be remedied. In addition, the knowledge that such a review will occur can also motivate staff and leaders to take greater care in handling their nonprofit's finances. Thus, an audit requirement seems a natural fit for clubs concerned with improving their member nonprofits' financial accountability.

Whether a club's adoption of an audit requirement will assist principals and create benefits for club members depends, however, on how this requirement interacts with principals' existing standards regarding auditing. There are states that require large nonprofits to obtain audited financial reports and submit them to regulators (Mass. Gen. Laws ch. 12 § 8F; Cal. Gov. Code § 12586). More do so for those nonprofits that solicit charitable contributions from the public (Fremont-Smith, 2004). Additionally, at least some private funding principals bargain for contractual terms requiring audits and reports on their findings. Both government and foundation grants can include such conditions. Further, audit requirements place relatively straightforward demands on nonprofits that should be easy for them to understand.

Compliance with an audit requirement is also fairly transparent. Principals need only to demand that the required audit be submitted to them. If a nonprofit fails to submit required audits, public principals may levy fines, eliminate its special status, or revoke its license to solicit donations. If required documentation is not provided to a funding principal, negotiated remedies may allow it to withhold promised funds or possibly sue for the return of funds previously disbursed. Therefore, noncompliance is quite risky even in the absence of the club.

A club establishing a duplicative audit requirement seems unlikely to provide private benefits, owing to the clarity of principals' audit requirements to nonprofits and the transparency of compliance for at least some principals. Club membership could make a nonprofit's otherwise-mandated decision to obtain an audit more transparent to nonfunding private principals or convey to them the importance of audits. Thereby, it could offer some incremental branding benefits.

In this circumstance, as in many in the financial accountability area, clubs can offer additional gains by establishing and enforcing more stringent standards than principals have done. A club might adopt standards requiring members to maintain a particular set of internal controls, to insure against failure of those controls, or to rotate auditors on a regular basis. When the CRC described by Bies revised its accountability standards in the early 1960s, it required not only audited accounts, but also itemized budgets and reasonable fundraising campaign expenses. More stringent standards, even without an increase in the potency of swords, allow a club to offer branding and private benefits to members. The club can provide previously unavailable information to principals and additional financial accountability guidance to club members. Of course, clubs could also provide benefits to principals and members by adopting more powerful swords than principals tend to use. For example, they could provide for peer or third-party review of audit reports or unscheduled visits to review financial operations.

When fashioning their institutional design, clubs must also always consider cost. As the stringency and potency of the standards and swords adopted rises, the number of nonprofits that will desire and be able to meet them will decline. For clubs targeting a narrower range of nonprofits, seeking to provide deep assurances of financial accountability to principals, standards greatly in excess of those expressed by principals may be appropriate. For broad-membership clubs, they would prove unworkable. As such, club standards and swords addressing financial accountability can be designed to offer a range of useful benefits. Yet, the financial accountability gains clubs can provide will be limited by the necessity of providing either only incremental benefits to a broad membership or substantial gains to a much narrower group.

Greater potential gains in organizational accountability

Clubs could also be designed to fill gaps in organizational accountability. A club's chosen standards and swords will again interact with the baseline of existing legal obligations and enforcement mechanisms available to principals. Club designers must respond to and complement this baseline in order to shape standards and swords that send the most useful signal to principals, and generate net branding and private benefits for members.

Principals commonly establish organizational accountability standards, but seldom enforce them. States and their AGs are particularly active here, demanding that a governing body be seated and function predictably. Yet, these public principals do not – and should not – articulate standards prescribing the details of nonprofits' operational processes. While they have some tools and authority to enforce organizational accountability, public enforcement in the area remains lacking. Funding principals may also exert some influence in this area, but their efforts will be inconsistent and will be hampered by limited remedies. Further, funding principals' incentives will not encourage them to enforce broad norms of organizational accountability.

In this context, clubs have the potential to offer substantial benefits. Bowman's study in this volume (chapter 3) suggests that at least some clubs have taken up organizational accountability by focusing on governance as a major issue, particularly as it intersects with financial issues. Designing clubs in the complementary manner advocated here will make their efforts more effective. Again, even duplicating principals' existing standards can be helpful in ensuring standards are implemented. Without significant enforcement, these standards may not be well understood by targeted nonprofits. Consider a nonprofit that fails to understand or comply with standards requiring a board to be seated and hold meetings. A duplicative club standard may communicate this requirement and the desire to join can compel compliance. Thereby, the nonprofit will improve its governance practices, a valuable private benefit. If comprehension of and compliance with this legal requirement is not widespread, simply providing member nonprofits with this information and emphasizing its importance may be significant.

Clubs can offer further improvements in organizational accountability if they can also increase transparency as to compliance. The lackluster enforcement of organizational accountability standards may lead busy nonprofit leaders to ignore them. Further, as they pertain to the internal operations of an organization, compliance with these standards will be difficult for principals to determine. With their existing authority and resources, they also may be difficult or costly for principals to enforce. Duplicative club standards provide valuable information to principals if clubs can more successfully police and signal compliance. Doing so will confer branding benefits on members that would have complied with the standards anyway, and will provide branding and private benefits to those who would not. Club designers can choose among a variety of swords by which to monitor and enforce compliance, ranging from self-certification to disclosure for third-party review. Selecting among these will require consideration of both effectiveness and cost. In this context, however, even weak monitoring and enforcement of organizational accountability norms will represent an improvement over existing efforts by principals.

In addition, of course, clubs can complement existing enforcement by setting more stringent standards than principals would require. Rather than simply requiring boards to be seated or to meet, clubs might require particular sets of director qualifications, independence criteria, or set a minimum number of meetings per year. They might require directors to undergo training on governance best practices at the outset of their board tenure or at intervals throughout their terms. Again, cost-benefit analysis should guide design and adoption of more stringent standards.

The optimal strength of standards and swords addressing organizational accountability is an institutional design question for each club to consider. In this context, public principals will frequently have articulated minimum standards. Funding principals may also have done so, but all principals will underenforce. Thus, even clubs that duplicate existing standards can have an impact, particularly if clubs can wield stronger or more effective swords than principals employ. More stringent standards can create even greater benefits if a club can adopt them and remain attractive despite increased costs. Therefore, the club model offers greater potential gains in the organizational than in the financial accountability area, provided that club designers stay attuned to the baseline and craft standards to complement it.

Greatest relative gains in mission accountability

The greatest relative accountability gains from the club model, however, can be made in the area of mission accountability. Significant relative gains are available here because the baseline of principal enforcement is so low. Principals articulate mission accountability standards that are vague or conflicting and their enforcement capacity is at best minimal and at worst counterproductive. As such, clubs can provide much-needed information about mission accountability to principals, and thereby generate significant branding benefits for nonprofit members. In addition, clubs offer substantial private benefits in the mission accountability context as their standards and swords guide member nonprofits through articulation, evaluation, and legitimate transformation of their missions. Although mission accountability does not yet appear to be a major focus area for many clubs, the CRC described by Bies has, in the past decade, begun to focus on mission standards. Still, this process has been difficult and the CRC standards remain more focused on financial and organizational accountability, as do those of the clubs explored by Tschirhart and Bowman. As clubs are created and modified, their designers should consciously orient them to fill the crucial mission accountability void.

Public principals engage in very little legal regulation touching on mission accountability. Public mandates require only generic statements of purposes to be generated and filed with state and federal tax authorities.

Fulfilling these mandates in turn provides weak, if not negligible, signals regarding mission accountability to public and private principals who may access them. Enforcement mechanisms are likewise nonexistent or unreliable. Regulatory and judicial action touching on mission change might offer valuable information, but is too infrequent and inconsistent to provide reliable enforcement of mission accountability. Moreover, government regulators are particularly unsuitable to serve as everyday enforcers of mission accountability.

Of course, private principals can all make their own assessments of how well a nonprofit is hewing to its mission. Any type of private principal – donors, beneficiaries, partner organizations, and the general public – may in a particular case be vocal in demanding that a nonprofit heed its own concerns regarding mission. They can enforce their mission accountability claims by withdrawing their support. The opinions of funding principals may be especially loud and persuasive on this topic. Yet, evolving or cabining mission to serve the squeaky wheel is not true mission accountability. Rather, pursuit of mission accountability demands engagement with a process by various principals, to examine and test claims regarding the need to hew to or change mission, and hashing out the unavoidable conflicts among these principals through dialogue. Thus, while some principals may be able to articulate or enforce mission accountability standards in service of their own idiosyncratic goals, they are also unsuited to play this role for the larger society.

With the understanding that mission articulation, evaluation, and legitimate transformation are all processes, a club can adopt a range of standards requiring members to adopt and utilize them. At the very least, a club can adopt a standard requiring that organizations maintain a mission statement beyond the generic statement of purposes required by law. In order to earn membership, nonprofits will have to undertake at least this first step toward tracking mission. Because principals' standards in this area are so bare, this slight uptick can offer real improvements in the signal principals receive regarding mission accountability. Thus, there will be branding benefits of even this feeble club standard. It also can provide limited private benefits to the extent it induces nonprofits to engage in mission articulation activities that they would not otherwise have undertaken.

Clubs can provide greater branding benefits regarding mission accountability by adopting more stringent standards, utilizing strong swords, or both. Clubs can adopt standards demanding that mission be interrogated by member nonprofits' boards on a timeline, perhaps annually. These demands can be backed up with swords demanding submission of supporting documentation and review of these documents. This review, of course, should be limited to confirming that the required dialogue has occurred. External review of how a particular nonprofit balances the demands that it defer to and legitimately evolve its mission is deeply problematic. Still, these requirements will provide branding benefits by signaling the fact that the board is engaged in an ongoing debate on the content of the nonprofit's mission. Further, these standards will sensitize nonprofit leaders to the crucial question of mission accountability and give them a set of points at which to reflect upon it. Thereby, nonprofits will be empowered to improve their mission accountability, to the private benefit of individual groups and to general benefit of the nonprofit sector.

Even more stringent standards could mandate the adoption and use of procedures to encourage ongoing discussion about mission fulfillment among a nonprofit's various principals. A club could require intermittent meetings to allow principals to voice their concerns on how the nonprofit is pursuing its mission, and to provide them with the opportunity to hear the positions of others. It could mandate that notice of these meetings be given to various groups of principals, including publication in a newspaper or posting on the organization's website. Again, assuming that swords suffice to make club membership a reliable signal, these requirements would reassure principals of their ability to voice positions on mission on a regular basis. As such, these standards offer additional branding benefits. However, the private benefits of offering member nonprofits a framework to generate dialogue among principals about mission and resolve conflicts about mission evolution are likely more substantial.

Clubs might also set standards limiting the means by which a member's mission may be changed, demanding notice, deliberation, documentation, and perhaps consensus. Member nonprofits could be required to invoke such legitimate process for considering impact on mission as a prerequisite to changing a mission statement, adopting or discontinuing a program, or other similar events implicating mission change. A standard demanding the opportunity for debate among principals in advance of actions that could transform mission would reassure principals concerned about nonprofits veering off the rails. It would send a powerful signal to principals that some warning system exists to protect their interests. Moreover, additional private benefits will be gained by educating nonprofits about those moments when mission should be assessed, and ways in which it can legitimately be transformed.

Clubs could adopt varying swords to enforce any of these mission accountability standards. A club may wish only to require members to certify they have complied with the relevant standard. If a club chooses to review these certifications, it again should look only for adequate process. It is important to be aware of the danger of arrogating to the club authority over the proper substantive course of the mission of its member nonprofits. As the MCN experience described by Bies demonstrates, clubs attempting to rate substantive compliance with mission will meet strong resistance. Any mission accountability review also will need to be speedy. It cannot be allowed to create delays that hinder the ability of club members to respond to the needs of their constituencies.

As in the financial and organizational accountability context, as clubs increase the stringency of mission accountability standards and their swords to compel compliance, the clubs' expenses and fees for membership will also rise. These upsurges in cost will have predictable consequences. Some nonprofits may be priced out and, therefore, will not be able to receive the branding and private benefits of membership. Owing to network effects, if too many nonprofits are priced out of membership, the value of the club's branding benefits will be reduced. Club designers should be cautious not to adopt standards or swords so stringent or potent that the mission accountability benefits of club membership will be available to only a small number of nonprofits. The need for greater mission account-ability is too great.

Furthermore, club designers must be wary of unintended consequences. If a proposed change of program or mission statement engenders fear in club members – fear that their membership is at risk, or even fear of the costs of compliance with the club's mandated process – evolution of nonprofit mission may be inappropriately hampered. One great value of nonprofits lies in their ability to balance the competing policies of preserv-ing their original values and evolving to meet society's current needs. Thus, it is paramount for club designers to consider the impacts of the standards and swords they select on their members' ability to play this important role.

The club framework has the greatest potential to improve nonprofit accountability in the mission context, as a result of the extremely low baseline of standard articulation and enforcement by principals in this area. Clubs that require members to institute some process for expressing and evaluating mission offer information to principals and resulting branding benefits to nonprofits. This is true even if standards are relatively weak and accompanied by few swords to incentivize ongoing compliance. By sensitizing nonprofit leaders to the importance of tracking mission, and giving them a framework in which to undertake this process, mission accountability standards also offer significant private benefits. Additional mission accountability gains may be available by increasing the stringency and potency of the standards and swords selected. As throughout the process of club design, however, consideration of costs and consequences is vital. With such a limited baseline of standard articulation and enforcement by principals, clubs should seize the opportunity to fill the perilous gaps in mission accountability.

Conclusion

Clubs have the potential to complement nonprofit accountability enforcement by principals. Among the multiple principals relevant to nonprofits, public and funding principals are the only ones who will consistently have the authority and resources to establish and enforce accountability standards. Thanks to their own mandates, incentive structures, and resources, these principals will concentrate their efforts on financial accountability. Organizational activity will receive some secondary, although suboptimal, attention. Club standards and swords could be consciously designed to fill the gaps in principal enforcement in these areas. In the mission accountability context, articulation and enforcement of standards by public and private principals is negligible or counterproductive. Therefore, club design is even more pivotal and designers have a somewhat freer hand to craft standards and swords in this area.

This volume conceptualizes accountability relationships between principals and nonprofits as consisting of standards for behavior, flows of information, and a set of potential responses to that information. This chapter shows how accountability clubs can play a critical role as mediators of information between nonprofits and their principals, even when they do not engage in beyond-compliance standard-setting. When principals have little means of enforcing existing standards, a club brand can provide a credible signal to principals about nonprofit compliance. The chapter argues that organizational and mission accountability are the least occupied accountability spaces in the United States, and posits that clubs have the greatest potential to improve accountability relationships in this area. A key question for the rest of the volume is the extent to which clubs take up this opportunity.

REFERENCES

ABA Section of Business Law. 2002. *Guidebook for Directors of Nonprofit Corporations*, edited by George W. Overton and Jeannie Carmadelle Frey. 2nd edn. Chicago: American Bar Association.

Ascher, Mark L., Austin Wakeman Scott, and William Franklin Fratcher. 2008. *Scott and Ascher on Trusts*, 5th edn. New York: Aspen.

Atkinson, Rob. 1998. Unsettled Standing: Who (Else) Should Enforce the Duties of Charitable Fiduciaries? *Journal of Corporation Law.* 23: 655–699.

Blasko, Mary Grace, Curt S. Crossley and David Lloyd. 1993. Standing to Sue in the Charitable Sector. *University of San Francisco Law Review.* 28: 37–84.

Bob Jones University v. United States, 461 U.S. 574 (1983).

Bograd, Harriet. 1994. The Role of State Attorneys General in Relation to Troubled Nonprofits. Program on Nonprofit Organizations, Yale University, Working Paper No. 206, August. Accessed via http://ponpo.som.yale.edu/work.php.

Brakman Reiser, Dana. 2003. Dismembering Civil Society: The Social Cost of Internally Undemocratic Nonprofits. *Oregon Law Review* 82(3): 829–900.

2004. Enron.org: Why Sarbanes–Oxley Will not Ensure Comprehensive Nonprofit Accountability. *University of California, Davis Law Review* 38(1): 205–280.

Brody, Evelyn. 1996. Agents without Principals: The Economic Convergence of the Nonprofit and For-Profit Organizational Forms. *New York Law School Law Review* 40(3): 457–536.

1998. The Limits of Charity Fiduciary Law. *Maryland Law Review* 57: 1400–1501.

2002. Accountability and Public Trust. In Lester Salamon, ed. *The State of Nonprofit America*. Washington, DC: The Urban Institute Press, pp. 471–498.

2004. Whose Public? Parochialism and Paternalism in State Charity Law Enforcement. *Indiana Law Journal* 79: 937–1036.

2007. From the Dead Hand to the Living Dead: The Conundrum of Charitable-Donor Standing. *Georgia Law Review* 41: 1183–1276.

Bucholtz, Barbara K. 1998. Reflections on the Role of Nonprofit Associations in a Representative Democracy. *Cornell Journal of Law and Public Policy* 7: 555–603.

Cal. Gov. Code § 12586.

Charity Oversight and Reform: Keeping Bad Things from Happening to Good Charities: Hearing Before the Subcomm. on Finance of the S. Comm. on Finance, 108th Cong. (2004).

Chisolm, Laura B. 1995. Accountability of Nonprofit Organizations and Those Who Control Them: The Legal Framework. *Nonprofit Management & Leadership* 6: 141–156.

Crimm, Nina J. 2001. A Case Study of a Private Foundation's Governance and Self-Interested Fiduciaries Calls for Further Regulation. *Emory Law Journal* 50: 1093–1196.

de Tocqueville, Alexis. 1969. *Democracy in America*, trans. by George Lawrence; edited by J. P. Mayer. Garden City, NY: Anchor Books.

Fishman, James J. 2003. Improving Charitable Accountability. *Maryland Law Review*. 62: 218–287.

Fishman, James J. and Stephen Schwarz. 2006. *Nonprofit Organizations*, 3rd edn. New York: Foundation Press.

Fremont-Smith, Marion R. 1965. *Foundations and Government*. Hartford, CT: Russell Sage Foundation.

2004. *Governing Nonprofit Organizations: Federal and State Law and Regulation*. Cambridge, MA: Harvard University Press.

GuideStar nonprofit reports and Forms 990 for donors, grantmakers, and businesses. Accessed via www.Guidestar.org/.

Hansmann, Henry B. 1980. The Role of Nonprofit Enterprise. *Yale Law Journal* 89: 835.

1981. Reforming Nonprofit Corporation Law. *University of Pennsylvania Law Review* 129: 479.

Internal Revenue Service, Rev. Proc. 90–12.

IRC §§ 170(c), 170(f)(8), 501(c)(3), 4943, 4944, 4958, 6115.

IRS Form 990 and Instructions. 2007 and new 2008 versions. Accessed via www. irs.gov/charities/index.html.

Manhattan Eye, Ear & Throat Hospital v. *Spitzer*, 715 N.Y.S.2d 575 (1999).

Mass. Gen. Laws ch. 12 § 8F.

Panel on the Nonprofit Sector. 2005a. Interim Report Presented to the Senate Finance Committee. Accessed via www.nonprofitpanel.org/about/interim/ PanelReport.pdf.

2005b. Strengthening Transparency Governance Accountability of Charitable Organizations: A Final Report to Congress and the Nonprofit Sector. Accessed via www.nonprofitpanel.org/Report/final/Panel_Final_Report.pdf.

2006. Strengthening Transparency Governance Accountability of Charitable Organizations: A Supplement to the Final Report to Congress and the Nonprofit Sector. Accessed via www.nonprofitpanel.org/Report/supplement/ Panel_Supplement_Final.pdf.

Phelan, Marilyn E. 2000. *Nonprofit Enterprises: Corporations, Trusts, and Associations.* St. Paul, MN: West Group.

Revised Model Nonprofit Corporation Act (RMNCA). 1998. §§ 2.02–03, 2.05–06, 7.01, 8.01, 8.20–25.

Ross, Lynne M., ed. 1990. *State Attorneys General: Powers and Responsibilities.* Washington, DC: National Association of Attorneys General.

Siegel, Jack B. 2006. *A Desktop Guide for Nonprofit Directors, Officers, and Advisors.* Hoboken, NJ: John Wiley & Sons.

Silber, Norman I. 2001. *A Corporate Form of Freedom.* Boulder, CO: Westview Press.

Strom, Stephanie. 2003. Accountability: New Equation for Charities: More Money, Less Oversight. *New York Times*, November 17: F1.

Swords, Peter. 1998. The Form 990 as an Accountability Tool for 501(c)(3) Nonprofits. *Tax Lawyer* 51: 571–574.

Treasury Regulation § 53.4958–6.

Weitzman, M. S., N. T. Jalandoni, L. M. Lampkin, and T. H. Pollak, eds. 2002. *The New Nonprofit Almanac and Desk Reference: The Essential Facts and Figures for Managers, Researchers, and Volunteers.* San Francisco: Jossey-Bass.

3   Trends and patterns in third-party accreditation clubs

Woods Bowman

An important group of accountability clubs are accreditation clubs. These clubs try to influence the behavior of member organizations using tools ranging from codes of conduct to intensive and sophisticated accreditation processes. This chapter uses the club framework developed by Gugerty and Prakash in this volume (chapter 1) that combines an agency perspective on accountability with club theory and signaling theory to describe the various types of voluntary standard-setting and enforcement in the nonprofit sector. The particular focus of this chapter is on the health and education sectors in the United States where such clubs are quite prevalent. A principal who delegates a task to an agent has a right to expect the agent to perform according to her specifications. When the self-interests of the principal and her agent diverge, as they often do, the agent has an incentive to shirk. Asymmetric information between the general public and its agent (a nonprofit) places the public at a disadvantage in giving, volunteering, and seeking service. Asymmetric information is a fact of life where the most important characteristics of services are not readily observable and/or not easily evaluated by lay persons – as is typical of education and healthcare services. Gugerty and Prakash identify competence asymmetry as an additional component of the information problem. Even if one has information on an organization, one might not be able to evaluate competence as it is unclear how well that information measures organizational competence. As Brakman Reiser points out in chapter 2, claims for financial and organizational accountability by both public and private nonprofit principals are restricted by both legal and practical limitations.

Principals can redress information asymmetries by monitoring, but monitoring is costly and it does not help redress competence asymmetries. This is where accreditation clubs add value. Club sponsors, who have the

Results of the research presented in this chapter were originally reported in "Accountability through Self-Regulation in the Nonprofit Sector: A Preliminary Report," presented to the Association for Research on Nonprofit Organizations and Voluntary Action at Miami (December 1, 2001).

technical competence necessary to evaluate programs, serve as the managers of such programs. To ensure that members fulfill club expectations, sponsors collectively develop standards which they may supplement with monitoring. Without complete information on the reliability of a club's sponsors, the public and other stakeholders can assess a club's credibility only by observing its design. A club with clear standards but without monitoring is likely to be judged to be a weak club and marginally credible, whereas a club that monitors compliance is stronger, but a club with clear standards that monitors and imposes sanctions for noncompliance is a strong club and likely to be judged credible. For example, the federal government makes use of accreditation by the Joint Commission (formerly the Joint Commission on Accreditation of Health Care Organizations) to identify hospitals that are eligible for Medicaid funds. The emphasis here is primarily on strong clubs, and the Joint Commission will be used to illustrate main points. The Joint Commission is a 501(c)(3) tax-exempt organization that surveys and accredits numerous types of healthcare organizations including general medical-surgical hospitals. It is arguably the most significant accreditation club in the United States because billions of federal dollars are contingent upon its accreditation.

A club's standards and its enforcement must be sufficiently stringent to affect perceptions of participant quality, but not so stringent that few organizations seek accreditation. The word "club" seemingly implies a formal membership that exercises direct control over the group through election of officers, like the American Hospital Association, but this need not be the case. Some accrediting clubs, like the Joint Commission, do not have members in this sense. Instead, their members are an amorphous group of organizations with common interests that are furthered by accreditation.

All clubs provide a brand identity for their members. Strong clubs protect the brand's value by preventing nonconforming members from free-riding (a form of shirking). The Joint Commission, like other strong accreditation clubs, is self-conscious about its brand identity. As its website says,

Joint Commission accreditation and certification is recognized nationwide as a symbol of quality that reflects an organization's commitment to meeting certain performance standards ... The website now reflects The Joint Commission's new brand and logo, as well as our new tagline, Helping Health Care Organizations Help Patients. The new brand reflects The Joint Commission's continuing efforts to improve the value of accreditation and its utility as a mechanism for improving the quality and safety of patient care. (www.jointcommission.org)

A typical nonprofit organization has numerous stakeholders, all vying for a role as principal with accountability claims on the nonprofit. If their demands are not mutually conflicting, all is well, but this situation is not assured. If their demands are in conflict, there are two possibilities. Either

(1) the organization's managers make trade-offs, which satisfies everyone in part but also disappoints everyone in part, or (2) a dominant principal emerges whose interests take precedence. As this chapter reveals, the education and healthcare subsectors together have more strong accreditation clubs than the balance of the nonprofit sector. I argue that this is because the federal government, as the single most important source of funds to healthcare and education, plays the role of dominant principal.

A dominant principal has the power to grant significant benefits to club participants, or to wield a sword that can create significant penalties. As mentioned above, the federal government makes use of Joint Commission accreditation to identify hospitals that are eligible for Medicaid funds. To be denied Medicaid funding is a virtual death sentence for most hospitals and this gives the Joint Commission's work teeth. The threat of this sanction makes nonprofits willing to participate in strong certification programs and makes this certification credible to external stakeholders: although they cannot directly observe participant quality, they recognize that organizations will not want to jeopardize their funding and are therefore likely to adhere to the standards set by the Joint Commission. Another example: according to the website of the Higher Learning Commission (HLC) of the North Central Association of Colleges and Schools, the United States Department of Education is "threatening" not to provide financial aid for any instruction site submitted to the Department of Energy (DoE) but not registered with HLC.

Research method

To identify the sample of accountability clubs in the USA, I searched on key words such as accreditation, certification, and common variants, in the mission statements of all 23,000 associations in the United States listed in the internet edition of Gale's *Encyclopedia of Associations* (Gale's). Because the main purpose was to study accreditation programs among nonprofit organizations, selection excluded associations that certify individuals in a professional capacity (e.g. architects, doctors, accountants, nurses). Also excluded were umbrella associations such as the Boy's and Girl's Clubs, Goodwill Industries, United Way, etc. that set standards for their affiliates. This group has already been studied by Young *et al.* (1996) who likewise used Gale's to identify candidates.[1] However, Gale's does not classify nonprofits by industry, so this study assigned candidates to industry groups

---

[1] They conclude that most umbrella associations act like trade associations, providing service to their members without exerting control. Only one in three umbrella associations attempts to regulate its affiliates.

Table 3.1 *Focus of accreditation clubs in sample*

	Candidates	Respondents
Education	118	29
Health	52	37
Welfare	12	9
Technical	8	5
Cultural/recreation	4	2
Government	2	1
Other	6	1
Unclassified/anonymous	14	14
Total	216	98
No standards	17 (est.)	8
Net	199 (est.)	90

based on their names and inferences drawn from their mission statements.[2] This method of selection is likely to identify most of the strong clubs. The mission statements of weak clubs may be silent on promulgating standards.

The search, conducted from February through May of 2001, resulted in 216 candidates. The resulting list likely overlooks some accreditation clubs, but the power of electronic search engines provides a reasonable basis for believing that it is sufficiently extensive to reveal broad trends and patterns. After a pretest involving twenty candidates, a ten-question survey was mailed to the others. It was deliberately kept short to maximize the response rate; consequently a number of issues remain unexplored. The survey instrument can be found as the appendix to this chapter. The postal service returned 10 percent (n = 21) as undeliverable. Fifty percent (n = 98) responded. Of respondents, 5 percent (n = 11) are not involved in this activity or did not respond to the question. The method of searching on mission statements probably missed most of the weak clubs, but it likely identified most of the strong clubs. If so, we can say that the universe of strong accreditation clubs is somewhat larger than two hundred. (See Table 3.1.) This estimate is a dynamic figure, likely to be growing.

From Table 3.1 it is obvious that accrediting clubs whose primary focus is education at any level (55 percent) or healthcare (24 percent) predominate. Nearly a third of the education accreditation clubs (n = 35) have a secondary focus in healthcare by training healthcare workers. For reasons that are unclear, the response rate for education accreditation clubs is lower than their prevalence among possible candidates.

---

[2] Some names permitted unambiguous classification because they contained words like "education," "colleges," or "healthcare," but others were more inferential, such as "rehabilitation facilities."

Curiously, the number of accreditation clubs in education is nearly double the number in health, although healthcare service providers are more numerous than private education institutions. This difference might be explained by the fact that the Joint Commission is a powerhouse accreditation club that dominates healthcare, surveying and accrediting a diverse set of healthcare institutions providing ambulatory care, behavioral healthcare, critical access hospitals, disease-specific care, general medical-surgical hospitals, healthcare staffing services, home care, laboratories, long-term care, and office-based surgery practices.

There is no comparable multi-institution accrediting club in education. In fact, education exhibits extreme fragmentation. My own university is an example. It is accredited by the Higher Learning Commission of the North Central Association of Colleges and Schools. Several schools and colleges within the university are accredited separately by other organizations. For example, the American Bar Association accredits its law school, and the Association to Advance Collegiate Schools of Business accredits its College of Commerce, and so forth. Departments and degree programs are separately accredited as well. The program in which I teach is accredited by the National Association of Schools of Public Affairs and Administration (NASPAA), which requires periodic self-studies backed up by on-site peer reviews. It is also a member of the Nonprofit Academic Centers Council (NACC, a club of teaching and research centers in nonprofit studies), which uses curricular guidelines to screen programs for membership, but lacks an ongoing enforcement mechanism like NASPAA's. In the terms used here, NASPAA is a strong club, NACC is a weak one. This is consistent with the findings of Young in this volume (chapter 5), who examines the accountability club run by NACC and finds it to be particularly hesitant to engage in strong monitoring and enforcement of members.

Table 3.2 shows that, of ninety-five respondents to my inquiry, eight are false positives – that is, despite the occurrence of one of the key words in

Table 3.2 *Use of passive standards v. accreditation by clubs in sample*

	Passive standards		
	No	Yes	Total
Accredit. No	8	10	18
Accredit. Yes	47	30	77
Total	55	40	95

Note: Three respondents answered "Not sure" to one or both of these questions.

their mission statement, they neither establish passive standards nor accredit with verification. Eleven percent (n = 10) are clubs with weak enforcement, relying solely on passive standards to do the job. The remaining 81 percent (n = 77) have strong enforcement, accrediting with verification. Forty percent of the latter group (n = 30) supplement with passive standards such as codes of ethics and best practices that are not part of the formal accreditation process.

Historical trends in club monitoring and verification

Given that passive standards tend to give rise to weak clubs, while accreditation with verification is associated with stronger clubs, the survey distinguished between these two groups. Figure 3.1 shows growth rates for different types of accreditation clubs. The values are the numbers of clubs in the sample based on self-reported dates of first use of passive standards and accrediting with verification. As sample data, they underreport actual population. However, assuming that the reported number is proportional to the actual population in each time period, the slopes should give us a reasonably accurate picture.

Passive standards form the older accreditation tool – the earliest date reported for this practice by a respondent was 1890. The "reluctant clubs"

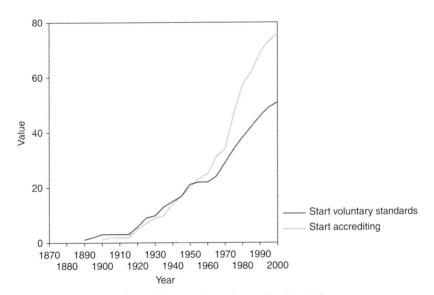

Figure 3.1 Cumulative number of accreditation clubs

of infrastructure organizations, which Dennis Young discusses in this volume (chapter 5), and the weak clubs of state associations, which Mary Tschirhart analyzes (chapter 4), promulgate passive standards. Independent Sector provides hyperlinks to more than a hundred such codes on its website. This section, however, focuses on strong clubs that verify compliance.

The exceedingly high proportion of accreditation clubs found in the fields of education and healthcare is striking. This phenomenon seems to depend more on money than on the number of organizations operating in a field because the revenues of healthcare and education providers have soared relative to those of other reporting public charities, while numerically these organizations have become a smaller fraction of the nonprofit universe. The amount of money flowing to healthcare and education institutions overwhelms the revenues of all other charities combined. In 2000, healthcare and education revenues comprised 74 percent of all reported charitable revenue, up from 41 percent in 1977. However, between 1954 and 2000, healthcare and education service providers fell from comprising 44 percent of all reporting public charities to 32 percent, implying lower than average growth rates in these sectors.

Figure 3.2 shows the growth rates of the strong accrediting clubs in both fields. As in Figure 3.1, values are the numbers of clubs in the sample

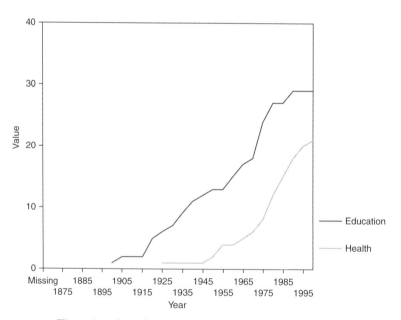

Figure 3.2 Cumulative number of education and health accrediting bodies

based on self-reported dates of first use of accrediting with verification. (Passive standards are not represented.) As sample data, they underreport actual population. However, assuming that the reported number is proportional to the actual population in each time period, the slopes should give us a reasonably accurate picture.

The presence of a dominant principal influences the type of club that emerges. This chapter argues that a key reason for the increased prevalence of stronger accreditation clubs in the healthcare and education fields is the strong influence of federal funding. Growth patterns depicted in Figures 3.1 and 3.2 seem to correlate with major changes in federal funding. The following paragraphs sketch the history of federal funding in healthcare and education.

Passage of the 1946 Hill–Burton Act, which financed new hospital construction, coincided with the formation of new accreditation clubs in healthcare. The Joint Commission was created in 1951. Growth of new healthcare accreditation clubs accelerated upon the launch of Medicaid and Medicare in 1965. The federal government moved from being a bystander to being a principal of healthcare organizations and, as its financial commitment grew, it quickly became the dominant principal of the Joint Commission. In 2001, the federal government spent $348 billion on Medicaid and Medicare.[3] Nonprofit institutions of all kinds received approximately $199 billion of this amount, which constituted 88 percent of all their total income. Nonprofit hospitals alone received $167 billion, with two-thirds coming from Medicare.

The federal government has been funding higher education longer than healthcare. Milestones are: the Hatch Act (funding for agricultural research) in 1887, Smith-Lever Act (cooperative extension) in 1914, GI Bill in 1944, National Defense Education Act in 1958, Economic Opportunity Act (work-study) in 1964, and Higher Education Act in 1965 (the foundation of all current federal student aid programs). The last has been amended and extended several times. It is hard to track federal dollars flowing to higher education because much federal support is in the form of subsidized loans to students who then pay the college. Accreditation clubs in education increased their numbers at a relatively steady rate from 1915 onward until a surge occurred in 1975. It is noteworthy that three out of the four education accreditation clubs formed after 1975 were involved in education for the health professions.

An interesting contrast to these histories is the Standards of Excellence program of the Maryland Association of Nonprofit Organizations

---

[3] Public funding data in this paragraph are calculated from Figure 5.1 and Table 5.3 in Bowman and Fremont-Smith (2006).

(MANO), which has no dominant principal holding the whip hand. In 1988 MANO obtained foundation support to establish an institute to replicate Standards of Excellence nationwide (Bowman and Bies, 2005). Participating nonprofits must apply, agree to abide by the standards, submit to evaluation by the institute's local replication partner, and pay a fee. Accredited nonprofits are authorized to use the institute's seal. The institute can withdraw authorization to use the seal if a nonprofit fails to live up to the Standards for Excellence. However, after a decade only a few dozen charities in Maryland are in this program – mostly small local groups or chapters of national nonprofits (Phillips, 2005).[4] Nationwide, participation numbers in the hundreds, not thousands. Given that participation is costly, lack of participation suggests that nonprofit decision-makers see low or highly uncertain marginal benefits of the program. If participants reported increased donations, or if a dominant principal insisted, participation would undoubtedly increase.

Patterns in club standards: monitoring and verification

Here we return to the survey data discussed above to evaluate patterns of club structure in terms of membership, standards, and enforcement. The survey allowed each respondent to decide what constitutes a member of its own organization. To keep the survey short it asked simply "Is yours a membership association?" Seventy-three percent responded affirmatively. This is consistent with Gugerty's finding in this volume (chapter 10), that many accreditation clubs are membership-based. The median membership among strong accreditation clubs is 906. As discussed below, most verification is undertaken through peer mechanisms. The high median size suggests that most membership-based accrediting clubs have an adequate pool of trained professionals to draw upon for the demanding tasks of developing standards, setting benchmarks, and evaluating applicants for accreditation. Of course, outsiders may be involved in the accrediting process to lend a public perspective. In designing the survey instrument it was assumed that most membership-based accrediting clubs restrict accrediting with verification to their own membership and, if they

---

[4] This paragraph is from Bowman and Bies (2005). Jordan Silvergleid (2003) of The Advisory Board, an association of healthcare systems and medical centers, questions whether donors care about ratings. Using statistical techniques, he was unable to detect a relationship between American Institute of Philanthropy ratings of various organizations and the amount of donations they receive. In Minnesota, donations to regional charities apparently respond to whether they meet the standards of the Minnesota Charities Review Council, but his sample is too small for this result to be convincing.

offered accrediting with verification for nonmembers, they would provide a cost advantage to their members.

Accreditation tools

The survey asked whether the club utilized self-assessment, site visits by staff, and/or site visits by peers. It turns out that accrediting with verification is substantially peer-driven. Only one accrediting club that performs verification does not use a self-assessment tool in conjunction with a site visit by staff or peers. Consequently use of self-assessments is not reported in Table 3.3. Of those accrediting clubs that utilize site visits, only three rely exclusively on staff. (The Joint Commission, which did not respond to the survey, exclusively relies on paid surveyors.) The others are evenly divided between utilizing only peers and utilizing peers and staff, as we see in Table 3.3. Other analyses (not tabulated) compared the use of peers by membership organizations and nonmembership organizations. It found both types of accrediting clubs are equally likely to use peers.

Standards

The categories of standards emphasized in the accreditation process are shown in Table 3.4, which is arranged by prevalence of a category among respondents. (Each category is presented as it was worded in the survey.) Overall program quality, credentialing, and program outcomes are the most frequently mentioned, followed closely by ethics. Public disclosure, governance, and financial management are decidedly less popular, but still mentioned by at least three-fifths of respondents. Only fundraising drops out of sight at 19 percent, which is interesting because fundraising ratios are of great public interest and fundraising practice is the top concern in many European clubs. A plausible explanation is that education and healthcare are largely federally subsidized fee-based programs and

Table 3.3 *Participants in site visits*

	Use site visit by peers		
	No	Yes	Total
Use site visit by staff – No	1	35	36
Use site visit by staff – Yes	3	34	38
Total	4	69	74

Note: Twenty did not answer these questions and one answered "Not sure."

Table 3.4 *Categories of standards (in percent, except minimum number)*

	All	Education	Healthcare
Program quality	94	97	91
Credentialing of personnel	88	90	90
Program outcomes	87	97	76
Ethics	78	87	67
Public disclosure	71	80	67
Governance	69	90	57
Financial management	62	83	38
Fundraising	19	27	0
Minimum number of responses	76	30	21

Table 3.5 *Correlations between categories of standards*

	Credentials	Outcomes	Ethics	Disclosure	Governance	Finances	Fundraising
Quality	**0.51**	**0.44**	**0.33**	**0.37**	0.16	0.12	0.13
Credentials		**0.44**	**0.47**	**0.43**	0.18	0.12	0.07
Outcomes			0.07	**0.34**	**0.29**	0.09	0.17
Ethics				**0.30**	**0.30**	**0.34**	0.17
Disclosure					**0.29**	**0.35**	**0.22**
Governance						**0.63**	**0.33**
Finances							**0.30**

Notes: Categories are paraphrased to save space. Bold and italic indicates significance at the 0.01 level (2-tail t-test); bold only, significance at the 0.05 level. In other words, there is less than a one-in-twenty chance that bold-faced values are zero or have the opposite sign.

therefore donors are not dominant principals. There are interesting differences between different types of institutions. The categories in Table 3.4, except fundraising, are more or less of equal interest to education bodies. In healthcare, program quality and credentialing predominate.

These categories cluster in revealing ways as the correlation coefficients in Table 3.5 show. The numerical value of a correlation coefficient indicates the strength of a relationship between variables. A positive value means the variables tend to change in the same direction (both up or both down), whereas a negative sign would mean they tend to change in opposite directions (one up, the other down). A plus one or a minus one indicates that it is possible to predict with perfect accuracy the change in one variable knowing only a change in the other. A zero correlation indicates that regardless of how a variable changes, the other is as likely to increase as to decrease, making accurate predictions impossible. It should be emphasized that a high correlation between two variables does not imply that one causes the other.

In Table 3.5 disclosure correlates with nearly every other variable. Unlike the other categories, disclosure is a sword. The accountability club framework suggests that disclosure punishes "bad" organizations by publishing information that principals will find negative. This result can be interpreted in several ways that are not mutually exclusive. Disclosure by a strict accreditation program is a signal to the public that it is reliable. For less strict programs, it is a way to enlist the market as a policing mechanism. It also economizes on monitoring costs since disclosure requirements do not require extensive monitoring or investigation. Interestingly, membership organizations and nonmember-based organizations are equally likely to have disclosure standards (approximately 70 percent).

This table also shows two partially overlapping clusters of variables that are mutually correlated to a significant degree, suggesting the existence of two unobserved causal variables (one corresponding to each cluster). One cluster consists of quality, credentials, outcomes, and ethics. Governance, finances, and fundraising form another cluster. Disclosure correlates significantly with everything except fundraising. In other words, when an accreditation club sets up a program, it tends not to pick and choose from the full menu of standards, but rather to focus on standards belonging to categories in one or the other cluster. I used a multivariate technique called discriminant analysis to find the combination of standards that best differentiated healthcare and educational institutions.[5] It only confirmed what was evident from casual inspection of the data: having financial standards is a key distinguishing characteristic. In general, education accreditation clubs have them; healthcare clubs do not.

Twenty-five of the thirty education accreditation clubs have standards that include financial management, while only eight in twenty-one healthcare accreditation clubs have financial management standards. Neither the US Department of Health and Human Services (HHS) standards nor the Joint Commission's standards include financial management. Why? Hospitals cannot turn away patients, so they must maintain excess capacity, but universities operate at capacity because they can be choosy about whom they admit, and they admit more than they can accommodate, expecting that some will decline their offer. These differences have implications for their finances.

---

[5] I subjected the data for education and healthcare to a step-wise discriminant analysis using the Wilkes' Lambda method and identified financial management as the single discriminating factor. The discriminant function evaluated at the centroid of each group yielded $+0.43$ for education and -0.62 for healthcare, a significant difference at the 0.01 level in view of the large $F = 13.6$.

Hospitals receive 88 percent of their income from program services[6] and their key challenge is to fill empty beds. If accreditation succeeds in improving a hospital's quality, its average daily census is likely to increase, bringing it more revenue. As long as the margin on each occupied bed is positive, increasing quality will automatically improve a hospital's bottom line. However, universities receive only 56 percent of their revenue from program services,[7] suggesting that many of their programs lose money. Thus expansion is counterproductive in most cases. Unlike hospitals, universities typically have more applicants than openings. If accreditation succeeds in increasing a university's quality, it will increase the number of applicants without bringing additional revenue. Ergo, increased quality does not automatically lead to improved finances for universities. This may also explain why 27 percent of accreditation clubs in education have fundraising standards compared with none in healthcare.

The viability of an average educational provider depends on its success at exploiting and managing diverse income streams from nonprogram sources. This is a daunting task where elementary management miscues can have catastrophic consequences. Differences in the administrative skill pools magnify the financial dangers inherent in university management. Most healthcare institutions are managed by professional administrators, whereas the principle of shared governance in higher education has resulted in colleges and universities being run by tenured faculty who, for the most part, are not trained in business administration. Accreditation serves a teaching as well as a policing function and in education, more so than in healthcare, teaching is needed in financial management.

Case study: the Joint Commission

Survey data provide an overview of accreditation activity, but they leave unanswered many interesting questions about how the relationship between principals and agents affects club design. Case studies are useful for filling in the blanks. This chapter concludes with a short history of the Joint Commission's role in accreditation of hospitals.[8] The Joint Commission is a good place to start because of its long history, its pivotal role in accreditation of healthcare institutions, and its complex relationship with the federal government. This section will address the question: why did the federal government turn to accreditation clubs in the nonprofit sector instead of directly regulating it, like the Food and Drug

---

[6] Calculated by the author from Wing *et al.* (2008), Tables 5.13 and 5.15.   [7] See note 6.

[8] Unless otherwise noted, the information in this section is from Sprague (2005).

Administration regulates the pharmaceutical industry or the Department of Agriculture inspects food-processing plants?

The Joint Commission derives 91 percent of its revenues from program services, charging hospitals between $6,250 and $26,000 every three years depending on their size. Nearly all of its other income is investment-related.[9] According to the American Hospital Association, of 5,585 hospitals (including public and for-profit) in 2003, 4,671 were accredited, and 80 percent of these were accredited by the Joint Commission. The 914 unaccredited hospitals, mostly located in sparsely populated rural areas, cited cost as the main reason for forgoing accreditation. These costs may not be limited to the expense of a survey, but may also refer to compliance costs.

The Joint Commission's history actually begins long before it incorporated. When the American College of Surgeons was founded in 1913, hospital standardization was one of its goals. In 1918 it established five minimum standards, which only 20 percent of hospitals could meet at the time. By 1935 this figure had reached 90 percent when the federal government adopted its first standards for hospitals, but these were limited to maternity and childcare.

The Hill–Burton Act of 1946 required the receiving states to establish minimum operational standards. At this time most states did not license hospitals. The American College of Surgeons, the American Medical Association, the American Hospital Association, and the American College of Physicians combined in 1951 to sponsor the Joint Commission on Accreditation of Hospitals (the Joint Commission's original title). The American Dental Association became a sponsor in 1979. Then, in 1965 Congress amended the Social Security Act to create Medicare and Medicaid. As a major funding source the federal government would be implicated if anything went wrong in the hospital system, creating problems for elected officials. Congress authorized the Secretary of the US Department of Health, Education and Welfare (HEW, now Health and Human Services or HHS) to promulgate minimum standards for hospitals – known as Conditions of Participation (COPs).

In 1965 the Joint Commission was accrediting 60 percent of hospitals. These hospitals did not want to be subject to two sets of regulations, and they let their legislators know. So, "legislators are reported to have assured the hospital community that hospitals meeting [Joint Commission] standards would automatically be eligible for Medicare participation" (Sprague, 2005: 4). The law required participating hospitals to undergo

---

[9] Data are from the Joint Commission's 990 form which is publicly available at www. Guidestar.org.

a federal regulatory review to determine whether they satisfied the minimum federal standards, but hospitals accredited by the Joint Commission were automatically "deemed" to meet them.[10] In 1972 Congress gave the Secretary of HHS authority to establish higher standards than those of the Joint Commission and to conduct "validation" (or "look behind") surveys of Joint Commission-accredited hospitals to verify compliance. Initially, HHS subcontracted this responsibility to the states. In 1986 the Reagan administration adopted less restrictive, but broader, COPs and introduced the concept of quality assurance (QA). In 1997 a new rule formally required hospitals to have a Quality Assessment and Performance Improvement Program.

In 1999 the Inspector General for HHS issued a report pointedly subtitled "A Call for Greater Accountability." On the one hand it praised the Joint Commission for being "an important vehicle for reducing risk and fostering improvement" (Brown, 2003: 2). But the main point of the report was a finding that "Joint Commission surveys are unlikely to detect substandard patterns of care or individual practitioners with questionable skills." It noted that "the hospital review system is moving toward a collegial mode of oversight [focusing on education and improved performance] and away from a regulatory mode," citing the Joint Commission as a leader of the movement. The report concluded by saying "The emerging dominance of *the collegial mode may undermine the existing system of patient protection afforded by accreditation and certification practices*" (emphasis added).

The Inspector General observed that the Centers for Medicare and Medicaid Services (CMS) – at the time called the Health Care Financing Administration (HCFA) – "relies mainly on validation surveys conducted, at [its] expense, by the State agencies. But for a number of reasons, these surveys have been limited" (Sprague, 2005: 4). HHS began conducting its own validation surveys on a sample basis. In 2003 it conducted seventy-one validation surveys of hospitals accredited by the Joint Commission, finding twenty-three to be out of compliance with one of the twenty-two COPs. In response, the Joint Commission points to the 1,539 COPs that are validated (71 hospitals times 22 COPS minus 23 COPs not validated). Prior to 2006 the Joint Commission scheduled on-site surveys in advance. Currently, its accreditation process consists of an annual self-assessment and an unannounced triennial on-site survey.

---

[10] The Secretary of HEW (HHS) promulgated regulations in 1966 "deeming" the American Osteopathic Association's (AOA) standards as well. The AOA currently accredits 139 hospitals.

In this brief review of the history of the Joint Commission, we have discovered why the federal government turned to accreditation clubs in the nonprofit sector instead of directly regulating various healthcare institutions. By the time the federal government created Medicare and Medicaid, the Joint Commission was already accrediting 60 percent of American hospitals. (It is now 80 percent.) These new healthcare programs transformed the federal government into the dominant purchaser of healthcare – in other words, a dominant principal in the healthcare field. By endorsing the Joint Commission's process, the federal government accomplished two goals: it placated the hospitals that wanted to avoid duplicate regulation and it saved itself the cost of a monitoring bureaucracy.

However, this review suggests that over time relationships among HHS, the Joint Commission, and the hospitals became cozier. What started as a hard-nosed regulatory process morphed into a collegial process of education and improvement. Although the Inspector General acknowledged that both modes have positive qualities, she argued that "quick-paced, tightly structured, educationally oriented surveys afford little opportunity for in-depth probing of hospital conditions or practices" (Brown, 2003: 2). As a result of this stinging report, HHS exercised its prerogative as dominant principal and took direct charge of more aggressive monitoring of the monitors.

Further thoughts

Education and healthcare nonprofits have plenty of reasons to cooperate to control quality and set exclusive standards since growth in competition can drive down prices and uncontrolled expansion may invite low-quality operators that threaten the reputations of incumbent nonprofits. This may explain why the accreditation clubs in these subsectors favor accreditation with strong verification instead of passive mechanisms. It is tempting to speculate that strong accreditation clubs in healthcare and education have suppressed the growth of for-profit enterprises in these fields.

The discussion of financial management above suggests a dilemma inherent in standard-setting, especially for strong accreditation clubs: the costs of compliance. Higher quality is a good thing, but it comes at a price. This is consistent with signaling theory: credible signals are costly to send. Accreditation clubs must understand the cost structures of their industries and be careful not to increase quality faster than the market can pay for it. Clubs may gain power by increasing their size, but in the short run they must be careful that this does not come at the expense of standards or enforcement. Clubs must also be responsive to incumbent members. Making standards tight enough to restrict market entry is likely to be more popular than making standards so tight that they force incumbents out. The fact that most accreditation clubs in health and education are membership clubs might also raise fears about collusion and watering down of certification, as the Joint Commission case suggests.

My empirical results suggest that accreditation in education and healthcare is extensive. The federal government is a major financer of hospital services and when its interests are threatened, it can force stricter adherence to standards. This is consistent with Tschirhart's hypothesis in chapter 4 of this volume that government tends to support only those associations that serve a role in helping to promote good practices and policies through presentation of codes or statements. She was looking at state associations that, at best, promulgate passive standards. In this volume, Tschirhart, Young (chapter 5), and Gugerty (chapter 10) all find that most membership associations are engaged in recruiting and providing services to members, and these types of associations are less likely to sponsor strong accountability clubs. One reason, they hypothesize, is that such clubs are beholden to multiple principals who may have conflicting standards. In addition, it may be easier for members to pressure club sponsors to weaken standards and verification. Thus Angela Bies in this volume (chapter 9) finds that in Minnesota, two kinds of clubs have emerged. The nonprofit association there sponsors a club focused on education and improvement of nonprofits, while the main donor watchdog agency sponsors a club aimed at providing signals of quality to donors.

This chapter extends these findings: where a dominant principal, like the federal government, funds a specific program and this program is engaged in production of public goods, the dominant principal is more likely to demand strong verification measures. If there is no clear dominant principal in a nonprofit sector, accreditation clubs may be slower to emerge and may be weaker. If the government felt it was in its interest to do so, it could clearly increase the pressure on nonprofits (by means other than funding) and they might likely respond. But in our diffuse, federal system that seems unlikely.

Nonprofits outside of education and healthcare are starting to realize the value of accreditation clubs, and/or are feeling pressure and are starting to experiment with new structures. The Greater Kansas City Community Foundation recently developed DonorEdge, a file on nearly six hundred charities with data on both financial and nonfinancial performance metrics, verified through site visits. This is a hybrid model: no standards but verified data on program performance. Donors with funds managed by the foundation have access to DonorEdge through a password-protected portal on its website. DonorEdge does not establish standards, but most foundations in Kansas City require charities to participate in DonorEdge as a precondition for funding.[11] Word probably gets around about the applicants rejected by foundations because this or that metric was not "good enough." Over time de facto standards will probably emerge. This speculation deserves further research because the William and Flora Hewlett Foundation is financing an expansion of DonorEdge to seven additional cities.

A lingering question is: does accreditation boost public confidence? René Bekkers in this volume (chapter 11) finds that individuals in the Netherlands who are aware of the main accountability club in the country have higher confidence in fundraising nonprofits and increase the level of their donations. Unfortunately, similar data are not available for the USA. The most detailed surveys of public confidence in institutions were conducted in California between 1973 and 1997 by the marketing and public opinion polling firm Field Research Institute.[12] Since California is a microcosm of the nation, these data are worth considering. Although they are somewhat dated, they are consistent with recent national data collected by other polling organizations. Field measured the degree of public confidence (a lot, some, not much) in thirty-four different public and private institutions. In 1997 it reported that 37 percent of the general public had "a lot of confidence" in universities and colleges and 32 percent had "a lot" of confidence in hospitals. To put these numbers in perspective, universities and colleges ranked sixth of thirty-four institutions, just behind local police departments (39 percent) and just ahead of the medical profession (36 percent). Hospitals ranked eighth of thirty-four institutions, just behind the medical profession and tied with the US Supreme Court (32 percent).

These data are consistent with a national Harris poll conducted in 2006[13] showing 38 percent of the public had "a great deal" of confidence in "major educational institutions, such as colleges and universities." Hospitals were not included in this poll, but 31 percent reported "a great deal" of confidence in the medical profession, and 33 percent reported

[11] Private communication with Dr. David Renz, a nonprofit scholar at University of Missouri at Kansas City.

[12] Accessed via www.field.com/fieldpollonline/subscribers/COI-97-Sep-Institutions.pdf, August 25, 2008. Field also calculated a confidence index which it reported for 1981, 1984, and 1997. In the years 1981 to 1997, the index ranged between 308 and 420 for universities and colleges, for hospitals it ranged between 180 and 229, for local police departments between 270 and 370, and for the US Supreme Court between 170 and 220.

[13] Survey on confidence in institutions, published in 2007. Accessed via www.harrisinteractive. com/harris_poll/index.asp?PID=646, April 2, 2010.

"a great deal" of confidence in the US Supreme Court. All of these data are in line with the corresponding California results, so we may be cautiously optimistic that hospitals retained their position along with the medical profession. High public confidence in universities and hospitals surely helped them in maintaining satisfactory levels of public funding. It seems that funding and accountability have a positive and reciprocal relationship in the fields of education and health. This feature, together with the presence of a dominant principal in the form of the federal government, may help to explain the strong clubs in these sectors.

Appendix: Survey

This survey is about standard-setting for institutions, or organizations, or programs. If you do not verify compliance, it is called voluntary standard-setting. If you verify compliance, it is called accreditation.

1 Do you (check one or more)
   (a) Set voluntary standards? (do not verify compliance) Yes __No __ Not sure__
   (b) Do accreditation? (verify compliance) Yes __No __Not sure__
If you answered No or Not sure to both, stop here, but please return the survey. Thank you.

2 Is yours a membership association? Yes___ No ___ If yes, how many members? _____

3 What year were you founded? _____ (In case of merger, give earliest founding year.)

4 What is the earliest year you or your predecessor began to:
   (a) Set voluntary standards for institutions, organizations or programs? ____
   (b) Accredit institutions, organizations or programs? ____

5 Are you exempt from the federal corporate income tax? Yes __ No __ Not sure __
If you do not accredit, stop here, but please return the survey anyway. Thank you.

6 Including provisional and probationary status, how many entities do you currently accredit?_____

7 Do the people who develop standards also decide whom to accredit? Yes __No __Not sure__

8 Do you conduct periodic reviews utilizing (check all that apply)
   (a) Self-assessment? Yes __ No __ Not sure __
   (b) Site visit by staff? Yes __ No __ Not sure __
   (c) Site visit by peers? Yes __ No __ Not sure __

9 In which of the following categories do you promulgate standards for accreditation:
  (a) Governance? Yes __ No __ Not sure __
  (b) Ethics? Yes __ No __ Not sure __
  (c) Public disclosure? Yes __ No __ Not sure __
  (d) Program quality? Yes __ No __ Not sure __
  (e) Program outcomes? Yes __ No __ Not sure __
  (f) Credentials of personnel? Yes __ No __ Not sure __
  (g) Fundraising? Yes __ No __ Not sure __
  (h) Financial management? Yes __ No __ Not sure __
10 If you accredit in conjunction with another organization, please identify it by name (otherwise, leave blank)_____

REFERENCES

Bekkers, René. 2003. Trust, Accreditation, and Philanthropy in the Netherlands. *Nonprofit and Voluntary Sector Quarterly* 32(4): 596–615.
Bowman, Woods and Marion R. Fremont-Smith. 2006. Nonprofits and State and Local Governments. In Elizabeth T. Boris and C. Eugene Steuerle, eds. *Nonprofits and Government: Collaboration and Conflict*, 2nd edn. Washington, DC: Urban Institute Press, pp. 181–217.
Bowman, Woods and Angela Bies. 2005. Can the Charitable Sector Regulate Itself? *Nonprofit Quarterly* 12(special issue): 39–43.
Brown, June Gibbs. 2003. *The External Review of Hospital Quality: A Call for Greater Accountability*. Washington, DC: U.S. Department of Health and Human Services, Office of the Inspector General. Accessed via http://oig. hhs.gov/oei/reports/oei-01–97–00050.pdf.
Encyclopedia of Associations: A Guide to Nearly 23,000 National and International Organizations. Accessed via http://galenet.gale.com.
Independent Sector. 2002. *The Nonprofit Almanac and Desk Reference*. Washington, DC: Independent Sector.
Phillips, Michael M. 2005. Big Charities Pursue Certification. *Wall Street Journal*, March 9: A1+.
Silber, Norman I. 2001. *A Corporate Form of Freedom: The Emergence of the Nonprofit Sector*. Boulder, CO: Westview Press.
Silvergleid, Jordan E. 2003. Effects of Watchdog Organizations on the Social Capital Market. *New Directions for Philanthropic Fundraising* (special issue: *Exploring Measurement and Evaluation Efforts in Fundraising*) 41: 7–26.
Sprague, Lisa. 2005. *Hospital Oversight in Medicare: Accreditation and Deeming Authority*. National Health Policy Forum Issue Brief No. 802 (May 6). Washington, DC: George Washington University.
Weisbrod, Burton A. 1988. *The Nonprofit Economy*. Cambridge, MA: Harvard University Press.

Wing, Kennard T., Thomas H. Pollak, and Amy Blackwood. 2008. *The Nonprofit Almanac*. Washington, DC: Urban Institute Press.

Young, Dennis, Neil Bania, and Darlyne Bailey. 1996. Structure and Accountability: A Study of National Nonprofit Associations. *Nonprofit Management and Leadership* 6(4): 347–365.

4 Self-regulation at the state level: nonprofit membership associations and club emergence

Mary Tschirhart

Concerns about unethical and poor performance in the nonprofit sector have led to discussions of accountability and regulation, along with varied attempts to promote principles of best practice, codes of conduct, and ethical guidelines for the sector. Incentives are being crafted to encourage organizations to adopt specific practices beyond what is legally or administratively required (Gugerty, 2009). The sources of standards for practice include watchdog agencies such as the Better Business Bureau, agencies attempting to serve as the voice of the sector such as Independent Sector, and others. Attempts to shape nonprofit organizations have included simple statements of best practices, basic codes of ethics, customized standards of practice, and comprehensive certification programs. The specificity of the guidelines offered and the mechanisms for monitoring compliance vary greatly. No set of standards or principles has achieved a level of prominence and acceptance that suggests it has become widely institutionalized. What appear to be among the most endorsed and democratically produced efforts (e.g., The Donor Bill of Rights, The Accountable Nonprofit Organization, and Independent Sector's ethical guidelines) have all been characterized as failing miserably (Bothwell, 2001). Not only may bad behavior go uncorrected if standards and principles are not enforceable, the principles themselves may be criticized for not allowing adequate flexibility or, conversely, for being too vague.

In the business sector, accountability programs created and managed through industry and trade associations to signal members' quality and adherence to standards have come under increasing scrutiny by researchers. These clubs have been promoted as a method for avoiding government regulation, collectively reducing pooled risk, and preventing negative externalities from unfettered production activities of businesses in the industry. Researchers have questioned why firms join these accountability programs (e.g., Lenox, 2006) and whether the programs actually influence firm behavior (e.g., Potoski and Prakash, 2005; Rivera *et al.*, 2006), as well as their actual value as accountability signals for participants and nonparticipants (e.g., King and Terlaak, 2006). Studies suggest that free-riding by nonparticipants, adverse selection in which participants join to disguise low quality, and moral hazard, in which participants engage in only symbolic efforts rather than real compliance, can be problems in these clubs, particularly when they are sponsored by industry or trade associations (Lenox, 2006; Lenox and Nash, 2003; King and Lenox, 2000). There is some evidence that associations interested in regulating members' behaviors may require state involvement to be effective (Brockman, 1998) and that association leaders often have little confidence that members adhere to their association's ethical codes of conduct (Tucker *et al.*, 1999).

As pointed out by Gugerty and Prakash in the introductory chapter of this volume, nonprofits face the challenge of signaling organizational accountability to their external principals. Faced with media criticism, nonprofits are almost obligated to demonstrate to external principals that they are deploying funds and adopting policies that cohere with the organizational mandate. One could speculate that very much like the for-profit sector, which has faced similar challenges, nonprofit associations would be the likely actors to sponsor such accountability mechanisms. After all, accountability scandal in one nonprofit can create negative spillovers for others (Prakash and Potoski, 2007).

Nonprofit associations provide an array of benefits to their nonprofit members including economies of scale through purchasing discounts, protection from government interference, increased capacity, educational programs, a strong voice to influence government, and professional networks. Accountability club obligations could be bundled with these other benefits, as is done by trade associations in the for-profit sector. Compared with efforts to understand accountability signaling through clubs by businesses, however, there is a paucity of data available on nonprofits' use of accountability signaling through clubs, despite the fact that many nonprofits face the challenge of multiple stakeholders such as donors, clients, service partners, and politicians demanding accountability. These stakeholders typically have limited information with which to judge the nonprofits. To establish a positive reputation with these stakeholders, nonprofits could join a club to share a brand that conveys quality and accountability.

Provision of multiple benefits may be problematic in associations for nonprofits owing to lack of resources. Further, the sponsorship of accountability clubs may not cohere with the overall objectives and expertise of these associations. It is questionable whether nonprofit associations can effectively serve many purposes, which makes it useful to examine whether they tend to develop and sponsor accountability clubs. Indeed, this chapter finds that state nonprofit associations' efforts to address accountability concerns in the nonprofit sector using club mechanisms are limited.

State nonprofit associations' primary members are nonprofit organizations operating in the state. In the United States, regulatory jurisdictions over nonprofits exist at both the federal and state level. The fifty state governments in the United States independently set rules for the nonprofits operating in their states. Moreover, the vast majority of nonprofits in the USA are small and local with little interest in activities or claim on resources outside their state. For these reasons, one might expect state-level accountability clubs to emerge in response to accountability demands by state-level actors. By coming together at the state level, nonprofits can collectively attempt to influence a potential regulator. In addition, joining an association with other nonprofits in the same state may be useful for nonprofits seeking to network with local partners and jointly contract with local suppliers. Donors may limit their funding to nonprofits in a particular state, suggesting that state boundaries may be relevant to nonprofits seeking to shape their philanthropic environment, and the use of a state-level association to do this may be helpful.

In this study, I examine whether states have a state-level nonprofit association with or without an accountability club. I am interested in how, if at all, state nonprofit associations shape and signal the accountability of members through the promotion of standards and principles of behavior among the members and the larger nonprofit sector in the state. Do the associations present ethical or practice codes created by other entities, oversee the creation by members of a code, coordinate a statement that association members endorse a code, or implement a system in which some of the members are certified if they demonstrate practices and policies consistent with the code? Are there other means by which accountability is fostered and signaled?

Differences across states in nonprofit membership associations

To examine the research questions, I looked at all US states to determine whether they had one or more statewide membership associations serving the nonprofits in the state. I used website searches and the National Council of Nonprofit Associations to identify relevant associations. Once the associations were identified, data were collected from the associations through personal interviews and an examination of their tax records, websites, annual reports, and brochures. Data were also collected on the states to examine environmental factors that might affect association membership numbers, policies, and practices. Specific sources of state-level data are described in the discussion of analyses.

In the summer of 2008, only thirty-five states (70 percent) had associations that gave voting rights to the member nonprofit organizations and were not limited to specific nonprofit mission domains, professions, or geographic areas within the state. Some states had nonprofit organizations that seem similar to state nonprofit associations but are not incorporated as membership associations; of these, at least one is in the process of converting to a membership form of organization. In one case, a state recently lost its state nonprofit association as a result of its inability to sustain itself, and an examination of the financial statements of current state nonprofit associations suggests that others might be in jeopardy given financial vulnerabilities. Figure 4.1 shows the distribution of state nonprofit associations at the time of the study reported in this chapter, along with the highest level accountability signaling mechanism in use by each state association (certification, codes of standards or ethics, or award for excellence).

All state nonprofit associations are similar in that they claim to exist to strengthen and support the nonprofit organizations in their state and have nonprofit organizations as members who have specific rights and benefits. Thus, they can be considered to offer benefits that are both instrumental (focus on influencing nonmembers) and expressive (satisfying the private interests of members) (Tschirhart, 2006). The National Council of Nonprofit Associations serves a network of some of these state nonprofit associations. The Council's website explains what its members do:

These associations provide valuable services to nonprofits, including: leadership and convening, with local nonprofit networking opportunities such as annual conferences, roundtables, and listservs; discounted quality products and services that provide reduced prices and referenced quality on insurance, office supplies, and more; advocacy and public policy through monitoring issues on the local, state, and national levels that affect all nonprofits, including taxes, regulation, and accountability; management training and professional development, with frequent workshops in core subjects that are essential for running a nonprofit organization; research, information, and referral to elevate the profile of the sector and respond to questions about effective nonprofit management; communications through newsletters, reports, and electronic updates, keeping nonprofits informed, and providing valuable insights into management issues.
(Text adapted from www.ncna.org, March 22, 2008)

To assess the extent to which state nonprofit associations sponsor accountability clubs, I reviewed the services they provide as indicated on their websites and promotional materials. This review reveals that not all associations are involved in accountability efforts, defined as activities to

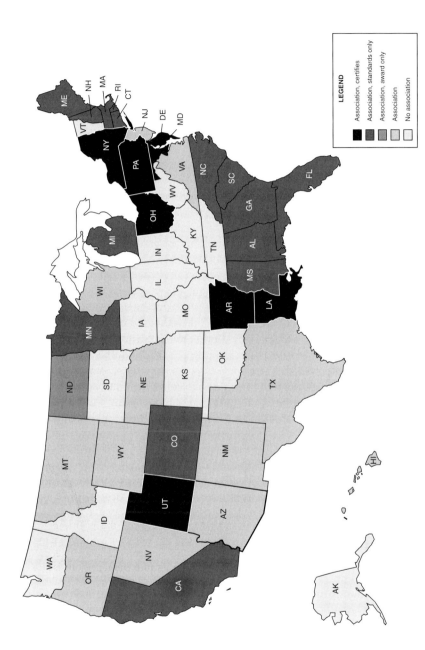

Figure 4.1 US states and nonprofit accountability programs

promote ethics and standards of practice among nonprofit organizations in their state. The efforts that do exist take a variety of forms.

The strongest possible form of accountability club involves certification of compliance and publicity about which organizations have received certification; these clubs include monitoring mechanisms that may result in removal from the list of organizations that do not continue to comply with standards. The stricter the standards, the stronger can be the signal of accountability for those organizations in the certification club. Even an association without a certification program can promote and signal accountability. At the simplest level, the mere existence of standards communicated to members and nonmembers may support desired norms and values (King and Lenox, 2000). Associations that provide members with access to information on standards or principles of behavior in a forum accessible to the public are implicitly suggesting to key stakeholders (i.e., the principals for a nonprofit in a principal–agent relationship) that the nonprofit will adhere to the guidelines. The weakest club is seen when an association provides members with codes set by other entities and does not require members publicly to endorse or to agree to abide by those standards. Slightly stronger is an association-sponsored club in which the association develops its own standards and encourages members to adopt them. Even stronger is the association that asks members to pledge that they will abide by the standards, with those that pledge being part of the club.

At the time of the study, there were no state membership associations requiring that a nonprofit agree to abide by a code in order to be a member of the association. The associations had no mechanisms to force nonprofit organizations in the state to join and comply with association standards and principles. For the state nonprofit associations that do have guidelines, compliance is on a voluntary basis. I found no active monitoring systems in which members are identified and ostracized if they do not come into compliance with association standards or principles. In other words, I found no strong accountability clubs. Figure 4.2 indicates the forms that accountability efforts take among state nonprofit associations. The most common means is to offer ethics or practice guidelines. Twenty nonprofit associations offer standards or codes of ethics or practice, created either by the association or by other entities. Eight associations offer an award for excellence, indicating that the association is encouraging and evaluating quality and accountability. Five state nonprofit associations offer certification for nonprofits initially meeting established standards.

While state nonprofit associations can act as accountability clubs for nonprofits, these clubs are at best weak, and some are borderline clubs.

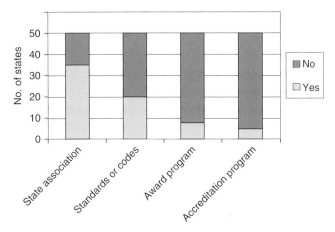

Figure 4.2 Accountability efforts by state nonprofit associations

There are few associations that have a certification program with a subset of members which have been screened for compliance with standards or have self-affirmed that they meet the standards. Even those associations offering this certification are relatively weak clubs, given that for the subset of certified members, compliance cannot be guaranteed and certification, once given, is typically not withdrawn. Certified members can choose to free-ride; once in the club they may fail to maintain the standards that they met as affirmed by a screener, or claimed to have met if they were self-certified, in order to gain entry to the club. These certification programs can be considered clubs because they produce a nonrival collective good for those that participate. The reputational signal provided by the program benefits all participants without reducing the reputational benefits available to other members. These programs are also excludable since some organizations can be excluded from membership and thus are not able to take advantage of the signal of quality that members of the club enjoy. The certification programs run by US state associations are not strong clubs because compliance is not rigorously enforced. Associations that offer standards without requiring endorsement are borderline clubs. There is the possibility that the existence of standards is enough to signal quality even for those association members that do not choose to take the extra step to became formally certified as following the standards or even endorse the standards. It may be unclear to principals that not all members of the association are certified as compliant with the standards or are committed to the standards. If this is the case, the club can be deemed to have failed in that members who do not meet the standards have not been excluded from obtaining the benefits intended for members who have met or are attempting to meet the standards. Over time, if true members are not being distinguished from free-riders, principals may fail to see a quality distinction and thus the credibility of the club likely will suffer.

Given the leniency with which standards are enforced, state nonprofit associations are not credible accountability signalers. To be more credible, the associations need swords such as third-party monitoring and complaint systems for reporting bad behavior, or public postings of the level of compliance with standards. Though the associations may signal quality to external principals by suggesting that nonprofits in their state are following standards or principles, overall, their lack of enforcement mechanisms may do little to reassure principals with limited information on the quality and ethics of individual nonprofits. The existence of an award for excellence program may give the impression to the public and key stakeholders that all the members of the association strive to be award winners. However, not all of the eight associations that use this mechanism communicate the criteria for winning an award to the general public, reducing the value of the award program as an accountability signal.

There are other means, besides certification programs, ethical and practice standards, and awards, for strengthening the accountability of nonprofit organizations through an association. The association may offer training programs for staff and board members and indirectly support the adoption of desired practices and policies by fostering connections among nonprofit organizations. Networks may facilitate the transfer of best practices, and foster conformity with standards to avoid exposure of bad behavior and public shame. All the state nonprofit associations offer at least some opportunity for nonprofit organization representatives to network, at minimum through a membership directory, and offer educational resources, at least through provision on their website of educational materials related to desirable practices. Encouragement of sharing of information among members by a state nonprofit association may help to shape understandings of appropriate behaviors and thus foster accountability. These approaches cannot be considered clubs, however, given that they are not using an excludable membership form to signal accountability.

Preliminary findings

Overall, it is clear that there is little effort on the part of state nonprofit associations to offer strong accountability signals for nonprofit organization members. In this section, I offer results from preliminary analyses

Table 4.1 *Descriptive variables for preliminary analyses for subset of states with state nonprofit association*

Variable	Descriptive information
Present standards or ethical code	20 associations
Use certification program	5 associations
Use awards for excellence program	8 associations
Association establishment date	Ranges from 1927 to 2007, mean is 1990 (s.d. 16.2)
Size of association staff	Ranges from 0 to 28, mean is 8.62 (s.d. 8.3)
Size of association board	Ranges from 7 to 41 , mean is 17.7 (s.d. 6.4)
Size of nonprofit sector in state, all registered nonprofits	Ranges from 4,418 to 152,963, mean is 29,000 (s.d. 28,382)
Number of 501(c)3 registered organizations in state	Ranges from 2,757 to 115,338, mean is 19,900 (s.d. 20,857.9)

exploring factors that might influence the emergence of clubs. Table 4.1 provides descriptive data on the variables used in the analyses.

There are a number of reasons why accountability clubs, even if weak, might be more likely to emerge in some states rather than others. To test hypotheses, I conduct simple correlation analyses. First, market potential for a club might influence accountability signaling by state nonprofit associations, with associations in states with a large number of nonprofits more likely to sponsor a club. I find no significant correlation between size of the nonprofit sector in a state and whether the state's nonprofit association offers standards, an excellence award program, or a certification program. This is true when size is captured by number of 501(c)(3) registered organizations and when the measure is all types of registered nonprofits in the state, with the sizes drawn from the National Center for Charitable Statistics. The relative size of the market for an accountability club does not appear to influence its establishment by a state nonprofit association. However, what this quick analysis does not reveal is the effect of relative sizes of subsectors of the state nonprofit sector on use of accountability clubs. A more nuanced look at the subpopulations of nonprofits in the state might reveal that specific information asymmetry problems for nonprofit subsets may influence the establishment and maintenance of accountability clubs by state nonprofit associations, as well as which types of nonprofits are most likely to join the association and participate in a certification club within it.

Is the organizational capacity of associations a predictor of their ability or willingness to sponsor accountability clubs? Association age, number of staff, and number of board members are not related to existence of accountability clubs. Controlling for these factors, state nonprofit sector size is still not correlated with the existence of accountability clubs. Simple correlation analyses do not reveal any direct or indirect effects of these capacity proxies, though effects might emerge if other variables were controlled.

A third hypothesis is that resources for offering accountability signals might be available through affiliations with other organizations. The most likely candidate to provide resources is the National Council of Nonprofit Associations (NCNA). Twenty-eight of the thirty-five state nonprofit associations belong to this organization. However, NCNA membership is not significantly correlated with offering certification, excellence awards, or standards.

Additional propositions

Given the largely untapped potential of the club form as an accountability signal for nonprofits, it is useful to develop propositions that may help in more closely examining the dynamics of accountability efforts by state nonprofit associations. Correlation analyses are only a first step in evaluating possible predictors, and more nuanced measures and analyses than I have offered in this chapter are needed. In particular, consideration of budget information and revenue sources may be helpful in revealing patterns in accountability signaling activities. The literature suggests ideas about which membership associations will be more likely to engage in efforts to shape the behaviors and perceived accountability of their members. In the next sections, I review relevant theories and suggest a few propositions for future testing.

Signaling in response to information asymmetries

Certification programs may emerge to help nonprofits and their principals deal with information asymmetries. Showing compliance with standards can help an organization signify superior unobservable qualities, thus giving it a competitive advantage in its markets (King and Terlaak, 2006). Donors and clients important to a nonprofit organization may be impressed that an organization has been certified by or is a member of an association that promotes accountability standards. The value of this signaling effect is likely to be greater for nonprofits that exist within a larger population where the information asymmetries may be greater. This corresponds to King and Terlaak's (2006) argument and finding among for-profit firms that the larger the industry, the greater the benefit from certification. This suggests that nonprofit leaders facing greater competition to build and maintain positive perceptions of their nonprofit may be more likely to seek out and even collectively invent mechanisms to signal quality, such as membership in an association promoting account-ability standards. Demand for signaling mechanisms by prospective and current members may encourage an association of nonprofits to promote standards as one aspect of its mission. If an association offers a certifica-tion program or has other weaker forms of accountability signaling such as standards or principles, the association may be more successful in attract-ing nonprofits that wish to stand out in a crowded field. The effect may be especially strong if the nonprofits belong to an industry in which account-ability is commonly questioned as a result of scandal or controversy. In addition, the more difficult it is for principals to judge their accountability and the more likely the principals may assume lack of accountability given limited information, the more likely nonprofits may participate in a state nonprofit association's certification program or adopt the association's standards as a means to address information asymmetries.

Dependency on government

Associations may find that government is receptive to the idea of voluntary self-regulatory programs. Corrupt or inefficient nonprofits have the potential to tarnish other nonprofits' reputation and incite pressure for government scrutiny and constraints on the entire sector. An account-ability program sponsored by a state nonprofit association may satisfy state government that direct regulatory oversight is not needed, or may complement state regulatory efforts as Brakman Reiser notes in this volume (chapter 2). A program applicable to all types of nonprofits is likely to be more appealing to government than one that is designed for a specific type of nonprofit since it will have larger regulatory coverage (Gugerty, 2008). Given that a voluntary program can offer cost benefits to government, a state nonprofit association that is attempting to guide the behaviors of nonprofits in the state by offering formal standards may be more likely to be supported by government than one that is not taking this role as part of its mission. Therefore, I propose that the greater the proportion of its government funding, the more likely it is that a state nonprofit association will promote formal standards.

Member self-interest

Mancur Olson's (1965) classic argument is that members join associa-tions in order to attain selective benefits that exceed the cost of member-ship. State nonprofit associations may offer a variety of benefits to members, including discounts, networking opportunities, promotion venues, consulting, and training. Those that offer a formal certification program may be particularly attractive to potential members because of the opportunity to use affiliation with the association to signal quality and credibility. Membership in such an association may give the nonprofit the opportunity to influence certification processes and standards so that they are more aligned with the nonprofit's interests. Nonprofit leaders may feel they can protect their organization from unfair or unwelcome evaluation if their nonprofit has the opportunity to influence criteria and processes as an association member.

However, membership density, that is, the number of members compared with the number of potential members, may be negatively affected by the potential diversity of interests within a prospective membership base (Olson, 1965). Given that the nonprofit sector in a state is diverse in missions and operations, it may be that a certification program loses attractiveness if it appears to be too narrowly focused on the needs of certain types of members over others. We might expect that the positive effect on membership of having an accountability program may be diminished if the standards are perceived to be specific only to certain types of nonprofits. On the other hand, greater diversity of the membership base may be associated with greater generality and vagueness of accountability standards in order to increase likelihood of acceptance among all current and prospective members. A certification program may lose attractiveness if it is seen as only a weak signal of accountability because the standards are too weak. However, given that compliance to any set of standards may be in name only (Lenox, 2006; Lenox and Nash, 2003; King and Lenox, 2000), and that there may be some signaling benefits in belonging to a group that promotes standards even if one does not meet them or if all organizations can meet them, I expect that offering an accountability program is positively associated with number of nonprofit organization members.

Discussion

More theorizing and in-depth data collection is needed to see whether a richer story can be told about the development of accountability clubs sponsored by state nonprofit associations. Clearly, the potential exists for the use of these clubs. Five state nonprofit associations have certification programs, albeit with no enforcement of continued compliance and no requirement that members join these clubs. This chapter suggests that in the United States, state nonprofit associations, at present, do not have much leverage in improving the accountability of the nonprofit sector.

The focus of these associations is more on providing direct benefits to members, such as discounts on products, than on monitoring nonprofit accountability to standards and codes of conduct. In many respects, this story is similar to the story of Independent Sector, discussed by Dennis Young in this volume (chapter 5). Associations that are dealing with a diverse membership and engaged in recruiting and supporting members may not be good candidates to develop strong accountability clubs. And as Dana Brakman Reiser notes in chapter 2, most state attorney general offices have very low capacity for enforcement of existing charity laws and requirements, so that the threat of increased regulatory interference appears low. Independent Sector, like the foundations discussed by Peter Frumkin in chapter 6, moved toward establishing an accountability club only when the threat of increased regulation was imminent.

At present, state nonprofit association activities that address accountability concerns in the nonprofit sector are limited to at best weak club mechanisms. Still, the majority of state nonprofit organizations in existence do offer standards or principles of practice for the nonprofits in their state. These guidelines could be the basis for the creation of stronger clubs that ensure member compliance. As Angela Bies demonstrates in chapter 9, there is also potential for state associations to play an important role in the development and dissemination of standards, while parallel initiatives serve monitoring and compliance functions. This appears to be part of the story in Minnesota, where the state nonprofit association has developed extensive standards, while the charity watchdog agency has developed an accountability club aimed largely at donors. As Brakman Reiser also argues in chapter 2, there is significant potential for associations to develop standards that complement and go beyond the requirements of state regulatory offices which are often quite weak. As pressures for accountability grow, associations offering standards and principles may find greater interest by nonprofit members in visible, branded conformance to the guidelines.

REFERENCES

Bothwell, R. O. 2001. Trends in Self-Regulation and Transparency of Nonprofits in the U.S. *International Journal of Not-for-Profit Law* 2(3). Accessed via www.icnl.org/journal/vol2iss3/arn_bothwell.htm, November 2007.

Brockman, J. 1998. Fortunate Enough to Obtain and Keep the Title of Profession: Self-Regulating Organizations and the Enforcement of Professional Monopolies. *Canadian Public Administration* 41(4): 587–621.

Gugerty, M. K. 2008. The Effectiveness of NGO Self-Regulation: Theory and Evidence from Africa. *Public Administration and Development* 28(May):105–118.

2009. Signaling Virtue: Voluntary Accountability Programs among Nonprofit Organizations. *Policy Sciences* 42: 243–273.

King, A. A. and M. J. Lenox. 2000. Industry Self-Regulation without Sanctions: The Chemical Industry's Responsible Care Program. *Academy of Management Journal* 43(4): 698–716.

King, A. A. and A. Terlaak. 2006. The Effect of Certification with the ISO 9000 Quality Management Standard: A Signaling Approach. *Journal of Economic Behavior and Organization* 60: 579–602.

Lenox, M. J. (2006). The Role of Private Decentralized Institutions in Sustaining Industry Self-Regulation. *Organization Science* 17: 677–690.

Lenox, M. and J. Nash. 2003. Industry Self-Regulation and Adverse Selection: A Comparison across Four Trade Association Programs. *Business Strategy and the Environment* 12: 343–356.

Olson, M. 1965. *The Logic of Collective Action*. Cambridge, MA: Harvard University Press.

Panel on the Nonprofit Sector and Independent Sector. 2007. Principles for Good Governance and Ethical Practice: A Guide for Charities and Foundations. Washington, DC. Accessed via www.nonprofitpanel.org, November 2007.

Potoski, M. and A. Prakash. 2005. Green Clubs and Voluntary Governance: ISO 14001 and Firms' Regulatory Compliance. *American Journal of Political Science* 49: 235–248.

Prakash, A. and M. Potoski. 2007. Collective Action through Voluntary Environmental Programs: A Club Theory Perspective. *Policy Studies Journal* 35(4): 773–792.

Rivera, J., P. de Leon, and C. Koerber. 2006. Is Greener Whiter Yet? The Sustainable Slopes Program after Five Years. *Policy Studies Journal* 34: 195–221.

Tschirhart, M. 2006. Membership Associations. In W. W. Powell and R. Steinberg, eds. *The Non-Profit Sector: A Research Handbook*. New Haven: Yale University Press, pp. 523–541.

Tucker, L. R., V. Stathakopolous, and C. H. Patti, 1999. A Multidimensional Assessment of Ethical Codes: The Professional Business Association Perspective. *Journal of Business Ethics* 19: 287–300.

Part II

Club sponsorship and club design

5 Nonprofit infrastructure associations as reluctant clubs

Dennis R. Young

In his 1992 book, Peter Dobkin Hall argued that the nonprofit sector in the United States was "invented" in the latter half of the twentieth century (Hall, 1992). Of course, no one would assert that nonprofits did not exist before then. Indeed, they preceded the founding of the republic. What Hall meant was that the multi-industry collection of charitable and philanthropic, service, advocacy, and intermediary organizations that we now think of as the nonprofit sector in the United States developed its collective identity in that period. As Hall (1992), O'Connell (1997), Brilliant (2000), and others have documented, and as Peter Frumkin discusses in this volume (chapter 6), much of the impetus for this identity formation originated with Congressional pressure to regulate and limit the influence of foundations, ultimately leading to the building of infrastructure organizations such as Independent Sector, the Council on Foundations, academic centers like the Program on NonProfit Organizations at Yale, the Nonprofit Sector Research Fund of the Aspen Institute, and other organizations designed to coalesce common interests in defending the sector and understanding and improving its functioning. Many of these organizations take the form of associations whose members are constituent organizations that subscribe to a common set of interests or goals.

This chapter examines the evolution of two of these infrastructure associations – Independent Sector (IS) and the Nonprofit Academic Centers Council (NACC) – from the point of view of club theory. The intent is to assess the extent to which these associations can be understood as manifesting the behavior and embracing the functions of voluntary accountability clubs, what insights club theory offers into their development, and what limits apply to club theory as a lens for understanding these associations. A common theme is that associations such as these

I wish to thank Russ Cargo, Evelyn Brody, Amy McClellan, Brian O'Connell, Virginia Hodgkinson, Eleanor Brilliant, Diana Aviv, Mary Kay Gugerty, and Aseem Prakash for their helpful comments and suggestions, and Lewis Faulk and Lindsay Romansanta for their research support.

evolve in their functioning over their life cycles. Associations such as IS and NACC were established largely for reasons other than for the purpose of establishing "accountability clubs" to address standards, rules of behavior, and accountability of their members, although they both embraced from the outset the goals of enhancing the visibility and public image of those members and signaling their importance and integrity to external constituencies. However, as they have matured as organizations, and as their environments have changed over the years, an implicit temptation to embrace the functions of an accountability club has gained strength in IS and NACC, in some tension with other goals. This tension has played out through the establishment of new program initiatives that promote accountability and set standards without directly enforcing them. Ultimately, these associations must reconcile the club function with other goals that require greater tolerance for inclusiveness, diversity, support, and accommodation of their members.

Nonprofit clubs

From the perspective of this volume, clubs are institutions that create benefits which are shared by all members (i.e., that are nonrival), but which nonmembers are excluded from enjoying. According to this perspective, clubs perform three functions – they set standards for their members beyond what is legally required of them; they impose additional costs on their members such as fees and costs of implementing club requirements; and they provide benefits not otherwise available to nonmembers, such as the implicit seal of approval deriving from club membership. These functions are designed to make members more attractive to their supporters (principals) by enhancing reputation or providing assurances of quality that principals have difficulty obtaining in other ways. This perspective on clubs derives from a view of accountability based on the relationships between nonprofits as agents and government, donors, the public, and other stakeholders as principals making claims on nonprofits.

The key elements that define a club are the definition of common standards for behavior and the attempt to signal outsider principals or stakeholders. While clubs can range widely in the degrees to which they set and enforce strict standards, impose fees and other costs on their members, and offer significant benefits not otherwise obtainable by members, there are certain underlying implications of the club model for the behavior of membership associations. Clubs must be willing to limit their membership, discipline errant members, and reach consensus on a set of standards of operation and behavior. More generally, they must accept the notion that their members are agents to some common group of principals to which they are accountable and whom they can better serve if the principals have greater confidence in their membership as a whole.

These assumptions apply in varying degrees to the intents and purposes of infrastructure organizations that evolved with the growth and development of the nonprofit sector in the latter part of the twentieth century. For the most part, the focus of these organizations has been on the growth, development, and protection of their memberships and on increasing their public visibility, understanding, and support. The two cases discussed here are particular kinds of associations for which the club model may pose particular challenges: as infrastructure organizations their members are other organizations, not individuals. This affects how they operate, the scope of activities they can undertake, and the obstacles they face. In particular, they must reach for an elusive common ground without treading on the turf of member groups or taking positions that satisfy some members at the expense of others. Nonetheless, as pressures from government and from competitive forces outside their memberships have increased, there has been a growing inclination to emphasize standards, exclusivity, and best practices, so as to protect existing members against adverse public criticism and governmental oversight, and to preserve or expand their market shares.

Independent Sector and the Nonprofit Academic Centers Council are very different cases in point. The former emerged in 1980 as a grand coalition designed to provide a public face to the sector, give it a voice in Washington, and enhance public understanding of the sector. IS is an older and much larger association which encompasses a much more diverse membership than NACC. (Indeed, IS served as an incubator for NACC as well as a catalyst for the establishment of some of the academic centers belonging to NACC.) In contrast, NACC was organized in 1991 by a small group of directors of new academic centers devoted to study of the nonprofit sector. While NACC has grown considerably over time, it is still a small association with a relatively homogeneous membership, designed to help its members gain support within their own universities and in various academic disciplines by promoting the rigor, relevance, and overall academic legitimacy of this field of study. Both associations have enjoyed some success, but neither is likely to develop a strong club-like character or hold inordinate sway over its members. Indeed, while certain environmental forces encourage self-regulatory initiatives for their respective memberships, other factors, including membership diversity, market pressures favoring inclusiveness, and resistance of members to infringements on their autonomy, serve as brakes on full-scale emergence of voluntary club behavior.

The Nonprofit Academic Centers Council (NACC)

According to its website, NACC "is a membership association comprised of academic centers or programs at accredited colleges and universities that focus on the study of nonprofit organizations, voluntarism and/or philanthropy." It grew out of a series of informal meetings over a six-year period, facilitated by the Vice President for Research of Independent Sector, to share ideas and discuss common issues. NACC was established in 1991 (and officially incorporated in 1995) by directors of some of the earliest established nonprofit academic centers, including those at Case Western Reserve University, Tufts, the University of San Francisco, The New School, the University of Missouri at Kansas City, New York University, and Indiana University (NACC, 2001). Recognizing that they faced common challenges in maintaining and developing their centers within the contexts of their universities, their academic disciplines, and the funding and nonprofit communities at large, the original members of NACC viewed the organization as a kind of mutual support group through which they could collaborate, exchange ideas, testify to the importance of their agendas, and build the academic legitimacy and societal relevance of the field together. The idiosyncratic nature of academic centers and the significant challenges of running centers within traditional university structures were central issues that bound this group together. So too, establishing the nonprofit sector as an important, distinct, and substantial area of study for university programming was seen as a common challenge for this group to address. The latter was especially frustrating because of the interdisciplinary character of nonprofit studies: on the one hand, several different existing disciplines claimed the territory; on the other hand, none of those disciplines, with the arguable exception of public administration in some places, gave priority to this subject relative to other topical areas of study.

All this points to a complex picture of accountability for NACC members that involves accountability claims by a number of principals. The members of NACC are the academic centers themselves, which by NACC rules can be represented at NACC meetings and in NACC decisions only by their directors. As leaders of academic centers within their respective universities, directors are generally responsible to their deans or provosts and to the faculties to which they belong and whom they engage in the work of their programs. As self-standing units usually expected to pay for themselves, the centers are also accountable to external funders who provide grants and contracts to support center operations. As contributors to degree and nondegree programming, many centers also have accountability relationships with current and potential students and alumni. Finally, as aspects of their relationships with funders, obligations to students, and often in their roles as community service emissaries of their universities, centers are also accountable to the regional and sometimes national and international nonprofit communities with which they work. This web of accountability claims clearly involves tensions – between the objectivity and rigor demanded by the academic community and the more practical needs and self-interests of the nonprofit community, and between the immediate practical concerns of funders focused on helping their nonprofit organization grantees and the longer-term and more fundamental interests in knowledge building of the academy. On balance, university administrators and external funders are the main principals to which NACC members are accountable, but the mix of emphasis varies considerably from one center to another.

Given the primacy of establishing the academic legitimacy of the field and strengthening the role of centers, it is not surprising that an early requirement for joining NACC was that a center must have its own full-time director and that it must have a distinct research program. Thus, NACC members wanted to distinguish themselves from nominal so-called "centers" that consisted only of a telephone number and a course offering or two that touched on nonprofit issues. The emphasis on research also illuminated how nonprofit centers could contribute to existing university programming, by engaging faculty and students in a variety of existing programs in ways that would contribute to advances in their home disciplines such as management, public administration, economics, political science, history, social work, and sociology.

Given these defining parameters, NACC's early aspiration was clearly to grow its membership from the small handful of founding members to a more substantial group that would be more fully representative of the national university community and would ultimately include greater representation of the top schools in the USA. NACC began modestly, with the IS Research Office serving as its secretariat in the early years. A watershed was reached in the mid-1990s with the membership of Harvard University and some years later, with members from Canada, the UK, and Australia. As the field of nonprofit studies grew, NACC became a popular venue for new centers to join because membership became a source of leverage within their own universities; in short, it signaled that they were part of a network with other respected universities and it offered access to the deeper pool of expertise and experience of other centers.

Over time, NACC's expansion (more than forty-seven centers and counting) helped fuel the growth of educational programming in the field, particularly in nonprofit management, although some critics questioned the efficacy of nonprofit studies in addressing the leadership and other needs of the sector. Some asked whether the new programs really resulted in more qualified nonprofit managers and whether graduates of the new programs were successful in gaining positions of leadership and management responsibility in the sector (Haas and Robinson, 1998; Mirabella and Wish, 1999). Others decried the shift toward managerialism in the sector and called for a different kind of education emphasizing values, voluntarism, social change, and leadership rather than emulation of the business management model (Bradley Center, 2005). Not coincidentally, NACC's agenda began to shift in the early part of the new century toward a focus on educational content.

A major grant from the David and Lucile Packard Foundation in 2001, designed to stabilize NACC as a support system for nonprofit academic centers and for education in the sector at large, enabled NACC to make a quantum leap in its development as a formal organization and to wean itself from its incubation by Independent Sector. NACC was able to hire its first paid executive director and, following a competitive bidding process, relocated to the Mandel Center for Nonprofit Organizations at Case Western Reserve University, one of NACC's founding members. In particular, this funding permitted NACC to undertake new initiatives, and as nonprofit management programs were emerging in growing numbers across the country, NACC decided to focus on defining a standard curriculum as a resource to guide these programs. Hence, more attention was necessarily paid, in meeting discussions and membership decisions, to curricular content and less to issues of research or to the organizational and management challenges of center directors. The dramatic growth in membership through the late 1990s and early 2000s also changed the dynamics of NACC's meetings. Meetings became more structured, no longer the intimate and relatively informal gatherings of old friends. Some of the original center director members became disaffected, and others retired, and the cogency of the original issues waned in comparison with curricular concerns, administrative matters, and new membership application evaluations. New leaders of NACC concentrated on creating curricular models and guidelines that would help to codify the field – first at the graduate level and later at the undergraduate level (see Nonprofit Academic Centers Council, 2007a and 2007b), providing fellowships to encourage scholarship among faculty of color, defining characteristics of strong, sustainable academic centers (see Nonprofit Academic Centers Council, 2006), and examining membership criteria to maximize the influence of NACC in developing the field. (This is not to say, however, that recent NACC deliberations wholly neglected organizational and management challenges. For example, meeting agendas in 2005 and

2006 included discussions of institutional support as well as governance of academic centers.)

Hence, beginning in the late 1990s, NACC began to engage in some club-like programming, particularly with regard to standard-setting. There was no intention of imposing curricular standards as a condition of membership but a clear implication of NACC's work is that these designs should be used as guides in developing professional nonprofit management and leadership curricula at the master's degree level. The curricular standards were developed through committee work and open discussions at NACC meetings. The intent was to identify the areas of knowledge felt to be essential to prepare students for professional work in the sector. It was understood that the standards, basically areas of curricular content, would be suggestive and instructive and could be incorporated, all or in part, in various ways by individual master's degree programs. Although it was recognized that this exercise was relevant to the question of accreditation, it was not meant to displace existing accreditation mechanisms such as the accreditation of MPA (Masters of Public Administration) programs by NASPAA (National Association of Schools of Public Affairs and Administration). In fact, a NACC committee worked with a NASPAA accreditation committee to inform and improve the latter's requirements.

In truth, there was sympathy among some NACC members to wade into the murky waters of accreditation because other accreditation bodies do not recognize the overall integrity of nonprofit studies as a field of its own; moreover, the nonprofit studies field itself is split up among several different sponsoring disciplines including public administration, business management, political science, social work, and the like. A result of this lack of coherence is that there is no overall ranking system available for nonprofit programs, only the separate ratings provided within other groupings such as Schools of Public Affairs or Schools of Management as rated by *US News and World Report*. While there may have been interest on the part of some members of NACC to promulgate an independent accreditation process for graduate programs of nonprofit study, potential advocates realized that such a movement would be heavily resisted by existing accreditation agencies and their member schools. Moreover, it would test the loyalties of NACC members themselves, many of which were based in schools directly governed by established accreditation bodies.

To date, the implications for undergraduate work remain unclear, and consensus among NACC members less strong, with new guidelines intentionally bifurcated between career-oriented study and more general liberal arts appreciation of the role of the sector in society. These developments solidified a professional agenda for field building, particularly in the educational arena, and diverted, at least temporarily, earlier penchants for NACC to serve as a collegial forum for discussion of research and center management issues.

In short, the NACC curricular guidelines suggest a movement of NACC toward club-like structures in a number of ways. Members of NACC can allude to these guidelines as standards of excellence in making arguments for curricular reform or development within their own institutions. Moreover, new centers that manage to achieve NACC membership can point to this as a kind of seal of approval within their own universities. The process of applying for NACC membership has become more formalized and arguably more rigorous over the years, and there may also be some growing tension over whether to expand NACC's membership much further. While new members bring in more revenue (to help support the fixed cost of permanent staffing) and prestigious new members, especially from abroad, help solidify NACC's own institutional status and reputation, the growth of NACC may ultimately threaten its usefulness as an intimate leadership peer group venue. It may also dilute NACC as a standard-setter if rigorous admission criteria are not maintained. Moreover, given the diversification that is taking place in the field of "third sector" studies, which now includes social enterprise and corporate social responsibility programs in business schools, further growth of NACC could dilute its original focus on study of the nonprofit sector. In addition, there is some bifurcation taking place between universities that are incorporating nonprofit studies basically as a teaching and service function, with little emphasis on research, and those that emphasize research as a major dimension of their nonprofit programs. These stress lines raise the question of where and how tightly NACC should craft its membership criteria. A broadly construed set of criteria would embrace teaching as well as research-based programs and centers and institutes that focus generically on social purpose programming (in business schools, etc.) as well as those defining themselves strictly in nonprofit terms. These choices pose alternative dangers for NACC: failure to accommodate the new modalities could ultimately court irrelevancy, while too much accommodation could risk ambiguity. In particular, by broadening its criteria, NACC could lose its "brand" as a group of research-based centers identified specifically with education and research on the nonprofit sector. But by being inflexible NACC could abdicate its central place as a forum for university-based "third sector" studies. The option regularly raised in this debate at NACC meetings, given the organization's growth trajectory, is to establish affinity groups within the association so that diverse interests can be more effectively embraced without obfuscating NACC's essential identity.

Finally, another tension in NACC's debate over admissions criteria involves the membership of elite institutions including a number of Ivy League schools that have resisted or ignored opportunities for membership or active participation. The participation of such institutions is viewed by some NACC members as important for maintaining the aura of leadership in the field. But appealing to these institutions involves further dilemmas. Diluting membership criteria, for example by reducing emphasis on research, could decrease the likelihood of having this group of academic centers join or become more active in NACC since NACC would become a less elite group. However, it is unclear whether maintaining elite standards would actually have any effect on this group. Meanwhile, NACC depends on a growing membership to maintain itself.

In clubs theory terminology, the membership criteria debate in NACC reflects basic considerations of identity and branding that connect to defining who both the agents and the principals are, or should be. On the one hand, NACC could remain fairly static, adhering to the nonprofit label and strict interpretation of a center as having a strong research program. In this case its principals would be the current set of research universities and funders devoted distinctly to the nonprofit sector. On the other hand, NACC could broaden itself to encompass programs of social enterprise and corporate social responsibility in business schools, and a variety of teaching and service learning programs that do not emphasize research. Indeed, some of these latter groups have already knocked at NACC's door. Were NACC to accommodate these centers, substantial growth might follow, with a concomitant promise of greater financial strength for the organization; however, this would also substantially increase the diversity of principals and agents, requiring a new search for common ground. For the moment, these dilemmas of membership inhibit NACC from developing strong club characteristics.

Various other factors mitigate against NACC embracing the functions of a strong accountability club. Unless nonprofit studies becomes an institutionally autonomous area of study within universities, superseding its current status as an interdisciplinary field housed within a variety of academic structures, it will be difficult for NACC ever to become a formal accrediting agency for nonprofit studies programs. In fact, NACC's membership has generally resisted this possibility, although, as noted above, it has pursued conversations with one accrediting agency (the National Association of Schools of Public Affairs and Administration) to influence the criteria that NASPAA uses to accredit schools of public affairs with concentrations in nonprofit management. This same strategy could be used with other accrediting groups such as AACSB (American Association of Colleges and Schools of Business) or CSWE (Council of Social Work Education). But in all likelihood, NACC will continue to lack this strong "sword" to discipline its members in the educational realm. Furthermore, by enforcing its particular set of standards, however broad and flexible they may be, NACC would leave itself open to growing more and more out of touch as multiple approaches to addressing social issues develop across universities' diverse disciplines and professional venues. By remaining flexible, pragmatic, and grounded in its historical mission, NACC may have a better chance to remain useful and relevant than if it tries to seize the levers of control over curricular matters that strong club programming would suggest. In the face of diversity in its own membership and those of related programs outside its membership, NACC appears to have found some strength rather as a guiding light or curricular resource that various parties can draw on as best suits them. It will be interesting to watch how this guiding light model develops in the future. If indeed NACC has a good product to sell, it might ultimately offer itself as an unofficial certifier of program quality that its own members and others can seek for their own purposes.

However, the present inclination to pursue this route seems tepid. In fact, with the winding down of the Packard grant, recent discussions point to a shift in NACC's agenda back toward a broader discussion of research issues, including collaborative projects among member centers, and the support of academic centers and faculty in pursuing nonprofit-related research. In some sense, NACC appears to be returning to its roots, albeit on a substantially larger scale. It continues to serve as an active issue forum for nonprofit academic center leaders. Moreover, it has become a kind of open-source mechanism for gathering, discussing, codifying, and promulgating ideas about nonprofit sector education and the broader questions of the roles of research and community and professional service in achieving excellence as an academic center. As such, its effectiveness as a club may ultimately grow, not out of its development of strong swords such as the policing of standards, so much as out of the formulation of good practices and promoting the benefits of collaboration. These are the "signaling" functions of a club to which NACC may be best adapted.

Independent Sector (IS)

The establishment of Independent Sector in 1980 reflected a long history of concern by philanthropic leaders over increased dependency of nonprofit institutions on government funding and a growing penchant for government to regulate and control the sector, especially private foundations (Nielsen, 1979). As far back as 1914 Congressional committees worried about some powerful foundations and sought to investigate and regulate foundations in various ways. Later, in the contentious period of anti-communist frenzy of the 1950s, Congressional committees sought to censure foundations on ideological grounds. Public debate began to heat up during the Truman administration and then ignited in Congress in the 1960s and 1970s with a litany of criticisms and skepticism about philanthropy, including concerns about abuse and effectiveness of philanthropic resources, political activity of nonprofit institutions, and questioning of the value of volunteering, much of this culminating in the Tax Reform Act of 1969 which imposed special requirements on private foundations including minimum payouts, restrictions on lobbying, and reporting requirements (O'Connell, 1997). The 1969 Tax Act set in motion a torrent of self-examination and organizing by the philanthropic community including, through the leadership of John D. Rockefeller III, the Peterson and Filer Commissions (Brilliant, 2000). The Peterson Commission was created specifically to confront the threats to philanthropy posed by the 1969 Tax Act while the Filer Commission, although staffed by a leading Washington tax attorney and endorsed by the US Treasury Department, eventually addressed its inquiry to a broader understanding of the full range of nonprofit and philanthropic activity in the USA. A flurry of debate and activity followed the Filer Commission's work, including deliberations on how best to follow up with some kind of organizational structure that could oversee and speak for philanthropy at the national level (Brilliant, 2000). In this connection, there was a difference of opinion on several key issues, particularly with respect to whether the entity should be public or private and to what degree it should take on regulatory authority. However, by now there was substantial recognition that a national organization should be concerned with both philanthropy (foundations) and the charitable (501(c)3 and 501(c)4) nonprofit recipients of that philanthropy.

Ultimately, two existing private sector organizations were merged and redesigned to address these needs – the Coalition of National Voluntary Organizations representing operating nonprofits, and the National Council on Philanthropy (NCOP) representing foundation interests. Independent Sector was born of this marriage and was considered to be the heir to the work of the Filer Commission, although it was not the quasi-public commission that some had hoped for. Given the circumstances surrounding this birth, the primary motivation was to enhance the credibility of philanthropy, voluntarism, and the nonprofit sector in the context of public misunderstanding and loss of confidence in philanthropic institutions, as well as to serve as a counterforce to both increasing government scrutiny and nonprofit dependency on government funds. It is no surprise, therefore, that the original goals of Independent Sector emphasized these concerns in the following order: public education; communication within the newly designated sector to identify and pursue shared problems; tending to the relationships between the nonprofit sector and government; research to develop a body of knowledge about the sector; and encouragement of effective operations and management of nonprofit institutions (O'Connell, 1997: 48). It is the last-named goal, of course, that relates most directly to whether IS would function as voluntary accountability club. Would it develop standards for its members and how would those standards be promulgated and enforced?

There is no question that, even in its early stages, IS grappled with the parameters of a voluntary club. Specifying membership criteria was one challenge. Dues structure was another. And a third was the issue of standards and promulgation of good practices. These parameters would define what it meant to be a member and hence who the principals and agents of a club might be.

In order to be effective in its mission to promote the interests of the whole sector, IS chose to be inclusive in many ways and somewhat exclusive in others. It would include as members both funders and organizations that were recipients of philanthropy, but it would focus in these early years on organizations that were national in scope rather than compete for nonprofits that would be members of other (e.g., field-specific or regional) umbrella groups. Hence, United Way of America would be a member but not necessarily local United Ways, etc. And dues structure would be scaled so that it reflected the ability to pay of different kinds and sizes of institutions. These parameters were implemented in a flexible and pragmatic way and evolved in their implementation over time. It is clear, however, that in terms of its potential functioning as an accountability club, IS faced significant challenges because of its necessarily diverse membership. The clear mandate to be inclusive and universal in its relevance to institutions across the whole of the nonprofit sector made the development of common ground within this membership more elusive.

To its credit, even in the early days, IS did not neglect the issues of self-regulation and standard-setting, although it had precious few strong swords that it could wield on behalf of these goals. Clearly, the history of conflict in the public policy arena leading to the establishment of IS and the threat of further government regulation and oversight motivated this attention. Setting standards and promoting models of excellence were important because the battle was for the public's perception of the sector, which in turn would be reflected in public policy affecting the sector. This battle reflected a steady loss of public confidence in the sector stemming from a variety of concerns, such as scandals in major nonprofit institutions and controversies over executive salaries and commercial practices in various subsectors, and the willingness of various watchdog groups and public officials to press these issues by calling for greater public accountability and transparency. In this context, Congress and the public at large could be seen as the group of principals to which nonprofits needed to respond. Compared with NACC's better-defined group of principals (e.g., university officials and funders), the principals to which IS's members were accountable were in one sense more diffuse and in another sense more delineated. Congress was a clear and present danger, and a very significant principal, but the more general issue of public opinion required a much broader approach to transparency and promotion of a positive public image for the sector that appealed to a wide variety of donor, client, and taxpayer groups. As such, IS needed at least to signal to nonprofit stakeholders and association members that certain good practices were essential to the welfare of the nonprofit sector and society at large.

Early IS projects included the development of various publications on the nature of leadership in the sector, good governance practices, organizational evaluation, and profiles of excellence that documented successful voluntary operations and provided examples and guidelines for practice. A "Give 5" campaign promoted charitable giving in the country at large, helping simultaneously to bring awareness of the good works of charitable institutions. IS also promoted standards of excellence indirectly by helping to foster the development of other institutions that would specifically address good practices. For example, IS was instrumental in organizing the National Center for Nonprofit Boards (later called BoardSource) and it played a catalytic role in helping to start some of the early university academic centers that would educate students and produce more competent future nonprofit sector managers and leaders.

Still, IS, despite good intentions, was not in a very strong position to fully assume the functions of a voluntary accountability club for the nonprofit sector, despite growing concerns about the efficacy and honesty of nonprofit institutions. In the context of general losses of public confidence in major American institutions, scandals ranging from the United Way debacle in the early 1990s, to the Covenant House and Catholic Church pedophile scandals, to self-serving financial abuses of some foundations, eroded confidence in the nonprofit sector. While other efforts by state associations of nonprofits, private groups such as the Better Business

Bureau Wise Giving Alliance, the Association of Fundraising
Professionals, and BoardSource took up some of the challenges in piece-
meal fashion by creating codes of good practice, IS struggled to find its
voice in this area. Having achieved much in creating awareness of the
sector throughout the 1980s and early 1990s, and having helped to build
the research and educational infrastructure of the sector, it now searched
for a way to remain relevant itself.

In retrospect, several factors seemed responsible for the hiatus of the
late 1990s. IS was membership driven and its members were many and
diverse. The interests of granting organizations conflicted with those of
operating nonprofit groups and there was resistance by many members
to self-scrutiny. IS's governance structure was fairly standard for a
nonprofit organization, yet its governance was complex because the
structure allowed not only for general membership participation but
also the substantial influence of powerful corporate and philanthropic
groups. While voting membership was open to all nongovernmental
organizations with philanthropic interests, and all voting members had
the same rights, dues were graded according to the financial size of the
organization, implicitly favoring larger organizations that could bring
more resources to the table. The board of directors, consisting of twenty
to twenty-four individuals elected by the voting membership upon nom-
ination by the board's nominating committee or by petition by 10 percent of the voting members, had the power to approve new members.
(Originally the board consisted of more than forty voting members but
was reduced over time.) A board development committee had the
responsibility to identify and recruit new board members and a six-
member executive committee functioned to make decisions subject to
full board approval. A membership committee was charged to identify
and solicit prospective members. In the early days there was a clear
mandate to favor national-level nonprofit organizations, umbrella associations, foundations, and corporations, though this distinction was
never clear and began slowly to erode as resource support became
more of an issue. For example, individual universities were encouraged
to join, not just national associations representing institutions of higher
education. Eventually some ambiguity developed between the membership mandate of Independent Sector and the more recently established
National Council of Nonprofit Associations, which represented the
state-level associations of nonprofit organizations and whose members
generally constituted smaller, locally based organizations; of note, many
of the state associations also joined IS. Given this complex governance
picture, Independent Sector required strong and visionary executive
leadership, which it clearly received from its well-respected founding

president, Brian O'Connell. After O'Connell's retirement, however, IS struggled to find a new direction. At first, recognizing its structure as a membership organization and its obligation to support the general organizational maintenance needs of its members, IS stressed membership development and information services, but lost some of its voice in the policy arena and had difficulty finding an attractive package of services that members would continue to support. In particular, it had already helped to develop the general infrastructure of the sector through the establishment of other organizations and no longer took primary responsibility for pioneering efforts in research, database development, policy analysis, or organizational management and leadership practices. It took almost a decade and new leadership by its third president, Diana Aviv, to redefine and refine its niche as a sector convener and a locus of connection between the sector and the federal government.

Still, there were some notable accomplishments over the early years of IS in the area of accountability and organizational practices. Several of IS's publications emphasized themes of accountability and ethics (see O'Connell, 1997). In 1991, IS organized a major coalition of national leaders that produced a report entitled *Ethics and the Nature of Responsibility: Obedience to the Unenforceable*, which offered a blueprint for proper organizational behavior in the aftermath of the United Way scandal. Later, IS worked hard for the implementation of "intermediate sanctions" legislation which provided IRS with more refined tools for policing violations in the sector rather than having to resort to the draconian measure of removing tax-exempt status.

However, it has only been within the current decade that IS has really begun to develop its capacities as a voluntary club, by exploiting its special competencies as a convener and as a central voice of the sector in Washington. It is in this context that the issue of voluntary self-regulation as an answer to threats of increased governmental regulation has now risen to prominence in IS's agenda. By the mid-1990s, IS had a strong government relations unit which informed members of relevant government actions. This helped IS move deftly into the vacuum created by the Sarbanes–Oxley legislation, which had created common concerns across the sector about how nonprofits could respond to calls for responsible governance while avoiding heavy-handed governmental enforcement. Although Sarbanes–Oxley did not apply directly to nonprofit institutions, nonprofits clearly saw the writing on the wall. Indeed, the US Senate Finance Committee began actively examining the issues associated with the oversight and governance of tax-exempt organizations in the early years of the new century and IS quickly engaged the committee in dialogue about these issues.

In October 2004, and with the encouragement of the US Senate Finance Committee leadership on both sides of the aisle, IS organized the Panel on the Nonprofit Sector, representing a broad cross-section of US charities and foundations. The Panel consisted of twenty-four respected nonprofit sector leaders. These individuals were picked to represent a broad cross-section of the nonprofit sector, with diversity of location, mission, and scope, and with a level of prestige that would draw wide respect from Congress and IS's broad and diverse constituencies. The panel was co-chaired by a foundation executive (the president of the Hewlett Foundation and later by the president of the New York Community Trust) and the CEO of the American Heart Association, and staffed by the president and a senior vice president of Independent Sector. The Panel created several mechanisms to ensure broad input to its deliberations, including an Expert Advisory Group, a Citizens' Advisory Group, and five Working Groups, each focusing on a particular issue area. In the spring of 2006 the Panel created an Advisory Committee on Self-Regulation of the Charitable Sector, also widely representative of the nonprofit community.

The purpose of the Panel was to make recommendations to Congress and to nonprofits generally, on the subjects of governance, accountability, and transparency. It utilized a number of different processes to collect information and advice including a series of field hearings, a place on Independent Sector's website for site visitors to make comments, and it held a series of national conference calls to keep interested parties informed of its work. The Panel's deliberative process was open and participatory, accessible to all with an interest in expressing opinions and providing relevant information. The Panel issued three reports – a report to Congress in June 2005 entitled *Strengthening Transparency, Governance, and Accountability of Charitable Organizations*, a supplemental report by the same name in April 2006, and a report entitled *Principles for Good Governance and Ethical Practice: A Guide for Charities and Foundations* in October 2007.

The recommendations of the first report covered a wide range of issues including: (a) greater funding of the IRS for enforcement of existing law and funding for states to increase oversight and education for charitable organizations; (b) improvement of the IRS 990 tax form to produce more accurate and timely information; (c) requiring that larger nonprofits conduct audits and file audited financial statements; (d) greater reporting by nonprofits on their websites of operations and evaluation of their programs; (e) tighter regulation and transparency of donor-advised funds, including a new payout requirement; (f) minimum distribution requirements and stronger governance and regulation of supporting organizations; (g) curbs on abuse of tax shelters involving tax-exempt organizations; and (h) strengthening of rules governing contributions of appreciated property, conservation, and historic façade easements, and contributions of clothing and household items to nonprofit organizations. The Panel also recommended *against* a new periodic review system to verify a charitable organization's qualification for tax-exempt status.

In its supplemental report to the Congress, the Panel addressed nine issue areas: international grantmaking; charitable solicitation; compensation of trustees; prudent investor standards; nonprofit conversions; tax on sales of donated property; consumer credit counseling organizations; disclosure of unrelated business activity; and federal court equity powers and standing to sue. Notable recommendations within these areas include: (a) a set of practices that charitable organizations should follow to guide their international work; (b) a recommendation that Congress authorize funding to create a national uniform electronic filing system for charitable solicitation registration and annual reporting; (c) a recommendation to state charity officials, attorneys general, and state commissioners to work together to update the Model Charitable Solicitations Act; (d) recommendations to Congress to amend self-dealing regulations applying to private foundations in connection with trustee compensation; (e) a recommendation to IRS to revise the 990 tax form to clarify compensation to individual trustees; (f) a recommendation to Congress to revise regulations applying to private foundations in order to reflect the "prudent investor standard"; (g) recommendations to states to enact legislation providing disclosure of all proposed nonprofit to for-profit conversions; (h) a recommendation to state attorneys general and charity officials to develop guidelines for the role of state charity officials in nonprofit conversions; (i) a recommendation to Congress to amend federal tax laws to require qualified appraisals of donated property; (j) a recommendation to Congress to remove exemptions of consumer credit counseling organizations from federal consumer protection statutes; (k) recommendations that the IRS amend the 990 tax form to increase information on unrelated business income; and (l) a requirement for public charities to report situations in which a nonprofit officer, director, or trustee owns 10 percent or more of an entity in which the charity also has a 10 percent or greater ownership.

Since the issuance of its supplemental report, the IS Panel is continuing to work with government officials and sector representatives in key areas including self-regulation, improvement of financial reporting, ethical standards, and the revision of the 990 tax form. According to the Supplemental Report, the Panel intends to "identify sample policies on codes of ethics, conflicts of interest, reporting of misconduct, executive and board compensation, audit committees, and records retention to assist charitable organizations in improving governance and standards of practice" (Independent Sector, 2006: 3)

Clearly these numerous recommendations are a grab bag of suggestions collected from a considerable outreach effort by the Panel. Overall, the recommendations place a burden on government to take various actions that would be acceptable to most nonprofits and would move the field forward in terms of bolstering public confidence in the sector. More stringent requirements on the sector such as periodic review of the tax-exempt status of individual charities would be perceived as burdensome, intrusive, and threatening, and clearly would not have passed muster with IS's membership. Thus, the recommendations succeed in signaling the intent of the sector to improve its practices, without accepting onerous provisions, while acknowledging and embracing solutions to problems and putting the burden on an outside principal (government) to take action, invest resources, and serve as policeman.

Despite the recent efforts of IS to engage with government policy-makers and to use this as leverage for greater self-regulation of the nonprofit sector, IS remains weak in its efforts to implement the parameters of a voluntary accountability club, mainly for structural reasons. First, IS's membership is hugely diverse, restricting it to a very narrow common agenda. Moreover, within this membership there are important divisions – e.g., grantmakers and grantseekers – across which agreement is often difficult. Indeed, IS is so broad that members often identify more closely with their own subfields of activity than with the sector as a whole. As a result, membership in IS does not serve as a valued brand per se that can easily be used to induce compliance with codes of practice or behavior. Nonetheless, its principles of good governance documents have been a popular download from IS's website and widely circulated, suggesting substantial voluntary interest in IS's recommendations.

There are also policy reasons for IS's shying away from a strong voluntary accountability club role. Its board has explicitly avoided having the organization become an oversight agency or watchdog, favoring instead the role of providing a leadership forum for setting standards and developing strategy for the sector. There is, however, a common fear of government regulation and stringent policy action across the sector, especially among larger philanthropic institutions, and IS has strategically positioned itself to respond to that concern by aligning itself with government. Government needs a handle on the complex mass of institutions qualifying for tax exemption, and IS gives it that handle, especially when it can orchestrate the debate and bring coherent and comprehensive views of the sector into the halls of Congress. Similarly, IS needs government to generate support for itself among its diverse constituencies; without pervasive concerns about government regulation, IS would have much less leverage to bring its diverse constituents to the table, despite the considerable credibility it has achieved from its work on the Pension Protection Act and other policy issues over the years. Even its leverage derived from government involvement is highly constrained: IS has focused its efforts primarily in Washington and not on the state and local governments which also affect nonprofits in important ways. Moreover, IS's influence in Washington is intrinsically limited, given that it is prohibited from buying access to policymakers through the campaign finance process.

Nor is IS especially inclined to serve as a policeman for the sector, seeing itself more as protector and promoter, recognizing that the best way to do this is some combination of relatively benign government oversight combined with the promulgation of voluntary standards and codes of behavior that improve the public perception of philanthropy and non-profits as trustworthy and effective agents for the public good.

A stronger accreditation or certification process for nonprofits was never really on the table, for several reasons. First, accreditation would put IS in competition with various subsector groups, in fields such as healthcare, education, and social services, which already provide accreditation for nonprofits in their fields of service. Second, as an accrediting body, IS would be caught in the tension between its role as a broadly supported advocate for the sector, and having to police and penalize some of its members for nonconformity to recommended practices. From an organizational maintenance point of view, this balance was always tenuous, especially given strong feelings among major institutions in the sector to maintain their autonomy and, to some degree, their privacy. From its beginnings, the founders of IS failed to embrace the recommendation of the Filer Commission for a quasi-public body that would regulate the sector. However, all along, IS has walked a very thin line, coaxing the IRS to take a stronger but still gentle hand in overseeing the sector while moving its own members toward a voluntary consensus around good policies and practices. That is, IS has tried to resolve the tension surrounding nonprofit regulation by separating membership and advocacy for the sector, and its own organizational maintenance, from the accountability issue. There is some doubt, of course, as to whether any system of purely voluntary standards can work effectively. There is evidence from other countries such as the Netherlands (Bekkers, 2003; see also chapter 11 in this volume) and the Czech Republic (Ortmann and Svítková, 2007; see also chapter 7 in this volume) that strong regulation requires an independent body not beholden to the sector itself. This has been implicitly recognized by IS in its sympathetic and collaborative approach to the

IRS and the Senate Finance Committee which favors a stronger role for government.

It is important to recognize that IS has little incentive to limit its membership or to discipline members by excluding them from membership. Indeed, the political strength of IS depends very much on the numbers of organizations and individuals it can claim to speak for; hence the more members, the better. To witness, bylaws have been changed recently to include local nonprofit organizations, and the size distribution of membership has broadened conspicuously as a result. Conversely, IS or its general membership would be little damaged by the bad behavior of a few of its members, with the exception of very large and prominent organizations such as the Red Cross or a large foundation. Thus, an IS good housekeeping seal or a threat to suspend members would not have much weight. Rather, IS's leverage depends on the public imagery it can create through voluntary codes, awards for good behavior, and the promulgation of sympathetic government oversight, as well as the political might it can claim through the numbers of its participants in the policy advocacy process. In terms of collective action theory (Olson, 1965), IS has little coercive leverage over its members, nor does it have available many selective incentives it can offer to members to support its program for improving the performance and public image of the sector. Indeed, it is challenged even to define the public goods which all of its members value in common, given the tremendous diversity of its constituencies. It does, however, have the support of what Olson termed its "privileged members" – those larger philanthropic institutions that would be seriously affected by heavy-handed government regulatory policy, especially given that such policy would likely take a "one size fits all" approach typical of policymaking in a democratic setting governed by majority rule. By deftly inserting itself as a sympathetic and credible mediator between broad sector interests as a whole and the federal government, IS may have found the only effective way to build its capacity to function in part as a voluntary accountability club.

Clubs and the life cycle of infrastructure associations

Independent Sector and NACC are examples of what might be termed "field-building" organizations designed to coalesce, support, grow, protect, and even help clarify the identity of newly emerging fields of service. The mission of IS was to give a broad, diverse, and ill-defined segment of society an identity as a sector, and to help that sector defend itself from threats of political opposition and heavy-handed governmental regulation. In helping to develop the nonprofit sector, IS's task was to help assemble the preexisting components of the field (e.g., philanthropy, charitable organizations, etc.), give them a collective shape, and find ways, through programs and infrastructure development, to nurture and protect them. This was a somewhat different task than that addressed by NACC, which was to support the enterprises of academic entrepreneurs to develop a new, more narrowly defined field within higher education, to help build and secure acceptance for that field, and possibly, ultimately, to protect it from other variants competing for the same academic territory. Nonetheless, seen through the lens of clubs, IS and NACC are similar in the sense that their missions from the outset were primarily to carve out, define, gain respect, and secure new organizational territory for, rather than simply protect, an existing set of organizations or industries. Hence the likelihood of membership associations like IS and NACC sponsoring strong accountability clubs seems low, given the competing interests within these associations. These organizations began as coalitions of entities with common interests at junctures when issues of standard-setting and self-regulation took a back seat to self-identification, building of membership, gathering of support, and pursuing strategies for survival and growth. The development of these infrastructure organizations has important parallels to the development of the foundation field as discussed by Peter Frumkin in chapter 6 of this volume. Like IS, the Council on Foundations and related regional organizations have remained focused on field development, professionalization, and networking, and the willingness to sponsor strong accountability clubs has been limited by these conflicting incentives. In the case of NACC, club development has also been limited by competition from other accrediting bodies that serve the universities of which NACC members are a part.

However, NACC and IS also give us a common perspective on the life cycle of associations and the inflection points when club functions become more trenchant. In IS's case, standard-setting and self-regulation were on its list of priorities from the beginning, though not at the top. More pressing were needs to build the identity of the sector, grow its membership, stimulate the development of other sectorwide infrastructure, create public knowledge of the sector, and give voice to sectorwide interests. Part of this, of course, was the intent to signal the quality and importance of the sector, essentially a club-related function. And when external threats to the sector accelerated, the voluntary club function gained a stronger foothold and issues of standards and self-regulation rose to the top of IS's agenda. This again parallels the foundation field, which began to develop principles of conduct only in the face of threat of additional government regulation.

In NACC's case, there really was no constituency at the beginning out of which a self-regulatory accountability club function could have been developed – only a handful of academic centers with a new idea and a desire to gain a foothold within the university setting. This necessarily required a focus on field building – an expansion of their numbers in many more universities around the country and eventually around the world, and a clarification of what distinguished them from other academic programs and organizational units. By the 1990s, however, there were several hundred university programs of nonprofit study (Mirabella and Wish, 2001), many still challenged to establish themselves firmly, as well as alternative programs contending to define the field (such as programs in social enterprise and corporate social responsibility in business schools, and programs on the social economy or civil society in universities in other parts of the world). Driven by both internal resource needs and sector interests in bringing some order and sense to the cacophony of university programs claiming to offer nonprofit sector education, NACC stepped more assertively into the realm of curricular guidelines and standards for academic centers. These guidelines have been a distinguishing contribution of NACC, though its focus on this agenda did not enjoy the full enthusiasm of its original membership, nor are they intended to impose uniformity or require certain levels of performance by its members.

For both NACC and IS, club behavior became more manifest after the fields of activity to which they addressed themselves gained some maturity. Hence there appears to be a life cycle dimension to voluntary clubs associated with newly emerging fields. The club agenda makes sense once there is a clearly defined and robust field to protect. However, the process of building that field seems necessarily to create certain restraints that hold infrastructure-building associations back from developing a full-fledged voluntary accountability club capacity with strong swords to maintain and enforce standards and regulations. To a certain degree, IS and NACC share in common the fact that building membership necessarily requires flexibility in criteria for admission, and inclusiveness in developing program agendas. Early in the life cycle at least, there is little stomach for disciplining errant members or excluding them from the group. The best that can be achieved is the articulation of models of good practice so as to guide member development positively and to put the best foot forward for the field as a whole. The same phenomenon is observed by Tschirhart in this volume (chapter 4). She finds that among US states with nonprofit associations, very few of those associations have developed accountability clubs and those that do exist are relatively weak. Like IS and NACC, many state associations represent a diverse set of organizations, and the associations themselves are often engaged in a struggle for membership and revenue that makes them unwilling to take on monitoring and sanctioning behavior that will be off-putting to some potential members.

Another common notion that links the IS and NACC cases is the effectiveness of building alliances with external agents in the membership environment. Rather than assuming the full functions of clubs themselves, these organizations show signs of becoming agents who can influence the important principals to which their memberships owe fealty, giving themselves important leverage in the process. An alliance with Congress, for instance, has maneuvered IS into a strong position to have a moderating effect on public regulatory policy toward nonprofits as well as strong support from its membership to serve as a central voice for the sector.

In the case of NACC, this partnership strategy is less clear. Recent conversations between NACC and the accrediting body NASPAA suggest that NACC can gain leverage by providing the substantive curricular information that NASPAA needs to oversee its many member schools of public affairs that have concentrations in nonprofit management. Similarly, NACC may be able to gain leverage with other associations such as American Humanics, which is influential in shaping undergraduate programming in nonprofit studies, or with AACSB (Association to Advance Collegiate Schools of Business) which accredits schools of management.

In summary, if NACC and IS are an indication, nonprofit infrastructure associations charged with establishing and building new fields of endeavor are at best reluctant about fully assuming the functioning of accountability clubs. They do in some stages of their life cycles pursue initiatives to develop guidelines and standards of practice and encourage self-regulation of their members. But the strategies they pursue to build their fields necessarily contain elements (inclusiveness and diversity, for example) that ultimately constrict their effectiveness as regulatory clubs with strong swords. Rather it seems more likely that these organizations will build alliances with other sources of regulatory power so that they can achieve protection for their members and a moderating influence on the regulatory process, while continuing to signal to both their principals and agents preferred practices and behaviors.

REFERENCES

Bekkers, René. 2003. Trust, Accreditation and Philanthropy in the Netherlands. *Nonprofit and Voluntary Sector Quarterly* 32: 596–615.
Bradley Center for Philanthropy and Civic Renewal. 2005. Nonprofit Management Education: Required Course or Off Course? Edited transcript. Washington, DC: Hudson Institute, September 13.

Brilliant, Eleanor L. 2000. *Private Charity and Public Inquiry*. Bloomington and Indianapolis: Indiana University Press.

Haas, Peter J. and Maynard G. Robinson. 1998. The Views of Nonprofit Executives on Educating Nonprofit Managers. *Nonprofit Management and Leadership* 8(4): 349–363.

Hall, Peter Dobkin. 1992. *Inventing the Nonprofit Sector*. Baltimore: Johns Hopkins University Press.

Independent Sector, Panel on the Nonprofit Sector. 2005. *Strengthening Transparency, Governance, and Accountability of Charitable Organizations: A Final Report to Congress and the Nonprofit Sector*. Accessed via www.nonprofitpanel.org, June 2005.

2006. *Strengthening Transparency, Governance, and Accountability of Charitable Organizations*. Accessed via www.nonprofitpanel.org, April 2006.

2007. *Principles for Good Governance and Ethical Practice: A Guide for Charities and Foundations*. Accessed via www.nonprofitpanel.org, October 2007.

Mirabella, Roseanne M. and Naomi B. Wish. 1999. Educational Impact of Graduate Nonprofit Degree Programs. *Nonprofit Management and Leadership* 9(3): 329–340.

2001. University-Based Educational Programs in the Management of Nonprofit Organizations: An Updated Census of U.S. Programs. *Public Performance and Management Review* 25(1): 30–41.

NACC (Nonprofit Academic Centers Council). 2001. The History of NACC, draft working paper.

2006. *In Pursuit of Excellence: Indicators of Quality in Nonprofit Academic Centers*. Accessed via www.nacouncil.org.

2007a. *Curricular Guidelines for Graduate Study in Nonprofit Leadership, the Nonprofit Sector, and Philanthropy*, revised 2nd edn. Accessed via www.naccouncil.org.

2007b. *Curricular Guidelines for Undergraduate Study in Nonprofit Leadership, the Nonprofit Sector and Philanthropy*, 1st edn. Accessed via www.naccouncil.org.

Nielsen, Waldemar A. 1979. *The Endangered Sector*. New York: Columbia University Press.

O'Connell, Brian, 1997. *Powered by Coalition*. San Francisco: Jossey-Bass.

Olson, Mancur. 1965. *The Logic of Collective Action*. Cambridge, MA: Harvard University Press.

Ortmann, Andreas and Katarina Svítková. 2007. Certification as a Viable Quality Assurance Mechanism in Transition Economies. *Prague Economic Papers* 16 (2): 99–114.

6   Foundation accountability clubs and the search for philanthropic standards

Peter Frumkin

Today, private foundations in the United States number more than 68,000, control $500 billion in assets, and make grants totaling more than $20 billion annually. Foundations often provide critical early capital to nonprofit organizations seeking to start new programs or projects. By virtue of their wealth and influence in the broader nonprofit sector, foundations have long occupied a privileged position and tend to be treated with deference not just by the organizations that depend on their grants, but by government which recognizes the significance of these private funds directed at solving public needs. In many of the chapters in this volume, foundations play the role of principal, making accountability claims on their grantees. This chapter examines how accountability issues play out when foundations themselves face their own set of accountability claims.

Accountability issues in the foundation field differ in a number of ways from those facing nongranting nonprofits. A key concern of nonprofit organizations is securing the financial resources needed to carry out their programs. Thus donor organizations tend to be important nonprofit principals. Foundations are grantmaking organizations with their own endowments and are resource independent. The accountability claims on foundations differ from those made on other kinds of charitable organizations because of this independence. Foundations are more insulated from accountability claims from the public at large because they are not directly using public funds to carry out their programs. While foundations do not have financial principals, the public sector has historically acted as a key authorizer and legitimizer for the sector. Governments wield important regulatory instruments regarding rules for foundation payout and give foundations their charitable status. As a consequence, foundations pay a great deal of attention to relevant legislative processes and regulatory policy. As this chapter shows, potential changes to the regulatory systems governing foundation operations have been met with concerted collective action and the development of new accountability programs.

Over the past forty years, the foundation field has been remarkably successful in fending off government regulation, in part through the use

125

of accountability club structures. In several cases, existing external standards and rules related to the management of foundations have been relaxed or removed at the instigation of the field. Today, national associations of foundations, state and regional associations of grantmakers, and a broad array of affinity groups constitute a rich and tight fabric that provides support to the field. This chapter explores the role of foundation associations in establishing accountability clubs as the foundation field has evolved. The chapter first presents a quick sketch of the evolution of government–foundation relations, which sets the stage for an examination of the current landscape of foundation clubs and a consideration of the roles these accountability clubs play in organizing foundation work. Throughout, the aim is to provide a critical assessment of the challenges to self-governance and self-regulation in a field where the institutions are wealthy and completely resource independent.

Origins of foundation accountability clubs

The Council on Foundations, the main professional organization that represents the foundation world, has played a critical role in defending the autonomy of the field. More than twenty years ago, the Council took a lead role in attempting to fashion a voluntary accountability system based on the promulgation of principles and practices to guide the work of foundations. More recently, the Council has worked collaboratively with Congress to develop new rules to ensure the effective stewardship of these special institutions. Looking at several episodes in the Council on Foundations' long-term work to defend and organize the field, we conclude, however, that the claims of principals have not to date been sufficiently strong to encourage foundations to define and enact – on a voluntary basis – meaningful accountability measures for the field.

The turning point for foundation accountability was the passage of the Tax Reform Act of 1969 (TRA 1969). The legislation signed into law on December 31, 1969, put in place a new and far-reaching set of taxes, regulations, and operating requirements that signaled the first major public challenge to the independence and autonomy of America's philanthropic foundations (Labovitz, 1973). Before this Act, foundations enjoyed a lax regulatory environment and were able to operate largely under the radar of government. The Act included new regulations on foundations bearing on reporting, self-dealing, the grant payout rate, and other issues (Edie, 1987), and signaled that American foundations would no longer be trusted to monitor themselves.

The process of mounting a credible defense of philanthropy, however, ultimately had a powerful organizational effect on American foundations.

The complex legislative ordeal culminating in the passage of new regulations propelled foundations toward the realization that they needed to join together to form a more organized and cohesive field if further government intrusion into the voluntary sector was to be avoided. Although foundation officials began their debate with Congress over the future of philanthropy as representatives of individual institutions each having its own interests and agenda, these same officials emerged at the end of the process with a determination to operate as a unified and cohesive community (Andrews, 1973). The fight over the Tax Reform Act of 1969 and the regulations it proposed for foundations thus turned out to be the deciding moment in the history of organized philanthropy (Nielsen, 1985; Frumkin, 1999).

Several prior Congressional investigations of foundations failed to produce new regulations (Lankford, 1964), but Congressman Wright Patman's decade-long inquiry produced the first serious regulations bearing on the governance of private foundations (US Congress Senate Finance Committee, 1969a and 1969b). As a result of this shock to the system, an elaborate infrastructure of associations and groups was built to constitute a new infrastructure for the field. In a series of hearings, Patman triumphantly unmasked a few troublesome incidents of abuse and self-dealing, and succeeded in placing foundations on the public radar screen. The tide of negative publicity coming out of the Congressional investigation of foundations eventually led a few foundation officials to argue that in order to stave off harsh punishment from government, foundations needed to adopt a proactive stance. By 1968, the Foundation Center, under the direction of Manning Pattillo, suggested that the best course of action was for philanthropy to set in place voluntarily a new set of regulations and principles for foundation governance. Key to Pattillo's plan was a system of accreditation, one that would mirror in many respects that used by higher education. Under this system, foundations would submit themselves to regular review, agree to meet certain standards and practices, and be accredited by a board of experts.

Pattillo put forward a six-point plan to develop an accrediting system for foundations. The plan included the following elements:

1. Formation of a nucleus of foundations considered by informed observers to be well administered. A group of about ten or twelve would be sufficient.
2. Election of a committee on standards and accreditation.
3. Formulation of a set of standards which could be applied with reasonable objectivity.
4. An invitation to other foundations to apply for accreditation or certification.
5. Inspection of the applying foundations by committees selected from the staffs of the original members.
6. Publicizing of the standards and the roster of accredited foundations.

(Pattillo, 1968: 20)

At the Seminar on Foundation Administration, jointly sponsored by
New York University and the Foundation Center in 1968, some progress
was made toward establishing a uniform set of standards for all foundations, that is, step three in Pattillo's scheme. Fourteen "Principles of
Foundation Management" were prepared at this meeting, then published
and debated. However, no other concrete steps were taken to put the
Pattillo plan into action. By the end of 1968, it became clear that the
Foundation Center's attempt to set up standards and a system of accreditation lacked the broad-based support it needed to get off the ground.
Other factions within the foundation community were emerging – not
all of which were committed to a rigorous program of self-regulation.
The most influential foundations, that is, Carnegie, Rockefeller, and
Ford, had each developed its own opinions about government regulation
and none was willing to join the Council on Foundations in order to
speak in one voice. Nor were these leaders eager to place their full weight
behind the Foundation Center's proposed accrediting plan. Instead, as
Congressional hearings got underway in 1969, foundation officials from
all over the country arrived in Washington with separate agendas and
proposals (Andrews, 1973; Pifer, 1984; Committee on the Foundation
Field, 1970). The result was a bruising defeat for foundations and the
enactment of a first major package of regulations for the field by Congress.

With the passage of TRA 1969, foundations faced a new payout requirement, limits on the holding of concentrated stockholdings, prohibitions on
self-serving transactions, and a host of reporting and transparency requirements. Even though a forty-year death sentence for all foundations was
avoided and the proposed 7.5 percent tax on income had been reduced to
4 percent (later to be further reduced), the effect of the regulation on the
psyche of American philanthropy should not be underestimated.
Foundations were crushed by the outcome of their year-long struggle
with Congress. In the pages of *Foundation News* immediately following
the passage of the Tax Reform Act, a sense of dire concern is obvious, as
article after article outlined the damage done by the legislation. As one
foundation executive put it, "Suddenly we realized we were not the
conscientious, silent do-gooders we thought we were, but a vast array of
extremely diverse organizations – with little or no constituency to come to
our collective defense. Even more eye opening was the sudden realization
that we needed defense – and needed it badly" (Wallace, 1971: 1).
Significantly, the sense of shock and despair experienced by foundations
also brought with it a desire for change and a resolve to oppose more
effectively future government challenges to philanthropy (Simon, 1974).
In the decade of the 1970s, foundations strengthened and expanded their
communal defense and emerged as a more closely knit force. As one

foundation professional observed: "The Tax Reform Act of 1969 strength-ened foundations, creating a sense of national and regional foundation 'community' where none had existed" (Shakely, 1980: 19). Foundations also established a powerful, permanent, and unified lobbying presence in Washington, one that would represent the interests of an emerging foundation community and work to professionalize the field.

Impacts of the Tax Reform Act of 1969

In the years immediately following the passage of the Tax Reform Act, the Council on Foundations would also transform itself. The Council's membership would double, then triple, as its presence and influence in Washington increased. Alongside the strengthening of the Council on Foundations, the 1970s witnessed an explosion in the formation of regional associations for grantmakers. While the Kansas City Association of Trusts and Foundations was founded in 1949, it was not until the 1970s that the idea caught on in other cities around the country. Soon there were regional associations of grantmakers in cities across the country working to build ties among foundations. These new associations were often set up and funded by large local foundations interested in increasing their local public presence.

Another effect of the legislative process was to broaden the sights of foundations. Foundations no longer saw themselves as islands of privilege immune from outside pressure (Council on Foundations, 1977). During the 1970s, the fate of foundations was linked to the fate of the entire nonprofit community, which would become known as the independent sector. The fact that the legislation, with its tax on income, was seen to be a threat to educational and scientific organizations was instrumental in pushing this process along. Foundations began to portray themselves as part of a bigger picture, part of a voluntary or independent sector. The advantage of this repositioning is clear: it is harder to make the charge of elitism stick to foundations when they portray themselves as working "in partnership" with grassroots nonprofit organizations delivering services to communities (Frumkin, 2006b).

During the years after 1969, there were many proposals to merge asso-ciations and groups to build a more cohesive infrastructure for the field. While the proposed mergers never took place, the Council on Foundations eventually moved to Washington, DC, where it could have more direct access to Congress, the Treasury Department, and the IRS (Olasky, 1993). The idea that philanthropy organize itself around a single association was realized when the National Council on Philanthropy was merged with the Coalition of National Voluntary Organizations into Independent Sector. The Council on Foundations thus became the sole spokesperson for the foundation community. While allowing for some overlap, the division of labor between the two groups was clear: the Council would represent the interests of organized philanthropy and Independent Sector would pursue issues of interest to the entire nonprofit sector.

One key sign of professionalization and the creation of an accountability club is the propagation of a code of ethics that governs the behavior of its members (Abbott, 1988; Colvard, 1961; DiMaggio and Powell, 1983; Wilensky, 1964). In philanthropy, the adoption of a code of ethics represented the final step toward instilling a new ethos of openness. A code of ethics was slow in coming for two reasons: first, the Council did not want to impose a code unilaterally too soon after 1969 for fear of alienating its new and growing membership; and second, foundation officials prided themselves on their independence and were generally resistant to outside parties seeking to influence a foundation's policies. However, many foundation officials felt there was a need for some kind of statement from the field as a whole, which would outline acceptable foundation practices and demonstrate to the public that foundations were capable of self-governance and self-regulation.

The Council made a first effort after TRA 1969 at laying down operating principles for foundations in 1973. It published in *Foundations News* "Some General Principles and Guidelines for Grantmaking Foundations: A Policy Statement of the Directors of the Council on Foundations" (Council on Foundations, 1973: 2). The principles were nonbinding and generally sought to reinforce the notion that foundations must make special effort to be open and accountable. Included in the principles was a clear reference to TRA 1969 as a lesson not to be forgotten:

Despite the "overkill" contained in these provisions – which one must hope will prove open to Congressional adjustment as working experience with the effects of the Tax Reform Act of 1969 become clearer – the act's forceful reminders that foundations exist for the public benefit and must be so directed have to be recognized as necessary and for the good. (Council on Foundations, 1973: 3)

The policy pronouncements of 1973 set in place the cornerstone on which a more ambitious effort to develop operating principles for foundations was built six years later when the board of directors of the Council on Foundations began developing a true code of professional ethics in mid-1979 by appointing a special committee. Meeting often over the course of a year, the committee worked through numerous drafts and presented them at meetings of various regional gatherings and at the Council's annual meeting in Dallas. The Council was clear about the purpose of the code: "The purpose of the statement is to provide practical counsel to new foundations just establishing their operating guidelines and to existing foundations and other donor organizations that may be re-examining their policies and procedures" (Council on Foundations, 1980: 8).

The statement of "Recommended Principles and Practices for Effective Grantmaking" also served an important public relations function. In the aftermath of regulation, the Council went to considerable lengths to help its members increase their public profile and improve relations with recipient organizations. The code fit well into this plan. The Council noted: "It draws heavily on the experience and insights of foundation executives and corporate giving administrators and is couched in terms of what has proved useful in the successful handling of grants and in the maintaining of good relations with the various publics with which grantmakers must be concerned" (Council on Foundations, 1980: 8).

The eleven principles and practices amounted to complete endorsement of the view that private foundations have important public responsibilities and must be governed in the public interest. These principles formed the basis for an emerging consensus on foundation standards for governance and performance, though the principles did not contain any provisions for monitoring and enforcement. The first three principles urged foundations to establish a set of policies that clearly define fundamental objectives, to appoint a board of directors committed to implementing these objectives, and to set up processes for receiving, examining, and deciding on grant applications. These first three principles all emphasized the importance of clear objectives, policies, and procedures.

The fourth, fifth, sixth, and seventh principles focused on accountability and accessibility. The Council urged that foundations recognize their public responsibilities to a broad range of constituents, including recipient organizations, state governments, and the IRS. Open communication with the public and grantseeking organizations was recommended, including prompt and honest responses to all grant requests and the publication of an annual report. These ideas flowed directly from the experience of foundations during the 1960s, when an inability to communicate the good work of foundations opened the door for Congressional attacks.

The ninth, tenth, and eleventh principles supported commonsense measures aimed at improving foundation performance. The Council recommended the periodical evaluation of foundation programs, the careful avoidance of any transactions that might appear self-interested, and active participation in the Council, regional associations, and organizations representing the entire nonprofit sector.

Ten of the eleven principles and practices were thus uncontroversial and predictable in that they pushed the Council's accountability and openness agenda, while seeking to ensure that foundations continue to improve and professionalize their grantmaking practices. One of the eleven principles did, however, cause some controversy and provoke some resistance: the eighth principle urged foundations to seek diversity in their staffs:

8. It is important that grantmakers be alert and responsive to changing conditions in society and to the changing needs and merits of particular grantseeking organizations. Responses to needs and social conditions may well be determined by independent inquiries, not merely by reactions to requests submitted by grantseekers. In response to new challenges, grantmakers are helpful if they use the special knowledge, experience and insight of individuals beyond those persons, families or corporations from which the funds originally came. Some grantmakers find it useful to secure ideas and comments from a variety of consultants and advisory panels, as well as diversified staff and board members. In view of the historic under-representation of minorities and women in supervisory and policy positions, particular attention should be given to finding ways to draw them into the decision making processes. (Council on Foundations, 1980).

Three years after the Council on Foundations propounded its principles and practices, it required all member foundations to agree – in writing – to embrace these guidelines as a condition for membership in the association. This essentially turned what had been a passive code of conduct into an active club. Even if monitoring and reporting provisions were weak, by signing up to the guidelines foundations were opening themselves up to peer scrutiny. Although most foundations were already hiring women and minorities in significant numbers, a few more conservative members of the Council objected to the eighth clause and did not embrace the Council's conception of foundations as public trusts. Because philanthropy had always prided itself on the plurality of visions and approaches which it encompassed, the Council's attempt to impose a single set of operating principles was naturally met with resistance by some foundations.

A small rival foundation group, the Philanthropy Roundtable, emerged in 1983. The group included the handful of openly conservative foundations, including the Olin, Scaife, and Richardson Foundations, as well as a number of smaller individual donors and corporate members. Although Irving Kristol and other well-known conservatives were involved in the Roundtable, membership remained small for several years as the group launched a newsletter and began organizing conferences. While the Roundtable survived and even increased its membership to two hundred by 1990, its relationship with the Council actually improved to the point where cooperation between the two groups now occasionally occurs in event planning.

Many observers have interpreted the schism caused by the Council in purely political terms, seeing in the Council's endorsement of liberal notions such as affirmative action the cause of the departure of a block of more conservative foundations from the Council's ranks. In reality, the dispute embodied more than just politics. It pitted two fundamentally different perceptions of the nature of philanthropy and the role of self-regulation and accountability in the field: the minority view believed foundations did not need an outside agent interfering with the internal affairs of private foundations. The majority view embraced the new openness and welcomed the Council's input.

The alienation of a small number of Council members in 1983 was a small price to pay for having a large number of private foundations publicly endorse the Council's ethics code (Joseph, 1983). Ten years after the move to require Council members to subscribe to the principles and practices, the Council noted: "The fact that the vast majority of our members had, indeed, affirmed the statement on principles and practices was not lost on our elected officials. No public presentation by the Council or other witnesses was as effective as this demonstration of commitment to responsible foundation practices in making the case for less government regulation" (Council on Foundations, 1990). This suggests that even standards without enforcement can have some useful signaling properties. The decade of the 1970s was a turning point in the development of modern philanthropy. The new regulations brought about two significant shifts in foundation theory and practice. First, foundations embraced a new self-understanding of their status as public trusts that were to be operated for public purposes and with responsibilities to that public. Thus the public was clearly acknowledged as a foundation principal, with foundations as agents acting in broad accordance with public wishes. With the Council pushing for greater reporting and better relations with grantees, foundations fundamentally redefined their work. The tendency toward secrecy and aloofness was challenged and weakened. In its place was a new sense of the public responsibilities of foundations. The strengthening of the Council on Foundations and the promulgation of explicit norms and standards for behavior ushered in a whole new conception of private foundations as public trusts, open and accountable to all. In addition to the strengthening of this central accountability club, the decades following TRA 1969 were also a period when other associations and smaller regional accountability clubs were established. Together, these institutions constitute today a large and complex institutional and accountability infrastructure for the foundation field.

Structure and function of foundation clubs and associations today

Foundation associations allow members to gather together without preconditions. If they choose to sponsor clubs as well, they must define codes and standards to which members must subscribe. Foundation associations and accountability clubs currently operate at both a national level and a regional level. Most foundation associations restrict membership to funders only and do not allow nonprofit organizations that might seek foundation support to be members. The main reason for this exclusive approach is to give foundation leaders a place where they can drop their guard and speak to their peers freely. Foundation associations fulfill many purposes, but the three most important include networking and information sharing; new staff training; and policy work and lobbying. Foundation accountability clubs fulfill these three purposes and add to this list a fourth: norm- and standard-setting. In this sense the diversity of their responsibilities is quite similar to the state associations discussed by Tschirhart in chapter 4 of this volume.

Professional networking and information sharing

Through annual events, special meetings, weekly brownbag lunches, lectures by outside experts, and a host of other events, foundation clubs allow members to associate with one another. The relationships that are built between program staff and leaders of foundations at these events can sometimes provide a basis for interorganizational collaboration around special grantmaking initiatives or they can simply be a place for foundation workers to build their peer network. Foundation associations act as clearinghouses for new approaches to persistent problems and a place where best practices are shared. Foundation members can learn from outside subject experts or seasoned philanthropy insiders what works and what does not in a range of fields. Interest in learning about best practices is fueled often by a desire to learn from the successes and failures of others before philanthropic funds are committed to a project or cause. Because robust and compelling metrics are often elusive, grantmakers frequently will fall back on anecdotal evidence and personal experience when seeking to convey best practices. In this way, many clubs are places where war stories and cautionary lessons are shared right alongside promising new approaches to public problemsolving.

Training newcomers to the field and professionalization

As foundations have added professional staff over the past four decades since TRA 1969, there has been a growing need for professional education and development programs for newcomers to the grantmaking field. Associations can and do offer introductory training services to new program staff, exposing them to topics such as how to conduct a site visit, how to analyze a budget, and how to make coherent and strategic grant decisions.

This commitment to professional development and preparation has also been pushed along by a growing sense that grantmaking is fast approaching the status of a profession. Just as one would not practice any other established profession such as law, accounting, or nursing without adequate training, so too in philanthropy is there a sense that sound preparation is essential to effective and responsible philanthropy.

Lobbying and shaping policy

Foundation associations can and do play policy roles at the national and state levels. As interested onlookers to the making of policy both as it affects the fields in which they fund and the regulatory environment around foundations themselves, clubs keep close watch on what policies are being discussed and what bills are being considered in state legislatures and on Capitol Hill. In recent years, as the Senate Finance Committee began to look closely at some of the rules surrounding supporting organizations and the annual reporting to the IRS that foundations have long undertaken, there was a period of intense interest within both the Council on Foundations and the Philanthropy Roundtable in these deliberations. Lobbying and policy work are important to the field because they represent attempts to advance the interests of all foundations, not just a small number of the largest and most influential foundations. This work creates a sense of community and solidarity across the field and defends the freedoms that foundations guard jealously.

Defining and promulgating norms and standards

A final function of accountability associations is to sponsor clubs, that is, to define what good philanthropic practice entails and to make the case that adhering to norms or standards is important to the advancement of the field and its long-term legitimacy. The norms that are promulgated by foundation clubs are almost always procedural rather than substantive. Clubs do not tell their members what kinds of programs to fund or what areas of focus to develop. Not only would no one listen to such advice, it would be viewed as a violation of the freedoms that foundations guard closely to determine how private wealth will be directed to solve particular public problems. The norms and standards that are advanced are thus typically related to good management, communication and transparency, and ethical behavior. They are intended to define professional grantmaking conduct, not dictate or shape the content of philanthropic decisions. By adhering to norms, foundations gain something very important in exchange, namely legitimacy. Floating atop large multimillion- and in an increasing number of instances multibillion-dollar endowments, foundations face the question of what gives them the right to choose particular problems and then to select and support organizations that will work on these problems. Adhering to norms helps foundations address the question of the legitimacy of philanthropic power (Frumkin, 2006a).

Foundation associations usually fulfill – with varying degrees of commitment – each of the first three functions. Foundation associations become accountability club sponsors when they carry out the last function – norm- and standard-setting – along with the other three functions as well. This is the critical difference between foundation associations and accountability clubs.

Foundation accountability clubs are different than nonprofit accountability clubs in several important respects. Nonprofit clubs seek to mediate between stakeholders and nonprofit organizations by giving nonprofits a way of building confidence in the sector and sending signals to stakeholders about nonprofit quality. Accountability is pursued and built as a means to secure external support for the nonprofit sector from individual donors, foundation corporations, and government funders. By providing information about nonprofit practices to the broad group of stakeholders that surround nonprofits, clubs work to help improve and build the flow of information and resources into a sector that is often ridden by competition for scarce funding. Accountability through clubs is thus a means of responding to the problem of resource dependence and the information requirements of nonprofit principals with the expectation that financial donors will be willing to reward club participation with increased funding.

When it comes to private philanthropic foundations, this resource dependence rationale (Emerson, 1962; Pfeffer and Salancik, 1978) for participation and compliance is simply not present. Foundations are endowed in almost all cases in perpetuity; they have no need for the approbation of the recipient organizations or support from the communities in which they operate. There will always be a long line of nonprofit organizations eager to relieve foundations of their surplus wealth by accepting their grants. Similarly, foundations do not need financial support from any external source. Permanent endowments largely shield the foundation world from financial pressures and transform the role of accountability clubs from one oriented to outside stakeholders controlling resources to one more oriented to actors within the field and to the political and regulatory environment. Foundation accountability clubs are oriented toward legitimacy and awareness. Clubs are designed to improve the effectiveness of the field, legitimize foundations and build public understanding of the field, and, most importantly, protect foundations from further regulation.

The landscape of foundation accountability clubs and associations today

The associational landscape of philanthropy has three major levels. First, national associations and clubs sit across the entire field and work with foundation staff and board members to advance the field. Second, at the state and regional level, foundations are linked to one another through regional associations of grantmakers (RAGs), some of which take the form of loose associations, while others operate more like accountability clubs with standards. Third, the foundation field is supported by a large number of associations that are focused on fields of interest within philanthropy, such as health, education, and the arts. At each level, these associations and clubs almost always fulfill the first two functions outlined above: professional networking and idea sharing, training newcomers to the field. Some engage in policy work and a few engage in real accountability work, either by defining norms or setting standards.

National-level groups

The Council on Foundations remains today the largest and most influential accountability club in the foundation field. Since its founding in 1949, through its involvement in a range of legislative battles, and carrying on today as it works with members to strengthen the quality of foundation management, the Council has worked to find a compromise between defining and enforcing rules for the field and simply suggesting best practices.

The Council defines its mission as providing "the opportunity, leadership and tools needed by philanthropic organizations to expand, enhance and sustain their ability to advance the common good." The Council has 2,100 members today and charges dues based on a sliding scale keyed to the size of the foundation member, ranging from $500 to $55,000. These member fees support an annual budget of $20 million and this scale reflects that the larger foundations have a greater stake in the preservation of the current loose but supportive regulatory environment compared with the smaller foundations.

Major activities of the Council today include an annual conference, a community foundations conference, a corporate grantmakers summit, and a family foundation conference. The Council does offer professional development programs and sponsors an extensive array of research projects and publications related to grantmaking. To protect and defend the field effectively, the Council engages in a range of advocacy and lobbying work, including a Foundations on the Hill day, which began in 2003 and gives grantmakers the chance to meet their federal lawmakers in Washington, DC.

Meetings are scheduled so grantmakers can personally discuss their work with policymakers. There are also regular legislative updates and newsletters for members covering policy issues related to foundations.

The Council's principles and practices represented the first major attempt to bring norms of professional conduct and self-regulation to the field, but by 2005 the Council had adopted the following modified "Statement of Ethical Principles" that constitutes the linchpin of the accountability club for the sector:

- Mission: Our members are committed to the public benefit and to their philanthropic purposes and act accordingly.
- Stewardship: Our members manage their resources to maximize philanthropic purposes, not private gain; and actively avoid excessive compensation and unreasonable or unnecessary expenses. They pursue maximum benefit through their work, how they work, and by supporting the work of partners, colleagues and grantees.
- Accountability and transparency: In carrying out their philanthropic activities, our members embrace both the letter and the spirit of the law. They welcome public interest, take responsibility for their actions and communicate truthfully.
- Diversity and inclusiveness: Our members seek diversity and inclusiveness in order to reflect the communities they serve and to ensure that a range of perspectives contribute to the common good and the development of their mission in a changing society.
- Governance: Our members' governing bodies understand and embrace their responsibility to oversee the mission, strategic direction, finances and operations of their respective organizations, and do so honestly and with integrity. They establish clear and understandable policies and ensure that they are followed.
- Respect: Members interact respectfully with grantees, colleagues, donors and peers.

Members are required to adhere to these principles and, unlike in the earlier incarnation, the club contains some enforcement mechanisms. Members are subject to disciplinary action if they violate legal or ethical practices. At the decision of the Council president, Council staff will conduct an initial inquiry and submit a report. A review panel comprising six appointees will consider these cases in teams of two. They can choose to take no action, recommend further investigation, or recommend sanctions. Possible sanctions include: private censure; probation; suspension; public censure; and revocation of membership. This statement of ethical principles and the attendant sanctions for violation of these norms represent the single clearest and most meaningful form of self-regulation in the foundation field today, although the standards remain fairly broad.

For foundations that do not have enormous assets or that prefer the company of smaller, family-governed foundations, there is an alternative to the Council on Foundations. The Association of Small Foundations (ASF) was founded in 1995 by a group of small grantmakers who felt that modestly endowed institutions, with few or no staff, faced a set of challenges distinct from those of larger foundations. It became a 501(c)3 in 1996 and established its headquarters in Washington, DC. Today it has three thousand dues-paying members and defines its vision as follows: "ASF enhances the power of small foundation giving by providing the donors, trustees, and staff of member foundations with peer learning opportunities, targeted tools and resources, and a collective voice in and beyond the philanthropic community." ASF emphasizes networking and member education through conferences, smaller events, and publications, and undertakes some legislative updating for members. However, given that many smaller foundations do not feel as enmeshed in that broader policy and regulatory debate related to philanthropy, ASF is less political than the Council on Foundations. And because it does not have robust and enforceable norms it remains more of an association and not an accountability club.

Alongside the two national associations are two more politically oriented groups of grantmakers. The Philanthropy Roundtable has a membership of 550 and has from the start sought to "foster excellence in philanthropy, to protect philanthropic freedom, to assist donors in achieving their philanthropic intent, and to help donors advance liberty, opportunity, and personal responsibility in America and abroad." Like other membership groups, the Roundtable hosts conferences and meetings of donors. But unlike other groups in the field, the Roundtable has distinctive interests that more often than not represent a conservative or at least free market approach to public problemsolving. In the areas of K-12 education reform the focus is on choice and charter schools. In higher education the focus tends toward preserving excellence and fighting political correctness. Since it does not believe in strong norms for the field but rather in an increase in autonomy and freedom for donors, the Roundtable does not act like an accountability club. It is, in effect, an association for donors who do not want to be part of the Council on Foundations and for whom legitimacy and accountability are not central concerns.

The National Network of Grantmakers (NNG) was for years the countervailing political force in the foundation landscape to the Philanthropy Roundtable. NNG is an organization of funders committed to supporting social and economic justice. The Network "values individuals, projects, and organizations working for systematic change in the US and abroad in order to create an equitable distribution of wealth and power, and mutual respect for all peoples." NNG works primarily within organized philanthropy to increase financial and other resources to groups committed to social and economic justice (Odendahl, 1990). The NNG was founded in 1980 and incorporated in 1987. In 2007, the organization encountered financial difficulties and called on members to pay their dues early to keep it on its feet. It has struggled since and its website is now closed. NNG actively sought to influence its members to fund social justice organizations, and to simplify and standardize grant application processes, and it advocated for increasing the payout requirement for foundations to ensure that more funds reached the broader nonprofit sector. While at its peak it had several hundred members, NNG struggled with the challenge of attracting and retaining in its membership foundations committed to its progressive and activist agenda. In its heyday, NNG was a progressive accountability club for a small set of socially committed donors.

Regional associations

Today, the accountability movement of foundations is advanced not just by the major national associations, but also by an array of regional associations of grantmakers or RAGs. The associations draw membership from single states (e.g., New York Regional Association of Grantmakers) or broader multi-state regions (e.g., Conference of Southwest Foundations). Many of these RAGS were founded in the late 1960s through the 1970s, with founding events continuing to the present. Though some RAGs predate TRA 1969, the largest wave of foundings was in the decades following the new foundation regulations of 1969 (Magat, 1990), as shown in Figure 6.1. The organizing work across the country that the

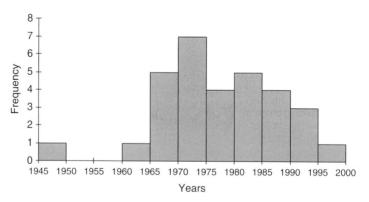

Figure 6.1 Founding dates of regional associations of grantmakers

Council undertook in the years that followed passage of the TRA helped increase the demand for field-building activity and new organizational connections.

The handling of norms and codes of conduct is the single most significant differentiating factor between regional associations that fulfill large professional development functions and those that sponsor accountability clubs. The mix of functions fulfilled by RAGs ranges across all four of the core activities outlined earlier. All RAGs promote professional networking and the sharing of best practices. Some RAGs offer formal training programs for new foundation staff members and trustees, and an ever smaller number do policy work on behalf of other members. A tiny select few engage in norm-setting and enforcement, which elevates them to the status of an accountability club (Figure 6.2).

To illustrate the spectrum of approaches to the questions of norms and codes of conduct in RAGs, it may be useful to consider three different RAGs, including one that follows the most basic and loosest of codes, one that has more expectations associated with its behavioral standards, and one with an ethics code that has real teeth to it and which displays behavior associated with a pure accountability club.

Indiana Grantmakers has a voluntary set of standards that it encourages its member to adopt. Acceptance of these standards is not a requirement for membership nor is failure to follow these standards a basis for termination of membership. Indiana Grantmakers "encourages all grantmakers to adopt their own standards" that include *at least* the following:

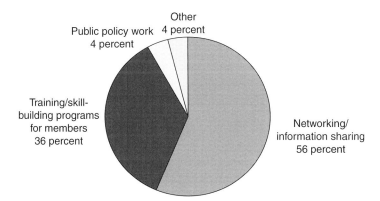

Figure 6.2 Reported activities of regional associations of grantmakers

- fulfill all fiduciary responsibilities and comply with all legal requirements;
- strive for the highest standards of ethical behavior;
- operate with an identifiable, active governing board;
- maintain constructive relationships with applicants, grantees, donors and the public based on mutual respect, candor and confidentiality;
- make basic information about their grantmaking readily available; and
- within the grantmaker's operation guidelines, strive to include the perspectives, opinions and experiences of a broad cross-section of people to inform the foundation through its grantmaking, governance/staff structure and business practices.

Indiana Grantmakers is clearly a membership association first and foremost and it does not constitute a true accountability club. However, in the case of the Arizona Grantmakers Forum (AGF), the issues become less clear-cut. The AGF sums up its approach as follows: "Members of the Arizona Grantmakers Forum (AGF) recognize that we play an important role in our communities, that our role is sustained by the public trust, and that certain obligations follow from that trust. We are committed to basing our work on principles that reflect those obligations." Its statement continues:

As AGF members, we endorse the following principles of grantmaking: to deal respectfully with applicants, grantees, peers and members of the general public; to be accessible and to respond clearly, promptly and as fairly as possible to requests from the community; to make readily available basic information about our programs, funding priorities, and application requirements; to respect the confidentiality of applicants, grantees and peers and to use discretion in communications with others about specific organizations and individuals; to be thoughtful and purposeful in our grantmaking and to periodically review and evaluate our respective missions, priorities, policies and practices; to recognize the cultural diversity of the communities we serve and, within the limits of our individual charters, to seek to reflect this diversity in our work; to adhere to the highest standards of ethical behavior and to maintain an appropriate conflict of interest policy for staff and board members; and to understand and fulfill our fiduciary and legal responsibilities.

Thus, the approach of the AGF is a compromise one. It sets out principles that members accept but does not elaborate fully on what the consequences might be for failing to observe these principles. They are simply those that the membership has collectively defined as important for foundations to embrace as part of their membership in the AGF. There is an intent present to create an accountability club but not all the operational elements are fully in place.

The strongest example of an association-sponsored accountability club is the Council of Michigan Foundations (CMF), which states simply that "because foundations should strive to maintain the public trust in fulfilling their respective charitable purposes, the CMF Board of Trustees adopted seven Guiding Principles as a condition of membership effective April 1, 2004." To make the code more central to the identity and work of the CMF, its members are asked to "endorse, work to achieve and demonstrate" each of the principles in their foundation's operations. These principles are:

1 adhere to the highest standards of ethical behavior in all foundation actions;
2 honor donor(s) intent;
3 have an identifiable active governing board – a decision-making body that sets and regularly reviews policies on: governance, including conflict of interest; grantmaking; finance and administration, including audit; and communications;
4 be accessible by having basic grantmaking information readily available regarding funding priorities and application requirements;
5 build constructive relationships based on mutual respect, candor, confidentiality and understanding with the public, applicants, grantees and donors;
6 strive to include the perspectives, opinions and experiences of the broadest possible cross-section of people to inform the foundation through its grantmaking, through the composition of its board, committees, staff and advisors/consultants and through its business practices; and
7 support continuous learning on the part of trustees, staff and grantees.

To gain a broader perspective on the normative content of RAG behavior, the content of the RAG statement of principles can be analyzed. When these kinds of data are scrutinized (Figure 6.3), it becomes apparent that the most central elements of RAG operational identity are ethical behavior, rule following, and responsive customer service for grant applicants. Only one RAG endorsed boldness and innovation and three stated that equity and justice were core guiding principles. What this analysis reveals is that the central concerns of RAGs are focused on procedural issues in foundation philanthropy, not substantive ones. RAGs help build the accountability of regional foundation fields by bringing these institutions together around common commitments to behavior that will reflect well on the field and build confidence in the broader nonprofit field that philanthropic power is being wielded sensibly.

The RAGs play an important role in the foundation accountability system today. They bring together foundations that have geography in common and help these institutions find ways to do their work more effectively. In some cases, they take on the role of accountability clubs and move their membership toward greater levels of professionalism and transparency, while in other instances they fall short of enforcing standards of conduct and play a more socializing and networking role. In either case, RAGs push the associational infrastructure of foundation philanthropy

Figure 6.3 Reported guiding principles of regional associations of grantmakers

deeper into the field than the Council on Foundations could ever do, by reaching smaller and more locally focused funders.

Affinity groups

The RAGs are not alone, however, in building relationships among foundations at a different level than the national groups. Affinity groups bring foundations together around shared interests. Affinity groups are organized around field of interest (e.g., Grantmakers for Education), a specific skill or challenge in grantmaking (e.g., Technology Affinity Group), or identity group (e.g., Native Americans in Philanthropy). In each case, foundation staff and trustees are drawn to these associations by the promise of meeting other grantmakers working on similar issues. Most affinity groups host annual meetings and smaller seminars where their members have a chance to talk to one another and hear from experts in their chosen field. While they do not promulgate explicit standards for grantmaking, these groups often do define best practices, and by singling out issues and approaches, the affinity groups shape the conceptual frameworks and priorities of their members.

The affinity groups are the most recent additions to the foundation support infrastructure. The decades of the 1980s and 1990s witnessed the

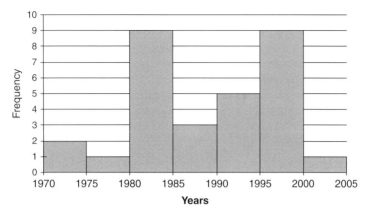

Figure 6.4 Founding dates of foundation affinity groups

heaviest number of affinity group foundings (Figure 6.4). This process of growth was accelerated and supported by the Council on Foundations as a way to ensure that members with well-defined funding interests were being engaged and assisted. While some of the affinity groups take stands on social justice issues, none is set up to drive accountability among members or to replace other regulatory bodies. In this sense, affinity groups are associations first and foremost and really not accountability clubs at all.

The number of affinity groups working on one issue or another is substantial. A partial list includes: Grantmakers for Children, Youth and Families, Grantmakers for Education, Grantmakers for Health, Grantmakers Concerned with Immigrants and Refugees, Environmental Grantmakers, Funders Concerned about AIDS, Grantmakers in Aging, International Funders for Indigenous People, and Africa Grantmakers. Each of these groups aims to inform and improve the practice of philanthropy within a defined substantive boundary. In some cases, the issues and approaches to public problemsolving can be filled with politics and contention. In other cases there may be a fair degree of consensus among members. Grantmakers for Children, Youth and Families has as its goal "to increase the ability of organized philanthropy to improve the well-being of children, youth and families." It works with foundation staff and trustees who are committed to working on early childhood education, youth development, and family support issues. Beyond field building, the group, which has more than five hundred members – making it one of the largest affinity groups – serves a broader purpose: it is "a forum to review and analyze grantmaking strategies, exchange information about effective programs, examine public policy developments and maintain ongoing discussions with national leaders." This goal of deepening connection within the foundation field and between the foundations and the outside policy and practice environment is what many of the smaller emerging affinity groups seek to accomplish.

In the skills-building category of affinity groups, one example is the Communications Network. It defines its mission as: "To improve the effectiveness and accountability of foundations by promoting and strengthening the strategic practice of communications philanthropy." Members of this group meet to share best practices and learn about what practice leaders outside the foundation world are thinking and doing in the area of strategic communications. The Technology Affinity Group has both a skills and a substantive focus. It both "seeks to advance the capacities of philanthropic organizations through the use of technology" and conducts educational programs with the goal of providing information to grantmakers working with technology issues.

Finally, in the identity group category of affinity groups, race is a common unifier for funders who are or work with minority groups. Asian Americans/Pacific Islanders in Philanthropy, Native Americans in Philanthropy, and the Association of Black Foundation Executives all give members an opportunity to learn and network together around issues of identity and philanthropy.

To give a single snapshot of what goes on in affinity groups, data were collected from thirty affinity groups related to their services and activities (Figure 6.5). Across all three different kinds of affinity groups, one thing is consistent: the main emphasis is on social and professional networking and idea sharing. The affinity groups give their members a chance to delve deeper into their main philanthropic interests and to learn from peers and experts in the field about the latest and most significant developments in their chosen area of interest. While some affinity groups do offer training, and while there is advocacy work undertaken by affinity groups, the main focus remains on networking and information sharing.

Foundation accountability clubs and associations: then and now

Looking back over the past half-century of foundation field infrastructure building, it becomes clear that there have been at least three major periods or phases. The earliest phase of self-regulation occurred in the 1970s in the aftermath of the Tax Reform Act of 1969 (TRA 1969), which imposed the first real set of government regulations on foundations. Acting on a few highly publicized cases of financial and grantmaking abuses, Congress set

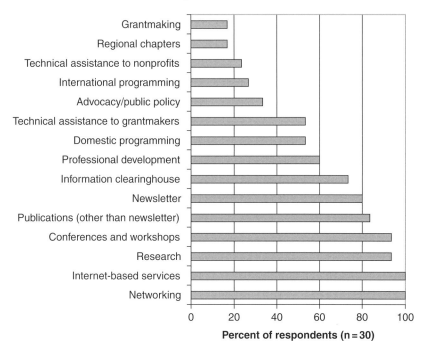

Figure 6.5 Services offered by foundation affinity groups

in place limits on the ownership of stock in one company, prohibitions on self-interested transactions by board members, a mandated minimum grant payout rate, and new reporting requirements. Reacting to this stunning incursion into the field, the Council on Foundations led a national effort to improve public understanding of the work of foundations, to encourage professional management of these institutions, to expand evaluation practices, to ameliorate relations with recipient organizations, and to redefine private foundations as "public trusts" to be governed for public purposes. This was also the time when RAGs began to take hold around the country and drive foundation accountability down to the regional level.

Later, in a second phase focused on norm building in the 1980s, the Council promulgated a more far-reaching code of conduct, what it termed "principles and practices for effective grantmaking," and made acceptance of them a condition of membership in the association. During this period, the foundation field attempted to wrest the initiative for overseeing the foundation field from Congress and place it squarely in the hands of the foundations themselves. By mandating acceptance of the principles and practices – including procedural transparency in grantmaking, diversity in staffing, and standards for stewardship – as a condition for membership, the Council on Foundations attempted to preempt government responsibility for foundation oversight. During this phase, the affinity groups began to proliferate and deepen the range of connections within the field, though they did little on accountability issues or to move the field toward greater self-regulation.

A third phase of foundation self-regulation occurred very recently. After years of little new government regulation of foundations, there has been renewed interest in Congress in looking at the foundation field and revisiting regulatory issues. Again, a small number of publicized abuses reported in newspapers around the country led to Congressional interest in foundation governance. For a field that had thought the case for self-regulation and self-patrolling had been made and won, this was a surprising turn of events. In 2002, the Sarbanes–Oxley Act was passed in response to a number of major corporate and accounting scandals, such as those affecting companies like Enron and WorldCom. These scandals resulted in a decline of public trust in accounting and reporting practices in the private sector. The legislation is wide-ranging and establishes new or enhanced standards for all US public company boards, management, and public accounting firms. The Act establishes a new quasi-public agency, the Public Company Accounting Oversight Board, or PCAOB, which is charged with overseeing, regulating, inspecting, and disciplining accounting firms in their roles as auditors of public companies. While Sarbanes–Oxley did not apply to nonprofits, some nonprofit agencies and large foundations began asking whether they should adopt similar rules voluntarily to bolster public confidence in their financial integrity. Eventually Senator Grassley began investigating and holding hearings about nonprofit and foundation accountability issues. Draft legislation was advanced bearing on reporting and governance issues. Throughout this entire process, the Council on Foundations, along with Independent Sector, the trade association for the broader nonprofit sector to which many foundations also belong, crafted responses to proposed reforms and even outlined their own policy recommendations for Congressional consideration. In contrast to the confused and chaotic response of the field to TRA 1969, the Council has shown in recent years just how organized and prepared it is to make the case against greater regulation of the field.

While there can be little doubt that the foundation field is well defended today, there remains a lingering question about whether the accountability clubs in the foundation field actually work to ensure ethical conduct and sound philanthropic practices. There is little doubt that grantmakers have wrapped themselves in the cloth of transparency and accountability and that they have used both national and regional associations to project an image of responsible self-regulation and self-policing. There remains, however, some question about how meaningful and enforceable these voluntary systems and measures really are (Frumkin, 2008).

The largest stumbling block to the development of strong and viable accountability clubs in the foundation field comes from the lack of a real incentive to change behavior in light of any outside standard or pressure. While foundations were shocked by the regulation that hit the field in 1969, the number of professionals in the field today who lived through that period is small. Many of the leaders of the largest foundations come to their work without the specter of another TRA 1969 hanging over their heads. In the context of a field that is awash in hundreds of billions of dollars and has no real way of failing, foundations can and do coast along comfortably, working at their own pace on issues of their own choosing. Like the infrastructure accountability clubs studied by Young (chapter 5) and the nonprofit state associations examined by Tschirhart (chapter 4) both in this volume, foundation accountability clubs are currently embedded in membership associations that need to represent and be responsive to a broad spectrum of organizations. This helps to explain the reluctance of foundations to develop stronger accountability clubs. But it is the resource independence of foundations and the lack of strong demands from principals, apart from government, that is the strongest explanation for the weakness of the accountability clubs that currently exist. The foundation field also exhibits some parallels with the humanitarian agencies discussed by Zarnegar Deloffre (chapter 8). She finds that the principle of independence embedded in the humanitarian imperative is strong enough to create real resistance among agencies to pressure from principals for strong accountability clubs. As with foundations, the clubs and standards that emerged were the product of an intense intra-sector debate about the nature and obligations of the field.

In the end, there are no real performance standards or social impact metrics to which foundations are held accountable, no independent groups in a position to make real demands on the field's money, and few critics looking over the shoulder of the field and asking tough questions. In short, there is very little pressure at all on foundations. Thus, as foundations continue making a limited number of grants while rejecting the entreaties of masses of nonprofit organizations pleading for funding, it is far from clear that the presence of codes on conduct and even peer pressure from fellow travelers in accountability clubs represent a meaningful control mechanism for the field. Exclusion from an association will hardly change anything for a resource-independent organization that needs nothing from the environment around it. Still, the foundation field has built an elaborate web of infrastructure organizations, including

both accountability clubs and associations, designed to support and protect foundation philanthropy. From the perspective of the foundation
field, this work must be judged successful, given that no new significant
regulations of foundations have been passed since 1969 and many of the
regulations that were put in place forty years ago, including the payout
requirement, have been relaxed over the years. Whether the rise of
accountability clubs and associations has benefited the nonprofit sector
and the broader public interest is a deeper and more complex question.

REFERENCES

Abbott, Andrew. 1988. *The System of Professions: An Essay on the Division of Expert Labor*. University of Chicago Press.

Andrews, F. Emerson. 1973. *Foundation Watcher*. Lancaster, PA.: Franklin and Marshall College.

Colvard, Richard. 1961. Foundations and Professions: The Organizational Defense of Autonomy. *Administrative Science Quarterly* 6: 167–184.

Committee on the Foundation Field. 1970. Report of the Committee on the Foundation Field. Unpublished manuscript on file at the Foundation Center.

Council on Foundations. 1973. *Some General Principles and Guidelines for Grantmaking Foundations*. Washington, DC: Council on Foundations.

1977. Private Foundations and the 1969 Tax Reform Act. In *Research Papers, Sponsored by the Commission on Private Philanthropy and Public Needs, Vol. III.* Washington, DC: Department of Treasury.

1980. Recommended Principles and Practices for Effective Grantmaking. *Foundation News* 21(5): 8–10.

1990. *Principles and Practices of Effective Grantmaking*. Washington, DC: Council on Foundations.

DiMaggio, Paul and Walter W. Powell. 1983. The Iron Cage Revisited: Institutional Isomorphism and Collective Rationality in Organizational Fields. *American Sociological Review* 48: 147–160.

Edie, John. 1987. *Congress and Private Foundations: An Historical Analysis.* Washington, DC: Council on Foundations.

Emerson, Richard. 1962. Power-Dependence Relations. *American Sociological Review* 27(1): 31–41.

Frumkin, Peter. 1999. Private Foundations as Public Institutions. In Ellen Condliffe Lagemann, ed. *Studying Philanthropic Foundations: New Scholarship, New Possibilities*. Bloomington, IN: Indiana University Press, pp. 69–98.

2006a. Accountability and Legitimacy in American Foundation Philanthropy. In Kenneth Prewitt, Mattei Dogan, Steven Heydemann, and Stefan Toepler, eds. *The Legitimacy of Philanthropic Foundations*. New York: Russell Sage Foundation, pp. 99–122.

2006b. *Strategic Giving: The Art and Science of Philanthropy*. University of Chicago Press.

2008. Wielding Philanthropic Power Responsively. In Amy A. Kass, ed. *Giving Well, Doing Good*. Bloomington, IN: Indiana University Press.

Joseph, James A. 1983. Why the Concern with Principles? *Foundation News* 24(6): 64.

Labovitz, John R. 1973. 1969 Tax Reform Reconsidered. In Fritz Heinman, ed. *The Future of Foundations*. Englewood Cliffs, NJ: Prentice Hall, pp. 101–131.

Lankford, John. 1964. *Congress and the Foundations in the Twentieth Century*. River Falls, WI: Wisconsin State University.

Magat, Richard. 1990. Born in Outrage and Pride: NYRAG Rose to Conquer. *NYRAG Times*, Winter.

Nielsen, Waldemar. 1985. *The Golden Donors: A New Anatomy of the Great Foundations*. New York: E. P. Dutton.

Odendahl, Teresa. 1990. *Charity Begins at Home*. New York: Basic Books.

Olasky, Marvin. 1993. *Philanthropically Correct: The Story of the Council on Foundations*. Washington, DC: Capital Research Center.

Pattillo, Manning M. 1968. *How Can Foundations Be Improved?* Foundation Center Annual Report. New York: Foundation Center.

Pfeffer, Jeffrey and Gerald Salancik. 1978. *The External Control of Organizations: A Resource Dependence Perspective*. New York: Harper and Row.

Pifer, Alan. 1984. *Philanthropy in an Age of Transition: The Essays of Alan Pifer*. New York: The Foundation Center.

Shakely, Jack. 1980. Tom Troyer Appraises the Tax Reform Act of 1969. *Foundation News* 21(3): 19–24.

Simon, John G. 1974. Are Private Foundations an Endangered Species? *Foundation News* 15(1): 11–18.

US Congress Senate Finance Committee. 1969a. Improper Payments by Private Foundations to Government Officials, Hearings before the Committee on Finance, 91st Congress. Washington, DC: US Government Printing Office.

1969b. Tax Reform Act of 1969, Hearings before the Committee on Finance, 91st Congress. Washington, DC: US Government Printing Office.

Wallace, Martha R. 1971. The Foundation Meets the Fund Raiser. *Foundation News* 12(1): 1–5.

Wilensky, Harold L. 1964. The Professionalization of Everyone. *American Journal of Sociology* 70: 137–158.

7 Do self-regulation clubs work? Some evidence from Europe and some caveats from economic theory

Andreas Ortmann and Katarina Svítková

> We also wanted to make sure there was transparency in the donation system. People must know where their money goes and what it's really spent for.
>
> (Pavlína Kalousová, executive director of the Czech Donors Forum)

Quality assurance for goods and services relies often on direct reputations, or indirect reputations provided by ratings systems, certification systems, or self-regulatory programs. (It might also rely on warranties or other more tangible mechanisms.) Ratings systems are involuntary systems established by watchdogs that rate the sellers in a particular market according to some set of criteria or standards. The sellers typically do not take part in the definition of the set of standards, or in the evaluation of their performance in meeting these standards, and thus ratings programs are not voluntary programs. In contrast, various certification systems (e.g., ISO 9000, ISO 14001, Fair Trade coffee, organic certification, or certification systems for charitable organizations) and various self-regulatory programs rely on voluntary participation, at least on the part of those that are certified or take part in such programs. Thus the incentives facing both the designers and the participants in these systems will differ. Complementing our previous work on certification systems (e.g., Ortmann and Svítková, 2007), here we ponder the relative advantages of the competing forms that voluntary participation can take, particularly among nonprofit organizations. Befitting the title of the book to which our chapter contributes, we look at a particular case of a nonprofit accountability club of sorts. Accountability clubs can be thought of as a kind of quality assurance program for nonprofits, in which the buyers are the various nonprofit principals who are "purchasing" or contracting for nonprofit services. Just as buyers face information challenges in ascertaining the quality of products, nonprofit principals face challenges in obtaining good information on the quality of nonprofit services.

Our study is motivated by the curious fact that in many European countries, one finds certification of charities by a third party, a form of accountability club that does not rely on self-regulation. The evidence of such entities – the existence of a stable and growing set of currently about a dozen such certification agencies in as many countries (e.g., Guet, 2002; Ortmann and Svítková, 2007), their documented beneficial effects (e.g., Bekkers, 2003, 2006, and chapter 11 in this volume; see also Chhaochharia and Ghosh, 2008), and the absence of self-regulatory entities in those same countries (Wilke, 2005) – suggests a quick answer to the title of this chapter. Interestingly though, the evidence against self-regulation clubs is restricted to the older European Union member states.

In the member states that only recently acceded to the European Union – often called transition countries – one does find variants of accountability clubs that rely on self-regulation, and indeed seem to be successful. The Czech Donors Forum is the poster child, and facilitator, of that development and therefore our point of departure for a discussion of a phenomenon that important theoretical work (e.g., De Marzo *et al.*, 2005; Nunez, 2001 and 2007) suggests will be a transitional one.

At the same time, one does not find in transition countries certification of charities by a third party. This curious constellation – certification prevailing in the older European Union member states, and self-regulation clubs prevailing in the newer European member states – seems worth investigating. We are specifically interested in better understanding whether the Czech Donors Forum and related self-regulation clubs do indeed deserve their label, why they have managed to emerge in this part of the world, and whether their existence suggests that the relevant theoretical work is in need of revision. A better understanding of self-regulation clubs, and the circumstances under which they seem to thrive, will also shed light on the claim that voluntary certification and self-regulation are essentially the same thing, with the difference simply being that of sponsorship.

Below, after having reviewed the environment in which it operates, we discuss the case of the Czech Donors Forum and, then, the commonalities of, and differences between, certification agencies and self-regulatory entities, as well as theoretical and empirical work on self-regulatory entities and the (non)feasibility, and (un)desirability of self-regulatory entities, as arguably exemplified by the Czech Donors Forum and similar self-regulatory entities in transition economies.

Accountability clubs in a transition economy

To make the reader appreciate the difficulties of quality assurance in transition economies, a brief sketch of the realities of institutional enforcement in the market for nonprofit and nongovernmental organizations in the Czech Republic is in order. Pospisil (2006) is a relevant reference. After having mapped the nonprofit sector in the Czech Republic (www.e-cvns.cz/en/), Pospisil and his co-workers at the Center for Nonprofit Sector Research concluded that, in spite of its impressive growth, the

Czech civil society sector remains a terra incognita in 2005. There were fewer than one thousand "mass social organizations" left at the end of the communist era, today we have perhaps 80,000 or 110,000 civil society organizations, depending on the definition used. And yet there are no reliable empirical data about them, there has been no systematic research, and debates about civil society, be they academic or public policy, lack both substance and quality as a result.

When Pospisil and his colleagues sent out questionnaires to all 1,225 foundations and endowment funds[1] that were registered in 2002, they found that the contact data for 60 percent of them were not valid. Pospisil and his colleagues ended up, after significant prodding, with a return rate of 10 percent. Using a complementary strategy of checking with the regional courts (with which foundations and funds by law have to register their annual reports), they found that only about a third did so. Even though the foundation law is quite explicit about the compulsory content of the annual report, only about 15 percent of those reports contained what they were required to contain. Almost 40 percent contained no hard facts whatsoever and were at best public relations material. What little hard data Pospisil and his colleagues could compile suggested that "most Czech foundations and funds do not have endowments or other assets large enough to generate substantial annual incomes. They depend on annual fundraising, like other types of nonprofit organizations, which they also resemble in their mission statements, goals and activities." In other words, although the foundation law requires it, "Czech foundations and funds are typically not grant-makers." In fact, about two-thirds of these foundation-like organizations are not independent institutions but were "established by, and/or affiliated to, other institutions. Their main function is to fulfil the role of fundraising and supporting agencies to their 'parent' institutions …

---

[1] Endowment funds are legal entities similar to foundations, the main difference being that endowment funds may use all their property for the charitable purposes while foundations must maintain at minimum 500,000 Czech koruns in their endowment. As of the writing of the final version of this chapter (December 2008), that amounts to about $25,000.

A small number of foundations (20–30) have gradually built endowments of their own that have enabled them to become independent."

As Pospisil makes clear quite bluntly, the publicly available data on nonprofits are a mess and this state of affairs is no coincidence:

Very few NPOs file the required information with the registers or keep the information updated. The registers do not penalize the offenders. There is a general low level of respect for law in the society, and NPOs are obviously no exception to the rule. Equally poor is the law enforcement … Most NPOs are bad at monitoring and evaluating their work and at strategic planning: that is why they do not value research and why they are not willing to complete questionnaires … The fact that many NPOs are weak at monitoring and evaluating their work and at strategic planning and the fact that most do not publish annual reports mean that they do not have the required information available. To provide it would represent a lot of hard work in old untidy files, finding and putting together the data would almost amount to a new "project" for the organization … Respondents in public administration are typically poorly qualified to fill in questionnaires about NPOs … the nonprofit sector is of only very marginal importance to legislation, public administration, public policy, and the general public. This has the result that the sector is neglected and badly treated in the judiciary, in the executive, in public registers, in national statistics, in politics and in public debate … Respondents in both public administration and in the NPOs themselves remain inexperienced in, or unaccustomed to, keeping structured records and providing accounts. If systematic research of the nonprofit sector is to succeed in the Czech Republic, it has to be expanded to include the development of sources of data, the improvement of legislative and administrative tools and mechanisms, and the education and training of administrators and respondents.

Of course, the situation in the Czech Republic, as in many transition economies, is unusually dire, at least in comparison to western European countries. As Pospisil points out, "the rich tradition of associational life, philanthropy and citizen initiatives before the Second World War was brutally annihilated by the two successive totalitarian regimes of Nazism and Communism." In addition, the (almost) two decades since the 1989 revolution were a hectic growth phase that was often driven by lack of enforcement and poorly structured incentives that led to curious phenomena such as the temporary ballooning of the number of foundations to more than five thousand since there was hope that state money that was to come from privatization would freely be spread (Brhlikova, 2004).[2] However, now that the Czech Republic has acceded to the

---

[2] Brhlikova (2004) recalls the rapid increase in the number of foundations in the Czech Republic throughout the 1990s. Before 1989 there was only one foundation (which was not active). By 1998, five thousand foundations were registered. In 1998 a new Act – since revised – on foundations and foundation funds succeeded in reducing that number to fifty-five in less than a year. Fric and Goulli (2001) have argued that profit-motivated

European Union one would, and should, expect that terms like accountability and transparency are being taken seriously. Enough is at stake: about 1 billion Czech koruns (at the time of the writing of this article, about $50 million) in tax-effective donations (individuals can deduct donations up to 10 percent from the tax base, firms up to 5 percent of theirs). And that is not counting donations that are not deductible, or have not been deducted, or were in kind.

The Czech Donors Forum

The Czech Donors Forum (CDF) is a self-regulatory association of almost sixty foundations and endowment funds and nineteen company donors.[3] It is divided into four membership divisions (foundations, endowment funds, company donors, and patrons). Formally, the CDF is a civic association (which has implications for state-mandated reporting requirements, those for civic associations being at a minimum) with the four "divisions" informally also organized as associations. (Of these only three are currently active since the patrons' division has not found any takers so far.)

CDF came into existence in 1995 as a voluntary platform for the cooperation of foundations and donors; historically it was meant to be an umbrella organization for philanthropic activities in the Czech Republic. It became a civic association in 1997. Its most important division, the Association of Foundations, was established by eleven foundations in 1999, and at the end of 2007 numbered thirty-eight foundations (which was slightly up from two years earlier). The Association of Endowment Funds was established in 2003, and at the end of 2007 totaled nineteen members (also slightly up from two years earlier), while the Association of Corporate Donors was reported to have seventeen members at the end of 2007 (slightly down from two years earlier).

The formal membership conditions for both foundations and endowment funds are very similar: the organization has to be registered in

entrepreneurs opted for the foundation form in order to receive money from the Foundation Investment Fund (FIF) which was created in 1991 by the government to support activities of the nonprofit sector through 1 percent of the returns from the privatization of state property. These funds were paid out in 1999 (CzK 500 million to thirty-eight foundations) and 2002 (CzK 850 million plus a similar amount from the proceeds of the sale of remaining FIF stocks (electricity and gas companies, Czech Airlines) to sixty-four foundations, with some of them being able to go for a second helping). Altogether seventy-three foundations received a contribution (about 20 percent of all registered foundations). Foundations had to use FIF contributions to create an endowment and spend the annual income (20 percent for administration and 80 percent for grants); they also had to make grants through an open, public grantmaking process. So much for the theory.

[3] According to www.donorsforum.cz, accessed December 15, 2008.

compliance with the foundations and endowment funds law no. 227/1997 and adhere to all its terms, grant support on a regular basis, and abide by principles of ethical conduct that the CDF Associations of Foundations and Endowment Funds have issued (www.donorsforum. cz/clenstvi-nadace for foundations, www.donorsforum.cz/clenstvi-nf for endowment funds; see also www.donorsforum.cz/principy-zakladajici-listina for company donors).[4] In this respect, the CDF is a self-regulatory club in each of its divisions, as well as in toto in that membership is voluntary.

According to the annual report for 2007, at the end of that year the CDF employed thirteen people, impressive growth for an organization that was incorporated only about a decade before (1997) and that, for the most part, is financed from grants and donations. For comparison purposes, it is noteworthy that certification agencies in Europe – often serving much larger populations and charitable sectors – make do with fewer personnel (see Ortmann and Svítková, 2007).

It is also important to note that the CDF operates in an environment characterized frequently by noncongruence of formal and informal decision power. So here, too: formally, the Annual Assembly of all members of the three active divisions is the managing body of the Czech Donors Forum. The representatives of the member organizations select the CDF Executive Board for a period of three years. In turn, the Executive Board formally appoints the executive director. It is, however, unlikely that the informal structure of the CDF is as bottom-up as the official description implies; rather the anecdotal evidence suggests that the CDF is run top-down by a powerful executive director.

The CDF is not only a self-regulatory and self-help entity as suggested by the formal structure and our focus in this chapter. As mentioned, the CDF was initially established by several important foundations as an umbrella organization meant to promote philanthropy and giving: "a development agency for philanthropy" (Kalousová, 2007). In support of this goal, the CDF has undertaken various activities: it introduced public rankings of top donors and persuaded newspapers to report on these rankings (even giving awards to journalists who wrote about these activities) and has worked hard to persuade corporations that supporting charitable activities as part of a company's general business strategy makes good business sense. It organizes training and seminars for nonprofits to increase their visibility and professionalism, and established an

---

[4] The ethics guidelines are available in Czech only; they differ somewhat for endowment funds, foundations, and donor companies, but stipulate, by and large, what one would expect: minimization of administrative costs, regular contributions to the public good, accountability (including publication of annual reports), transparency, etc.

information center for foundations and foundation funds. The CDF also came up with the innovative idea of allowing people to make donations through sms messages (the "Donors Message Service") – an idea that seems fairly unique and was so successful that the CDF could pressure the government into exempting these messages, starting in 2006, from excise taxes.[5] Moreover, the CDF functions also as a lobbying group for its members, and works hard to influence the fiscal policies of the government in ways favorable to its members, for example it lobbies hard for a 1 percent tax designation – making it possible for individuals to directly designate 1 percent of taxes to nonprofit organizations; it lobbies hard to allow firms to spread their tax-effective donations over a three-year window; and it also had its hand in the distribution of government support for nonprofits (so-called FIF funds, about which more below).[6]

Increasingly, the CDF has tried to strengthen its position as mediator of donations and umbrella organization/representative of the Czech non-profit sector, trying to identify "partnerships [that] can be formed between NGOs, companies and the government" and to conceptualize "a strategy for the development of the nonprofit sector": "We are the ones who create giving trends" (Kalousová, 2008). Generously funded by foundations such as the Mott Foundation, the CDF has started to export its business model to other central and eastern European (CEE) countries[7] and it is engaged in multiple development efforts on the European level (participation of its executive director in the Worldwide Initiative for Grantmaker Support (WINGS) and the European Foundation Centre (EFC) both headquartered in Brussels).

---

[5]   According to Kalousová (2008), the Donors Message Service, or DMS, is a project of the Czech Donors Forum and all telecommunication operators (Telefónica-O2, T-Mobile, and Vodafone). Since the DMS was launched in April 2004, more than 120 foundations and nonprofit groups have participated. Altogether, through 2007 more than 5.6 million messages were sent in a country of about 10 million inhabitants only. Donors gave more than $7 million for areas such as helping physically disabled people, homeless people, and refugees, and giving money for environmental protection, monuments, and disaster relief.

[6]   There is little doubt that many of these activities have been useful (for example, in enticing new donors through the innovative sms project – www.darcovskasms.cz – and securing funds on various levels through European and other international networking) and had their benefits. Even the use of more professional marketing and communications methods seems not a bad thing per se.

[7]   In 2005, the CDF prepared a project called CEENERGI – Central and Eastern European Network for Responsible Giving. CEENERGI is currently developing company donations in eight countries of central and eastern Europe: besides the Czech Republic, these are Bulgaria, Hungary, Poland, Romania, Russia, Slovakia, and Ukraine. The CDF is a regional center for CEENERGI and the mother of all donor centers in those countries: see www.mott.org/publications/Mott%20Mosaic/April%202007%20v6n1/cs%20April%202007.aspx.

A recent activity of the CDF is the partnership with the London Benchmarking Group (LBG),[8] which is meant to promote the LBG methodology in the Czech and Slovak republics. The LBG methodology aims to measure the size and impact of philanthropic contributions by companies to society. The project is particularly relevant for this chapter because the LBG methodology claims to be one of the best measures of philanthropic activities for corporations (it is difficult to assess using the publicly available information to what extent this is true) and as such presents a tool for self-regulatory agencies to assess their members. The CDF, at this point, does not require its members to employ the LBG methodology but it strongly recommends it. It will be interesting to follow future developments – requiring members to employ the methodology would mean strengthening the requirements for membership (regardless of the requirements of the methodology it will be more stringent than the current one), thus increasing the quality of the signal but possibly decreasing membership in the club. Nevertheless, employing the LBG methodology remains far from the ideal requirement for an accountability club: according to the available information, the measure is designed to help with the marketing of charitable activities both internally and externally. This may help to promote philanthropy, but will not foster accountability of the participating organizations (it may even go in the opposite direction) as long as there is no third party evaluating the reported information. The CDF does not seem to be interested in doing this job.

In sum, the self-regulatory function of the CDF seems to be of only secondary importance, a supplement that was meant to formalize the membership of foundations in the association. The arrangement allowed the CDF to collect annual membership dues and it allowed members to enjoy the CDF's good reputation, a particularly valuable "commodity" for at least two reasons: first, the Czech nonprofit sector experienced a turbulent period during the 1990s, when the reputation of foundations in particular was harmed by several scandals, which resulted in a change in the regulation in 1998 (see Brhlikova, 2004, and recall Pospisil, 2006). Second, foundations and endowment funds in the Czech Republic have relied more heavily on donors than have their western counterparts. Foundations in the CR were younger and without any significant endowments; as such, they had (and often still have) to function as fundraising organizations, raising donations from various sources. In order to maintain the good reputation of the CDF and its new division(s), it was important to argue that the condition for membership in the association

---

[8] See www.standard-lbg.org; see also www.lbg-online.net/index.php/lbg/top_menu/about_the_lbg/introductory_booklet.

was quality and ethical behavior. What is interesting in this case is the extent to which this argument appears to have succeeded, at least for the moment, in spite of the CDF undertaking very little in the way of monitoring its membership.

Notwithstanding the various education and training courses that the CDF offers its members and that are meant to enhance their viability, and notwithstanding the required commitment to adhere to ethics guidelines provided by the CDF, there is no clear-cut enforcement and/or monitoring mechanism that would guarantee that the member organizations are actually behaving according to CDF's standards of ethical behavior, and that the raised funds are spent in ways that could be considered efficient and wise. In other words, while all activities are meant to create favorable conditions for giving, none seems geared toward a consistent pattern of accountability and transparency. Interestingly, even the CDF fails to meet the basic requirements of accountability and transparency such as making publicly available its annual report. While we were working on an earlier version of this chapter (in the spring and fall of 2008), the latest annual report available on the CDF site was from 2005. As we write the final version of this chapter in March 2010, the annual reports for 2007 and 2008 have been made available (but not the one for 2006).

Notwithstanding the evidence of the difficult circumstances in which it operates, in light of its stated goal of accountability and transparency it seems surprising that throughout 2007 and much of 2008 the CDF had online as the most recent annual report only the 2005 one. It is also noteworthy that the 2005 report is not exactly a template for transparent accounting of where funds came from (e.g., no breakdown of sources is given) and how they were spent (e.g., no salaries for the top administrators, etc.), and that there is no guarantee that the funds raised through the CDF were spent in ways that could be considered efficient and wise. The 2007 report shows some improvement – it lists the most important donors and their donations; however, the other reservations remain. In sum, while it does fulfill some useful functions, and has done some innovative work, the CDF is hardly a poster child for accountability and transparency. It resembles more a self-serving organization whose major purpose is to channel and control donor activities to the maximum extent. It seems questionable whether such an organization is the one most suited to develop a grand design for the Czech nonprofit sector.

As an aside, and in the interest of full disclosure, we note that, in collaboration with the Czech branch of Transparency International, we attempted a couple of years ago to develop a tool that would help increase the trustworthiness, and effectiveness, of the entire Czech NGO sector. The project was undertaken in light of the perceived lack of transparency of the actors populating the field at that point, including the CDF and its members. Taking inspiration from certification models already existing in other European countries (presented at the workshop by representatives of certification agencies in the Netherlands, Germany, Austria, and Switzerland), we introduced the basic idea through a two-day workshop on certification systems for nonprofit organizations in May 2005 (www. transparency.cz/index.php?lan=ukandid=2700). While we expected implementation of such a system in the Czech Republic to be an uphill battle, we were surprised by the intensity of the opposition coming from the representatives of the NGO sector (including the executive director of the CDF). Some of the objections – that certification might be used by the state to further regulate activities of nonprofit organizations – could not be dismissed out of hand given the particular situation and history of the Czech nonprofit sector. However, since such intervention is not a problem in the Netherlands, Germany, Austria, and Switzerland, or for that matter any of the other countries where certification systems are currently being used, it seems an unpersuasive argument. Throughout the workshop, and also from conversations afterwards with various participants, it seemed that some CDF representatives were feeling quite comfortable with the current lack of accountability and transparency. If you believe in the self-interest postulate of economic theory, then this state of affairs encourages inferences that are not pleasant. In the next section we show that the literature on the economics of self-regulation suggests that the potential for self-regulatory clubs to make strong contributions to non-profit accountability or to solving the trust problem in philanthropy is limited.

The economics of self-regulation and some anecdotal evidence about the (non)feasibility, and (non)desirability of self-regulatory clubs

The agency perspective on accountability used in this volume argues that incomplete information between principals, such as donors, and non-profits as their agents creates opportunities for low-quality organizations to enter the market and ultimately to damage the reputation of high-quality organizations. If this is the case, principals may be unwilling to trust that nonprofits will use funds in accordance with their wishes. One possible way to establish the trustworthiness of commercial and donative nonprofits under these circumstances is through establishing a direct reputation. However, reputation is a solution to the notorious credibility problem that charitable organizations face only under conditions of extra-ordinarily good information flows, the production of goods with experience (rather than credence) characteristics, a relatively small number of producers, and fairly homogeneous producers and products (Klein and Leffler, 1981; Kreps, 1990; Ortmann, 2001; Ortmann and Svítková, 2007 and references therein). Regulation is another solution, but because of information asymmetries it is typically not applicable in situations where information flows are wanting, goods have credence good (rather than experience good) characteristics, producers are many, and producers and their products are heterogeneous to boot (Ortmann and Svítková, 2007 and references therein).

In these situations self-regulation and certification emerge as the main contenders for an institutional solution. (As mentioned before, they can be thought of as indirect reputation mechanisms.) Ortmann and Myslivecek (2010) identify important commonalities of these two institutions: they feature third parties of sorts that address a severe information asymmetry through a signal of quality. So, one way to think about these certification and self-regulation institutions is to take them to be essentially the same thing, with the difference simply being their sponsorship. There are important differences though: certification agencies are, conceptually at least, exogenous and independent entities, while self-regulatory organizations are endogenous and dependent entities. Theoretical work suggests strongly that these differences affect the internal organization and dynamics.

The relevant economics literature on self-regulation is small but important. The earliest work of interest here is Shaked and Sutton (1981), whose major message is that a self-regulatory profession has an incentive to increase its income by reducing size/restricting entry. Shaked and Sutton do assume that quality of production of each producer is fixed. In this manner, they eliminate the hidden action problem that is at the heart of the gift-exchange interaction, or principal–agent relation.

Nunez (2001) analyzes the incentives of self-regulatory organizations to monitor their members and reveal (imperfectly) observed fraud. Nunez (2001) is essentially a special case of Nunez (2007) which adds to the dynamic game of incomplete information the possibility of self-regulatory organizations being bribed by members who have been identified as cheaters. Clearly, in contrast to Shaked and Sutton (1981), Nunez allows for the quality of production of each producer not being fixed. He moves the hidden action problem squarely back on to centerstage, where in our view it rightly belongs.

For his corruption-free benchmark, Nunez shows that there is always an equilibrium in which self-regulatory organizations do not invest in monitoring and do not reveal fraud. Essentially this is the case when there are no reputation gains to be had from exposing fraud. While Nunez identifies other equilibria, he concludes that there are scant incentives to monitor quality and expose fraud for self-regulated industries. While there are situations where vigilance, fraud deterrence, and fraud exposure might occur, it is not clear how likely these situations are. The same problem exists when he adds the possibility of corruptibility of self-regulatory organizations. Nunez concludes that "a significant amount of fraud may in practice go undetected or may be concealed in self-regulated activities" (Nunez, 2007: 229). To determine how likely these situations are would require some calibration of the model – one of the big challenges for microeconomists. An additional complication might be that Nunez assumes throughout that self-interest and profit-maximization would drive behavior of the self-regulatory organization. Other assumptions (e.g., altruistic behavior and other objective functions) might weaken these results (e.g., Svítková and Ortmann, 2006), although we believe it would be a mistake to build the analysis of nonprofits on such assumptions (e.g., Ortmann, 1996; Ortmann and Schlesinger, 2003).

DeMarzo *et al.* (2005) study the extent to which government oversight influences, theoretically, the effectiveness of self-regulation. They find, quite intuitively, that "government oversight of self-regulation can benefit customers by leading the SRO to engage in more aggressive enforcement. The SRO would choose an enforcement policy that is just aggressive enough to pre-empt the government doing its own enforcement" (p. 702). This is an interesting result that seems to characterize well the Independent Sector's activities between 2005 and 2007 that Young (chapter 5 in this volume) has documented (see also Ortmann and Svítková, 2007 on this issue). It will be interesting to watch how many of the well-intentioned measures to improve governance, accountability, and transparency of the nonprofit and voluntary sector will indeed be implemented if the immediate threat of the government conducting its own enforcement subsides. Relatedly, Stefanadis (2003) and Maxwell *et al.* (2000) also study self-regulation as an attempt to undermine a perceived need for regulation.

Kleiner (2006) collects empirical evidence on the effects of one particular form of self-regulation, occupational licensing. He shows that occupational licensing is a growing phenomenon in many markets: for example, a larger proportion of the workforce in the USA is now licensed than is in unions. And, by and large, the evidence that he presents suggests that licensing increases wages and decreases employment, without a corresponding increase in the quality of the products. The answer to the question asked in the subtitle of Kleiner's book therefore is: licensing occupations, rather than ensuring quality (as they apparently tend to do in the beginning), does (in the long run) restrict competition and thus reduce consumer welfare. This result is roughly in line with the kind of arguments that Shaked and Sutton (1981) made. One possible explanation is in the argument made formally by Nunez (2001 and 2007). If indeed that is the relevant explanation, it would support the claim that the sponsorship of accountability clubs, whether they are based on third-party certification or self-regulation, gives rise to different signaling mechanisms. Thus certification and self-regulation have very different incentive properties for many relevant parameterizations. Licensing, of course, is a particular form of self-regulation because it is mandatory and therefore does not fulfill the club definition of voluntary compliance meant to create a particular "brand" or identity of its members. Yet, we believe that there are useful lessons to be learned from this particular form of self-regulation and its attempt to solve the quality assurance problem.

Of obvious interest in the present context are the results by Potoski and Prakash (2005a and 2005b) who find that US companies that joined the International Organization for Standardization (ISO) voluntary environmental compliance program (ISO 14001) reduced their pollution emissions relative to those that did not. The ISO compliance program has relatively weak monitoring and sanctioning mechanisms, but the standards for participation and the reporting provisions are much stronger than those of the CDF discussed here. That said, it has to be noted that the effect of voluntary compliance programs seems fragile. Banerjee and Duflo (2000) show, for example, that ISO certification does not seem to help to overcome the asymmetric information problems that plague the Indian software industry. The potential for a relatively weak club to generate the effects reported in Potoski and Prakash (2005a and 2005b) may be due, as conjectured by the authors, to the high reputational benefits such voluntary compliance might generate because of consumer concern with firms' environmental performance, or it might be an attempt to stave off government intervention, and hence more unpalatable forms of regulation. These pressures may be stronger for environmental protection than for software. We reiterate that the work both of Kleiner (2006) and of Potoski and Prakash (2005a and 2005b) is not concerned with accountability clubs that rely on self-regulation in a strict sense.

Challenges to self-regulatory clubs in transition economies

As we have seen, the Czech Donors Forum is a multipurpose organization whose self-regulatory function seems of secondary importance. While its member organizations are expected to live up to the precepts of the "Principles of ethical conduct" that the CDF Associations of

Foundations, Endowment Funds, and Corporate Donors have issued, their enforcement does not seem to be undertaken through means of systematic quality assurance measures. Standards seem weakly enforced at best. This impression is also communicated through the CDF's own practice which does not live up to what it preaches: "People must know where their money goes and what it's really spent for" (Kalousová, 2008).

Even though the CDF is not legally required to publish its annual report because it is an association, having in the fall of 2008 only the annual report for 2005 posted online is hardly an example of responsible and responsive stewardship; nor is the choice of an organizational form that minimizes the degree of public accountability and transparency. (The public benefit organizational form would be more suitable.) Arguably, an organization that wants to increase the quality of the nonprofit sector should lead by example and be the first to disclose details about its operation. The lack of a clear-cut enforcement and/or monitoring mechanism that would guarantee that raised funds are spent in ways which could be considered efficient and wise is troubling.

It is also not clear to what extent the CDF has succeeded in its intention to guarantee standards of good practice in giving and increase the trustworthiness of charities: notwithstanding increasingly sophisticated means of raising donations and increasing wealth in the population, giving in real terms has stagnated over the past few years. Anecdotal evidence also suggests that the Donors Forum has not been completely successful in preventing misbehavior among some of its members, confirming some of Nunez's dire predictions. Quite possibly this is responsible for the modest growth of donations in the Czech Republic. There is also a widespread belief that the Donors Forum, while acting as a club, erects undesirable barriers to entry, confirming some of the dire predictions that can be derived from Shaked and Sutton (1981). We can only speculate to what extent it has also contributed to stagnation in giving.

As we have seen, the CDF is involved in various other activities (such as being a lobbying group for its members, a self-anointed representative/developer of the Czech nonprofit sector, an international lobbyist/mediator of donations/representative/developer, as well as a franchisor of this business model to other CEE states). This multiplicity of activities and agendas is problematic to handle under one roof. While, if managed correctly, it may result in synergies and further enforcement of the individual functions, it does open the door to lack of attention to the core functions and also invites cross-subsidization and other inefficiencies of a similar nature. There is no hard evidence that we can rely on, but it seems clear that the authentication function of the CDF is of subordinate importance and overshadowed by other functions. This parallels the findings of Tschirhart and Young in this volume (chapters 4 and 5), who also observe that membership associations tend to have multiple functions that can potentially conflict with the development of standard-setting and enforcement mechanisms.

Conclusions

Does self-regulation of the charitable sector in the Czech Republic work? It was the curious constellation of certification prevailing in the older European Union member states and self-regulation clubs prevailing in the newer European member states that motivated our contribution. We conclude that the accountability club called Czech Donors Forum has, for all we can assert, weak monitoring and sanctioning mechanisms involving only a very small fraction of nonprofit and nongovernmental organizations. We have argued that, because of its various other functions, the self-regulatory function is insufficiently developed. The less than accountable and nontransparent behavior of the CDF itself, the choice of an organizational form that minimizes accountability and transparency requirements, and its members' opposition to a certification with some bite, all make the theoretical literature on the undesirable incentive properties of accountability clubs that rely on self-regulation (e.g., Nunez 2001 and 2007; Shaked and Sutton, 1981) look persuasive.

Does self-regulation of the charitable sector in the Czech Republic work? There is no hard or direct evidence that we could use to answer this question with some confidence. What seems obvious is that donors in the Czech Republic rarely know where their money goes and what it is really spent on. At this point it can only be conjectured that this state of affairs is instrumental for the stagnating of giving in the Czech Republic. We would not be surprised to see eventually in the Czech Republic what we see in the older European Union member states: certification of charities by a third party, a form of accountability club that does not rely on self-regulation.

REFERENCES

Banerjee, A. and E. Duflo. 2000. Reputation Effects and the Limits of Contracting: A Study of the Indian Software Industry. *Quarterly Journal of Economics* 115(3): 989–1017.
Bekkers, R. 2003. Trust, Accreditation, and Philanthropy in the Netherlands. *Nonprofit and Voluntary Sector Quarterly* 32(4): 596–615.

2006. The Benefits of Accreditation for Fundraising Nonprofits. Accessed via www.cbf.nl/Downloads/Bestanden/Algemeen/benefits%20of%20accredita tion%20artikel%20Rene%20Bekkers.pdf.

Brhlikova, P. 2004. The Nonprofit Sector in the Czech Republic. CERGE-EI Discussion Paper No. 128.

2007. Essays on Competition and Entrepreneurial Choice between Nonprofit and For-profit Firms. CERGE-EI dissertation. Accessed via www.cerge-ei. cz/publications/dissertations/brhlikova_dissertation.asp.

Chhaochharia, V. and S. Ghosh. 2008. Do Charity Ratings Matter? Working paper, Florida Atlantic University.

DeMarzo, P. M., M. J. Fishman, and K. M. Hagerty. 2005. Self-Regulation and Government Oversight. *Review of Economic Studies* 72(3): 687–706.

Drucker, P. 1992. *Managing the Non-Profit Organization.* New York: HarperCollins.

Fric, P. and R. Goulli. 2001. *Neziskovy sektor v Ceske republice.* Prague: Eurolex Bohemia.

Gibelman, M. and S. R. Gelman. 2004. A Loss of Credibility: Patterns of Wrongdoing among Nongovernmental Organizations. *Voluntas* 15(5): 355–381.

Guet, I. H. 2002. *Monitoring Fundraising: A Comparative Survey of ICFO Members and their Countries.* Berlin: ICFO.

Kalousová, P. 2007. 10 Questions with ... *Prague Post.* April 20. Accessed via www.the prague post.com/articles/2007/11/21/10-questions.php.

2008. Contribute to Charity. *Prague Post.* January 3. Accessed via www. thepraguepost.com/articles/2008/01/03contribute-to-charity.php.

Klein, B. and K. Leffler. 1981. The Role of Market Forces in Assuring Contractual Performance. *Journal of Political Economy* 89(3): 615–641.

Kleiner, M. M. 2006. *Licensing Occupations: Ensuring Quality or Restricting Competition?* Kalamazoo, MI: W.E. Upjohn Institute for Employment Research.

Kreps, D. M. 1990. *A Course in Microeconomic Theory.* Princeton University Press.

Maxwell, J., T. Lyon, and S. Hackett. 2000. Self-Regulation and Social Welfare: The Political Economy of Corporate Environmentalism. *Journal of Law and Economics*, 43(2): 583–617.

Myslivecek, J. 2008. *Comparing Certification and Self-Regulation.* Unpublished manuscript.

Nunez, J. 2001. A Model of Self-Regulation. *Economics Letters* 74(1): 91–97.

2007. Can Self Regulation Work?: A Story of Corruption, Impunity and Cover-up. *Journal of Regulatory Economics* 31(2): 209–233.

Ortmann, A. 1996. Modern Economic Theory and the Study of Nonprofit Organizations: Why the Twain Shall Meet. *Nonprofit and Voluntary Sector Quarterly* 25(4): 470–484.

2001. Capital Romance: Why Wall Street Fell in Love with Higher Education. *Education Economics* 9(3): 293–311.

Ortmann, A. and M. Schlesinger. 2003. Trust, Repute, and the Role of Nonprofit Enterprise. In H. Anheier and A. Ben-Ner, eds. *The Study of Nonprofit Enterprise.* Kluwer Academic/Plenum, pp. 77–114.

Ortmann, A. and J. Myslivecek. 2010. Certification and Self-Regulation of Non-Profits, and the Institutional Choice between Them. In B. Seaman and D. Young, eds. *Handbook of Research on Nonprofit Economics and Management.* Cheltenham: Edward Elgar, pp. 280–290.

Ortmann, A. and K. Svítková. 2007. Certification as a Viable Quality Assurance Mechanism in Transition Economies: Evidence, Theory, and Open Questions. *Prague Economic Papers* 16: 99–115.

Pospisil, M. 2006. Mapping the Czech Nonprofit Sector. *Civil Review* 3(3–4): 233–244.

Potoski, M. and A. Prakash. 2005a. Covenants with Weak Swords: 14001 and Facilities' Environmental Performance. *Journal of Policy Analysis and Management* 24(4): 745–769.

2005b. Green Clubs and Voluntary Governance: ISO 14001 and Firms' Regulatory Compliance. *American Journal of Political Science* 49(2): 235–248.

Shaked, A. and J. Sutton. 1981. The Self-Regulating Profession. *Review of Economic Studies* 48(2): 217–234.

Stefanadis, C. 2003. Self-Regulation, Innovation, and the Financial Industry. *Journal of Regulatory Economics* 23(1): 5–25.

Svítková, K. and A. Ortmann. 2006. Certification as a Viable Quality Assurance Mechanism: Theory and Suggestive Evidence. CERGE-EI Working Paper No. 288.

Tirole, J. 1996. A Theory of Collective Reputations (with Applications to the Persistence of Corruption and to Firm Quality). *The Review of Economic Studies* 63(1): 1–22.

2006. *The Theory of Corporate Finance.* Princeton University Press.

Wilke, B. 2005. Transparenz im Spendenwesen: Siegel, Selbstregulierung, Watchdogs. Ein Vergleich USA, Grossbritannien und Deutschland. In W. R. Walz, H. Koetz, P. Rawert, and K. Schmidt, eds. *Non-Profit Law Yearbook 2004.* Calogne: Carl Heymans Verlag, pp. 181–206.

8   NGO accountability clubs in the humanitarian sector: social dimensions of club emergence and design

Maryam Zarnegar Deloffre

In the 1990s humanitarian nongovernmental organizations (NGOs) began questioning how to demonstrate that they were doing good. NGOs looked for ways to improve their performance and the quality of humanitarian aid, and started work on a number of programs aimed at enhancing NGO accountability (Zarnegar Deloffre, 2010).[1] This increased activity resulted from the shared belief that something had changed. Working in a more complex environment characterized by an exponential increase in the number of NGOs, a surge in the amount and types of funding for humanitarian activities, the participation of nontraditional actors, such as militaries and private contracting firms, in aid delivery, and heightened media attention to NGO activities, NGOs came to the conclusion that good intentions were no longer enough. They began defining standards for doing good and created numerous accountability clubs to institutionalize these standards.

In the analytic framework for this volume (chapter 1), Gugerty and Prakash argue that NGOs create and join accountability clubs in response to agency dilemmas – between principals (stakeholders) and agents (NGOs) – that result from information asymmetries. Agency dilemmas, such as shirking, arise when agents pursue their interests over the interests of principals. Gugerty and Prakash contend that NGOs create accountability clubs, defined as "rule-based institutions that create benefits that can be shared by members," to signal to principals that they are performing per their specifications. In this conceptualization, principals are generally

I would like to thank Deborah Avant, Jennifer Brinkerhoff, Martha Finnemore, Susan Sell, Hans Peter Schmitz, Jennie Schulze, Christi Siver, Carrie Booth Walling, and the editors for their insightful comments and thoughtful criticisms. Earlier versions of this chapter were presented at the annual meetings of the Association for Research on Nonprofit Organizations and Voluntary Action (ARNOVA), November 15–17, 2007, in Atlanta, GA and at the International Studies Association (ISA), March 26–29, 2008, in San Francisco, CA.
[1] See, for example, Ebrahim (2003: 820); Lloyd (2005); Naidoo (2004: 15–16).

external actors contracting with NGOs to perform certain functions; because they are external, principals cannot easily assess NGOs' efforts to meet these obligations. Accountability relationships consist of the set of standards for behavior, flows of information about that behavior, and the resulting actions that can be taken by principals after evaluating nonprofit behavior.

This chapter provides a counterpoint to the accountability clubs framework elaborated in this volume by investigating how ethical considerations and principles shaped humanitarian NGO efforts to define collective accountability standards. In the aftermath of the humanitarian relief response to the 1994 Rwandan genocide, humanitarian NGOs worked to provide emergency care to refugees located in camps in neighboring countries, including the Goma camps in Zaire. Upon realization that numerous perpetrators of the genocide had infiltrated the Goma camps and hijacked aid distribution systems, humanitarian NGOs were confronted with an ethical dilemma: should they continue to distribute relief assistance with the knowledge that they were abetting war criminals and possibly fueling the conflict by bolstering the insurgency; or should they leave the camps and deny innocent victims vital food and medical services? This chapter argues that the ethical arguments advanced during these debates subsequently influenced how humanitarian NGOs formulated two competing collective accountability standards: the Sphere Project and COMPAS Qualité.

The humanitarian imperative to prevent and alleviate human suffering wherever it may occur defines the moral duty of humanitarian NGOs. This moral duty defines "for what" humanitarian NGOs are accountable. NGOs founded accountability clubs in the humanitarian sector because they believed that they failed to meet their moral duty in response to the refugee crisis that resulted from the 1994 Rwandan genocide. This perception of failure resulted from a shift in performance standards – defined as how NGOs know whether they are meeting their moral duty – from a charitable "good enough" standard to a "humanitarianism plus" standard. These performance standards are socially constructed expectations used by principals as well as NGOs to assess NGO activities. The good enough standard maintains that NGOs should alleviate human suffering by providing basic necessities and does not define a role for NGOs beyond the alleviation of immediate suffering. In contrast, the humanitarianism plus standard recognizes that humanitarian aid may adversely affect the course of humanitarian crises by prolonging conflicts and increasing human suffering. In order to meet the humanitarianism plus standard NGOs must not only provide basic goods and services to alleviate human suffering but also ensure that their interventions do no harm.

NGOs viewed their response to the Rwanda conflict as problematic because they were unable to separate the Hutu militia, many members of which were guilty of committing the genocide, from other refugees. As a result, Hutu militia present in the camps co-opted aid distribution systems, diverted aid, and then used it to bolster their efforts to launch attacks into Rwanda. Humanitarian NGOs grappled with the sentiment that they were complicit in prolonging the conflict and that they had failed to meet their moral duty as specified by the humanitarianism plus standard. This belief prompted NGO interest in forming accountability clubs.

This chapter provides an explanation for why NGOs created accountability clubs in the aftermath of the Rwanda crisis and how they designed these clubs. First, it argues that a global accountability culture and changing performance expectations of humanitarian NGOs shaped NGO and principal preferences for creating accountability clubs. Second, it argues that three factors shaped how NGOs designed accountability clubs: social interactions among NGOs, institutional donors, and academics during the Joint Evaluation Report (JER) of the Rwanda intervention; the principle of independence; and ideas regarding how to meet the moral duty of NGOs. Social interactions during the JER process resulted in the belief that humanitarian NGOs needed to act together to address humanitarian crises and led to the collective design of accountability clubs. The principle of independence shaped NGO preferences to pursue self-regulatory accountability clubs over other types of regulation such as third-party certification or accreditation. Although humanitarian NGOs agreed that the humanitarian imperative defined their organizations' ultimate end, after their experience in the Goma camps, they disagreed on the means to reach that end. This disagreement involved debating what constituted "good" and, in turn, how to define accountability standards that would determine whether they were indeed "doing good." I examine the design of two accountability clubs, the Sphere Project and COMPAS Qualité, which exemplify this contestation.

This chapter begins with a discussion of the humanitarian sector and explores elements that differentiate this sector from other nonprofit sectors, such as the principles of humanitarian action, which affect the emergence and design of accountability clubs. Next, it shows how two contextual factors, the rise of a global accountability culture and the shift in performance expectations from a good enough to a humanitarianism plus standard, explain the emergence of accountability clubs in the mid-1990s. The shift in expectations shaped the perception of both principals and agents that there was a problem in humanitarianism. The global accountability culture proffered a solution, accountability clubs, to solve the problem. The second part of the chapter examines the question of club design and shows how social interactions during the JER process and the principle of independence shaped NGOs' preferences for transnational self-regulatory accountability clubs. Finally, the chapter investigates debates regarding how to meet the moral duty of humanitarian NGOs and demonstrates how these debates affected the design of accountability clubs.

Overview of the humanitarian sector

The humanitarian sector includes NGOs that provide emergency relief assistance in response to complex emergencies, such as conflicts in the Balkans or Sudan, or natural disasters, such as the earthquake in Bam, Iran, or the tsunami in southeast Asia. According to the United Nations Office for the Coordination of Humanitarian Affairs (OCHA), a complex emergency is a "humanitarian crisis typically characterized by extensive violence and loss of life, massive displacements of people, widespread damage to societies and economies, and hindrance of humanitarian assistance by security risks and political and military constraints" (OCHA, 1999). This chapter considers humanitarian responses to complex emergencies, in Biafra, Nigeria, and in Rwanda, to show how performance expectations changed over time.

Humanitarian relief aid involves implementing short-term palliative measures in response to complex emergencies or natural disasters. Although many humanitarian organizations provide both relief and development assistance, this chapter focuses solely on the humanitarian relief activities undertaken by these organizations and the accountability clubs they have formulated to oversee these activities.

Though humanitarianism is not new and existed in myriad forms before World War II, a veritable system of organized and institutionalized humanitarian aid burgeoned after the war. The core beliefs that underlie the humanitarian sector include a universal definition of humanity, solidarity, or a belief that "we're all in this together," and the belief that the international community has the means and duty to alleviate the human suffering that results from humanitarian crises.[2] Four major principles, adopted from the seven fundamental principles of the International Red Cross and Red Crescent Movement, guide humanitarian action: humanity, impartiality, neutrality, and independence (Red Cross, 2008). Humanity, or the humanitarian imperative, states that humanitarian organizations have a duty to prevent and alleviate human suffering wherever it may occur. The humanitarian imperative defines the moral duty of humanitarian NGOs. Impartiality requires that humanitarians

---

[2] This argument is more thoroughly developed in Zarnegar Deloffre (2010), chapter 2: Humanitarian NGO Accountability in Historical Perspective.

provide aid based solely on need and not on individual characteristics such as nationality, religion, race, gender, class, or political opinions. The principle of neutrality directs NGOs to avoid engaging in racial, religious, or ideological conflicts or politics, so as to maintain access to those in need and inspire the trust of all parties. Independence requires humanitarian NGOs to maintain their autonomy from the influence of governments and political actors. The degree to which a given organization ascribes to each of these four principles varies; for example, an organization may accept government funding which compromises its independence, whereas another may refuse all government grants and increase its independence (Tong, 2004: 179–180). As a general rule, however, these four principles guide the operations of humanitarian NGOs.

Humanitarian NGOs take part in the international humanitarian system, which comprises a multitude of actors, including international organizations such as the United Nations or the World Food Program, official aid agencies such as the United States Agency for International Development (USAID) or the Department for International Development (DFID) in the UK, military forces, members of the Red Cross family, private contracting firms, and local NGO partners. Any one actor may participate in an array of activities ranging from funding to logistics to program implementation. In this complex environment, one implication for humanitarian NGOs is that they are simultaneously beholden to multiple principals including institutional donors, international coordinating bodies, host governments, local NGO partners, individual donors, and communities in both their home and host countries.

Accountability in the humanitarian sector

Accountability has multiple meanings, particularly in contexts such as the humanitarian sector where multiple stakeholders, or principals, color the landscape. In response to demands from numerous principals, humanitarian NGOs often think about accountability as "accountability to whom," a concept that has many dimensions such as upward accountability to donors, downward accountability to affected populations, horizontal accountability to other NGOs, or internal accountability to the organization.

This chapter considers "accountability for what" – for what are humanitarian organizations accountable, or in the language of the volume: what are the standards by which humanitarian action should be judged? Accountability for what includes performance accountability, financial accountability, and political/democratic accountability (Brinkerhoff, 2004: 374). Performance accountability involves assessing performance based upon measures or standards and emphasizes the results or outputs of

NGO activity. Financial accountability involves reporting to financial stake-holders on the allocation and use of financial resources. Political/democratic accountability refers to responsiveness to stakeholder demands, transparency, and equity of service delivery. This last form of accountability assesses important aspects of government actions and is increasingly used to evaluate NGO performance. This is especially applicable to the humanitarian sector where principals now expect NGO programs to be representative of the needs and interests of beneficiaries and aid to be distributed in an equitable manner.

As noted above, humanitarian NGOs paid increasing attention to accountability and created numerous accountability clubs in the 1990s. Principal–agent theorists argue that this change toward focusing on NGO accountability resulted from principal demands in the wake of several failures in humanitarian response, most notably in Rwanda (see, for example, Buchanan-Smith, 2003: 1–2). According to this logic, both principals (stakeholders) and NGOs (agents) saw increased regulation as a rational response aimed at correcting dysfunctional behavior, such as inefficient use of funds, ineffective programs, inappropriate aid, and redundant provision of goods or services. Principal–agent frameworks see accountability as a response to failure, a corrective and reactive measure aimed at standardizing the work of NGOs and increasing the credibility of the sector.[3]

One explanation for the emergence of accountability clubs post-Rwanda is that a proliferation of NGOs and funding for NGOs, particularly from government donors, amplified the visibility of the sector and led to increased demands – from principals – for demonstrating accountability. Although the humanitarian response to the Rwandan crisis was indeed of impressive scale, placed in historical perspective it is only one of many large-scale humanitarian interventions.

International responses to humanitarian crises in Biafra and Kosovo also elicited a proliferation of NGOs and funding. Ninety-six NGOs and forty-three national Red Cross societies participated in the relief efforts in Biafra, thirty countries donated money, supplies, food, or medicines, and UNICEF and the World Food Program (WFP) conducted limited programs there (Zarnegar Deloffre, 2010: chapter 2). The total amount of donations worldwide, including cash contributions by NGOs, UNICEF, WFP, and states, amounted to approximately US$170 million (USAID, 1969: 1; Davis, 1975). In Rwanda, 7 UN agencies, 250 NGOs, 80 military contingents, the ICRC, the International Federation of Red Cross and Red Crescent Societies (IFRC), and scores of national Red Cross and Red

---

[3] For a small sample see Edwards and Hulme (1996), Lindenberg and Bryant (2001), and Lewis (2007).

Crescent societies participated in the relief efforts (Borton *et al.*, 1996: 205–206). In the nine months of the emergency, from April to December 1994, more than US$1.4 billion was spent on refugee assistance and emergency relief efforts (Borton *et al.*, 1996: 1). Five years later, more than 285 NGOs registered to work in the international intervention in Kosovo, topping the record of 250 NGOs working in Rwanda (Wiles *et al.*, 2000: xvii; Independent International Commission on Kosovo, 2000: xviii). Another feature of the international response was the unprecedented amount of money donated to the crisis. Though exact figures of total expenditure are not known, an Oxfam report states that donor governments gave US$207 per person through the 1999 UN appeal for Kosovo while donating only US$16 per capita to Sierra Leone and US$8 per person to the crisis in the Democratic Republic of Congo (Oxfam, 2000). These data illustrate the progressive expansion of the humanitarian sector over time but they do not explain the emergence of accountability clubs. It is therefore important to keep in mind that although Rwanda witnessed a proliferation of NGOs and relief funding which increased the visibility and perhaps the scrutiny of the humanitarian sector, this factor does not stand alone in explaining why accountability clubs emerged in response to Rwanda. Instead, NGOs created accountability clubs post-Rwanda because they did not meet their perceived moral duty in the Rwanda crisis.

This chapter argues that although many of the same obstacles – such as access to affected populations, NGO coordination, and security – impeded NGO relief activities in both Biafra and Rwanda, it was not these performance failures that led to the emergence of accountability clubs. Instead, changing standards for humanitarian activity shaped NGO and principals' understandings of the Rwanda intervention and led to the perception that NGOs had failed to meet their moral duty. Embedded in a global accountability culture, principals and NGOs viewed accountability clubs as a potential solution to this perceived failure.

In this volume, Gugerty and Prakash adapt the principal–agent framework to the NGO sector and elaborate a theory of NGO voluntary clubs. The overarching argument of the volume is that accountability clubs seek to mitigate agency dilemmas resulting from information asymmetries that occur between agents and their multiple principals. Since principals do not have complete information about the activities of their agents, agents must demonstrate that they are delivering and governing per the specifications of the principal(s). Agents in the humanitarian sector have a strong incentive to address information asymmetries and resulting uncertainty because they are highly dependent on principals for funding which ensures their organization's survival. One way to address information asymmetry is by signaling to principals that they are reputable, credible, and efficient organizations. This volume examines one type of signaling, the creation of accountability clubs, that nonprofits undertake to allay the concerns of their principals.

Several features of the humanitarian sector make it a particularly good candidate for the clubs perspective: humanitarian nonprofit organizations are highly resource dependent; the outputs of humanitarian work are often intangible and difficult to measure; nonprofits have come under intense media scrutiny since the 1990s, increasing the potentially damaging effects of "bad apples"; humanitarian emergencies occur in far-off places making monitoring and evaluation difficult and costly; and the transactions, or services, provided by humanitarian nonprofits are often a one-shot occurrence. This chapter examines four hypotheses suggested by the voluntary club framework to explain the emergence and design of accountability clubs. First, the clubs framework expects that accountability clubs will emerge in response to information asymmetries and uncertainty. Second, since the provision of services in the humanitarian sector occurs at the transnational level, the club framework suggests that principals will demand transnational regulation. Third, the clubs perspective posits that clubs with third-party certification or accreditation will be perceived as more credible by principals, particularly in sectors that are highly resource dependent. Fourth, the framework predicts that club design will be most responsive to the preferences of the most salient principal. I address each hypothesis in turn.

The clubs framework predicts that NGOs will create accountability clubs in response to agency dilemmas as a means to signal to their principals that they are serving principals' interests. This chapter argues that a global accountability culture and shifting expectations for NGO performance and not a priori preferences of NGOs or principals led to the creation of accountability clubs. Both the global accountability culture and the shift in performance expectations are constitutive, or mutually reinforcing, factors. In other words, the global accountability culture constituted the preferences of NGOs and principals for creating accountability clubs to address problems in humanitarianism (see, for example, Wendt, 1987 and 1992). A shift in expectations from the good enough to the humanitarianism plus standard shaped beliefs regarding NGO performance in the Rwanda crisis and led to the shared understanding that there was a problem in humanitarianism. Although many of the same performance failures occurred in both the Biafran and Rwandan interventions, the shift in standards for humanitarian action led to NGO perceptions that they had failed in the Rwandan case. Embedded in a global accountability culture, NGOs and principals saw accountability clubs as a natural way to address this failure.

Next, the clubs framework suggests that principals will prefer transnational clubs in sectors, such as the humanitarian sector, where the provision of goods and services is transnational. This chapter concedes that NGOs do design accountability clubs at the transnational level, but not solely as a result of principal demands. The Joint Evaluation Report (JER), the major evaluation report of the international response to Rwanda conducted by official aid agencies, NGOs, and academics, highlighted a need for NGOs to address issues of accountability. The collective nature of the JER incited NGOs to examine the problems in humanitarianism with a collective lens (rather than attributing problems to specific organizations) and led to collective solutions such as accountability clubs. In other words, social interactions, among funders, academics, and NGOs, during the JER shaped the preferences of NGOs to design accountability clubs at the transnational level, whereas in the past they had addressed accountability at an agency or national umbrella organization level.

From the club perspective, strong accountability clubs with independent sponsorship are expected to emerge in NGO sectors that are highly donor reliant such as the humanitarian sector. Despite principal preferences for third-party monitoring and certification articulated during the JER process, humanitarian NGOs primarily developed self-regulatory accountability clubs, ranging from lenient codes of conduct to stringent standards, and resisted the use of independent sponsorship and third-party certification. This chapter argues that a fundamental principle of humanitarian action, independence or autonomy from outside influence, precluded third-party certification as an option for regulating the sector.

Finally, the volume hypothesizes that the preferences of the most salient principal may be the most important factor in explaining club design. For example, Bowman in this volume (chapter 3) finds that accreditation clubs in the health and education sectors in the USA are highly responsive to the US federal government as the dominant principal. In contrast, this chapter argues that ideas regarding how to meet the moral duty of NGOs, shaped by both the shift in standards for humanitarian activity and NGO experiences in Rwanda, are the most important factors in explaining club design in the humanitarian sector. Despite receiving funding from the same institutional donors, the NGO groups that founded Sphere and COMPAS Qualité disagreed on how they should meet their moral duty to alleviate suffering and meet the expectations of the humanitarianism plus standard. This contestation led to differences in club design.

Club emergence: the rise of an accountability culture

Increased calls for NGO accountability in the 1990s are not specific to the humanitarian sector but indicative of a broader normative shift in the public (government) and private (business) sectors as well. Although it is beyond the scope of this chapter to analyze the rise of accountability in the government and business sectors there is evidence that the attention to and the substance of accountability changed in all sectors in the 1980s and 1990s (for a few examples, see GAO, 2007; MacDonald, 2000; Florini, 2003).

Anthropologist Marilyn Strathern describes the rise of an "accountability culture" that burgeoned in the 1980s and is characterized by "the twinned precepts of economic efficiency and good practice" (Strathern, 2000: 1–2). Strathern and the contributors to her volume link the spread of an accountability culture to the permeation of new public management theories typically associated with the Anglo-Saxon world: the United States, the United Kingdom, Australia, and New Zealand (Strathern, 2000: 5, 8; MacDonald, 2000: 109, 115, 119–120). Though "Latin" countries of the European Union (France, Italy, Portugal, Greece, and Italy) and some French NGOs have resisted defining accountability in new public management terms, the need to address accountability issues is increasingly a concern for them as well. (MacDonald, 2000; Dubnick and Justice, 2004: 7; Grünewald *et al.*, 2001: 35).

New public management theories adopt a market-driven model of providing social services wherein individual offices of the state, such as schools or hospitals, compete for consumers. It employs models of consumer and contractual rights to define relationships and practices in public sector accountability systems (Darcy, 2004). In theory, consumers have access to significant amounts of information about providers and can choose or change their providers based on this knowledge (Pierson, 1991: 157). The end result is that states not only empower citizens to assess public services critically, but they also encourage service providers to improve performance standards, increase transparency, and improve responsiveness to clients (G. Drewery cited in Darcy, 2004: 117).

The accountability requirements of the new public management framework spilled over to the humanitarian NGO sector as states called on NGOs to provide social services in the 1980s and 1990s. NGOs promoted themselves as having a comparative advantage over governments because of their small scale, flexibility, ability to mobilize resources quickly, coordinate with local populations, and circumvent obstacles blocking access to vulnerable populations (Salamon, 1987;

Barrow and Jennings, 2001: 15–16; Brinkerhoff and Brinkerhoff, 2002: 5–6).[4] Failures in government and development agency programs in the 1960s and 1970s pushed governments in the 1980s to rely increasingly on NGOs to provide social services and implement development policies, shifting some responsibilities to NGOs (Lindenberg and Bryant, 2001: 8; Barrow and Jennings, 2001: 16; Lewis, 2007: 75).

In the 1990s, the international community – states and international organizations – viewed NGOs as the most efficient and effective tools to address "new" global problems. This new policy environment was characterized by economic globalization, a public fiscal crisis that led to increased privatization, the spread of democracy, which led to the diffusion of political and civil rights as well as the expansion of civil society, increased private giving, the rise of a global media system, which improved global communications, and the end of the Cold War (Lindenberg and Bryant, 2001: 9–11; Barrow and Jennings, 2001: 15–17; Wheeler, 2003: 32–41). Subcontracting to NGOs led to the development of a type of "international welfare system," and the privatization of service delivery magnified the role of NGOs as service providers. As NGO roles expanded so too did the number and types of stakeholders interested in holding them accountable (Duffield, 1994; Brinkerhoff and Brinkerhoff, 2002: 8; Barnett and Weiss, 2008: 17).

The rise of a global accountability culture affected the emergence of accountability clubs in the humanitarian sector in two ways: first, it redefined "accountability for what" for humanitarian NGOs, constituting in part a shift in performance expectations and standards. Second, the global accountability culture provided humanitarian NGOs with a model for addressing perceived problems in humanitarianism.

The global accountability culture, in redefining beliefs regarding NGO accountability, consisted of a shift from performance accountability to political/democratic accountability. For example, Niels Dabelstein of the Danish International Development Agency (Danida) states that the practice of evaluation during the JER shifted from "'traditional' evaluation with emphasis on impact, efficiency and cost-effectiveness," or an emphasis on performance accountability, to evaluation that included "qualitative analysis of cause-and-effect assessed in relation to contractual obligations or international legal norms," or a focus on political/democratic accountability (Dabelstein, 1996: 291). The global accountability culture, in constituting a shift in performance expectations for humanitarian NGOs, redefined their roles and responsibilities, and at the same time

---

[4] For brief presentations of critiques of this view see Brinkerhoff and Brinkerhoff (2002: 6) and Lewis (2007: 98).

provided humanitarian NGOs with the language to address failures to meet these new expectations. Subsequently, when confronted with the ethical delemma of what to do in the Goma camps, humanitarian NGOs viewed accountability as a natural or appropriate way to manage these new expectations. The following section will discuss the shift in perform-ance expectations from a good enough to humanitarianism plus standard by examining two cases, Biafra and Rwanda, where similar performance failures produced different assessments of NGO performance.

Club emergence: changing performance expectations for humanitarian NGOs

What are the expectations of the humanitarian sector? Ideas regarding poverty, welfare, and the extent to which states and other actors should intervene to alleviate human suffering justify and legitimate humanitar-ian action. One notable characteristic of the international humanitarian system – which encompasses states, international organizations, and the humanitarian sector – is that it is largely managed and funded by states and not nonstate actors (Porter, 2000; Calhoun, 2008: 79, 89). Institutional donors such as states and international organizations pro-vide the funding for humanitarian activity, conflict states provide access to affected populations, in some emergencies militaries provide logistical and security services, and legal covenants outline the social rights of humans and mandate states to provide these rights. Since international humanitarian law delegates the responsibility of providing social rights to states, the political activity (or inactivity) of states and other political actors may hinder or overshadow the efforts of humanitarian NGOs. In light of this, it is most useful to think of the activities of humanitarian NGOs as the fulfillment of a perceived moral duty, defined by the humanitarian imperative, rather than a legal responsibility.[5]

The nature and scope of NGOs' moral duty is defined by the ordering principles to which humanitarian NGOs ascribe: the humanitarian imper-ative, neutrality, impartiality, and independence. Although these principles order and inform humanitarian activity, they are dynamic and increasingly tested by new contextual challenges – such as the heavy use of military logistics in the humanitarian responses in Kosovo and Iraq, which under-mined the principle of neutrality – and debated by humanitarian NGOs. Performance expectations for humanitarian NGOs define how NGOs and others judge whether or not they meet their moral duty.

---

[5] See also Darcy (2004: 115) for a similar point.

This section investigates assessments of two international responses to humanitarian crises in Biafra and Rwanda and shows that expectations of humanitarian NGOs shifted from those based on charity (good enough) to more complex expectations that NGOs relieve human suffering while doing no harm (humanitarianism plus).[6] The good enough standard draws on the idea of benevolence and charity and directs NGOs to provide basic necessities and services to alleviate acute suffering (Zarnegar Deloffre, 2010). The humanitarianism plus standard, meanwhile, goes beyond requirements for short-term palliative assistance and requires NGOs to provide aid that is not only adequate and appropriate but also addresses the root-causes of humanitarian crises and does no harm. As discussed above, in the 1980s and 1990s, the global accountability culture molded new ideas about social service provision. These new ideas constituted a shift from thinking about accountability in terms of performance accountability, or a focus on outputs, to a political/democratic accountability focused on the voice of service recipients and the appropriateness and impact of aid.

To illustrate the difference between the two standards consider a situation where an NGO must intervene to alleviate famine. To meet a good enough standard, NGOs would deliver a specific quantity of food to meet the nutritional requirements for each famine victim. The focus would be on outputs (quantity of food delivered) and outcomes (lives saved). In contrast, to meet a humanitarianism plus standard an NGO would not only deliver enough food to meet nutritional requirements but also adapt its food distribution program to the context of the emergency, taking into consideration the cultural appropriateness and the environmental impact of food products (training famine victims how to use uncommon foodstuffs to minimize a waste of energy and food), and the interests of famine victims (i.e., providing famine victims foodstuffs they can use rather than foodstuffs donors are willing to provide).

The humanitarian responses in Biafra and Rwanda in comparative perspective

The mid-1990s is a critical juncture in debates about NGO accountability. To investigate how expectations of NGO performance changed, I examine one international humanitarian response that occurred before this juncture, Biafra 1967–1969, and one that occurred at the juncture, Rwanda 1994–1998 (George and Bennett, 2004: 166; Campbell and

---

[6] Humanitarianism plus draws on Mary Anderson's idea of "do no harm" (Anderson, 1996).

Stanley, 1963; Munck, 2004). Although the evolution of performance standards is a process, these cases occur at critical points and illustrate how the performance standards changed over time. Biafra was the first large-scale international response to a complex emergency and is illustrative of a larger set of cases of early humanitarian responses, such as Cambodia, Congo, and Ethiopia. Rwanda is the most prominent of several serious humanitarian crises that occurred in the 1990s including Bosnia and Somalia.

To investigate these cases I employed multiple qualitative methods and examined three categories of documents that assess NGO performance in the two crises: official aid agency and institutional donor evaluations of NGO performance, newspaper articles, and NGO memoirs and articles. These documents represent the assessments of three major principals: financial donors, the public, and NGOs. In addition I conducted semi-structured interviews with evaluators of humanitarian NGOs.

Biafra   The secession of the Ibo state of Biafra from Nigeria in May 1967 incited Nigeria to declare war on July 6, 1967 and impose a blockade on Biafra, which led to the outbreak of a famine.[7] The international humanitarian response to the Biafra crisis was the first time that the humanitarian sector undertook a large-scale international intervention in response to a humanitarian crisis. It was also the first time news outlets televised images depicting famine. These images incited communities around the world to act either by donating resources or by advocating for action from their governments (see for example Brauman and Portevin, 2006, and Rieff, 2001).

This publicity incited an impressive international response. Though some relief agencies such as the International Committee of the Red Cross (ICRC) and Catholic Relief Services began limited relief operations shortly after the outbreak of the civil war in July 1967, the international relief efforts did not pick up momentum until spring 1968. Joint Church Aid (JCA), a confederation of thirty-five mainly Catholic and Protestant relief organizations and others like Oxfam and Save the Children, began unauthorized relief flights in April 1968 and continued until the war's end in January 1970 (Forsyth, 1969; Terry, 2002; Brauman and Portevin, 2006). Though the true extent of the humanitarian crisis is contested, the most reliable estimate is that a million civilians died during the

[7] Space considerations limit a detailed discussion of the historical and political aspects of the two cases. Please see Zarnegar Deloffre (2010: chapter 2) for a detailed account of each case.

twenty-five-month humanitarian crisis and between 600,000 and 5 million were displaced (USAID, 1969: 1; Byrne, 1997: 162; Brauman, 2000: 58; Terry, 2002: 43).

The good enough standard shaped how NGOs interpreted how to carry out their moral duty during the Biafra crisis. Rooted in ideas about charity, the good enough standard directed NGOs to provide immediate palliative assistance to victims of the humanitarian crisis. NGOs focused on rapidly providing an adequate amount of aid to alleviate the human suffering resulting from the man-made famine, instead of focusing on the appropriateness or effectiveness of aid as they would later in the Rwanda crisis. Assessments of NGO performance by the three major stakeholder groups focused on outputs and viewed the major problem in relief operations as the inadequate and insufficient aid supply. A related problem was that aid did not reach victims fast enough to save lives.

Three obstacles hindered relief activities and prevented NGOs from providing adequate aid: political manipulation of aid proposals by both Biafran and Nigerian officials; impeded access to victims of the civil war; and logistical issues, namely a lack of adequate infrastructure such as operational landing strips in Biafra. These obstacles hindered humanitarian NGOs from providing both adequate and rapid relief to victims of the civil war. In order to meet the demands of the good enough standard and to fulfill their moral duty, Joint Church Aid and later the ICRC flew clandestine night flights into Biafra to deliver aid. Though major principals, such as the UK and US governments, expressed their disapproval of an airlift based on efficiency grounds, by December 1968 the airlift emerged as the sole solution to the humanitarian crisis because it was the only way to alleviate suffering rapidly (Mohr, 1968; Davis, 1975: 503; Welles, 1969; Department of State, 1969: 94; Thompson, 1990: 72, 87–90). International relief agencies, states, and the public supported the airlift, despite its problems and inefficiencies, because it rapidly delivered vital relief to the suffering Biafrans.[8]

Assessments of humanitarian relief efforts during the Biafran crisis illustrate how the good enough standard shaped understandings of NGO performance. Financial principals primarily expected humanitarian NGOs to meet a good enough standard of providing aid given the difficult logistical and political conditions resulting from the complex emergency. The good enough standard shaped evaluations of NGO performance by the United States, the largest government donor of aid during the Biafran

---

[8] On the numerous inefficiencies of the airlift see Lloyd et al. (1973).

crisis (Davis, 1975). For example, US Ambassador Clyde Ferguson, special coordinator of relief to civilian victims of the Nigerian civil war, states:

I would like to state emphatically that the efforts of the ICRC have been magnificent, especially given the difficult logistical environment in which the relief effort is working. The ICRC was effective and impartial in its humanitarian relief on both sides. The Red Cross airlift, together with that of Joint Church Aid, was literally the lifeline for millions of civilian victims of the war. (Department of State, 1969)

This quote is illustrative of the official assessments of the international response to the Biafran crisis and demonstrates the sentiment that relief agencies did what they could, or were "good enough" given the difficult logistical and political circumstances. Despite evidence of inefficiencies and inadequate aid supplies, financial stakeholders believed that NGOs met the expectations of the good enough standard.

Assessments of NGO performance in the press also illustrate the good enough standard, emphasizing the individual worth of each human being and the need to alleviate suffering through charitable means (Byrne, 1997: 63). Print media articles focused on the fact that NGOs were doing something to alleviate suffering, highlighting the charitable components of aid, and not the appropriateness of aid or its long-term impacts as they did later in Rwanda (Churchill, 1969).

Similarly, NGO self-assessments of the relief efforts in Biafra focus on the amount of relief aid dispersed and not on the effectiveness or appropriateness of aid. They concentrate on the rapid deployment of palliative aid and not on the long-term impacts of aid or its effects on beneficiaries as was the case in Rwanda. An incident that illustrates the strong normative power of the good enough standard involves a schism between how two factions of the JCA viewed the relief airlift. One faction of aid professionals believed that by providing food aid to Biafra, they helped bolster the secessionist regime and prolonged the war and suffering, thereby raising the issue of the adverse effects of humanitarian aid. In December 1969, the World Council of Churches announced that it "oppose[d] the continuation of mercy flights of food shipments to Biafra on the grounds that the aid is only prolonging the Nigerian civil war." And it "expresse[d] deep distress at the ambiguous position in which this tremendous effort has put the Christian people, churches and agencies because of its political side effects ... includ[ing] exposing the churches to the charge of prolonging the war and adding to the suffering of the people."[9] These charges

---

[9] "Churches Hint at Halting Biafra Aid," *The Times*, December 6, 1969; "Church Unit Cold to Biafra Relief," *The New York Times*, December 6, 1969.

were made by Nigerians as well as others in Africa, Europe, and North America.[10]

After making these explosive comments, the World Council of Churches attended a JCA meeting at Sandefjord, Norway where it expressed its views. A schism resulted among the attendees: a minority shared the World Council's view, while the majority felt that relief agencies should provide assistance to the starving regardless of political complications.[11] Father Tony Byrne shared the latter view:

> Churches were constantly criticized for keeping Biafra alive. I argued with them several times during television interviews that the churches were not keeping Biafra alive as such. What we kept alive were many people at risk, innocent civilians who happened to live in a country called Biafra. They had a right to life. They didn't start the war. They were its victims. (Byrne, 1997:122)

Byrne voices the viewpoint of the majority of relief agencies, clergymen, and the public who believed that keeping Biafrans alive was more important than the political side-effects of humanitarian action.[12] In other words, in the late 1960s, humanitarian NGOs were not yet ready to think about humanitarian action in terms of a humanitarianism plus standard. The development of a global accountability culture in the 1980s and 1990s changed the context in which humanitarian action took place and constituted new understandings of humanitarian aid that included reflection regarding the impacts of aid. The next section will show how this shift in expectations led NGOs to interpret their actions in Rwanda as a failure because they did not meet the provisions of a humanitarianism plus standard.

Rwanda The Rwandan civil war began in October 1990 when the Rwandan Patriotic Front (RPF), a group of Tutsi exiles, invaded Rwanda from its base in Uganda. In August 1993, the RPF and the Hutu-led Rwandan government of Juvénal Habyarimana signed the Arusha peace accords to end the civil war. The assassination of Habyarimana in April 1994 is considered to have been the catalyst for the genocide that ensued.

The genocide was planned in advance by Rwandan hardliners, including top government and military officials, local officials, and the police, who disputed and resented the power-sharing agreement set out in the Arusha peace accords (Terry, 2002: 155; Rieff, 2001: 157–158). These

---

[10] "New Biafra Plan Urged by Churches," *The Times*, December 14, 1969; "Churches Hint at Halting Biafra Aid," *The Times*, December 6, 1969.
[11] "Churches had Doubts about Biafra Airlift," *The Times*, February 2, 1970.
[12] "New Biafra Plan Urged by Churches," *The Times*, December 14, 1969.

hardliners organized and armed two militia groups, the Interahamwe and
Impuzamugambi, who carried out the extermination campaign by targeting members of the Tutsi minority and Hutu moderates who appeared to
support the power-sharing agreement. In the span of a hundred days,
these militia groups and their partners massacred an estimated 500,000–
800,000 individuals (see Borton *et al.*, 1996; Terry, 2002; Barnett, 2002;
Brauman and Portevin, 2006).

The humanitarian crisis in Rwanda began shortly before the defeat of
the Rwandan Armed Forces (Forces Armées Rwandaises, FAR) by the
Tutsi RPF in July 1994. The Rwandan government issued state directives
encouraging Hutus to flee Rwanda for fear of retaliatory attacks by the
RPF (Terry, 2002: 155). More than two million Hutus sought refuge in
the neighboring countries of Zaire (Congo), Tanzania, and Burundi, and
approximately one million Rwandans were displaced internally (Terry,
2002: 155). As discussed above, the presence of members of the Hutu
militia and perpetrators of the genocide in the camps compromised the
integrity of the relief operations. Unable to triage refugees, NGOs felt
complicit in prolonging the conflict and aggravating human suffering in
the camps. This sentiment led to the shared belief that they had failed to
meet their moral duty.

NGO reactions to perceived failures in Rwanda were more severe than
in the Biafra intervention, though many of the same problems, such as
capacity, coordination, and security, hindered NGO performance in both
emergencies. Though some aid groups working in Biafra did voice concerns that humanitarian relief aid prolonged the conflict by emboldening
Biafrans, their calls for reflection on the political and long-term effects of
humanitarian aid did not resonate in the humanitarian sector. In contrast,
NGOs in Rwanda reflected deeply about the long-term impacts of their
interventions.

The Rwanda case highlights a fundamental shift in the expectations of
humanitarian NGOs. The standard that emerged in Rwanda was one of
"humanitarianism plus," or the belief that NGOs should not only
alleviate suffering but also pay attention to root causes of suffering and
take into account the impacts of aid on local communities. As one
NGO employee states, "We now focus on root causes. After Rwanda,
there was a backlash against the 'band aid' or the 'truck and chuck'
approach" that characterized charitable interventions.[13] Another
humanitarian worker expressed the transition in expectations even
more clearly:

---

[13] Personal interview 1, April 16, 2008, Washington, DC.

[In] Biafra and Ethiopia 1984, [the humanitarian response was] very much a charitable act to someone in desperate circumstances. Rwanda [was] similar, but gradually we see an emergence of a human rights perspective. In the past we would say, "poor Africans, we did what we could" but now there is increasing dialogue that everyone has basic human rights and when they are not protected there is a moral and legal responsibility to do something about it.[14]

The shared belief that NGOs failed in Rwanda resulted from the challenges posed by the presence of former Forces Armées Rwandaises (FAR) refugees in the camps in Zaire, many of whom were active participants in the genocide. Not only did these former-FAR refugees receive aid, but in some cases NGOs, unaware of their identities, employed them to distribute aid. The former-FAR refugees used their positions in the distribution systems to control camps and to divert and stockpile aid. They later used this diverted aid to fuel insurgencies in the camps and raids into Rwanda (Terry, 2002: 164–165). NGOs believed that their well-intentioned actions led to the prolongation of the conflict and the suffering of refugees in the camps.

Though NGOs felt that they failed to meet the demands of the humanitarianism plus standard, they interpreted this failure in different ways. Two dominant positions emerged during the crisis: groups such as CARE-UK, the International Federation of Red Cross and Red Crescent Societies, Oxfam, and the Dutch and Belgian sections of Médecins Sans Frontières (MSF) felt that their moral duty justified staying in Rwanda. Others, like MSF-France and the International Rescue Committee (IRC), eventually pulled out of Rwanda because they believed that humanitarian aid was abetting the former-FAR refugees and prolonging the suffering. The two groups disagreed on how to meet their moral duty in Rwanda. Whereas the latter group acknowledged the potentially negative effects of well-intentioned actions, the former group believed that, above all, helping those in need superseded the problems associated with providing aid (Terry, 2002: 196–201; Degionanni, 1994; Hanley, 1997). Though a shift in performance expectations from the good enough to humanitarianism plus standard constituted NGOs' perceptions that they failed in Rwanda, how they interpreted that failure resulted in varying ideas about how to carry out their moral duty. Variation in ideas regarding NGOs' moral duty led these groups to design two different accountability clubs, as will be discussed below.

Official aid agency assessments of the international relief efforts in the Rwandan crisis also used the humanitarianism plus standard to evaluate NGO performance. As the crisis unfolded, the Danish International

---

[14] Personal interview 9, by telephone, May 21, 2008, Washington, DC.

Development Agency (Danida) proposed a joint evaluation of the humanitarian relief efforts in response to the situation. This was the first comprehensive evaluation of the collective humanitarian response to the
Rwandan crisis. Launched in January 1995 the collective evaluation was
an unprecedented multinational, multi-donor effort to assess relief efforts
systematically. A steering committee comprising thirty-eight members
representative of the international aid community managed the evaluation, and five countries, Sweden, Norway, Denmark, the United
Kingdom, and the United States, oversaw the day-to-day affairs of the
project. In all, five research teams conducted four substantive studies and
one synthesis report of the international humanitarian response to the
Rwanda conflict (Borton *et al.*, 1996: 7, 8, 47, 79; Dabelstein, 1996).

The JER identified the main problem in the Rwanda response as the
failure of the international community – states and international organizations – to intervene to prevent or stop the genocide. It does not single
out NGOs as being responsible for the failure and focuses instead on the
inaction of the international community. In its assessment of NGO relief
activities, the JER employs language shaped by the humanitarianism plus
standard. In contrast to assessments of the Biafra response, the JER
focused on the impacts of aid and the appropriateness of aid, or whether
or not relief aid was adapted to the context of the conflict and matched the
needs and customs of victims. In addition the JER considered the equitable distribution of aid and accountability to beneficiaries, issues that the
official aid agencies did not evaluate in their assessments of NGO performance in Biafra.

Assessments of the humanitarian response in Rwanda that appeared in
the press also focused mainly on the political inaction of the international
community and especially the misguided use of humanitarian aid to solve
political problems. Though the media did not attribute the failure in
Rwanda to NGOs it did examine problems in NGO performance. In
addition to the political inaction of the international community, which
led to a more severe refugee crisis and complicated the provision of aid,
the press discussed problems related to security, inefficiency/ineffective-
ness of aid, and access to conflict victims. Further, the press observed that
aid was, or seemed to be, prolonging the conflict. What is of particular
note is that NGOs themselves were most often the ones to voice concern
about the impacts of aid and NGO accountability in press articles that
discussed these issues.

This section has argued that NGOs created accountability clubs in the
humanitarian sector in response to their own perceptions that they failed
to meet a new moral obligation in Rwanda, rather than in response to
performance failures. It shows that though the same types of performance

failures occurred in both Biafra and Rwanda, a shift in performance expectations for NGOs from a good enough to a humanitarianism plus standard in Rwanda led to the shared belief that NGOs had failed to meet their moral obligation. Though principals, funders, and the media highlighted problems with NGO performance, it was the NGOs themselves that most severely criticized their role and failure in Rwanda. NGOs interpreted this failure in two ways and created accountability clubs to address the failure to meet their moral duty. The following section will discuss how NGOs designed these clubs.

Design of accountability clubs

The voluntary clubs framework advances multiple hypotheses regarding the design of accountability clubs; three are examined here. First, the clubs framework posits that principals will prefer clubs with jurisdictions that are congruent to their own because they will provide a more useful signal for nonprofit performance. In the case of the humanitarian sector, this means principals prefer that accountability clubs regulate at the transnational level. Second, the clubs framework predicts that accountability clubs with independent sponsorship and third-party certification will be more likely to emerge in sectors that are highly donor-reliant. Finally, the clubs framework suggests that the design of accountability clubs will be responsive to the preferences of the dominant principal. I examine each hypothesis in the sections to follow.

First, the clubs framework predicts that in the humanitarian sector where NGOs work at the transnational level, principals will find transnational signals most desirable. Empirically, this prediction bears out: NGOs have designed accountability clubs at the transnational level after the mid-1990s but not solely because of principal demands. This chapter provides an alternative explanation to the one advanced by the clubs framework as to why NGOs chose to self-regulate at the transnational level. It argues that social interactions during the JER shaped NGO preferences for transnational regulation over other possibilities.

The humanitarian relief community considers the international response to Rwanda and the subsequent JER report as important catalysts in the formation of accountability clubs (Buchanan-Smith, 2003; Walker and Purdin, 2004). This view is consistent with the predictions of the clubs framework which holds that the principals involved in the JER (institutional donors, states, etc.) influenced the design of the accountability clubs in the humanitarian sector. This section investigates *how* the JER affected and shaped the design of accountability clubs, and argues that the collective format of the JER and the social interactions among

NGOs, institutional donors, states, and academics led to the design of transnational accountability clubs.

The JER served as a focal point for humanitarian NGOs, and their experience in the JER process shaped NGO preferences to act in a collective fashion to address problems of standard-setting and accountability. Though NGOs began proactively discussing industry standards in the 1990s, the mechanism that brought these budding discussions to fruition was the collective format of the Joint Evaluation Report.[15] Prior to the JER, NGOs addressed accountability at the agency or umbrella organization level. Peter Walker and Susan Purdin (2004) discuss eight such NGO-led standards projects concurrently founded in the 1990s, as well as a plethora of agency-specific handbooks developed in the 1980s and 1990s. They contend that NGOs began proactively addressing changes in context and increasing pressures by the public and media to perform to new expectations by launching this eclectic set of projects (Walker and Purdin, 2004: 101–102). The importance of the JER is that it helped bolster and encourage discussions about the development of performance *standards* that had already debuted in 1993 in the humanitarian sector (Borton and Eriksson, 2004: 80; Buchanan-Smith, 2003: 7).[16]

The JER was the first time that official and institutional aid agencies, NGOs, states, and the UN came together to evaluate a humanitarian response. The collective nature of this endeavor and the interactions among members of the international humanitarian system prompted NGOs to seek collective solutions to the problems they identified in the humanitarian sector. As one interviewee states, "[After Rwanda] we [NGOs] were driven by a sense of doubt... [we were] driven by introspection and individual reflection. After the Joint Evaluation we started looking at these problems and our actions collectively. This is why the joint evaluation was important, it was a system-wide look at our work; we didn't look at each other as individual organizations anymore."[17] Many interviewees note the significance of these interactions and state that the JER led to increased dialogue in the NGO sector and the sentiment that "we're all in this together" or "we can't do this alone." The social interactions among participants in the JER and the collective nature of the process constituted NGO preferences to design accountability clubs at the

---

[15] Buchanan-Smith (2003: 12) also mentions this point.
[16] Lowrie (2000) states that the Joint Evaluation Report provided external impetus for discussions about NGO accountability and clubs like Sphere are an internally driven NGO initiative.
[17] Personal interview 12, June 11, 2008, Washington, DC.

transnational level. NGOs viewed transnational clubs as the appropriate or natural way to address accountability issues in the humanitarian sector. Second, the clubs framework posits that accountability clubs are more likely to have independent sponsorship and third-party certification or compliance mechanisms in sectors that are highly donor-reliant such as the humanitarian sector. The JER recommended two forms of regulation as a means to improve NGO performance: (1) self-managed regulation and (2) an international accreditation system (Borton *et al.*, 1996: 209). The report very clearly states that principals preferred an international accreditation system over self-regulation. NGOs, however, pursued self-regulatory accountability clubs instead of third-party accreditation programs. A subsequent assessment of the JER reaffirms the JER's recommendation to establish an accreditation system and notes the failure of NGOs to implement such a program (Borton and Eriksson, 2004: 78–81).

Despite being highly reliant on donors for funding and the clearly stated preferences of their principals for third-party regulation, humanitarian NGOs founded self-regulatory accountability clubs. The clubs framework as currently articulated does not provide an explanation why. I argue that the principle of independence, or the desire to maintain the autonomy of the sector from outside influence, constituted NGOs' preference for self-regulatory accountability clubs. Humanitarian workers stated during interviews that a third-party accreditation system threatened the independence of the sector and they pursued self-regulation as a means to protect their independence.[18] In sum, the principle of independence, and not the demands of principals, shaped NGO preferences for designing accountability clubs with self-regulatory compliance mechanisms.

Third, the clubs perspective predicts that agents design accountability clubs to resolve agency dilemmas and signal that they are performing per the interests of their principals. According to this logic, agents design accountability clubs in line with the preferences of their most salient principal. This chapter argues that humanitarian NGOs designed accountability clubs in order to meet their perceived moral duty, not in response to agency dilemmas. The divergent ideas regarding how to meet this moral duty led to variations in club design; two clubs, Sphere and COMPAS Qualité, are considered here.

---

[18] Personal interview 5, by telephone, April 18, 2008, Washington, DC; personal interview 11, by telephone, June 9, 2008, Washington DC; personal interview 12, June 11, 2008, Washington, DC.

Divergent ideas about how to meet NGOs' moral duty had implications for the process of promoting and elaborating accountability standards and clubs that were acceptable to all aid organizations. As discussed above, though NGOs viewed the humanitarian response in Rwanda as a failure to meet their moral duty, two ways of viewing the problem emerged and polarized NGOs into two camps. I contend that the contestation regarding accountability clubs and standards resulted from the two ways in which NGOs framed their moral duty during and after the Rwanda response.

The first camp argued that the humanitarian imperative obliged NGOs to stay in Rwanda, and NGOs needed to articulate a humanitarian space wherein they could do their jobs. Led by Peter Walker, then of the IFRC, and Nick Stockton, then of Oxfam, this group focused on two methods for improving humanitarian performance: the articulation of the legal duty of humanitarian NGOs and the elaboration of highly technical standards of performance. Both Stockton and Walker were vociferous critics of NGOs that left Rwanda and considered the actions of these groups as a failure to meet their moral duty (Terry, 2002: 200–201). In 1997, Stockton and Walker helped launch the Sphere Project in direct response to failures in Rwanda (Buchanan-Smith, 2003: 11).

Four hundred organizations in eighty countries participated in the process of developing the Sphere charter, standards, and handbook (Sphere Project, 2004). The handbook includes a humanitarian charter, based on international humanitarian and human rights law, which details principles of humanitarian action and the rights of affected populations. The minimum standards articulate standards and indicators in five key sectors of humanitarian activity: water supply and sanitation, nutrition, food aid, shelter, and health services. The baseline expectations for the development of the Sphere club standards were humanitarianism plus and a rights-based legal approach to meeting NGOs' moral duty.

Sphere is an example of a relatively strong club: it articulates rather stringent technical standards that aim to improve the quality of technical assistance and employs a self-certification compliance mechanism. Sphere includes a set of common standards that regulate a range of program components such as participation, initial assessment, response, targeting, evaluation, management, and monitoring and supervision. Further, it includes standards that regulate specific issue areas such as water and sanitation, food security, food aid, nutrition, shelter and settlement, health services, and nonfood items.

The humanitarian charter component of Sphere works to define "accountability for what" in terms of political/democratic accountability by establishing a legal duty for humanitarian NGOs and defining service standards in terms of entitlements (Darcy, 2004: 113). James Darcy delineates three fundamental ideational pillars of the Sphere club:

the first concerns the minimum requirements for sustaining human life with dignity; in other words, it concerns basic human needs. The second idea is that such needs are universal and must be understood as a minimal basis for universal human entitlements or rights ... The third strand of thought concerns human-itarian assistance and the quality of service delivery, linked to the achievement of the minimum requirements described above. (Darcy, 2004: 113).

The charter articulates these ideas in the handbook:

As humanitarian agencies, we define our role in relation to these primary roles and responsibilities. Our role in providing humanitarian assistance reflects the reality that those with primary responsibility are not always able or willing to perform this role themselves. This is sometimes a matter of capacity. Sometimes it constitutes a willful disregard of fundamental legal and ethical obligations, the result of which is much avoidable human suffering. (Sphere Project, 2004: 18)

This group of NGOs believed that their failure to meet their moral duty in Rwanda resulted from an absence of a humanitarian space wherein they could protect conflict victims and alleviate suffering. By including legal language in the Sphere charter and handbook, this group designed the Sphere accountability club to establish a legal space in which human-itarian NGOs could act. The claim that humans have a *right* to social assistance and that humanitarian NGOs have the *responsibility* to provide these rights is at the root of contestation regarding standard formation in the humanitarian sector.

The issue of how to monitor and enforce the Sphere standards led to considerable debate during the design process. Three groups articulated views on how the Sphere standards should be monitored and evaluated. One group felt that standards should be enforced through peer pressure, self-policing, and other noncoercive tools. A second group believed that some form of accreditation was needed to ensure the credibility of the standards. A third group argued that the Sphere standards should be separated from any type of enforcement mechanism and that the hand-book should not be imposed on humanitarian NGOs (Walker and Purdin, 2004: 109). According to Walker and Purdin, the issue of enforcement became the most difficult to resolve and was finally put to rest at the eleventh hour by prefacing the first edition (December 1998) of the Sphere manual with a letter that clearly explained that the manual would undergo field-testing before establishing any kind of accreditation system. As Gugerty suggests in this volume (chapter 10), this contestation has led to the inability of Sphere to enforce compliance with the minimum standards. The Sphere handbook remains largely a reference tool without enforcement or reporting mechanisms.

The second NGO camp included NGOs that left Rwanda in protest because they believed that humanitarian aid was abetting the former Rwandan government and prolonging the suffering. They also strongly believed that humanitarian aid coupled with political action was the only way to resolve the crisis. In essence, this second camp interpreted how to meet their moral duty in a fundamentally different manner than the first group; they felt that political contexts determined the degree to which NGOs could meet their moral duty. This camp believed that NGOs should cease aid efforts if aid prolongs a conflict or aggravates human suffering.

Headed initially by MSF, this group rejected the technical standards articulated by Sphere and formed an accountability club in 1999 in opposition to Sphere. MSF's primary objection was that Sphere linked issues of quality and accountability to technical standards (Buchanan-Smith, 2003: 15; Tong, 2004). In addition, MSF and others argued that a focus on technical standards overlooked fundamental problems in humanitarianism such as the lack of protection for victims of complex emergencies and the fact that in some instances humanitarian aid could prolong conflict and do harm. Further, NGOs in this camp objected to two other implicit assumptions in the Sphere charter and handbook, the first being the construction of consumerist notions of humanitarian aid where the victim is a client of a humanitarian organization. Second, they contested the legal validity of the humanitarian charter because it was based on an eccentric compilation of international law that implicated states and not nonstate actors (Dufour *et al.*, 2004). In short, this group did not believe that NGOs could meet their moral duty by using technical standards, establishing legal authority, or adopting a market-based model of serving conflict victims.

Two groups of French and other humanitarian NGOs launched two new accountability working groups, Projet Qualité and Synergie Qualité, in opposition to Sphere. The groups merged in 2001 to form the Quality Platform, which developed an accountability club called COMPAS Qualité.[19] The Quality Platform "advocates the enhancement of local participation, improved analysis of the political context and a better understanding of the impact of aid on the local environment, greater attention to staff training and a reaffirmation that states, not NGOs, have a primary responsibility for safeguarding their

---

[19] Veronique de Geoffroy, coordinator of COMPAS Qualité, personal communication, July 20, 2006.

citizens."[20] The emphasis on political context, the political responsibilities of states, and local impacts draws directly from how this group
interpreted NGO moral duty during and after the Rwanda crisis.

COMPAS Qualité is a weak club because it develops lenient standards
verified by self-certification. It elaborates a complex system of questioning
that encourages NGOs to improve the quality of humanitarian assistance
by considering each of twelve major themes. Instead of focusing on
technical delivery, the twelve themes are broad-based and allow NGOs
to consider the specific political, cultural, and humanitarian context of
their interventions. Examples of these themes include coherence of the
project with the organization's mandate and principles or appropriateness
of aid (La méthode COMPAS).

NGOs designed accountability clubs in order to address failures to
meet their moral duty during the Rwanda crisis. Competing interpretations of what this failure was and how to define NGO moral duty explain
why NGOs designed two different accountability clubs, Sphere and
COMPAS Qualité. The two camps discussed in this section contested
not only each other's interpretations of NGO failure in Rwanda and NGO
moral duty, but also how to design accountability clubs to address these
failures. In order for a legitimate normative structure, such as self-
regulatory codes of conduct, to emerge in the humanitarian sector,
NGOs need to agree on the interpretation of frames and appropriate
solutions. In highly competitive contexts, such as the humanitarian policy
context, like-minded actors who champion similar solutions may engage
in contentious debate regarding the dominant frame that legitimizes their
actions (Payne, 2001). As Gugerty argues in this volume (chapter 10),
contestation may diminish the regulatory potential of resultant accountability clubs and reduce the ability of clubs to enforce compliance.

Conclusions

This chapter examined four hypotheses posited by the voluntary club
framework to explain the emergence and design of accountability clubs
in the humanitarian sector. The club framework predicts that actors create
accountability clubs in response to agency dilemmas. I show that two
contextual factors, changes in the global accountability culture and in
performance expectations and standards for humanitarian NGOs, led to
the emergence of accountability clubs in the humanitarian sector.

[20] Grünewald *et al.* (2001); see also Terry (2000) and V. de Geoffroy, coordinator of
COMPAS Qualité, personal communication, July 20, 2006.

Whereas NGOs experienced many of the same performance failures in their responses to both the Biafran and Rwandan crises, these contextual factors shaped NGOs' own perceptions of their performance in Rwanda and their preferences to solve perceived problems by creating account-ability clubs. Embedded in a global accountability culture, NGOs saw accountability as a natural and appropriate solution to address perceived failures in the Rwanda crisis.

The club framework also advances hypotheses to explain the design of accountability clubs. It predicts that principals prefer transnational clubs to regulate agents who work at the transnational level. This chapter shows that social interactions during the Joint Evaluation Report and increased dialogue in the sector, not principal preferences, shaped NGO interests to create accountability clubs at the transnational level. Another prediction that the framework makes is that principals prefer third-party regulation in sectors that are highly donor-reliant such as the humanitarian sector. Humanitarian principals did exhibit a preference for third-party systems, but I show how the principle of independence shaped NGOs' preferences for and creation of self-regulatory compliance mechanisms.

Finally, this chapter argues that differing ideas regarding how to meet the moral duty of NGOs shaped the design of competing accountability clubs, Sphere and COMPAS Qualité, in the humanitarian sector. Unlike many of the clubs studied in this volume, in the humanitarian sector competing clubs arose at the same time and in direct opposition to one another. In the case of the Minnesota clubs examined by Bies in chapter 9, for example, competing clubs arose in part in response to the desires of two different sets of principals. In this case, two clubs emerged as a result of divergent NGO ideas regarding their ethical roles and responsibilities. On one hand, humanitarian NGOs that viewed establishing a legal responsibility for NGOs and technical standards as the best tools for meeting their moral duty founded the Sphere Project. NGOs that founded COMPAS Qualité believed that the best way to meet their moral duty was to adapt to political contexts, pressure states to intervene in humanitarian crises, and ensure that aid did not prolong conflicts. Thus the two clubs emerged not in response to demands by different sets of principals, but because of differing interpretations and definitions of moral duty by the NGOs themselves.

This chapter has theoretical and policy implications for the study of voluntary NGO accountability clubs. It shows that contextual factors such as the global accountability culture and a shift in performance expect-ations combined to create a situation where shared beliefs and principles for humanitarian action supported NGOs in overcoming collective action problems to create accountability clubs. As with the foundations studied by Frumkin in this volume (chapter 6), large shifts in how the public and key stakeholders viewed humanitarian agencies changed the agencies' own expectations of themselves and contributed to the belief that they would have to better account for their actions and behavior. Again, like foundations, humanitarian agencies were less subject to the demands of specific principals, but were able to articulate their own vision, principles, and standards by which performance should be judged.

The consequence of the contestation between the two clubs has been the reduced regulatory power of both accountability clubs. The contestation decreases the legitimacy of the accountability standards. Since both accountability clubs rely on noncoercive enforcement of the standards, decreased legitimacy lessens the regulatory power of the clubs. One policy implication is that accountability clubs may not be effective in improving NGO performance or the quality of aid because standards are not easily agreed upon. One way to increase the legitimacy of self-regulatory accountability clubs such as Sphere or COMPAS Qualité is to engage in dialogue aimed at resolving contestation and increasing consensus about these standards.

REFERENCES

Anderson, M. 1996. *Do No Harm: How Aid Can Support Peace or War*. Boulder, CO: Lynne Rienner.
Barnett, M. 2002. *Eyewitness to a Genocide: The United Nations and Rwanda*. Ithaca, NY: Cornell University Press.
Barnett, M. and T. G. Weiss. 2008. Humanitarianism: A Brief History of the Present. In M. Barnett and T. G. Weiss, eds. *Humanitarianism in Question: Politics, Power, Ethics*. Ithaca, NY: Cornell University Press, pp. 1–48.
Barrow, O. and M. Jennings. 2001. Introduction: The Charitable Impulse. In O. Barrow and M. Jennings, eds. *The Charitable Impulse: NGOs and Development in East and North-East Africa*. Bloomfield, CT: Kumarian Press, pp. 1–29.
Borton, J., E. Brusset, and A. Hallam. 1996. *The International Response to Conflict and Genocide: Lessons from the Rwanda Experience: Study 3 Humanitarian Aid and Effects*. London: Overseas Development Institute.
Borton, J. and J. Eriksson. 2004. *Lessons from Rwanda – Lessons for Today: Assessment of the Impact and Influence of Joint Evaluation of Emergency Assistance to Rwanda*. Denmark: Ministry of Foreign Affairs.
Brauman, R. 2000. *L'action humanitaire*. Paris: Flammarion.
Brauman, R. and C. Portevin. 2006. *Penser dans l'urgence: parcours critique d'un humanitaire*. Paris: Editions du Seuil.
Brinkerhoff, D. W. 2004. Accountability and Health Systems: Toward Conceptual Clarity and Policy Relevance. *Health Policy and Planning* 19(6): 371–379.

Brinkerhoff, J. M. and D. W. Brinkerhoff. 2002. Government–Nonprofit Relations in Comparative Perspective: Evolution, Themes and New Directions. *Public Administration and Development* 22: 3–18.

Buchanan-Smith, M. 2003. *How the Sphere Project Came into Being: A Case Study of Policy-Making in the Humanitarian Aid Sector and the Relative Influence of Research*. Overseas Development Institute, Working Paper No. 215, July.

Byrne, T. 1997. *Airlift to Biafra: Breaching the Blockade*. Dublin: The Columba Press.

Calhoun, C. 2008. The Imperative to Reduce Suffering: Charity, Progress and Emergencies in the Field of Humanitarian Action. In M. Barnett and T. G. Weiss, eds. *Humanitarianism in Question: Politics, Power, Ethics*. Ithaca, NY: Cornell University Press, pp. 73–97.

Campbell, D. T. and J. C. Stanley. 1963. *Experimental and Quasi-Experimental Designs for Research*. Boston, MA: Houghton Mifflin Company.

Churchill, W. S. Jr. 1969. Starving Millions Turned away from Relief Camps. *The Times*, June 26.

Dabelstein, N. 1996. Evaluating the International System: Rationale, Process and Management of the Joint Evaluation of the International Response to the Rwanda Genocide. *Disasters* 20(4): 287–294.

Darcy, J. 2004. Locating Responsibility: The Sphere Humanitarian Charter and its Rationale. *Disasters* 28(2): 112–123.

Davis, M. 1975. Audits of International Relief in the Nigerian Civil War: Some Political Perspectives. *International Organization* 29(2): 501–512.

Degionanni, B. 1994. Les ONG se défendant de traîner des pieds pour aider les Rwandais. *Agence France Presse*, July 11.

Department of State. 1969. Department Reviews U.S. Efforts to Aid Victims of the Nigerian Civil War. *Department of State Bulletin* No. 61, August 4.

Dubnick, M. J. and J. B. Justice. 2004. Accounting for Accountability. Paper presented at the Annual Meeting of the American Political Science Association, September 2–5, Chicago.

Duffield, M. 1994. The Political Economy of Internal War: Asset Transfer, Complex Emergencies and International Aid. In J. Macrae and A. Zwi, eds. *War and Hunger: Rethinking International Responses*. London: Zed, pp. 50–69.

Dufour, C., V. de Geoffroy, F. Grünewald, and H. Maury. 2004. Rights, Standards and Quality in a Complex Humanitarian Sphere: Is Sphere the Right Tool? *Disasters* 28(2): 124–141.

Ebrahim, A. 2003. Accountability in Practice: Mechanisms for NGOs. *World Development* 31(5): 813–829.

Edwards, M. and D. Hulme, eds. 1996. *Beyond the Magic Bullet: NGO Performance and Accountability in the Post-Cold War World*. West Hartford, CT: Kumarian Press.

Florini, A. 2003. Business and Global Governance: The Growing Role of Corporate Codes of Conduct. *The Brookings Review* 21(2): 4–8.

Forsyth, F. 1969. *The Biafra Story*. Baltimore, MD: Penguin.

GAO. 2007. The GAO – An Introduction. Accessed via www.gao.gov/about/history/introduction.htm, August 17, 2007.

George, A. and A. Bennett. 2004. *Case Studies and Theory Development in the Social Sciences*. Cambridge, MA: MIT Press.

Grünewald, F., C. Pirotte, and V. de Geoffroy. 2001. Debating Accountability. *Humanitarian Exchange* 19 (September): 35–36.

Hanley, C. J. 1997, Harming Those Who Do Good in the World. *Hobart Mercury* (Australia), January 4.

Independent International Commission on Kosovo. 2000. *Kosovo Report: A Report from the Independent International Commission on Kosovo.* Oxford University Press.

Lewis, D. 2007. *The Management of Non-Governmental Development Organizations,* 2nd edn. London: Routledge.

Lindenberg, M. and C. Bryant. 2001. *Going Global: Transforming Relief and Development NGOs.* Bloomfield, CT: Kumarian Press.

Lloyd, H. G., M. L. Mollerup, and C. A. Bratved. 1973. *The Nordchurchaid Airlift to Biafra 1968–1970: An Operations Report.* Copenhagen: Folkekirkens Nødhjælp.

Lloyd, R. 2005. *The Role of NGO Self-Regulation in Increasing Stakeholder Accountability.* London: OneWorldTrust, pp. 1–16.

Lowrie, S. 2000. Sphere at the End of Phase II. *Humanitarian Exchange* 17 (October): 11–14.

MacDonald, M. 2000. Accountability, Anthropology and the European Commission. In M. Strathern, ed. *Audit Cultures: Anthropological Studies in Accountability, Ethics and the Academy.* London: Routledge, pp. 106–132.

La méthode COMPAS. Accessed via www.compasqualite.org/, August 12, 2008.

Mohr, C. 1968. Johnson Asks Admission of Food into Biafra to Avert Starvation. *The New York Times,* July 12.

Munck, G. 2004. Tools for Qualitative Research. In H. E. Brady and D. Collier, eds. *Rethinking Social Inquiry: Diverse Tools, Shared Standards.* Oxford: Rowman and Littlefield, pp. 105–121.

Naidoo, K. 2004. The End of Blind Faith? Civil Society and the Challenge of Accountability, Legitimacy and Transparency. *AccountAbility Forum* 2, Special Issue on NGO Accountability and Performance: 14–25.

OCHA (United Nations Office for the Coordination of Humanitarian Affairs). 1999. *OCHA Coordination Handbook on Complex Emergencies.* New York: United Nations.

Oxfam. 2000. An End to Forgotten Emergencies. Accessed via www.oxfam.org. uk, November 21, 2008.

Payne, R. A. 2001. Persuasion, Frames and Norm Construction. *European Journal of International Relations* 7(1): 37–61.

Pierson, C. 1991. *Beyond the Welfare State? The New Political Economy of Welfare.* University Park, PA: The Pennsylvania State University Press.

Porter, T. 2000. The Partiality of Humanitarian Assistance – Kosovo in Comparative Perspective. *The Journal of Humanitarian Assistance,* June 17. Accessed via http://jha.ac/2000/06/17/the-partiality-of-humanitarian-assistance-kosovo-in-comparative-perspective/, March 30, 2010.

Red Cross. 2008. *The Fundamental Principles of the Red Cross.* Accessed via www.redcross.org, October 21, 2008.

Rieff, D. 2001. *A Bed for the Night: Humanitarianism in Crisis.* New York: Simon and Schuster.

Salamon, L. 1987. Of Market Failure, Voluntary Failure, and Third-Party Government. *Journal of Voluntary Action Research* 16(1): 29–49.

1994. The Rise of the Nonprofit Sector. *Foreign Affairs* 73(4): 109–122.

Sphere Project. 2004. *Humanitarian Charter and Minimum Standards in Disaster Response.* Geneva: Sphere Project. Accessed via www.sphereproject.org/index.php?option=content&task=view&id=27&Itemid=84, November 24, 2008.

Strathern, M. 2000. New Accountabilities: Anthropological Studies in Audit, Ethics and the Academy. In M. Strathern, ed. *Audit Cultures: Anthropological Studies in Accountability, Ethics and the Academy.* London: Routledge, pp. 1–56.

Terry, F. 2000. The Limits and Risks for Humanitarian Action. *Humanitarian Exchange* 17 (October): 20–21.

2002. *The Paradox of Humanitarian Action: Condemned to Repeat?* Ithaca, NY: Cornell University Press.

Thompson, J. E. 1990. *American Policy and African Famine.* New York: Greenwood Press.

Tong, J. 2004. Questionable Accountability: MSF and Sphere in 2003. *Disasters* 28(2): 176–189.

United States Agency for International Development (USAID). 1969. *Emergency Relief in Nigeria and the Biafran Enclave: July 1967 through June 30, 1969.* Washington, DC: USAID.

Walker, P. and S. Purdin, 2004. Birthing Sphere. *Disasters* 28(2): 100–111.

Waters, K. 2004. Influencing the Message: The Role of Catholic Missionaries in Media Coverage of the Nigerian Civil War. *The Catholic Historical Review* 90(4): 697–718.

Welles, B. 1969. Rogers Confers on Biafra Relief. *The New York Times,* January 23.

Wendt, A. 1987. The Agent–Structure Problem in International Relations Theory. *International Organization* 41(3): 335–370.

1992. Anarchy is What States Make of It: The Social Construction of Power Politics. *International Organization* 46(2): 391–425.

Wheeler, N. J. 2003. The Humanitarian Responsibilities of Sovereignty: Explaining the Development of a New Norm of Military Intervention for Humanitarian Purposes in International Society. In J. M. Welsh, ed. *Humanitarian Intervention and International Relations.* Oxford University Press, pp. 29–51.

Wiles, P., M. Bradbury, M. Buchanan-Smith, *et al.* 2000. *Independent Evaluation of Expenditure of DEC Kosovo Appeal Funds: Phases I and II, April 1999–January 2000,* vol. I. London: Overseas Development Institute and Valid International.

Zarnegar Deloffre, M. 2010 (expected). Defining Standards for Doing Good: NGO Accountability in the Humanitarian Sector. Unpublished PhD dissertation, George Washington University.

Part III

Club design and effectiveness

9 The impact of sponsorship on club standards and design

Angela Bies

This chapter examines the emergence, structure, and design of two non-profit accountability clubs in the state of Minnesota: the Charities Review Council, one of the oldest independent third-party certification programs in the USA, and the Principles and Practices for Nonprofit Excellence program of the Minnesota Council of Nonprofits, an accountability club sponsored by a statewide umbrella association of 1,850 nonprofit organizations. A key difference between the two clubs is the identity of the sponsors: the Charities Review Council (hereafter CRC) is sponsored by an actor who represents nonprofit donors. In contrast, the Minnesota Council of Nonprofits (or MCN) operates as an accountability club sponsored by a statewide nonprofit association. The perspective outlined by Gugerty and Prakash in the introductory chapter of this volume suggests that the accountability challenges nonprofits face can be viewed as agency dilemmas between nonprofits and their stakeholders, or principals. Accountability clubs arise to send signals to key principals about the quality and trustworthiness of the nonprofits that participate (and in some instances, those nonprofits that eschew participation). But the identity of club organizers, or sponsors, and the individual club's institutional context will shape the way in which club design reflects accountability claims, even in the same geographic and nonprofit context. Using a case study approach, this chapter investigates the impact of sponsorship on the emergence, structure, and desired outcomes in two voluntary clubs in Minnesota. The case studies illustrate how both the identity of principals and the accountability milieu in which nonprofits and their principals are embedded affect the manner in which accountability is defined and, consequently, how clubs as institutions respond to these definitions. The CRC and MCN clubs emerged at different time periods and initially exhibited marked differences in structure, participation norms, and desired outcomes that reflected different concerns and accountability demands. Nevertheless, the two clubs share several similarities. Both have emerged and operate in the same accountability domain, the state of Minnesota. Thus, they negotiate a similar regulatory-institutional environment. In addition, the two clubs share similar values which guide their mission and operational policies.

The CRC club is a relatively strong club that includes objective and measurable (although arguably minimal) standards as well as "strong swords" for monitoring and enforcement. In contrast, the MCN club centers on voluntary adherence to a set of expansive but not well-operationalized standards (the *Principles and Practices for Nonprofit Excellence*). It represents a much weaker club according to the typology proposed in the introductory chapter of this volume. But a number of factors present challenges to the strong–weak dichotomy developed in the club framework. The apparently strong CRC club has experienced a number of challenges as the number and diversity of its principals grow over time, as well as significant resource constraints that influence the enforcement and monitoring (and therefore the strength of its branding identity and signal) of club obligations. The MCN club, while seemingly weak and largely symbolic, has developed strong buy-in from member agencies and aligns well with the values and aspirations of its member nonprofits. It also offers added aspects of learning and mechanisms of self-study that may deepen the potential for club effectiveness and reputational benefits. Interestingly, as the chapter shows, the sponsors of each club have interacted in the design of the other, with the result being a coherent, yet resource-constrained, coexistence.

The chapter is organized around time periods that illustrate the changing role of nonprofit principals as well as changes in the nonprofit sector in Minnesota itself, particularly events affecting accountability dynamics. I use a long historical timeline, beginning with CRC's inception in 1946 in the post-World War II construction of institutionalized mechanisms of philanthropy, continuing through the emergence and design of MCN's club during the mid-1990s' accountability upsurge, and concluding with the present-day shift by CRC from a watchdog approach to a voluntary club, and the relative dormancy of the MCN club.

Method and data sources

The case study method was employed to trace the emergence and design of both accountability clubs in relationship to sponsorship. I collected archival data from the Charities Review Council and the Minnesota Council of Nonprofits from the period of the establishment of their accountability clubs (1946 and 1994, respectively). These data were drawn from the organizations directly and from their archival collections, housed at the Social Welfare History Archives of the Elmer Andersen Library at the University of Minnesota for CRC, and at the Minnesota

Historical Society for MCN. Documents examined include the organizations' articles and bylaws, mission statements, annual and financial reports, board meeting minutes, and minutes and other notes directly relating to the establishment and revision of standards and review processes.

I also conducted interviews with the current and all four former directors of the Charities Review Council, three CRC board members especially active in periods of transition for CRC, the founder and current executive director of MCN, and its policy director and board chair at the time of the establishment of MCN's accountability club. The interviews utilized a semi-structured interview protocol, which was developed, in large part, from themes that emerged through the initial review of documents. Such themes included: impetus for formation; key sponsors; conceptualization of vision and purpose of the accountability clubs and resultant program design and standards content; interactions and pressures from other nonprofit support entities (funders, the statewide nonprofit association, and management support centers), the media, and governmental regulators; and change over time. In addition, as then executive director of CRC and member of MCN's Accountability Task Force, I also observed the statewide, consultative process that resulted in the 1997 overhaul of CRC's standards and the 1999 formalization of MCN's accountability club standards, the *Principles and Practices for Nonprofit Excellence*.[1] In the case analysis and comparison that follows, three central goals were pursued: to convey how these two clubs emerged, changed over time, and interacted with each other; to determine how and to what extent CRC and the MCN program exhibit characteristics of nonprofit accountability clubs; and to ascertain the extent to which club theory helps to explain the clubs' differing origins and design aspects.

In both cases the evolution of the clubs responds to environmental demands and opportunities. For example, the formation of CRC by donors and civic leaders in post-World War II reconstruction in Minnesota was spurred on by a desire to "build philanthropy" and structure related institutions. Over time CRC's organizational design changed in response to a changing set of principals and their shifting expectations, namely the professionalization of foundation giving, the expansion and mass-marketing of individual fundraising techniques, and the surge of

---

[1] While my role as participant and observer in these processes provides access and working knowledge of a particular period of this history, there is risk of bias and subjectivity. Efforts to moderate this include careful reliance on archival documents and interview data for triangulation, fact-checking and verification with key informants, and use of objective research assistants for inter-rater reliability of data coding.

accountability expectations and increased interest by nonprofits in the work of CRC. The MCN club was born in the 1990s' nonprofit accountability milieu, which included similar initiatives to develop accountability clubs by other state nonprofit associations. MCN took a largely educational approach in its club standards and design, responding to its nonprofit members' need to understand what accountable behaviors might look like and to provide a set of benchmarks adaptable to members' own organizational situations and values. In this respect, the MCN approach is similar to that taken by the Independent Sector that Young describes in chapter 5 of this volume, as well as the approach of foundation clubs addressed by Frumkin in chapter 6. Moreover, MCN responded both to its members' preferences and to the preferences of the donors and state regulators in two ways. First, the MCN club signals its commitment not just to basic accountability, but to excellence by encompassing CRC's more minimal standards in the expansive MCN club standards. In this sense the MCN standards actually go beyond the baseline standards set in a more principal-driven club. Second, the MCN club signals the willingness of nonprofits to take a collective approach to accountability in Minnesota.

Yet the CRC and MCN clubs differ in key aspects. Differences in sponsorship bring forth divergent club design, particularly in relationship to obligations imposed by the club standards and especially in the monitoring and enforcement rules. Club standards typically are developed in response to the expectations of various nonprofit principals (individual and institutional donors), nonprofits themselves, and communities served by nonprofits (Brown, 2007). The monitoring, enforcement, and information-sharing activities of these clubs serve as mechanisms for nonprofit principals to hold nonprofit organizations to account and to align the interests of the nonprofit agents and their principals (Sloan, 2008). Explicit in the emergence and design of CRC is an attempt to reduce information problems that lead to agency slippages by the setting of club standards, third-party certification, and public provision of certification results. CRC is a strong club from the perspective of the club framework used in this volume; its effectiveness rests on the gold standard (strong swords) of independent monitoring.

In contrast, MCN has an explicit mission to serve its member nonprofits. As such, it is faced with a tension between advocating and policing nonprofits as it defines its accountability role vis-à-vis the expectations and needs of its member principals, a point also made by Tschirhart and Young in chapters 4 and 5 of this volume. MCN took the path of an advocate and formed what can best be described as a weak club, with high standards but essentially no enforcement. Yet implicit in MCN's setting of standards of "excellence" is the acknowledgment that its members and, by extension, the nonprofit sector itself, are concerned about nonprofit quality and seek to become accountable. By shaping accountability norms and expectations for members and signaling the value placed on accountability by members to varied principals, the MCN seeks to serve as an accountability club that signals the high quality of the nonprofit sector in Minnesota as a whole.

Findings and discussion

In this section, I examine the two clubs, with greater attention devoted to the longer, sixty-two-year history of CRC and related accountability shifts in the Minnesota landscape. This is followed by treatment of the salient aspects of the history of the half-century younger MCN club. An analysis of the contemporaneous evolution of the two clubs follows.

An interesting aspect of the two Minnesota clubs relates to their interaction. CRC is one of the few state-level nonprofit watchdog agencies. Interestingly, it emerged independent of any national watchdog agencies. MCN was one of the first state nonprofit associations to develop accountability principles. Subsequently, a number of associations have followed this model, with the Maryland Standards for Excellence being perhaps the best known (see chapter 4 in this volume by Tschirhart for detailed treatment of such clubs). While one might expect that these two clubs would emerge as competing systems, given the different objectives of their sponsors, this is not what has transpired in Minnesota. Contextual pressures (some local, others national in origin) and opportunities led to significant "accountability entrepreneurialism" in the form of two accountability club "firsts" on the state level, and to decisions eventually to "slice" the accountability pie in ways that attempt to address the varied preferences, exchanges, and control mechanisms available to their somewhat overlapping, multiple principals.

The Charities Review Council

Building philanthropy (1946–1960)   The Charities Review Council (originally known as the Minnesota Community Research Council but referred to as CRC throughout for simplicity) was established as a charitable nonprofit in Minnesota in 1946, with its initial sponsor being the Minnesota War Service Fund, Inc., a statewide arm of the National War Fund. The Minnesota War Service Fund, when disbanded, ceded its remaining funds and statewide volunteer infrastructure to the CRC, and formed its initial board of directors comprising business and civic leaders from throughout the state. To illustrate the guiding nature of the Minnesota War Service Fund to Minnesota Community Research Council, it is useful to consider the January 15, 1944 Minnesota War Service Fund Annual Report:

> Between October 18 and December 30, 1943, the people of Minnesota contributed about $5,725,000 in a united appeal for the 17 member agencies of the National War Fund and for state and local agencies concerned with character-building and welfare. Of this amount $2,504,000 was raised for the War Service Fund and $3,221,000 for local agencies … The accompanying report … sets forth in detail the procedure followed in enlisting the 2,937 chairmen and the 40,000 workers, outside the three cities, who volunteered to make the appeal in their communities, and in acquainting the people of the State with the work and needs of the Fund. Its analyses, conclusions, and recommendations will make it very helpful in any future campaign requiring state-wide organization. The success of our campaign was due primarily to the interest, loyalty, and hard work of the country chairmen and their associates. (MWSF, 1944: 2)

From this, CRC began under the auspices of a statewide philanthropic and civic network, with a direct mandate to build philanthropy in Minnesota. The Minnesota War Service Fund operated through a volunteer network of leaders involved in postwar rebuilding efforts, detailed reporting and transparency requirements associated with the War Fund's fundraising efforts, and a system of philanthropy characterized by commitment to processes of "analyses, conclusions, and recommendations."

As the Minnesota War Service Fund's work drew to a close, discussion took place as to how best to continue serving the development of Minnesota's charitable sector. In a June 3, 1946 memo to the directors of the Minneapolis, St. Paul, and Duluth Community Chests (forebears of United Way agencies), W. C. Walsh, state director of the Minnesota War Service Fund, set out the following as the basis for what would eventually become the Minnesota Community Research Council:

> The Trustees of the Minnesota War Service Fund have felt for some time that Minnesota was in need of an organization which would serve not only to protect the giving public from unfair and unwise solicitations but also to conserve the amount of available charitable funds to the end that our local agencies would receive adequate support. It is purposed to set up a representative statewide organization which would function for the following four essential purposes: 1) To investigate contemplated social and charitable money-raising campaigns (except religious or political agencies or organizations) for more than local or county-wide needs, and including campaigns covering gifts-in-kind; 2) To ascertain and indicate the percentage of the National goals for such fund raising campaign that should fairly be allocated to the State of Minnesota; 3) To ascertain by frequent studies the proper distribution by counties of state quotas; and 4) To

use its influence to prevent the over-lapping of money-raising campaigns in the state. (MCRC, 1946)

Upon incorporation, the Minnesota Community Research Council inherited initial funding of $60,000 from the Minnesota War Service Fund. Prominent leaders of the War Fund, representing donor interests, played key roles in the formation of the Council in its early years. J. Cameron Thomson, Chairman of Northwest Bank Corporation and former Chairman of the National War Fund Quota Committee, served as CRC's first board chairperson. W. C. Walsh served as its executive director from 1946 to 1966. Thomson and Walsh believed that Minnesota was expected to contribute a disproportionate share to support national organizations because of the state's history of generous participation in the War Service movement. Consequently, CRC was primarily concerned with establishing and controlling charitable fundraising quotas and reviewing fundraising campaigns in its early years. This preoccupation led to the initial architecture of what would become CRC's orientation to and process of standards-setting and monitoring of charities.

CRC developed standards during this era that were fairly spare in their definition, and required that nonprofits: (1) have a legitimate purpose; (2) have reasonable efficiency of management with an active and responsible governing body; (3) have proper financial controls; and (4) use ethical methods of fundraising. CRC leadership was concerned that "these standards be fair" and explicitly linked them with a desire to promote the growth of Minnesota's charitable sector. In its 1947 *Bulletin*, Chairman Thomson further described the CRC's approach with "the effectiveness of the work" of individual organizations and the charitable sector as a whole. Even at this early stage, CRC's role of gatekeeper, review of fundraising campaigns, and standards oriented toward legitimacy and efficiency are presented as being tantamount to effectiveness.

This era is also associated with CRC's explicit agenda to "build philanthropy" and "trust in civic organizations" in Minnesota and to achieve this throughout "every corner of the state." Between 1946 and 1966, CRC devoted the bulk of its resources to the initiation of more than sixty Community Chests, which later became United Ways. Beginning in the 1950s, CRC served as the review agency for the United Ways. Over time, the United Ways became the primary source of revenue for CRC and its primary sponsor or principal.

Analysis of the establishment and early formation of CRC reveals the presence of strong sponsor influence. The War Services Fund established an orientation toward public reporting and transparency, including fundraising quotas and a related focus on efficiency, the establishment of infrastructure and expansion of organized philanthropy throughout the state, and, in the 1950s, the application of (fairly minimal) accountability standards to nonprofits through review and analytical activities.

CRC as a donor service: nonprofit institutionalization (1960s–early 1980s)   By the mid-1950s, CRC had shifted its focus toward the analysis of nonprofits and fundraising campaigns. In 1961, Minnesota established charity registration laws, but they were not widely followed. By 1967, there were 360 nonprofits registered with the state and a task force was set up by the attorney general to enforce the state's registration laws. The executive director of CRC, Harold Adams (the second director, who joined the Council in 1966), served on the advisory committee of the task force to improve charity law enforcement. During this period, the Council continued to screen budgets of all charities in the state, moving toward a stronger monitoring and enforcement rules system to include the strong sword of "approving or disapproving" them based on their fundraising percentages. Association with the state also offered CRC reputational benefits as a club that served as a complement for government regulation. Aptly, one respondent described CRC's club role as "perceived as quasi-governmental," raising its "expert" status as an accountability club.

This period also marked the development of more formal and detailed CRC Accountability Standards, the expansion of the CRC's review services, and a move to serving a broader range of donors as primary constituents, particularly individuals and the newly expanding field of private and corporate foundations. During this period, there were also several scandals in Minnesota's charitable sector, most notably a fundraising scandal involving the Sister Kenney Institute, an organization serving people with disabilities. Pratt (1999) links this scandal with a brief downturn in philanthropic revenue and the rise of mistrust in charities. The mistrust engendered by this scandal was of concern to the board of CRC, particularly since nonprofit organizations were taking on greater civic duties and their growth strategies centered on increasing donative streams of revenue. This served to heighten the club's perceived utility and drove CRC's move toward a stronger donor service role. These dynamics also explain the move by CRC toward formalization of its enforcement and monitoring rules.

A move toward professionalization of certain segments of the nonprofit sector, notably among larger human service organizations, also increased funding of nonprofits by public agencies. The expansion and related institutionalization of federated nonprofits such as Scouting and other volunteer organizations are associated with this era and help to explain the actions of CRC to expand its volume of reviews for United Ways and private and corporate foundations. Nonprofit scandals and resulting mistrust, the formalization of Minnesota's philanthropic and nonprofit systems, and growth in fundraising demands on the public by nonprofits are cited in CRC's board minutes as the rationale behind the shift in direction. The Accountability Standards became more detailed during this time period, and centered on the following:

- Organizations must have an active and responsible governing body.
- They must have a legitimate purpose and reasonable efficiency of operation.
- They must have an itemized budget with audited accounts, reasonable campaign expenses and be willing to cooperate with other groups.

(CRC, 2001)

Until this point, CRC had received the majority of its funds from Community Chests and United Ways from throughout the state which viewed the CRC's work as promoting ethical fundraising. In the 1970s, the Council began to serve the needs of corporate and private foundations more directly, often providing data summaries and individual charity reviews at the request of institutional funders. In 1972, CRC changed its name from the Minnesota Community Research Council to Minnesota Charities Review Council to reflect its role as a review agency with a stronger system of monitoring and enforcement rules.

CRC also played an active role as "expert" to newly forming foundations and for the media. During this era, several important changes occurred in the realm of charity legislation in the state, most notably a 1970 requirement that charitable organizations register with the state Commerce Department. CRC's executive director again played an active role in the development of these regulatory initiatives.

CRC as watchdog/consumer protection club (later 1980s–1990s)   In the late 1980s, Gary Wolfe took over as CRC's executive director after more than twenty years of service by Harold Adams. Under Wolfe's tenure, the Council made a deliberate shift to strengthen its role as "watchdog," and Wolfe was hired with an explicit mandate for strengthening the consumer (i.e., individual donors) protection dimensions of the agency's processes. Interestingly, several interviewees described this transition in detail and with evocative language, noting the shift from a "bookish," "gray suit," "corporate-serving" CRC culture to a "modern," "information-age" orientation. One respondent said that CRC went from "building philanthropy to protecting it, like in a Clark Kent to Superman-Charity Avenger sort of way." This change in focus can be explained by four interrelated phenomena: the growing institutionalization of nonprofit and philanthropic norms, the ascent of high-stakes fundraising practices characterized by more distant relationships with donors, a general cultural shift toward a view of nonprofits as central to Minnesota's civic life and provision of human services, and the availability of new information technologies to respond to increased information demands on CRC. The selection of a new executive director also allowed CRC to reflect on its strategic position, principally the board's desire for relevancy, CRC's own resource constraints, and demand from a broader range of donors – institutional and individual – for quick and accurate information to help with giving decisions.

Direct marketing techniques were taking hold in Minnesota through sophisticated fundraising campaigns conducted by telephone and mail. Senior citizens became increasingly important consumers of CRC's services as they became a larger market for solicitation of charitable donations, and were a population targeted by unscrupulous fundraisers. A CRC tag line during this era was that CRC "represents the interests of you – the informed donor."

However, CRC also began to experience resource constraints as demand from new stakeholders increased, but revenue streams were in flux. CRC's services to United Ways began to be viewed as duplicative. As United Ways became more professional, they increasingly relied on their own paid staff and local civic panels for agency review and funding allocation decisions. In addition, the United Way of America began to provide some operational oversight and resources for capacity-building in local United Ways. Funding by United Way for nondirect service providers such as the Charities Review Council remained relatively static. To moderate these constraints, in the late 1980s, the Council conducted its first fundraising campaign to gain the support of individual donors for its work. But this expansion of sponsors was undertaken with some hesitation by the board of directors, who worried that CRC would be seen as competing with nonprofits for charitable contributions. Fundraising from individuals was rationalized by CRC's perception that it was doing more for individual donors and these efforts would be beneficial to "ethical and accountable" charities. CRC argued it was responsive to this new category of principal and, thus, worthy of resources and support. CRC began more intentionally to serve and advocate on behalf of the interests of individual donors through the development of educational brochures and a listing of all reviewed charities, thus increasing its signal that it was operating in ways coherent to the preferences and needs of these individual donor sponsors. CRC's board was also adamant that the agency not charge nonprofits for reviews, as they felt this would create a conflict of interest, threaten CRC's independence, and pose negative reputational effects. At this stage, individual donors were clearly conceptualized as the club's primary principal.

It was during this era that the CRC also began to provide summary financial data on nonprofits to donors, particularly comparison data on fundraising and administrative costs versus programmatic expenditures. Respondents noted that this may have reinforced the emphasis on efficiency, perhaps at the expense of larger organizational activities and program effectiveness. The change to this databank approach also reflected changes in information technology, the expectations of donors (perhaps created by CRC's approbation for "informed giving"), and, simply, the growth in numbers of charities registered to operate in Minnesota.

CRC also greatly expanded its status as "charity expert," ramped up its public profile, and not only reinforced but embraced its role as a watchdog by holding regular press conferences to announce egregious violations of its Accountability Standards. It began to serve as the "go-to" organization for information, and emphasized that its information was free and its reviews independent. CRC describes its own work during this era as having "addressed and brought many issues to the public's attention including unethical fundraising practices, inappropriate use of funds, high-pressured telemarketing, inadequate public disclosure, and insufficient governance" (CRC, 2001). Other actors active in the support of the nonprofit sector expressed concern that the Council was setting normative expectations for nonprofit behavior, arguing that it was focused on simplistic efficiency measures at the expense of more complex and particularistic aspects of nonprofit operations, management, and effectiveness. Although nonprofit principals continued to make their preferences known to CRC over the next two decades, CRC remained largely responsive to what it deemed its primary sponsor-principals: institutional and, increasingly, individual donors.

This orientation was reflected in the agency's mission: "The dominant purpose of the MCRC currently is substantiating the validity or integrity of existing funds or charities – a watchdog organization" (MCRC, 1982). Meeting minutes from this era are replete with references to community policing, protecting donors, and strengthening legislation to protect consumers. In this era CRC became a full-fledged watchdog agency, with a consumer protection focus operationalized through data provision, monitoring, and advocating for greater accountability and regulation of nonprofits. Yet even as ambitions to protect consumers grew, the CRC's resource constraints were heightened as the number of nonprofits grew and the discourse on what constitutes appropriate nonprofit behavior became more complex. In addition, potential substitutes for CRC began to emerge, as the state increased resources to the Charities Division, subfield accreditation activities provided greater depth, specificity, and monitoring, external auditing and evaluation firms grew in the market-place, and the state nonprofit association, the Minnesota Council of Nonprofits, formed a task force in the early 1990s to look at ways that it, too, could promote accountability.

Consumer education and nonprofit capacity (1993–2008) The years 1993–2002 brought significant change and three new executive directors to the helm of the Charities Review Council. Resource con-straints, growth in the numbers of nonprofits operating in Minnesota, and demand for services all grew during this era. CRC was also affected by the national United Way scandal, which, coupled with ongoing con-cerns about mass fundraising techniques, added to demand for its services.

In the early 1990s, CRC expanded its consumer education role, a design shift intended to extend CRC's work to protect individual donors. Research staff grew modestly, and consumer education became the end game for CRC's data analysis, review work, and public information pieces. CRC took on several prominent campaigns to educate donors about protection from fraudulent fundraising practices, produced reports on topics such as unethical practices in the international child relief industry and consumer fraud protection for senior citizen donors, and initiated a *Giving Guide* featuring a summary of reviewed charities. The *Giving Guide* represented a tacit endorsement of reviewed charities, which may have strengthened the club brand without any change in the strin-gency of the club standards.

CRC's work, internally and externally, was also affected by public demands that Minnesota nonprofits become more responsive to a broader and more culturally diverse population and to develop an out-comes orientation involving additional reporting on effectiveness and results. CRC's board began to be more introspective about the costs that reporting was imposing on nonprofits, given the levels of organiza-tional capacity and the potential burdens of competing evaluation requirements, especially during the economic downturn at the beginning of the 1990s. It was during this time that CRC first invited a nonprofit executive director to sit on its board of directors. This move was intended to signal a shift in CRC's orientation to nonprofits to be more inclusive and cooperative. Minutes during this time also reveal additional discus-sion about the appropriateness of current club standards. One board member described how CRC "began to recognize the limitations of its Accountability Standards. Yet it had trouble moving beyond a stance of objectivity. It was a situation of measuring what was measurable, not necessarily what or all that mattered. And the board began to recognize this." This discussion highlights how CRC began to wrestle with one of the key tensions facing accountability clubs: whether expanding and strengthening standards or shoring up monitoring and enforcement mechanisms (or some combination thereof) is the most effective way to promote nonprofit accountability and effectiveness. This tension was the primary driver of the comprehensive review of its operations that CRC undertook over the next decade. The comprehensive and consultative process described below brought a broader range of constituents' voices and perspectives to the table, but also complicated the agency's choices. While the CRC wanted to remain the premier evaluator of nonprofit quality, it also faced increasing resource constraints and a greater range of voices as nonprofit organizations played a larger role in the debate over accountability and standards.

Until 1997, CRC's monitoring and enforcement process focused mainly on tracking the number and nature of inquiries from the public, donors, and the media regarding the operations of nonprofit organizations, and initiating reviews based on public interest and, at times, public concern. In 1997, as CRC tried to be more responsive to nonprofits as a core constituency, it began carrying out reviews at the request of individual nonprofit organizations, but refrained from charging a fee for such services. The review and monitoring process involved CRC research staff gathering information on nonprofit organizations operating in Minnesota from data compiled from the attorney general's office, various donors, and the nonprofit itself to determine compliance with the CRC's Accountability Standards. CRC's monitoring and enforcement procedures were designed to foster due process and consistency of application. During this time several key nonprofit infrastructure heads, including the heads of the Minnesota Council of Nonprofits and the Minnesota Council on Foundations (a statewide association of private foundations), held seats on CRC's board of directors and arguably influenced a broader conceptualization of stakeholders and a more consultative relationship with the nonprofit sector.

In 1996–1997, CRC undertook a large-scale process to study and revise its Accountability Standards. First it created a "Donors' Jury" to understand the information needs of individual and institutional donors, which resulted in an initial draft set of Accountability Standards. Second, the Council convened a series of focus groups statewide with nonprofit staff members and boards to refine the proposed standards. The revised Accountability Standards that resulted from this process addressed four areas of management practice: public disclosure, governance, financial activity, and fundraising.[2] The standards also expanded to include more detailed governance standards and measures of internal consistency with mission standards (as a proxy for organizational effectiveness). The sixteen club standards were adopted in 1997 and are used today in the nonprofit-driven "Accountability Wizard" self-study program, described in greater detail below.

These standards included more detail, a more transparent set of guidelines for what the review process entailed, and a philosophy and set of related rationales for each Accountability Standard. Interestingly, for several standards the rationale was essentially a normative argument with limited data to support a link between the club standard and improved nonprofit accountability or donor support. CRC described its Accountability Standards as "indicators of effective, ethical and accountable management practices," even as CRC board and staff leadership continued privately to wrestle with the effects of its Accountability Standards and the logic of the review process model.

The issue of adding organizational effectiveness criteria had surfaced during the public deliberations and internal board examinations in the development of the 1997 standards. A staff respondent affiliated with CRC at the time indicated that "much of the accountability discussion in the practitioner literature and in various discussion groups indicated that many focus on financial accountability to the exclusion of other measures, such as effectiveness." CRC was concerned, not only about repeated calls for effectiveness criteria, but also by the possibility that its constituents, particularly individual donors, perceived that the club's standards actually measured organizational effectiveness. Even after extensive deliberation, the club's standards remained oriented toward efficiency and transparency criteria and did not overtly address issues of organizational effectiveness.

Even in the face of resource constraints, CRC remained unwilling to accept fees from nonprofits. These resource constraints also created a tension about whether and how to partner with what was then National Charities Information Bureau (NCIB) or Better Business's Philanthropic Advisory Service (now since merged into a single, national watchdog agency, operating under the auspices of the Better Business Bureau (BBB)). A decision was made to focus review efforts on Minnesota nonprofits, referring donors to national resources for large national charities, and reviewing national nonprofits only if they were engaged in large-scale fundraising in Minnesota. These efforts were stymied by the

---

[2] See www.crcmn.org/standards/index.htm for a full listing of the Council's Accountability Standards which includes background information on the philosophy underlying each standard.

eventual merger of the NCIB and BBB, and for several years CRC continued to try to review national organizations while taking requests from Minnesota-based nonprofits for review, further exacerbating awareness of its resource constraints. This period reflected a mixed orientation toward its principals, with CRC expressing a desire to "be a friend to nonprofits, a 'good cop' of sorts, a kind of community police model. Yet we couldn't quite escape the moniker of 'watchdog', but we were uncomfortable with it." It also highlighted the problem of resources and capacity, as CRC was not able to maintain the volume of reviews necessary to keep pace with demand for information from donors and interest in review by Minnesota nonprofits.

After this period of reflection and self-study, in 1999, Charities Review Council described itself as an independent nonprofit organization founded by citizens with a mission "to promote informed giving by donors who support charities that solicit funds in Minnesota" and further, CRC stated in its 1999 mission statement that it "exercises its mission by developing a set of 'Accountability Standards', reviewing nonprofits against the standards, and making the results of the reviews available to the public" (CRC, 1999: 1). From 1999 to 2005, CRC defined its key stakeholders as citizens, members of the media, researchers, nonprofit organizations, and individual and institutional donors, and its services as "individual, in-depth reports on some 300 nonprofit organizations; a database of nearly 7,000 nonprofits registered to solicit in the state of Minnesota with information derived from public and secondary data sources; educational activities such as training seminars related to nonprofit accountability issues; publications including a periodic *Giving Guide* which lists the results of the Council's reviews; and customized information services" (compilation of statistics from CRC annual reports from the period). Although CRC had a broad base of revenue from individuals, United Ways, corporations, and foundations, it continued to struggle with resource constraints. It launched a three-year capacity-building campaign to increase operating support from corporations and foundations, and was able to expand its research staff under its executive director, Rich Cowles, whose tenure began in 2000. At this stage, CRC had a well-developed but still minimal set of club standards, based on broad input and buy-in. The dilemma of how to address issues of effectiveness was left unresolved, however, as the issue was deemed a measurement morass. The dilemma was mitigated in part by the initiation of more expansive club standards developed by the accountability club of Minnesota's state nonprofit association, discussed below. Yet as CRC embarked on training and dissemination of its new club standards, it would continue to face the dilemma of sustainability and defining a meaningful scope of services.

Emergence and design of the MCN club (1994-present)

As noted above, an interesting characteristic of Minnesota's recent nonprofit landscape centers on the degree of cooperation and consistency that exists between the CRC club and a standards-setting initiative by the Minnesota Council of Nonprofits, emerging in 1994 and taking hold in 1999. MCN was founded in 1987 to inform, promote, and strengthen individual nonprofits in Minnesota. In 1994, the executive director of MCN, who had previously served on CRC's board and recently returned from a sabbatical to Harvard, was keenly aware of the national pulse toward nonprofit accountability and the competing and overlapping pressures faced by nonprofit organizations, MCN's primary constituency. MCN was in the process of expanding its membership base, developing an enhanced slate of services for member nonprofits, increasing its advocacy and research role, and strengthening relationships with Minnesota foundations. MCN's leadership described its nonprofit members as "expressing both a desire to be more accountable and fatigue from narrow and inexpedient accountability requirements."

MCN organized a cross-section of nonprofit and philanthropic leaders to study a potential role for MCN in the accountability milieu. It developed an initial set of standards in 1994, and "became the first state association of nonprofits to develop a set of accountability principles and management practices." There was significant pushback from Minnesota nonprofits, who worried that more inefficiencies and reporting burdens would be introduced into a rapidly expanding universe of evaluation, outcome, and performance reporting requirements. In fact, the MCN executive director observed that the MCN standards ended up in an article in the *Chronicle of Philanthropy* noting the reluctance of Minnesota nonprofits to have the statewide nonprofit association (i.e., MCN) play such an accountability standard-bearer role, especially in light of extant requirements and the established (although not universally endorsed) watchdog role of the CRC.

During 1997–1998, MCN engaged in a new, more consultative process to examine whether and how to push for nonprofits to adopt and use the accountability principles. Should MCN move into the business of monitoring and enforcement? Should it leave that up to CRC, where monitoring was more robust but club standards unsatisfactory because of their minimal nature? This process involved the then executive director of CRC, and paralleled CRC's extensive consultative study and adoption of new standards. The 2007 CRC board chair, a nonprofit executive himself, served as the chairperson of this 1997–1998 MCN Accountability Task Force. This task force worked together to expand the 1994 work, to create and issue in 2005 the Minnesota Council of

Nonprofits' *Principles and Practices*, which incorporated the CRC's Accountability Standards and also extended beyond them.

The task force and subsequent consultative process defined three key issues: MCN's *Principles and Practices* explicitly speaks to the pluralistic accountability needs and goals of its diverse nonprofit constituents; *Principles and Practices* explicitly addresses issues of mission and effectiveness; and MCN decided that it could not simultaneously be both reviewer of nonprofits and advocate for them. In the preface to the *Principles and Practices for Nonprofit Excellence*, the following points are emphasized:

1. The principles are based on fundamental values of quality, responsibility, and accountability.
2. The ten characteristic accountability principles distinguish the nonprofit sector from government and the business sector. The 133 management practices provide specific guidelines for individual organizations to evaluate and improve their operations, governance, human resources, advocacy, financial management, and fundraising.
3. The Principles have the following purposes: to provide individual organizations striving for excellence with a tool for strategic planning and operational evaluation relative to the rest of the nonprofit sector; to support the growth and quality of the sector; and to increase public understanding of the role and contributions of the nonprofit sector.

(MCN, Principles Introduction, 1998)

The *Principles and Practices* are set out in a twenty-four-page document that outlines the ten principles of nonprofit activity and provides detailed standards or practices for achieving each principle. These practices are characterized in one of two ways: legally mandated by state or federal law and "highly recommended" by the MCN. In this way, the MCN accountability principles help establish the "beyond compliance" standards that might signal quality to external principals, whom MCN calls "constituents." These relatively strong standards, however, are not accompanied by any "sword." MCN members are not even required to endorse these principles. The decision by MCN not to take on an assessment and monitoring role helped to clarify the respective domains of CRC's review and watchdog role (and its primary orientation as an advocate for donors, e.g., its club members) and MCN's primary accountability role as member advocate (e.g., nonprofits as its primary accountability club members). This decision by MCN runs contrary to the expansion that the Maryland Council of Nonprofits took, as witnessed in Maryland's expansion and franchising of its accountability program (see chapter 4 by Tschirhart in this volume).

To ensure that the principles were actively espoused and used by member organizations, MCN undertook a period of education on accountability, and continues to cooperate with CRC and other nonprofit infrastructure organizations on training and capacity-building relating to accountability. Critics argue that the MCN *Principles and Practices* approach has been largely symbolic. MCN's own language regarding the Principles speaks to the symbolic and political nature of setting accountability standards: "Given the blurring of the lines between the three sectors of the economy and the enormous growth of the nonprofit sector, this document is designed to support the effective functioning of our sector by recommending specific best practices" (MCN, 1998). While MCN claims that "The *Principles and Practices for Nonprofit Excellence* are not meant for use by funders or government to evaluate nonprofit organizations, nor are they intended as a substitute for the wisdom of directors or trustees of individual organizations" (MCN, 1998), others, among both MCN and CRC respondents, counter that the Principles have provided balance and complement to the narrow and minimal Accountability Standards of CRC. Table 9.1 provides a general summary of the club standards and Table 9.2 summarizes the path of club emergence traced here.

Complementary clubs?

Despite all the efforts on the part of both CRC and MCN to develop broadly acceptable club standards, a number of concerns remain, related to both the robustness of the club standards and the accountability models employed by the two accountability clubs as they share an accountability space. Bies (2002), for example, reports that 71 percent of participating nonprofits expressed disagreement with the proposition that CRC should add effectiveness criteria to its standards. But the pressures and desire for standards relating to effectiveness remained. Several nonprofits designated specific effectiveness criteria that should be added to the CRC's standards in such areas as outcomes, entrepreneurship, and pluralism. It was suggested that CRC, and similar review agencies, might need to define effectiveness criteria and then conduct further research, perhaps exploring feedback on several "scenarios" for how effectiveness could be reviewed. The expansive MCN standards served as a start for defining effectiveness, but without any real swords or incentives for implementation.

The demand from donors for more data on nonprofit operations, and the demand by many nonprofits for "certification," led CRC in 2005 to introduce the "Accountability Wizard" program, an online self-certification model. The Wizard was designed to "open up the charity review process to all nonprofits operating in Minnesota. The streamlined system allows us to shift the focus of our charity review role from judge to educator and helper. The Wizard is a self-assessment tool that measures an organization's performance in four critical areas: Public Disclosure, Governance, Financial

Table 9.1 *Comparison: club standards content*

Club	Time period	Standards
Charities Review Council	1946–1960	No explicit baseline. Standards oriented toward legitimacy and efficiency, and required nonprofits to have: (1) legitimate purpose; (2) reasonable efficiency of management with an active and responsible governing body; (3) proper financial controls; and (4) ethical methods of fundraising.
	1960s–early 1980s	Expansion of above to include approval or disapproval based on fundraising percentages, and requirements of nonprofits to have a reasonable efficiency of operation (i.e., 70 percent or more on "mission-related activities"), an itemized budget with audited accounts, reasonable campaign expenses, and demonstration of a willingness to cooperate with other groups.
	Later 1980s–1993	Similar to above, but expansion of content areas to include basic legal (registration and annual reporting). Financial standards also became more stringent to include required audits for nonprofits of a certain size, approbation of recurring deficits and accumulation of "excessive" net assets. Fundraising standards were explicit about coercive practices, honesty, and truthfulness in fundraising activities.
	1993–2008	Expanded to include public disclosure, governance, financial activity, fundraising, more detailed governance standards, and internal consistency with mission standards (as a proxy for organizational effectiveness). Introduction of a statement of philosophy and set of related rationales for each Accountability Standard. Accountability Standards described as "indicators of effective, ethical and accountable management practices."
MCN Club (*Principles and Practices for Nonprofit Excellence* program)	1994, initiation; 1998, establishment	Incorporate but extends beyond the CRC's Accountability Standards. Articulates ten characteristic accountability principles that distinguish the nonprofit sector from government and the business sector. Offers 133 management practices that provide specific guidelines for individual organizations to evaluate and improve their operations, governance, human resources, advocacy, financial management, and fundraising.

Table 9.2 *Comparison of accountability club emergence and design*

Club	Time period	Issues in nonprofit context	Sponsor(s)	Club type	Standards	Participation	Monitoring and enforcement rules
Charities Review Council	1946–1960	Building philanthropy and civic participation	Civic leaders, institutional donors, esp. United Ways	Certification club	Moderate	Mandatory (as a condition for United Way funding consideration)	Third-party certification; private provision of results
	1960s–early 1980s	Institutionalization of philanthropy and nonprofit sector; start of state charity registration	Corporate and private foundations	Certification club	Strong (focus on efficiency)	Quasi-mandatory on complaints basis	Third-party certification; public provision of results
	Later 1980s–1993	Mass fundraising appeals, weak state regulation, expansion of information technology	Individual donors, corporate and private foundations	Certification club	Strong (focus on efficiency)	Quasi-mandatory on complaints basis	Third-party certification; public provision of results
	1993–2008	Consumer protection and donor education; heightened accountability, evaluation, effectiveness, and capacity concerns	Individual donors, corporate and private foundations, nonprofits	Certification club	Strong (focus on efficiency plus learning)	Quasi-mandatory on complaints basis; voluntary from 2005 onward	Hybrid: Third-party certification and self-study; public and private provision of results; training and capacity-building resources provided as positive sword
MCN Club (Principles and Practices for Nonprofit Excellence program)	1994, initiation; 1998, establishment	Heightened accountability concerns, outcome evaluation push, effectiveness, and capacity concerns	Statewide nonprofit association; nonprofits	Minimal club	Weak (i.e., expansive, but not operationalized); Focused on excellence	Voluntary	None, aside from normative pressure to conform; some training and capacity-building resources provided

Activity and Fundraising" (CRC, 2008a). The Wizard is a voluntary, fee-based program in which charities sign up to provide information in the areas specified by the CRC. The CRC vets this information and if it deems the charity meets all standards, it issues a "Meets Standards" seal. The online system consists of an information portal and exchange that facilitates the provision of this information. CRC continues to pursue its traditional non-voluntary review process based on the scope of an organization's fundraising activity in Minnesota and on complaints, but these reviews occur far less regularly than in the past. CRC seems to be walking the line between acting as a watchdog for consumers (reducing information asymmetries) and as arbiter of quality (moderating moral hazard) and supporter of nonprofits.

The CRC has also spruced up its public communications and image to appeal to younger donors and web users, and to do so with greater cost savings and larger information impact. Referring to its web-based offerings as the "Smart Givers Web Site," CRC promises to "makes nonprofit information easily accessible to donors. Through the online searchable Giving Guide, users can search for organizations by name or category. Users can also research reviewed organizations' mission and programs at the online searchable Giving Guide, so they can be sure of what their money supports." The Smart Givers Web Site also features online resources for searching donations of goods, such as autos, and other noncash items, and has featured information pieces on timely issues such as donations for disaster relief. It also allows for users to establish personalized "Smart Givers accounts," which allow users to select among a set of giving and information preferences as well as to receive related periodic updates.

The CRC also continues its focus on institutional donors, stating "Grantmakers are an important element of the Smart Givers Network. We value your efforts to promote public trust in the nonprofit sector" (CRC, 2008a: 1). CRC has also developed tools for due process evaluation by foundations, including tools to foster sustainability for foundation grantees, to track monitored nonprofits, and to help nonprofits share resources with constituents, such as board members and employees. CRC continues to receive operating support from a fairly broad range of corporate and private foundations, suggesting that these entities remain important club principals.

MCN is publicly supportive of the Accountability Wizard approach, providing website links to CRC, the Accountability Standards, and the CRC online *Giving Guide*, an educational resource to help donors to understand the IRS Form 990. MCN also participates in the Accountability Wizard and displays on its website the CRC's "Meets Standards" seal. MCN's current executive director notes that it is useful to be able to refer donors to CRC, as MCN does not want to open itself up to internal conflict by evaluating its members and perhaps seeming to give preference to some over others. He also points out how MCN continues to find it useful to be able to refer to the external standards of CRC, particularly when there is an accountability scandal that might negatively affect perceptions of nonprofits. MCN can also point to its own *Principles and Practices*, which provide guidance for "nonprofits striving for excellence" and also help to define to the public and to donors what it means to be a nonprofit.

CRC and MCN also consistently collaborate on educational initiatives related to nonprofit accountability. The leaders of MCN and CRC initiated the Minnesota Nonprofit Accountability Collaborative, a working committee designed to strengthen the integrity of IRS 990 reporting. The committee consists of the leaders from the two agencies, as well as the Office of the Minnesota Attorney General, the Management Assistance Program for Nonprofits (a Minnesota-based management support center), the Minnesota Society of Certified Public Accountants, and the Internal Revenue Service.

In recent years, MCN has begun to focus more intensively on enhancing the capacity and effectiveness of the nonprofit sector in Minnesota, and on expanding the diversity of programs it provides to its nonprofit members, which now include conducting ongoing economic, employment, and giving research, convening a large and successful annual meeting, developing a range of operational and capacity-related training, and supporting a robust policy agenda. While accountability is implicit in this work, it has taken a backseat, rendering the MCN principles largely dormant as an accountability signaling mechanism. The *Principles*, however, continue to have an important educational function.

At the same time, CRC has expanded the number of reviews accommodated through the Wizard model, developed a rich set of educational resources, better dispatched staff resources for research and dissemination on key accountability issues, developed analytic tools for foundations, and attracted a modest revenue stream from nonprofit review fees and underwriting of such reviews by Minnesota donors. While the CRC club standards remain relatively lenient, the monitoring and enforcement swords and incentives have been strengthened. With the shared resource in the MCN *Principles and Practices* and the expanded monitoring swords and incentives of the CRC, executives from both agencies characterize the current scenario as highly functional. Despite this seeming functionality and numerous complementarities, at the start of 2009, CRC embarked on a periodic review of its Accountability Standards, a process which will be broadly consultative and representative of CRC's multiple principals. CRC executive director, Richard Cowles, describes the previous

Accountability Standards as "enduring," yet both CRC and MCN recognize the siren call of accountability as nonprofits must provide critical services in a period of significant economic contraction. How each club defines its primary sponsors in this shifting accountability and nonprofit capacity milieu – including the two clubs' perceptions of each other as a principal – promise to shape emergent club design and strategy. Greater polarization of roles may emerge around the competing sponsor expectations of the functions of watchdog (signals of trustworthiness and legitimacy through donor protection and informed giving conceptions) and nonprofit advocacy (signaling industry trade functions, with attention to capacity needs and effectiveness enhancement).

Conclusions

This chapter describes the development of two accountability clubs in the state of Minnesota, a relatively strong club sponsored by the Charities Review Council, and a relatively weak club sponsored by the Minnesota Council of Nonprofits. The comparative analysis suggested that the distinction between strong and weak clubs is complicated by a number of features. The apparent strength of the CRC club masks a complex institutional evolution. As the mix of nonprofit donors in Minnesota changed, the information signal that the club needed to provide changed as well, with different donors desiring different types of information. The ultimate result is a club with strong monitoring and enforcement but only moderately strong standards. The CRC's brand identity as the protector of donor interests led to a focus on information provision in the CRC, but the club may oversell the stringency of its standards and their ability to affect future nonprofit behavior.

The MCN club incorporates strong standards but with quite weak enforcement. This club reflects the values and interests of its members. It also provides a tool for members to judge their own quality and invests in club strength through related training and education activities. Moreover, the formation of the MCN club may have sent an important signal to donors and to CRC at a time when accountability concerns were heightened in Minnesota. This chapter demonstrates how the interaction between the two clubs informs the design of each. As the CRC club came under criticism for not addressing nonprofit effectiveness, the MCN developed principles that included effectiveness criteria. As donors demand more and higher quality nonprofit data and the MCN principles were criticized as largely symbolic, the CRC began to develop its online Accountability Wizard, which included verification mechanisms and greatly increased CRC's ability to provide information to donors. Thus a key finding of the chapter is that the sponsors of both clubs interacted in the design of the other, resulting in a division of the accountability landscape in Minnesota. This chapter also demonstrates how the articulation of accountability demands by key nonprofit principals is itself fluid and shaped by definitions of accountability that develop in the public sphere in response to the evolution of the nonprofit sector. The long timeline of the CRC case shows how changes in the structure and role of the nonprofit sector shift the definitions of accountability made by key nonprofit principals.

As in the cases discussed in the contributions of Young (chapter 5) and Frumkin (chapter 6) in this volume, a key motivation for the development of nonprofit clubs in Minnesota was the desire to professionalize the nonprofit field, and the definitions of accountability that emerged took place with these concerns in mind. In Minnesota, unlike in the other cases, however, the original concerns with accountability were mounted, not by a nonprofit membership association, but by a donor-driven association with a "watchdog" orientation. Not surprisingly, in this context the nonprofit membership association that developed, the MCN, took the accountability challenge seriously from the start, in part because it was responding to accountability initiatives from the CRC, and in part because it was responding to pressures on its member nonprofits from their donor principals for increased accountability. Thus the standards and principles developed by MCN were more detailed from the start than those developed by most state-level nonprofit associations, as discussed by Tschirhart in this volume (chapter 4), or those developed by the infrastructure associations discussed by Young and Frumkin. Like the humanitarian agencies discussed by Zarnegar Deloffre (chapter 8), MCN took a stance in favor of nonprofit autonomy and explicitly worked to carve out a niche for a set of standards aimed at education and learning. This was likely facilitated by an environment that already has a strong club run by a "watchdog" agency available for those nonprofits who wanted it. Unlike in the humanitarian sector, the accountability clubs in Minnesota have developed not in opposition to each other, but in tandem, with significant cooperation. The "carving up" of the accountability landscape in Minnesota is an interesting phenomenon and makes Minnesota an accountability "leader" among US states. It remains to be seen, however, what effect these clubs have on nonprofit accountability and effectiveness in the state, and at what cost to the organizations themselves.

REFERENCES

Bies, A. 2002. Accountability, Organizational Capacity and Continuous Improvement: Findings from Minnesota's Nonprofit Sector. In P. Barber, ed., *New Directions in Philanthropy*. Thousand Oaks, CA: Sage.

Brody, E. 2002. Accountability and Public Trust. In L. Salomon, ed., *The State of America's Nonprofit Sector*. Washington, DC: Brookings Institution and Aspen Institute.

Brown, D. 2007. Multiparty Social Action and Mutual Accountability. In A. Ebrahim and E. Weisband, eds., *Global Accountabilities: Participation, Pluralism, and Public Ethics*. Cambridge University Press, pp. 89–111.

Charities Review Council (CRC). 1999. *1999 Annual Report and History to Constituents*. St. Paul, MN: Charities Review Council.

　2001. History. In *2001 Annual Report*. St. Paul, MN: Charities Review Council.

　2008a. *Grantmaker Tools*. St. Paul, MN: Charities Review Council.

　2008b. *Report of Findings of a Survey of Minnesotans' Charitable Giving Habits and Perceptions of Charitable Organization*. St. Paul, MN: Charities Review Council.

Independent Sector. 2000. *Why Should Independent Sector Focus on Accountability?* Washington, DC: Independent Sector.

Kearns, K. 1994. The Strategic Management of Accountability in Nonprofit Organizations: An Analytical Framework. *Public Administration Review* 54 (2): 185–192.

Light, P. C. 2000. *Making Nonprofits Work*. Washington, DC: Brookings Institution.

Minnesota Charities Review Council (MCRC). 1982. *Annual Report*. Box Two, Minnesota Charities Review Council, Social Welfare History Archives, University of Minnesota.

Minnesota Community Research Council (MCRC). 1946. *June 3, 1946 Memo to the Directors of the Minneapolis, St. Paul, and Duluth Chests, from W.C. Walsh, State Director of the Minnesota War Service Fund*. Box One, MN War Funds Board of Trustee Minutes, 1943–1946, Minnesota Charities Review Council, Social Welfare History Archives, University of Minnesota.

　1947. *Bulletin, 1, 1*. Box One, MN War Funds Board of Trustee Minutes, 1943–1946, Minnesota Charities Review Council, Social Welfare History Archives, University of Minnesota.

Minnesota Council of Nonprofits (MCN). 1998. *Principles and Practices for Nonprofit Excellence*. St. Paul, MN: MCN.

Minnesota War Service Fund (MWSF). 1944. *Report on 1943 Campaign*. Box One, MN War Funds Board of Trustee Minutes, 1943–1946, Minnesota Charities Review Council, Social Welfare History Archives, University of Minnesota.

Naidoo, K. 2004. Coming Clean: Civil Society Organisations at a Time of Global Uncertainty. *International Journal of Not-for-Profit Law* 6(3): 1–3.

Najam, A. 1996. NGO Accountability: A Conceptual Framework. *Development Policy Review* 14: 339–353.

Pratt, J. 1999. The Case of Minnesota: Institutionalizing Public Spirit. In E. Clotfelter and T. Ehrlich, eds. *Philanthropy and the Nonprofit Sector in a Changing America*. Bloomington, IN: Indiana University Press.

Sloan, M. 2008. The Effects of Nonprofit Accountability Ratings on Donor Behavior. *Nonprofit and Voluntary Sector Quarterly*, May. Accessed via http://nvsq.sagepub.com, hosted at http://online.sagepub.com.

10   The emergence and design of NGO clubs in Africa

Mary Kay Gugerty

Challenges to nonprofit and nongovernmental organization (NGO) accountability are particularly acute in sub-Saharan Africa (hereafter Africa), a region often characterized by illiberal democratic governance, weak mechanisms of regulatory oversight, and nascent civil societies.[1] The combination of political liberalization and increased donor funding of nonprofits throughout the 1990s sparked a dramatic increase in the number of NGOs operating in most countries in Africa. In Kenya the estimated number of NGOs registered with the government grew from fewer than 500 in 1990 (Ndegwa, 1996) to nearly 3,200 in 2004 (National Council of NGOs, 2003). As a result of this growth, governments in Africa found themselves increasingly dependent on NGOs for the provision of key public services, but with few regulatory or coordination mechanisms at their disposal to influence or oversee the activities of these organizations (Barr *et al.*, 2005). Donors also found it increasingly difficult to assess the capabilities and potential of the many newly emerging organizations. The need for standard-setting and oversight was underscored throughout this period by the periodic eruption of high-profile nonprofit scandals that began to challenge the reputation and credibility of legitimate organizations (Kwesiga and Namisi, 2006; Gibbelman and Gelman, 2004; Naidoo, 2004). These scandals emphasized to donors, governments, and NGOs themselves the need for stronger standard-setting and credentialing mechanisms for the sector.

Efforts to develop voluntary NGO accountability programs in Africa have flourished, a somewhat surprising development in a region not often noted for the strength of its institutions. This chapter explores the factors underlying the emergence, design, and effectiveness of NGO accountability clubs in Africa using cross-national data from twenty-two countries in sub-Saharan Africa over the period 1990 to 2008, as well as seven shorter comparative case studies. The cross-national analysis shows how

---

[1] This chapter uses the terms nonprofit and NGO interchangeably, but NGO is used most frequently as it is the term most commonly employed in Africa.

clubs in Africa typically emerge in response to proposed changes in the regulatory environment by governments. The country case studies trace the emergence of clubs in seven national contexts, and show how the threat of new regulation interacts with the nature of club sponsorship in important ways. The chapter first lays out key features of the NGO accountability landscape and context in sub-Saharan Africa, then examines the cross-national and case study data on club emergence.

NGO accountability concerns in Africa

The NGO accountability context in Africa differs from industrialized country contexts in several respects, all of which suggest that accountability and oversight issues will be highly salient and particularly challenging. Unlike most charitable organizations in industrialized societies, African NGOs do not typically attract funds locally; rather, the bulk of NGO funding comes from international donors and NGOs. NGO principals are therefore quite distant from NGOs in many cases, creating particularly large information asymmetries. Those at most financial risk from corruption and mismanagement in NGOs are international donors, rather than the public or individual donors (although the public obviously stands to lose if services are not delivered). International funding, combined with high levels of unemployment in many countries, gives individual entrepreneurs, or "development brokers," the incentive to start NGOs as a means of employment, rather than as a means to serve the public good (Platteau and Gaspart, 2003). In addition, the legal status of NGOs in many African countries is precarious and the statutes governing the registration and operation of NGOs are often unclear or outdated (Armstrong, 2006). Thus, even if the nondistribution constraint were a sufficient check on managerial discretion, it is unlikely to be fully understood, binding, or enforceable in the African context. All these reasons suggest a strong rationale for donors to value credible signals of nonprofit quality and legitimacy.

The nature of the relationship between NGOs and governments in Africa further complicates issues of NGO accountability and oversight. Until relatively recently most NGO–government relationships have been characterized by a large amount of distrust, co-optation, and outright repression. NGO operations in many countries were often viewed by governments as a form of opposition (Fisher, 1997; Bratton, 1989). As many African countries experienced political liberalization throughout the 1990s, however, civil society organizations proliferated, easily outstripping the ability of governments to regulate them (Batley, 2006). Governments, often in the midst of fundamental transformations themselves, struggled to manage their relationships with nonprofits, often operating with laws dating back to the colonial period. During the 1990s and early 2000s, a number of governments therefore sought to update the legislation governing the operation of nonprofits, often with the goal of consolidating government control over the sector. Such legislation has been enacted in Kenya, Malawi, Tanzania, and Uganda, among other countries. Not surprisingly, many of these attempts at increased regulation were highly contested by NGOs. In the early years of political liberalization, donors tended to support NGOs in their attempts to counter interventionist regulation, viewing this issue as inextricably tied to issues of democratization and political liberalization.

Beginning in the late 1990s, the tenor of NGO relationships with these key principals – governments and donors – began to change. With the emergence of more democratic regimes, many nonprofit and civil society leaders were drawn from NGOs into the public sector. Donor funding began to shift back toward the public sector, and suddenly NGOs, like governments before them, faced the prospect of declining funding. Moreover as legitimate NGOs proliferated, so did "briefcase" NGOs, and donors became increasingly concerned with finding ways to identify legitimate and effective organizations to fund (Edwards and Hulme, 1996). Increased competition for donor funding meant local NGOs now needed ways to distinguish themselves from their competitors, a sign of the "end of blind faith" in NGOs (Naidoo, 2004).

This chapter examines the emergence and development of accountability clubs in this African context. The first wave of accountability initiatives in Africa emerged in the early years of political liberalization, largely in response to regulatory reform initiatives by government. Many early clubs were national in scope, intended to act as self-regulatory mechanisms for all NGOs in the country. These initiatives are similar in many respects to the accountability clubs studied by Young and Frumkin in chapters 5 and 6 this volume: they are sponsored by NGO membership associations that attempt to set standards and develop self-regulatory mechanisms in order to preempt government regulation. As these other chapters also note, self-regulatory accountability clubs sponsored by NGO membership associations face particular hurdles in developing credible monitoring and enforcement mechanisms since these associations confront conflicting incentives in attempting both to support and to monitor their members.

As this chapter shows, many of the national clubs that emerged in this period were quite weak. Because of these weaknesses, more recent attempts to develop voluntary clubs in Africa have focused on developing independently sponsored certification clubs that are intended to distinguish high-quality NGOs from low-quality or illegitimate counterparts. These initiatives tend to rely on more clearly articulated standards and stronger screening and enforcement mechanisms.

The rest of the chapter proceeds as follows. The next section documents the emergence of accountability clubs in Africa, using cross-national data on twenty-two countries. The section that follows outlines the institutional characteristics of the clubs that have emerged during the 1990–2008 period. Finally the chapter uses several short case studies to examine the factors underlying the emergence and design of accountability clubs in seven countries.

The emergence of accountability clubs in Africa

This chapter argues that the threat of increased government regulation is a key driver for the development of accountability clubs among NGOs in Africa. To examine this argument the chapter first explores the relationship between regulatory change, and the emergence of NGO clubs in Africa with data on twenty-two countries for which public data are available.[2] For this analysis, the broadest possible definition of a club was used: any attempt at publicly documented interorganizational standard-setting by NGOs or other nongovernmental agencies is considered as a club. In the section that follows, the nature and strength of these accountability initiatives are examined more closely.

Data were collected from a combination of key informant interviews, public records, online archives of national NGO organizations, and secondary sources. This method of data collection may have biased the sample toward countries with better information infrastructures and with English-language documentation; the cross-national results should therefore be generalized with caution. The first part of the analysis examines the bivariate association between club development and the threat of government regulation. This implicitly holds constant other country-level features that might affect the emergence of clubs, such as the size, capacity, and heterogeneity of the NGO sector, international factors at play in the timing of reform efforts, and government regime characteristics. Country-level variation is examined more closely in the subsequent section.

---

[2] Forty-seven countries in sub-Saharan Africa are eligible for World Bank concessional lending. A primary criterion for selection of the countries was the existence of a functional governmental regime for the majority of the period 1990–2008, during which self-regulation efforts emerged on the continent. Countries that experienced prolonged central governmental collapse or conflict during this period are excluded; this criterion excludes six of the forty-seven countries. Very small island nations are also excluded, which excludes four additional countries. There were insufficient public data available on the remaining fifteen countries to include them in the sample. In general, eastern and southern Anglophone countries are well represented in the sample, while central and west African and Francophone countries are underrepresented.

The full sample is presented in Table 10.1, which lists the countries and shows the incidence and timing of regulatory reform, the key NGO associations in each country, and their date of founding. Regulatory and legal reform initiatives include two potential components. First, governments may propose changes to existing statutes regarding the definition, registration, and operations of nonprofit/nongovernmental agencies (column 2). Second, governments may propose changes to national policy frameworks or the administrative structures governing NGO–state relationships (column 4). But these regulatory proposals may or may not be adopted; columns 3 and 5 indicate these outcomes. Of the twenty-two countries in the sample, regulatory reform or change was proposed in fourteen during the period examined. Ten of these initiatives proposed or enacted changes to the legal statutes governing nonprofit operations; in four countries governments promulgated new policy frameworks or guidelines for NGOs. Regulatory reform has been enacted or adopted in ten of these countries. For this analysis, however, the key variable of interest is the inception of changes to the regulatory framework, regardless of whether they are ultimately adopted.

Table 10.2 displays the twenty-two countries according to whether or not the country experienced a regulatory reform initiative during the period, and shows the countries in which credible attempts at club formation emerged. In spite of common pressures on governments and NGOs across the continent, attempts at accountability clubs emerged in a little more than half the countries in the sample. But clubs are much more common in countries that experienced attempts at regulatory reform, with twelve of the fourteen countries in this category witnessing the development of clubs, versus only one of eight countries where reforms were not proposed. Although this correlation should not be mistaken for causation, the pattern is suggestive. Among these twelve cases, however, the form that voluntary clubs have taken has varied and not all attempts at the development of accountability clubs have met with success. The next section characterizes the three types of clubs that have emerged in Africa and the section that follows traces club emergence in seven countries.

Types of accountability clubs in Africa

If increased government regulation is a key driver for the development of accountability clubs among NGOs in Africa, then such clubs can be expected to act as either a substitute for or a complement to government regulation. Clubs that are substitutes for government regulation may be more likely to emerge when NGOs seek to preempt additional regulation.

Table 10.1 *NGO legislation and umbrella associations in twenty-two African countries*

Country	Club sponsor or initiating organization	Year NGO umbrella association established (1)	Year regulatory reform introduced (2)	Year reform initiative passed or adopted (3)	Year NGO policy initiated (4)	Year NGO policy adopted (5)	Type of club (6)	Year club established (7)
Benin	Centre de Promotion des Associations et ONGs (CPA-ONG) (quasi-autonomous government agency)	2000			1999	2000		
Botswana	Botswana Council of NGOs (BOCONGO)	1995			2000	2001	Voluntary club	2001
Burkina Faso	Civil Society Organization Network for Development (RESOCIDE)	2002						
Ethiopia	Christian Relief and Development Association (CRDA)	1973	2001, 2008	2009			Voluntary club	1999
Gambia	The Association of NGOs (TANGO)	1983	1996		2003			
Ghana	Ghana Association of Private Voluntary Organizations in Development (GAPVOD)	1980	1995		2000		Voluntary certification club	In process

Table 10.1 (*cont.*)

Country	Club sponsor or initiating organization	Year NGO umbrella association established (1)	Year regulatory reform introduced (2)	Year reform initiative passed or adopted (3)	Year NGO policy initiated (4)	Year NGO policy adopted (5)	Type of club (6)	Year club established (7)
Kenya	The National Council of NGOs	1963	1990	1991	1990	1992, 2006	National club	1993
Lesotho	Lesotho Council of NGOs (LCN or Lecongo)	1990					Voluntary club	In process
Malawi	Council for Nongovernmental Organizations in Malawi (CONGOMA)	1985	2000	2001				
Mali	Comité de Coordination des Actions des ONG au Mali (Cca-Ong)	1983						
Mozambique								
Namibia	Namibia NonGovernmental Organizations Forum (NANGOF)	1991	In progress	1998[a]	1999	2005	Voluntary club	2003
Nigeria	Nigeria Network of NGOs (NNNGO)	1992	2001			Ongoing	Voluntary club	Date unclear

Country	Organisation						
Rwanda	Conseil de Consertation des Organisations d'Appui aux Initiatives de Base (CCOAIB)	1987					–
Senegal	Conseil des Organisations d'Appui au Développement (CONGAD)	1982	1993–1995	1995		Voluntary club	Date unclear
South Africa	South African National NGO Coalition (SANGOCO)	1995	1994	1997		Voluntary club	1997
Swaziland	Coordinating Assembly of NGOs (CANGO)	1983					–
Tanzania	Tanzania Association of NGOs (TANGO)	1988	1998	2003, amended in 2005	2001	National club	2008
	Tanzania Council for Social Development (TACOSODE)	1987					
	Association of NGOs of Zanzibar (ANGOZA)	1992					
	National Association of NGOs (NACONGO)	2003					
Togo	National Congress of the Civil Society in Togo (CNSC)	2002					–
Uganda	The National NGO Forum	1997	2001, 2004	2004 Act		Voluntary club	2001
	DENIVA	1988				Certification club	2006

Table 10.1 (cont.)

Country	Club sponsor or initiating organization	Year NGO umbrella association established (1)	Year regulatory reform introduced (2)	Year reform initiative passed or adopted (3)	Year NGO policy initiated (4)	Year policy adopted (5)	Type of club (6)	Year club established (7)
Zambia	National Council for Social Development (NCSD)	1974			1997			–
	NGO Coordinating Committee (NGOCC)	1985						
Zimbabwe	National Association of NGOs (NANGO)	1962	1995, 2004	2004 bill passed by parliament, not signed			Voluntary club	2006

Note: [a] Regulates foreign NGOs only. National NGOs do not need to register.

Table 10.2 *Regulatory change and the emergence of private governance in Africa, 1990–2006*

Panel A: Regulatory threat and club emergence	Changes to regulatory framework proposed	No changes proposed to regulatory framework
Credible attempts at club development	Botswana Ghana Malawi Nigeria South Africa Uganda	Lesotho
	Ethiopia Kenya Namibia Senegal Tanzania Zimbabwe	
No club development	Benin	Burkina Faso Mali Rwanda Togo
	Zambia	Gambia Mozambique Swaziland

Panel B: Types of clubs in Africa		
Certification club	Ethiopia Uganda Ghana (in development)	
National club	Botswana Kenya Malawi (attempted) Tanzania (in development)	
Voluntary club	Lesotho Namibia Nigeria South Africa Zimbabwe	

To be a credible substitute, such clubs must have national regulatory jurisdiction. In Africa, the most common institutional form is a national-level club in which government delegates some regulatory or oversight functions to a nongovernmental body, most commonly an NGO umbrella membership association. Attempts at national clubs have emerged in Botswana, Kenya, Malawi, and Tanzania, with varying degrees of success. These self-regulation clubs face collective action challenges because they must produce a public good (regulation) using private authority. The regulatory power of these systems is thus highly dependent on the strength of standards developed and the ability of the system to screen new entrants and enforce compliance, since they are typically unable to restrict participation. Governments may agree to such systems in order to achieve the regulatory coverage they desire and reduce their oversight burden, which is shifted to the NGO association charged with developing and maintaining NGO standards. For their part, NGOs may be able to assert more control over standard-setting and enforcement mechanisms under a club system. In many cases, however, governments retain control over the NGO registration process, but mandate participation in a self-regulation club. In this case, the sponsoring NGO association loses control over the screening process for entry. If governments have weak conditions for NGO registration, then club participation may carry little information about NGO quality. Thus national clubs face a trade-off: they must either develop effective oversight and reporting mechanisms or they must find a way to erect barriers to entry that serve to weed out illegitimate or poorly performing organizations.

An alternative approach is the development of a private voluntary standard-setting club created by NGOs or third-party organizations. In joining the club, participants agree to adhere to a set of standards, reporting requirements, and monitoring mechanisms. Unlike the quasi-voluntary national clubs described above, these clubs have no monopoly over entry and participation is voluntary, rather than mandatory. These clubs must therefore develop mechanisms to attract participants and overcome collective action challenges. They do so by creating a collective benefit that accrues only to participants. This benefit is the positive reputation or signal of quality that club participation provides. This signal depends upon the club's ability to limit membership and clearly distinguish participants from nonparticipants. One way in which clubs can limit membership is by setting high standards. In addition, clubs can develop a screen for entry, as through certification or accreditation. Such screening or certification clubs have been attempted in Ethiopia, Ghana, and Uganda. The signaling power of the club depends directly on the strength of the standards – but strength of standards will be inversely correlated with participation levels, since high standards may make it costly for many organizations to join.

Because of this more restrictive membership, voluntary standard-setting clubs may not be an attractive substitute for government oversight from a government perspective, although they may be a useful complement. For example, governments may use club membership as a requirement for government grants or contracts. Donors, however, may care more about the reputational signals the certification clubs can create. For NGOs able to participate, clubs may be an attractive mechanism for creating positive reputations that help to attract greater donor funding; such certification clubs may not be sufficient, however, to preempt additional government regulation. The collective action challenge for voluntary certification clubs is to develop strong standards, as well as monitoring and enforcement mechanisms that are credible enough so that stakeholders will reward members for participation.

The framework for this volume conceptualizes voluntary clubs as a mechanism for resolving agency dilemmas between nonprofits and their principals. If this is the case, we might expect clubs that are responding to government regulation initiatives to be national in scope and to have more inclusive membership policies. Alternatively, when clubs are responding to donor preferences, the focus will be on more voluntary certification clubs that help to distinguish high-quality from low-quality organizations. Of course in most African countries, NGOs feel both these pressures. What kinds of clubs result? We turn to this issue next.

Returning first to Table 10.1, columns 6 and 7 indicate the countries in which a club has emerged and characterize the club as either a national club, a voluntary club, or a certification club (a club that has developed specific screening or certification mechanisms). The table shows that twelve clubs have emerged across the sample of twenty-two countries. National clubs emerged in Botswana, Kenya, and Tanzania and such a club was attempted in Malawi. The most common type of club is the voluntary standards club, often referred to as one with a "code of conduct": seven countries developed this type of club, which involves developing a code of conduct or accountability principles, but without specific screening or certification procedures. Three countries, Ethiopia, Ghana, and Uganda, have attempted to develop more stringent certification clubs. What accounts for this variance in the emergence and structure of self-regulation across these contexts? To examine these questions, the next section presents brief case studies that describe the emergence of NGO clubs in seven countries. Data collection for the case studies in Uganda, Kenya, and Ethiopia incorporated fieldwork in all three countries that included interviews with fifty-five senior managers and program staff of nonprofits, donors, and governments. Data collection for Tanzania, Botswana, Ghana, and Malawi is based on review of publicly available government and nonprofit documents, secondary sources, and ten telephone interviews with key informants. Documents reviewed for all cases include reviews of available government legislation and national policy frameworks, nonprofit association evaluations, strategic plans, and annual reports; extensive secondary document review includes donor assessments and a comprehensive review of available media reports.

The emergence of national-level clubs

The first wave of attempted voluntary NGO regulation in Africa began in Kenya, the first country in Africa to wrestle formally with issues of voluntary regulation. In the wake of rapid growth in the NGO sector and in response to growing attempts at policy advocacy on the part of some NGOs, the authoritarian government of Daniel arap Moi introduced the NGO Coordination Act in late 1990. The Act was passed into law by parliament within two months. It vested large amounts of power in a government-controlled NGO Board with the sole power to register NGOs and created a national NGO council with no independent powers outside the state (Adiin Yaansah, 1997; Ndegwa, 1996). The interests of both domestic and international NGOs were threatened by the legislation (Ndegwa, 1996), and the NGO community, including both the larger domestic agencies as well as international NGOs, mobilized the support of the donor community and protested vociferously. A three-year process of contestation and consultation followed that ultimately resulted in the government increasing NGO representation on the NGO registration board and giving independent powers to the apex National NGO Council created by the legislation. Most importantly, the NGO Council was granted a legal mandate to develop its own governance structures and code of conduct (Adiin Yaansah, 1997).

The NGO code of conduct was subsequently developed by the NGO Council and established as Legal Notice no. 306 in 1995. All NGOs in Kenya are required by law to be members of the NGO Council and to abide by the provisions of the code upon registration with the government. The standards developed in the code of conduct itself are extremely broad, consisting of seven goals for NGO behavior: probity, self-regulation, justice, service, cooperation, prudence, and respect. NGOs are not required to document compliance with these goals and no detailed management standards for the goals were developed. Monitoring and enforcement power is vested in a regulatory committee within the NGO Council with power to act as a quasi-judicial tribunal to hear complaints brought against NGOs. If an NGO is found to be in violation of the code, the regulatory committee can verbally sanction the organization or recommend to the NGO Board that it be deregistered, or the general assembly can levy a fine or recommend suspension. Although the complaints review board does have strong powers that include the power to recommend deregistration, the detection of violations depends entirely on the public complaints process and it is not clear to what extent the public is aware of the code and their rights to bring a case against an NGO. In 2003, the last year for which data are available, the Council received thirty-four complaints; by the end of the year twenty-seven of those cases had been at least partly heard by the regulatory committee. The regulatory committee has been hampered in its enforcement in several respects. The NGO Council as a whole has suffered from funding problems; member organizations do not always pay their annual dues and the Council has limited mechanisms for enforcing the payment of dues. Estimates by NGO Council officials in 2004 suggested that only 400 of the approximately 3,165 member organizations had paid dues for that year. As a result, the level of staffing and financial resources available to the regulatory committee has been low and hence enforcement of the code has been weak. With the advent of multiparty democracy in 2002, a number of key leaders in the NGO sector, including staff from the NGO Council, joined the new government. In addition, the Council has suffered from severe leadership and capacity problems in recent years. In 2008, the Council was "relaunched" after a period of inactivity and controversy. While the Kenyan experiment was initially hailed as a model for the continent, the challenges faced by the Council in recent years highlight the challenges of sustaining an association-sponsored club absent the threat of an intrusive government.

Attempts to develop national clubs in Malawi and Tanzania also emerged in response to proposed changes in NGO regulatory frameworks. Both efforts drew on the Kenyan experience. In Malawi, the process began in the late 1990s when the recently elected democratic government began to draft a new act defining a regulatory system for NGOs. The government's stated goal was to develop a regulatory system in which NGO policy was formulated and implemented with NGO participation, similar to the self-regulatory system in place in Kenya. Unlike in Kenya, however, the process of developing a national self-regulatory system was initially characterized by a more collaborative consultation between NGOs and the government.

As in Kenya, the intent was to have the main NGO umbrella association, the Council for Nongovernmental Organizations in Malawi (CONGOMA), act as the sponsor for the club. During the consultative phase of legislative design, CONGOMA facilitated a series of meetings between nonprofits and government officials over the content of legislation. When the provisions of the proposed NGO Act were made public in late 2000, however, the contents were a surprise to many NGOs. The Act designated CONGOMA as the official coordinating body for NGOs, required all NGOs to join the association, and charged CONGOMA with developing and maintaining a code of conduct for the sector. Some NGOs felt the Act gave the government and CONGOMA excessive powers, and fifteen prominent NGOs issued a public appeal against the bill (Meinhardt and Patel, 2003).

When the Act was quickly passed by parliament in 2001, CONGOMA found itself in an awkward position, since some of its members had supported the Act while others were vocal opponents (Mkamanga and Fanwell, 2001). The short period between the tabling and enactment of the bill precluded a process for generating consensus among NGOs and the conflict ultimately led to the breakdown of the process. While CONGOMA remains the official umbrella body for nonprofits in Malawi, its authority over the sector remains weak and is not universally recognized; the association claims to have developed a code of ethics for NGOs but this code does not appear to be publicly available. The Malawi case illustrates another challenging feature of NGO association-sponsored national clubs: sponsoring associations must retain legitimacy and credibility with member NGOs. When the association is perceived as being in the government's "pocket," NGOs may be unwilling to participate and the association may not have the capacity for enforcement.

The process of club development in Tanzania has unfolded over nearly a decade. Attempts to agree on a national-style club have floundered and to date the club has not been fully institutionalized. Beginning in 1996, the Tanzanian government embarked on a process designed to produce a new NGO policy framework and regulatory system. The three major umbrella organizations, the Tanzanian Association of NGOs (TANGO), the Tanzania Council for Social Development (TACOSODE), and the Association of NGOs of Zanzibar (ANGOZA), were lead actors and organized workshops for NGO input on the content of a national NGO policy. As in Malawi, the issue of club sponsorship proved contentious. The process nearly broke down when the idea of creating a single umbrella body for nonprofits was proposed in 1999 by the head of the donor-supported Aid Management and Accountability Program (AMAP) (Mogella, 1999). The existing associations and their members threatened to pull out of the policy process altogether. The fifth draft of the policy was ultimately adopted in 2000 and a revised NGO Act was enacted in 2002, but without consultation with NGOs (Irish and Simon, 2003). The 2002 Act mandated the creation of a national umbrella association that would develop an NGO code of conduct; the National Council on NGOs (NACONGO) was subsequently formed in 2003. After passage of the Act, a behind-the-scenes consultative process continued, ultimately resulting in amendments to the Act in 2005 that reduced some of the more restrictive components of the original legislation (Iheme, 2005). But the experience left many NGOs distrustful of the process and the idea of a national apex body with self-regulating powers (Makaramba, 2007). Donors also were unwilling to support the effort, many preferring instead to support smaller thematic networks (Foundation for Civil Society, 2006). Moreover, had the government initially proposed more restrictive legislation, as in Kenya, NGO divisions might have been overcome in the quest to oppose the legislation. But the consultative process did nothing to assuage the fears of existing associations that they might be left out of the final institutional arrangements. NACONGO recently unveiled a National NGO Code of Ethics, which to date appears to be a passive code of conduct that does not spell out specific requirements for adherence or actions to be taken in the case of noncompliance. Again in Tanzania, as in Kenya and Malawi, the issue of sponsorship appeared to complicate national club development. In the Tanzanian case, competition among preexisting NGO associations for sponsorship presented an obstacle that was difficult to overcome.

These three cases highlight the difficulty of developing national-level clubs, which have often foundered over the issue of club sponsorship. A national system requires a sponsor with wide legitimacy and credibility. In the Kenyan case, such an organization was created in the face of severe threats to the NGO sector that gave NGOs the incentive to cooperate and to work under a single umbrella organization. In Malawi and Tanzania, initial state–NGO collaborations were ultimately perceived by NGOs to favor particular associations that did not have widespread legitimacy, and this fractured cooperation and trust among NGOs. These challenges may explain why no national-level clubs with strong self-regulating powers have emerged subsequent to the Kenya case. The national systems that have emerged in the subsequent period (for example, in Botswana, Namibia, and South Africa) are all voluntary national codes of conduct sponsored by a national NGO association.

The Botswana NGO code of conduct is a well-known example of a national code of conduct. The code was launched in 2001 and is sponsored by the Botswana Council of NGOs (BOCONGO). BOCONGO itself was formed in 1995 as the main NGO umbrella association in Botswana, with donor funding and support from the state. The code of conduct was developed in conjunction with a national policy on NGOs through a consultative process with participation of NGOs, donors, and government officials (Carroll and Carroll, 2004; Kaunda, 2005). The standards set forth in the code are broad, with the goal of setting a "prevailing standard of moral and social behavior" for NGOs. The code sets out broad guidelines governing values, governance, transparency, accountability, fundraising, and financial and human resource management. However, there are no provisions for NGOs to sign on to the code or to make other public commitments to adherence, and NGOs are expected to monitor their own adherence to it. The existence of a broadly accepted sponsor facilitated the process of developing the code in Botswana, but the code is quite weak in its signaling ability, given the poorly articulated standards. But its largest weakness lies in the lack of clear reporting, monitoring, and enforcement mechanisms. This relatively weak club structure is common to voluntary clubs in South Africa, Namibia, Lesotho, Nigeria, Senegal, and Zimbabwe.

The emergence of voluntary certification clubs in Africa

The difficulty of establishing national clubs and the resulting weakness of national voluntary systems may have prompted efforts in some countries to develop clubs that could incorporate stronger standards and enforcement mechanisms. The Ethiopian case is one example. The Ethiopian voluntary club consists of a code of conduct sponsored by the largest NGO association in the country, the Christian Relief and Development Association (CRDA). The impetus for the Ethiopian code was similar to that in many other African countries. As the number of NGOs in Ethiopia proliferated throughout the 1990s, government concerns with NGO oversight increased and the government instituted increasingly restrictive administrative requirements for NGO registration and operation. As concern over these provisions mounted among NGOs, CRDA spearheaded the development of a code of conduct that was ratified by a national consultative meeting of more than two hundred international and domestic NGOs (at that time a majority of registered NGOs in Ethiopia) in 1998. The original intent of the code was to establish a nationwide general assembly of NGOs that would elect a code observance committee charged with monitoring adherence to the code and hearing complaints. In practice, setting up such a separate body appeared to be a strong barrier to implementation, and so the code observance committee was housed at CRDA, at that time the largest, most representative NGO agency (CRDA interview, 2004). The implications of CRDA sponsorship, however, were different from association sponsorship in Malawi and Tanzania. At the time of the code development, CRDA was a relatively strong association that boasted a waiting list for membership. And unlike in Tanzania, where multiple associations competed for membership and authority, CRDA at the time was the only national umbrella association in existence in Ethiopia.

The standards developed in the code of conduct are also relatively strong in comparison with the Kenya case and other African national voluntary codes. The code lays out forty standards of conduct, including a requirement for a written constitution defining a mission, objectives, and organizational structure, and the requirement of an annual financial audit performed by an independent auditing firm and made public. Interviews with CRDA managers, however, suggested that the organization is not able to monitor compliance with this final requirement on an ongoing basis. Although CRDA has not been able to develop an ongoing code monitoring capacity, the code of conduct retains signaling power owing to the relatively significant screening process it uses to admit new members. Membership in CRDA is highly sought after because of important benefits associated with membership, including access to training programs, donor funding, and technical assistance. All members must pledge adherence to the code upon joining the organization, and the screening process for new entrants is relatively strict by African standards: NGOs must show proof of government registration, bylaws and memoranda of association, audited financial reports, and letters of support from three current CRDA members. Membership in CRDA provides a reputational benefit to NGOs because members are clearly distinguished from nonmembers, providing a signal about NGO quality to donors and to the government. Moreover, since a number of donors channel project funds through CRDA, the threat of loss of membership or investigation into fraudulent behavior carries the potential for significant financial losses. CRDA has incentives to engage in screening, since its own funding stream depends on its ability to recruit effective organizations to carry out donor-funded programs. Once NGOs have been admitted, the ongoing process of applying for funding provides a reasonably steady exchange of information between the organization and its members, even in the absence of well-implemented reporting mechanisms. Because CRDA is highly reliant on donor funding, it has every incentive to address quality problems among its membership once identified. The evidence suggests that donors find CRDA's signal credible; in 2006 the organization reported revenue of just over $4 million (compared with revenue of $319,000 in 2003 for the Kenyan NGO Council). This voluntary club model, however, involves one important trade-off: rather than having national coverage, the code applies only to association members. In the Ethiopian case, this is about 60 percent of the total population of NGOs in the country, and membership is likely oriented toward larger, national NGOs and international NGOs. The code has also not been sufficient to forestall additional government regulation; in 2008 the Ethiopian government introduced the Charities and Societies Proclamation which was subsequently passed by parliament in 2009. The Act has been widely condemned by a number of human rights organizations as severely restricting freedom of association and voice (Human Rights Watch, 2008; Amnesty International, 2008).

The Ugandan case also illustrates the trend toward the development of stronger clubs employing stronger enforcement mechanisms. Voluntary club development in Uganda has had two phases. In the first phase, parallel and weak voluntary codes were sponsored by the country's two main umbrella associations. The first association, DENIVA, was founded in 1988 as a support organization for indigenous NGOs. DENIVA had developed a code of conduct for members, but the code had no monitoring or enforcement mechanisms associated with it. The second association, the NGO Forum, was founded in 1997 to represent both national and international NGOs operating in Uganda and to provide a platform for NGOs to contribute to policy processes in the country. The NGO Forum launched a code of conduct for members in 2001. Like the DENIVA code, however, the NGO Forum code of conduct had no provisions for reporting, monitoring, or enforcement. In addition, competition between the two associations for membership and influence weakened the incentives of each association for developing compliance and oversight mechanisms that might exclude some potential members.

The need for a system to promote stronger NGO governance in Uganda was subsequently underscored by the government's decision in 2004 to reintroduce into parliament a long-dormant bill to amend the NonGovernmental Organizations Registration Act. The provisions of this Act gave the government more control over the activities of NGOs and narrowly defined the scope of allowable policy and advocacy activities. The bill was quickly passed by parliament and forwarded to the president for signature. The reaction among NGOs was swift. Rivalries among networks and associations were laid aside as NGOs formed the Coalition on the NGO Bill (CONOB). The Coalition held sectorwide meetings and conducted a media campaign against the bill. Although President Museveni ultimately did not sign the bill, the threat of the legislation had helped to galvanize coordinated action and to mobilize the support of international donors and NGOs. Ultimately, a new version of the Act was passed in 2006 and signed into law. The NGO Registration Amendments Act of 2006 created a government-appointed committee with the power to issue and revoke NGO registration permits, which many NGOs claimed could be used to suppress politically active organizations. These amendments went into effect in 2008. Alongside these events, several scandals tarnished the reputation of the NGO sector, including the 2005 suspension of funds from the Global Fund on AIDS and Tuberculosis on the grounds of corruption and misuse of funds. Subsequent investigations revealed that Global Fund resources administered by the government had been channeled though bogus NGOs linked to members of parliament, government ministers, and other government officials. The resulting scandal provided legitimate NGOs with a strong rationale for developing screening mechanisms that could separate legitimate from illegitimate organizations.

This combination of government threat, public scandals, and a new willingness among previously competitive NGO membership associations to work together gave additional support to ongoing efforts to develop a new system for NGO certification. With donor support, the two major umbrella organizations collaborated on the development of the Quality Assurance Mechanism (QuAM) in 2006. The QuAM is a certification system that includes detailed and specific standards for NGO behavior and a clear monitoring and enforcement system. To receive certification, NGOs must complete a detailed application and documentation process which is audited by district "quality assurance committees" that act as certification bodies.

A critical factor in the development of QuAM was the ongoing and consistent support for the process by a major international donor, DANIDA. In addition, the perceived strength of the regulatory threat gave the NGO Forum and DENIVA incentives to cooperate and to develop a district-level mechanism, even though the districts had been the site of the most intense competition between the two organizations. Finally, QuAM developers were able to draw explicitly on the experiences of other countries in developing self-regulation mechanisms unavailable in earlier periods (DENIVA, 2006). Because the QuAM is quite new, it has not yet begun accepting applications for certification. The ultimate effectiveness of the system in signaling legitimacy and forestalling additional regulatory initiatives will thus not be clear for some time.

Another certification initiative is underway in Ghana, where NGO–government negotiations over nonprofit regulatory frameworks have been ongoing since 1995, when a bill was unilaterally framed by government and placed before the Congress. The bill met with protest and strong dissent from NGOs and was withdrawn. Subsequent draft policies on the nonprofit sector were revised in consultation with NGOs each year from 2002 to 2005. These drafts proposed the development of a national commission for NGOs that would register NGOs, oversee NGO policy, and develop and implement a code of conduct for NGOs. To date, the national commission has not been established.

In a parallel process, NGOs, with donor support, have been developing a standards-based accreditation system, the Ghana NGO/CSO Standards for Excellence. The standards program is a joint effort of two of the largest nonprofit associations in Ghana, supported by the Ghana office of CARE International and USAID-Ghana. The initiative is developing a set of standards for nonprofit governance and management that draw explicitly on global standard-setting initiatives. The certification process will be overseen by a Standards Commission that will vet applications and award certification to nonprofits in compliance. The Commission is a peer review board composed of nonprofit managers from international and local NGOs. Applicant organizations will complete a self-certification process in which they document their adherence to detailed program standards for governance and management. Applications will be peer reviewed by a team of three reviewers drawn from previously certified organizations. The team makes a recommendation on certification to the Commission and recertification will take place after three years. The sponsors of the Ghana standards have been explicit about their desire to move away from a code of conduct and toward the development of specific, measurable standards that include mechanisms for monitoring and compliance. The Ghana standards program is also quite new, so it remains to be seen whether the program can be implemented as planned.

The Ethiopia, Uganda, and Ghana cases suggest a move toward the development of more stringent clubs in a number of African countries and may indicate a realization on the part of NGOs that stronger signaling mechanisms will require more exclusionary certification mechanisms. The willingness of some donors to invest substantial resources in supporting the development of these systems suggests that donors, the key financial principals of African NGOs, also recognize the value of accreditation. It is not clear how these initiatives will evolve in light of continuing attempts by some governments to impose additional controls on the NGO sector. These new certification systems would need to come to scale quite quickly to demonstrate to governments that the NGOs can adequately engage in self-regulation. Given the resource and capacity constraints that characterize most NGOs, however, this would seem to be an optimistic scenario at best.

Conclusions

The case studies presented above illustrate three distinct forms of voluntary clubs that have emerged in Africa. Panel B of Table 10.2 summarizes these club types by country. In the Kenyan case, the threat of repressive regulatory oversight was enough to galvanize NGOs behind a national accountability club with quasi-judicial enforcement potential. In Malawi, NGOs had doubts about the capacity and independence of the largest NGO umbrella organization to act in good faith as a club sponsor; when the government attempted to give this association self-regulatory power, NGOs were unwilling to accept the system. In Tanzania, the existence of three competing NGO membership associations meant that no association was willing to cede sponsorship of a code to another. As a result an entirely new association was created to sponsor the nascent national code of conduct, but without the broad-based support or participation of NGOs. Thus the legitimacy of club sponsors appears to matter a great deal to club development in Africa. Ortmann and Svítková make a similar point in their discussion of self-regulatory initiatives in the Czech Republic in chapter 7 of this volume.

More stringent certification clubs appear to be taking root in some African countries. Ethiopia developed one of the first clubs on the continent with significant signaling potential, although it was more a product of the dominance and relatively high capacity of the main umbrella association than of deliberate efforts at club design. In Uganda and Ghana, NGOs appear to be abandoning attempts to create nationwide systems and moving instead toward the creation of certification clubs with the support of NGO donors. This appears to reflect a new desire and willingness on the part of legitimate nonprofits to create mechanisms that may have the effect of excluding many organizations from participation.

Clubs in Africa do appear to be responsive to the interests of key NGO principals, namely governments and international donors. As hypothesized, threatened changes in the regulatory system played an important role in prompting club development in the majority of cases. This has parallels with the clubs discussed by Young and Frumkin in this volume (chapters 5 and 6), who also find that broad-based associations tend to initiate self-regulatory accountability efforts only when faced with the threat of increased regulation. But this chapter also finds that stronger clubs often emerged in the face of stronger perceived threats of repression, as in Kenya and Uganda. Where governments initially took a more consultative stance, particularly in Tanzania and Malawi, weaker clubs emerged. The threat of government regulation also interacted in important ways with club sponsorship. Relatively dominant NGO associations existed in both Ethiopia and Malawi, but a significant club emerged only in Ethiopia, where CRDA relied heavily on donor support and funding that gave it incentives to screen potential members. Tanzania and Uganda both had multiple competing associations, but in Uganda the recent threat of relatively repressive NGO legislation appears to have united these associations in the development of a certification club, whereas in

Tanzania the fragmentation of NGO associations led to competition over club sponsorship that could not be surmounted. In sum, while changes in regulatory frameworks are an important impetus for club development among NGOs in Africa, these effects are mediated by the perceived repressiveness of reform efforts, the nature and level of donor support, and interaction with preexisting NGO associations. Unlike the humanitarian clubs examined by Zarnegar Deloffre in chapter 8, and the foundation clubs described by Frumkin in chapter 6, there is little sign that NGOs in Africa are able to take an independent stance regarding self-regulation and the development of standards. NGOs remain highly donor-reliant and the threat of government repression is still significant in most countries. Accountability clubs thus emerge in an environment that is highly responsive to the interests of NGO principals.

The continuing threat of repressive government regulation in many countries suggests that NGO accountability clubs in Africa may ultimately evolve on a dual track. At the national level, NGOs will seek a voice with government over the design of national policy and regulations through national associations. Among themselves, NGOs may find it in their own interest to develop voluntary clubs with more stringent standards. While these systems will have more limited participation, the dissemination of stronger standards has the potential to raise the accountability expectations for NGOs, a point echoed by Bies in chapter 9 of this volume.

REFERENCES

Adiin Yaansah, E. A. 1997. An Experiment into Self-Regulation in Kenya. *Refugee Studies Programme*, mimeo, University of Oxford, March 1997.
Amnesty International. 2008. Comments on Draft Charities and Societies Proclamation, Ethiopia. June, 2008. AI index 25/005/2008.
Armstrong, Patricia. 2006. The Limits and Risks of Regulation: The Case of the World-Bank Supported Draft Handbook on Good Practices for Laws Relating to NGOs. In Lisa Jordan and Peter van Tuijl, eds. *NGO Accountability: Politics, Principles and Innovations*. London: Earthscan.
Barr, Abigail, Marcel Fafchamps, and Trudy Owens. 2005. The Governance of Nongovernmental Organizations in Uganda. *World Development* 33(4): 657–679.
Batley, R. 2006. Engaged or Divorced? Cross-Service Findings on Government Relations with Non-State Service Providers. *Public Administration and Development* 26(3): 241–251.
Bratton, Michael. 1989. The Politics of Government–NGO Relations in Africa. *World Development* 17(4): 569–587.
Carroll, Terrance and Barbara Wake Carroll. 2004. The Rapid Emergence of Civil Society in Botswana. *Commonwealth and Comparative Politics* 42(3): 333–355.

Charlick, R. B. 1998. Supporting Pluralism and the Voluntary Sector in Ethiopia. Mimeo, Cleveland State University.

Christian Relief and Development Association, 2001. Second Three-Year Program Plan 2002–2004. Draft, July 1. Accessed via www.crdaethiopia.org.

2004. Three Years Program Plan 2005–2007. Draft, July 1. Accessed via www.crdaethiopia.org.

Clark, J. 2000. *Civil Society, NGOs and Development in Ethiopia: A Snapshot View.* Washington, DC: The World Bank.

DENIVA. 2006. *NGOs Regulating Themselves: The Quality Assurance Mechanism.* Accessed via www.deniva.or.ug/files/_h_index.php?pageName=programme-governance_policies.html.

Edwards, Michael and David Hulme. 1996. *Beyond the Magic Bullet: NGO Performance and Accountability in the Post-Cold War World.* West Hartford, CT: Kumarian Press.`

Fisher, Julie. 1997. *Non-Governments: NGOs and the Political Development of the Third World.* West Hartford, CT: Kumarian Press.

Foundation for Civil Society, Tanzania. 2006. *Development Department Quarterly Report for Q2.* June. Accessed via www.thefoundation.or.tz.

Gibbelman, Margaret and Sheldon Gelman. 2004. A Loss of Credibility: Patterns of Wrongdoing among Nonprofit Organizations. *Voluntas* 15(4): 355–381.

Horning, Nadia Rabesahala. 2004. The Limits of Rules: When Rules Promote Forest Conservation and When They Do Not: Insights from Bara Country, Madagascar. PhD dissertation, Cornell University.

Human Rights Watch. 2008. *Analysis of Ethiopia's Draft Civil Society Law.* Accessed via www.hrw.org/node/88963, October 13 2008.

Iheme, Emeka. 2005. Strengthening Civil Society in the South: Challenges and Constraints; A Case Study of Tanzania – Response. *International Journal of Not-for-Profit Law* 8(1): 54–62.

Irish, Leon and Karla Simon. 2003. The Nongovernmental Organziations Act 2002, for the United Republic of Tanzania; Gazetted in the Official Gazette 4 October 2002. Comments by Leon Irish and Karla Simon. *International Journal of Civil Society Law* 1(1): 70–72.

Kaunda, J.M. 2005. Effective States and Engaged Societies: Capacity Development for Growth, Service Delivery, Empowerment and Security in Africa. Draft Report, Botswana Institute for Development Policy Analysis (BIDPA). Accessed via http://siteresources.worldbank.org/AFRICAEXT/Resources/CD_Botswana.pdf.

Kwesiga, J.B. and Harriet Namisi. 2006. Issues in Legislation for NGOs in Uganda. In Lisa Jordan and Peter van Tuijl, eds. *NGO Accountability: Politics, Principles and Innovations.* London: Earthscan.

Makaramba, Robert. 2007. The Legal Context for the Non-Profit Sector in Tanzania. Part of a report, *The Third Sector in Tanzania: Learning More about Civil Society Organisations, their Capabilities and Challenges.* Aga Khan Development Network, May. Accessed via www.akdn.org/publications/civil_society_tarzania_third_sector.pdf.

Meinhardt, H. and N. Patel. 2003. *Malawi's Process of Democratic Transition: An Analysis of Political Developments between 1990 and 2003.* Konrad Adenauer Foundation, Occasional Paper, November.

Mkamanga, G. and B. Fanwell. 2001. *Council for Nongovernmental Organizations in Malawi (CONGOMA) Consultative Appraisal.* GilEnterprise Consultants. Accessed via http://web.onetel.com/~fanwellbokosi/docs/congoma.pdf.

Mogella, C. 1999. The State and Civil Society Relations in Tanzania: The Case of the National NGOs Policy. Mimeo, Department of Political Science and Administration, University of Dar es Salaam (East African Comparative Research Project on Civil Society and Governance).

Naidoo, Kumi. 2004. The End of Blind Faith? Civil Society and the Challenge of Accountability, Legitimacy and Transparency. *AccountAbility Forum* 2 (summer): 14–25.

National Council of NGOs, Kenya. 2003. *2003 Annual Report.* Nairobi: NGO Council.

Ndegwa, S. 1996. *The Two Faces of Civil Society: NGOs and Politics in Africa.* West Hartford, CT: Kumarian Press.

NGO Forum. 2003. *The Road to a Collective Voice: A History of the National NGO Forum.* Kampala: NGO Forum.

Olson, M. 1965. *The Logic of Collective Action.* Cambridge, MA: Harvard University Press.

Pharano, G. 2001. NGO Codes of Conduct: The Case of Botswana. *Social Development Review* 5(3). Accessed via www.icsw.org/publications/sdr/2001-sept/ngo-reports.htm.

Platteau, Jean-Philippe and Francois Gaspart. 2003. Disciplining Local Leaders in Community-Based Development. Working Paper, CRED, University of Namur.

Sidel, M. 2003. Trends in Nonprofit Self-Regulation in the Asia Pacific Region: Initial Data on Initiatives, Experiments and Models in Seventeen Countries. Mimeo, University of Iowa Law School.

TANGO. 2006. District and Regional NGO Networks Defy the Odds. TANGO website, accessed February 14, 2007.

11 The benefits of accreditation clubs for fundraising nonprofits

René Bekkers

How can fundraising organizations signal trustworthiness to prospective donors? One way to do this is by conforming to standards of excellence and allowing a trusted, independent agency to monitor the organization with regard to these standards. The Central Bureau of Fundraising (CBF) in the Netherlands is an example of a club running such an accountability program. This chapter empirically investigates whether (1) awareness of the accountability program among donors increases donations by households; and (2) fundraising organizations that participate in the accountability program attract more donations than organizations that do not. To help understand the context in which the program operates, I will first briefly describe the regulation of fundraising in the Netherlands.

In contrast to the US context of many of the chapters in this volume, in the Netherlands the regulation of nonprofits can be described as a combination of few legal requirements, little government involvement, some self-regulation, and independent monitoring by a third party. The focus of the regulation that does exist is on fundraising practices. Nonprofit organizations that want to claim tax-exemption status have to register with the tax authorities, but are not required to submit audited financial statements or elaborate reports to obtain the status. To raise money in a door-to-door collection or in town, a permit from the municipality in which the collection is planned is required. Door-to-door collection is still a very common method of raising funds in the Netherlands. Such fundraising is done by unpaid volunteers for large, national fundraising organizations.

Previous versions of this chapter were presented at the 6th Workshop on the Challenges of Managing the Third Sector, March 12–13, 2007, in Venice; at the 35th Annual Conference of the Association for Research on Nonprofit and Voluntary Action, November 16–18, 2006, in Chicago; and at the Workshop on Certification Systems for Nonprofit Organizations, May 23–24, 2005, in Prague. I thank the Central Bureau of Fundraising for making available the data on income and expenses of fundraising organizations, and I thank Ad Graaman in particular for clarifications and additions to the database. I am also indebted to the editors, Richard Steinberg, Andreas Ortmann, Katarina Svítková, Dennis Young, Woods Bowman, Eddy Bekkers, Adri Kemps, and Ad Graaman who provided helpful comments on previous versions of this chapter. I thank Merel Ooms for research assistance.

About one in five volunteers in the Netherlands is active in raising funds (Bekkers, 2005). However, for national fundraising campaigns conducted via ordinary direct mail, email, or telephone no such requirements exist. National law prohibits selling or sharing of non-opt-in address lists between and/or among fundraising organizations and marketing agencies. Marketing agencies that are members of the Dutch Direct Marketing Association generally conform to the rule that they will not approach persons who have registered with Infofilter, a national database of "Don't call/mail me" addresses. Membership of the DDMA, however, is voluntary. Until recently, nonmembers did not have to conform to the "Don't call me" rule. Despite this liberal treatment of fundraising by nonprofit organizations, very few cases of fraud, abuse of funds, or other irregularities have been documented in the past decades. Such cases have involved only relatively small organizations.[1]

The relative absence of irregularities may be due to some extent to the accountability program run by the CBF. I briefly describe the program here. More details on the program are given in a previous study (Bekkers, 2003) and on the organization's website.[2] The CBF is an independent nongovernmental organization.[3] The CBF has no members and like many European accreditation programs, it receives a substantial public subsidy and relies on this income as well as income from fees for its revenue base (Wilke, 2003). The CBF develops standards for excellence, evaluates nonprofits on the basis of those standards, and issues a "seal of approval" to national fundraising organizations that have existed for at least three years and that meet the standards.[4] The standards include rules on board structure, the provision of financial statements issued by an external accountant, transparency to donors, complaint procedures, and a ceiling

[1] One of the few exceptions is the October 2007 case in which a volunteer for KWF Kankerbestrijding – a health charity fighting cancer and the largest fundraising nonprofit organization in the country – stole €15,000 from the door-to-door collection funds she helped to raise.

[2] See www.cbf.nl/Home/uk.php for more information.

[3] This has not always been the case. The CBF was established in 1925 as an office coordinating local fundraising activities of national fundraising organizations. The fifty-two weeks of the year were assigned to the major fundraising organizations such that citizens were not facing two collections for different organizations in the same week. The system still exists, but is managed by a different organization. It should also be noted that two members of the board represent the branch organization of fundraising organizations (VFI). One member represents the government (Department of Justice), three members represent the municipalities, and three members are not representing any institution or organization.

[4] Since its introduction in 1997, the CBF seal has been issued to 271 fundraising organizations. An additional 59 organizations have a "verklaring van geen bezwaar," which is issued to smaller fundraising organizations that are on their way to meet the same standards. These organizations are not considered as accredited fundraising organizations.

for fundraising costs (25 percent of fundraising income), among other things.[5] Recently, additional standards have been formulated as part of the evaluation procedure. These club standards go far beyond the legal requirements for fundraising organizations sketched above. The club standards are also much more stringent than those adopted by the national and state nonprofit associations (respectively) discussed in chapters 4 and 5 by Tschirhart and Young elsewhere in this volume.

Meeting the CBF club standards involves nontrivial costs.[6] The evaluation procedure requires a substantial time investment of the CEO and financial director to answer questions about the organization's activities, management, and expenses. In addition to the labor costs required to complete the procedure, nonprofit organizations pay fees. There is a fixed fee for the first evaluation procedure (€4,360) as well as a variable annual fee for the right to bear the seal, depending on fundraising income (ranging from €3,000 to €7,000). The accreditation is valid for five years. After this period, the organization has to complete the procedure again in order to retain the accreditation. The reevaluation procedure costs €2,195. The CBF evaluates the information provided and decides about accreditation.

The club has two main swords against failure to conform to the standards: press releases and, ultimately, withholding the seal. In the period 1994–2004, none of the accredited organizations was evicted or left the program voluntarily. In recent years, however, one international development organization with a religious background has left the program voluntarily, and three organizations were withheld the seal owing to irregularities and/or incapacity to produce the required information.

Because the procedure is costly and intensive, it is unlikely that organizations that have something to hide will enter and successfully complete the evaluation procedure. Though it is impossible to check, it is likely that the costs associated with accreditation limit entry of "bad apples" to the Dutch fundraising market. For these reasons, consumers can be expected

---

[5] The accreditation seal is not a trademark, nor is it strongly protected by law. Although the law does not prohibit fundraising organizations that do not abide by the standards of the CBF from bearing the seal, this has not occurred in practice. It is also very unlikely to happen because such organizations would be easily detected by the media, the Dutch donor association, the consumer association, and/or the CBF itself. The only legal arrangement concerning the seal is that the major national charitable lotteries cannot benefit organizations that are not accredited.

[6] As a purely anecdotal note: when I presented a previous version of this chapter in 2006 to an audience of fundraising directors, the representative of Greenpeace questioned the net benefit of the seal because of the "enormous amount of effort" required to complete the evaluation procedure. Several representatives of smaller organizations identified the effort required as a reason not to apply, despite the expected increase in fundraising income.

to be fairly confident that accredited organizations do not violate the standards set by the system.[7]

Another strength of the system is that the CBF is an independent nonprofit organization. Thus, donors are less likely to doubt the accreditation seal than information provided solely by fundraising organizations.[8] Results from a poll survey held in November 2005 among Dutch consumers revealed that 78 percent had "sufficient" or more confidence in the CBF, while 71 percent reported such confidence in national fundraising nonprofit organizations and only 49 percent said they had at least sufficient confidence in government (Zalpha van Berkel and WWAV, 2005). In September 2008, these figures were 77 percent, 68 percent, and 50 percent, respectively (WWAV, 2008).

Because the club standards are rather stringent, the signal that the accreditation seal sends out is credible. The purpose of the system according to the CBF is to enable donors to make more informed decisions. In other words, the accountability program reduces the asymmetry of information that donors face in their decisionmaking on charitable giving, viewing donors as the key principals the club is designed to serve. In terms of the club perspective, the CBF is a strong club. Club membership gives members a branding benefit – the right to use the seal in fundraising campaigns. The seal is a club good: it is a nonrival benefit for members, excludable for nonmembers. This does not imply that the benefits of accreditation accrue only to those who decide to join the program. Organizations that free-ride may benefit as well.

The trust problem in philanthropy

The effectiveness and efficiency of the services provided by nonprofit organizations are important factors in the eyes of donors when thinking about donations (Arumi *et al.*, 2005). However, donors face a high level of uncertainty about whether a nonprofit organization is effective and efficient

[7] This is not to say that accredited organizations make no mistakes, or work 100 percent effectively. Accreditation also does not guarantee that the organization abides by desirable standards that are not part of the accountability program. For instance, the public desires that fundraising managers and CEOs earn lower salaries than persons in comparable for-profit firms. However, there are no limits on salaries in the CBF standards.

[8] Ultimately, the CBF relies on reports provided by fundraising organizations themselves because the financial statements approved by external accountants are produced by accountants who are working for these organizations. Accountants would endanger their own reputation by approving financial statements that are grossly incorrect. However, as the Enron case shows, this is not a 100 percent guarantee against misrepresentations or fraud. Accountants may bend the rules for accounting in cooperation with the fundraising organizations that they work for (Wing and Hager, 2004).

because nonprofit organizations often provide services of which the quality is difficult to observe and evaluate. The introductory chapter of this volume outlines this problem of asymmetry of information. In the absence of accurate information about an organization's output, donors have to rely on their personal impressions of the trustworthiness of fundraising organizations. In many cases, donors are not recipients of services provided by nonprofit organizations, and donors and recipients of nonprofit organizations do not know each other personally. International development organizations or environmental and wildlife organizations are good examples of nonprofit organizations that provide services primarily to nondonors. In addition, they also work in distant areas. For decisions about donations to such organizations, the problem of uncertainty is most pressing. How can donors decide whether their contribution makes a difference? How can they know where their contribution is used most effectively? Donors want information about the nonprofit's mission, activities, overhead, and fundraising costs, and form an impression of an organization's efficiency using this information (Parsons, 2003), even though financial information is not necessarily indicative of quality (Steinberg, 1986).

Two problems with information about fundraising organizations reduce the likelihood that donors will put their charitable impulse into action: costs and credibility. The first problem is that for many donors, the search costs involved in the acquisition of such information are too high. Even in the USA, where information about fundraising organizations is publicly available through the internet (at www.guidestar.org), only a fraction of donors actively search for this information and use it (Arumi et al., 2005). Guidestar is not used by the majority of donors because gathering and interpreting the information is costly. Donors have to spend time on the internet obtaining the data, and they have to interpret and evaluate the data. This task is a difficult one that requires cognitive resources and time. Donors have to incur costs to "give wisely." Most donors are not prepared to incur these costs.

The second problem is that of credibility. How can donors be sure that the information they receive from fundraising organizations is accurate? The problem of credibility is a second reason why Guidestar is not often used. Guidestar is based on data provided by the nonprofit organizations themselves through the Form 990 that 501(c) organizations provide to the IRS in order to obtain tax-exempt status. Because the IRS has very few personnel to check the information provided, donors must rely on their personal impression about the organization. They cannot be sure that the data are accurate (Bowman and Bies, 2005). In contrast, donors in the Netherlands can be fairly confident that the data provided by fundraising organizations to the CBF are accurate.

The fundraising problem

From the perspective of nonprofit organizations that are trying to raise funds, the credibility problem emerges in a different light. For individual nonprofit organizations, the problem is how they can persuade donors of their trustworthiness. From the agency perspective, nonprofits must persuade donors that they are "accountable," meaning that they will do their best to fulfill donor wishes. Svítková and Ortmann (2006) call this the "fundraising problem." If fundraising organizations can show donors that they provide services of higher quality and that they are a more efficient organization, they will gain a competitive advantage in the market.

Donors may doubt the accuracy of information provided by nonprofit organizations themselves. The fundraising problem for fundraising organizations and the trust problem for donors can be solved if trustworthy information about fundraising organizations is available at no cost to donors. This is exactly what the program does. Generally speaking, seals of approval reduce search costs for consumers (Bennett and McCrohan, 1993). This also holds for decisions about donations to fundraising organizations. Fundraising organizations use the accreditation seal as a signal to donors that their organization is trustworthy, in the same way that for-profit firms use certification standards (e.g., ISO 9000; Terlaak and King, 2006).

The Dutch accountability club works as a reputation signaling system. When donors receive a fundraising appeal from a nonprofit organization, they can evaluate the trustworthiness of the organization by looking for the seal. If donors actually rely on the seal in their decisions on charitable contributions, it should give fundraising organizations that use the seal a competitive advantage over nonprofit organizations that do not use the seal: accredited organizations stand out as more trustworthy. The first hypothesis tested below is therefore:

H1 *Nonprofit organizations that participate in the accountability club increase fundraising income more strongly than nonprofit organizations that do not participate.*

The effect on donors is that the seal legitimates confidence in fundraising organizations among donors, and hence promotes giving. In the absence of an accountability program, donors have to rely on their casual impressions of the trustworthiness of nonprofit organizations, and they will worry about whether their confidence is justified. The public holds overly negative views on the fundraising costs of nonprofit organizations (Sargeant and Kähler, 1999; Bekkers, 2003). Such views are associated with (but do not necessarily cause) reduced donations (Bekkers, 2003).

When fundraising organizations are monitored by an independent agency, however, donors may correct their views. Independent monitoring provides an external piece of information that legitimates their confidence. A well-designed accountability program should therefore increase the level of charitable confidence among donors when they learn about the system. Such a system would be an alternative to joining an organization in order to obtain information about its trustworthiness (Bowman, 2004). The hypotheses tested below are:

H2   *Individuals who learn about the accountability club increase donations more strongly than individuals who do not learn about the program.*

H3   *Individuals who learn about the accountability club gain confidence in fundraising organizations more strongly than individuals who do not learn about the club.*

H4   *Individuals who learn about the accountability club increase donations more strongly than individuals who do not learn about the club because of enhanced confidence.*

Who responds to the accountability club?

There are good reasons to believe that accountability clubs are not equally important to all types of donors. One would expect that large donors would have stronger vested interests in accountability clubs. Generally speaking, people search for more information in decisionmaking about issues that are more important to them (Lanzetta and Driscoll, 1968). Those who give more to nonprofit organizations will find the trustworthiness of a fundraising organization soliciting contributions more important because they have a larger amount of money at stake. While Tinkelman (1998) found support for the hypothesis that large donors are more responsive to financial information from fundraising organizations in a study of corporate giving, Bowman (2006) did not find support for the hypothesis in a study of households. However, Bowman argues that his finding may have been the result of a low sample size. Donors who give large amounts to fundraising organizations will care more about the effectiveness of their contribution than donors who give small amounts. A large donation to an ineffective organization is a larger waste of money than a small donation. The hypothesis tested below is:

H5   *The higher the amount donated in previous years, the stronger the increase in donations upon learning about the accountability program.*

Who benefits from participation?

There are good reasons to believe that accreditation is not equally beneficial to all types of fundraising nonprofit organizations. One would expect that accreditation is most beneficial for organizations working beyond the donor's horizon, because they face a stronger asymmetry of information problem. The less visible the qualities of an organization's output are for consumers, the higher the potential benefits of external evaluations (Terlaak and King, 2006). Donors will have more difficulty judging the effectiveness and trustworthiness of fundraising organizations that operate in distant countries, or work for abstract causes like the environment and human rights. Progress in poverty relief and human rights protection is more difficult to see than progress in provision of welfare or arts and culture at the local level. In addition, poverty, ozone layer depletion, and human rights violations are likely to continue in spite of the efforts of nonprofit organizations. In such circumstances, donors may feel their support is legitimate when they know the organization is accredited. Local organizations, on the other hand, may not need accreditation because donors are able to gain an idea of the effectiveness of the organization themselves by paying a visit to the organization or through information from others who have contacts with the organization. Viewed from the perspective of the fundraising organization one arrives at the same hypothesis. Organizations that operate on a local level are more strongly visible to donors, and subject to control. Local organizations cannot afford mistakes because they would be noticed more easily. Thus:

H6   *International development organizations benefit more strongly from participation in the accountability program than do other organizations.*

The effect of accreditation on giving by households

In order to test the hypotheses on changes in donations among households, I use data from the Giving in the Netherlands Panel Study (GINPS), a longitudinal panel study of giving and volunteering behavior among households. The GINPS has been conducted in May biennially since 2002. Data are gathered in a computer-assisted self-interview (CASI). Thus far, three waves have been completed. In wave 1, 1,964 respondents completed the survey; 1,246 of the wave 1 respondents also completed wave 2, and 703 also completed wave 3. Total n in wave 2 was 1,316; n=1,474 in wave 3. I restrict the analyses to respondents who participated in at least two waves of the survey.[9]

---

[9] An important concern for the analyses is whether the group of respondents who participated in the second wave is representative of those who participated in the first wave. Selective panel attrition may endanger the validity of conclusions on the effects of learning about accreditation. A logistic regression analysis of panel attrition on the predictors of giving in 2004 used in the analyses showed only one significant effect: a negative effect of the level of education, indicating that university graduates were more likely to leave the

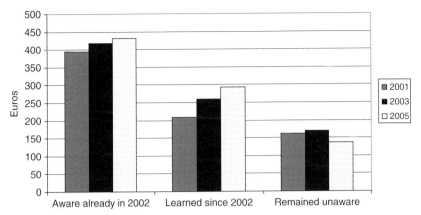

Figure 11.1 Mean amount donated in 2001, 2003, and 2005 by awareness of accreditation

First I estimate the influence of learning about the accountability clubs on charitable giving in 2003. I do so by comparing donations in 2003 and 2005 among those who had learned about CBF and those who had not, excluding those who already knew about the accreditation seal in 2002 because they cannot have learned about the system (see Figure 11.1).

Those who remained unaware of the system (n=621) gave €169 on average in 2003, which is about the same as two years earlier (€163). Those who learned about the system (n=183) gave €260 on average in 2003, which is substantially more than two years earlier (€209). Those who knew about the accountability program already gave on average €417 in 2003, a slight increase since 2001 (€394).[10] This pattern of results suggests that those who became aware of the CBF increased their giving, while those who remained unaware hardly did so. Looking at the subset of respondents who participated in all three waves of the survey (n=703), I

panel than those with lower levels of education. This is unfortunate because university graduates give more. The selectivity of panel attrition with regard to education will lead to an underestimation of the effect of education on giving in 2004.

[10] Logistic regression analyses were conducted to explore other differences between those who remained unaware of the system and those who were aware of it already in 2002 and became aware in 2004, respectively. Those who became aware of the system were younger, more highly educated, somewhat more likely to be members of an orthodox Protestant or other religious group, and significantly more trusting of others. Those who were aware of the system already in 2002 were more likely to be married or members of a small religious group, less likely to have children, more highly educated, more trusting of others, and more likely to attend church often. They also received more solicitations for charitable contributions.

Table 11.1 *Tobit regression of amount donated in 2005 (n=692; 586 uncensored, 106 censored)*

	Model 1		Model 2		Model 3		Model 4	
	Coeff.	p	Coeff.	p	Coeff.	p	Coeff.	p
Knew CBF already	218.3	***	116.5	***	128.9	***	129.9	***
Learned about CBF	133.9	*	114.7	**	121.3	**	121.9	**
Education	34.6	**	7.7		1.5		1.5	
Income (×10k)	20.1	**	12.0	*	12.2	*	12.2	*
Church attendance	7.1	***	3.2	***	3.2	***	3.2	***
Personal solicitations	1.3		−10.5		−8.2		−8.0	
Impersonal solicitations	45.1	*	22.9		25.6		25.5	
High trust	112.9	***	49.9		52.0	(*)	51.9	(*)
Amount 2001			.868	***	.785	***	.781	***
Confidence					37.8	(*)	29.3	(*)
Irritation					18.4		18.2	
Program spending					1.4	(*)	1.4	(*)
CBF* amount 2001							11.8	
Pseudo R square	.0309		.0680		.0712		.0712	

Notes: ***p<.001; **p<.01; *p<.05; (*) p<.10. Included in all regression models are controls for age, gender, marital status, working status, home ownership, town size, and religious affiliation.

find that those who remained unaware of the system from 2002 to 2006 (n=330) gave on average €136 in 2005, a slight decrease since 2003. Those who had learned about the system (n=114) gave €293 in 2005, substantially more than in 2003. Those who knew about the accountability program already gave on average €432, another increase.

Summing up: from 2001 to 2005, giving increased among the respondents who were already aware of the CBF system in 2002. But giving increased more strongly among respondents who became aware of the system. Giving slightly decreased among those who remained unaware.

A tobit regression analysis of the amount donated in 2005 on learning about the system (not shown in Table 11.1) shows that the gross effect of learning about the accountability program is €217.[11] When control variables are included, this difference is reduced to a still significant €134 (see Table 11.1, model 1). This result supports hypothesis 3. The major part of the relationship of learning about accreditation with the amount donated

---

[11] This relationship is significant, p<.000. The tobit model is used to take censoring of donations into account. The effect of learning about accreditation in the OLS model (€157) is somewhat smaller, but still significant (p<.006).

remains when the amount donated in 2001 is included in model 2. By including this variable the effects of the other variables can be interpreted as the effects on changes in giving. Thus, learning about the accountability program is associated with an increase in the amount donated of €115 in the period 2002–2006.[12]

When charitable confidence, irritation, and beliefs about program spending are included in model 3 the effect of learning about the accountability program remains about the same (€121). Thus, confidence hardly mediates the effect of learning about accreditation, despite the fact that it has a strong relationship with the amount donated. This result stands in contrast to hypothesis 4. The anomaly will be discussed below.

The results in model 4 do not support hypothesis 5, that learning about accreditation increases giving more strongly among those who gave larger amounts in the past. The interaction between learning about accreditation and the amount donated in 2001 is positive, but not significant. However, in an analysis of the amount donated in 2003 the interaction between learning about the system and the amount donated in 2001 is strongly significant (results available upon request). This result does support the hypothesis. Together, the results imply that there may be an additional effect of learning about accreditation among those who gave higher amounts in the past, but that it is short lived.

Differential effects on giving to religion and other causes

Table 11.2 shows the results of similar analyses separately for donations to religion and other causes. The analyses show that learning about the CBF accountability program affects donations to religion as well as causes other

[12] Because amounts donated are highly skewed I also ran analyses of the natural log of the amount donated. Results of these models show an effect of learning about the system of 75.2 percent, 64.0 percent, 60.8 percent, and 59.3 percent, in models 1–4, respectively. It may be argued that learning about the accreditation system is endogenous and that including the lagged amount donated and control variables still leaves room for unobserved heterogeneity to bias the estimates. Indeed a Hausman test for a regression of the amount donated on awareness of the accreditation system is highly significant, $\chi^2 = 100.05$ (df=1), p<.000. I conducted a fixed effects regression of the logged amount donated to assess this criticism and found that learning about accreditation increases giving by 15.3 percent (p<.081). This estimate is considerably smaller than the effect of learning about accreditation reported in model 2 of Table 11.1, which is about 70.6 percent (the €115 from model 2 in Table 11.1 divided by €163, the mean amount donated by households who were unaware of the system in 2002). The difference implies that to some extent unobserved heterogeneity is driving the results reported in Table 11.1, but not completely.

Table 11.2 *Tobit regression of amount donated to religion and causes other than religion in 2005*

	Religion		Other	
	Coeff.	*p*	Coeff.	*p*
Knew CBF already	73.2	(★)	91.7	★★★
Learned about CBF	119.7	★★	53.1	★
Education	2.2		4.5	
Income (×10k)	16.7	★★	4.1	
Attendance	2.4	★★★	−0.3	
Personal solicitations	−1.0		−6.4	
Impersonal solicitations	26.1		40.5	★★
High trust	26.9		37.7	★
Amount religion 2001	.862	★★★	.421	★★★
Amount other 2001	.050		.373	★★★
Confidence	−10.2		26.6	(★)
Irritation	−2.0		9.4	
Program spending	1.4		0.9	(★)
n (censored)	692 (432)		692 (115)	
Pseudo R square	.1197		.0490	

Notes: ★★★p<.001; ★★p<.01; ★p<.05; (★) p<.10. Included in all regression models are controls for age, gender, marital status, working status, home ownership, town size, and religious affiliation.

than religion; the former relationship appears to be somewhat stronger than the latter.

The results in the first column of Table 11.2 show that learning about CBF increased giving to religion in 2003 by about €120 when sociodemographic characteristics and donations in 2001 are taken into account. This finding is somewhat surprising. Despite the fact that none of the major churches in the Netherlands has the right to bear the accreditation seal, the churches did receive higher amounts from those who learned about the program. This finding suggests that there is an unintended positive externality generated by club participation. The purpose of the system is to enable donors to discriminate between organizations that are subject to monitoring and those that are not. Now it turns out that nonaccredited organizations also benefit from the system. Donors may have the apparently rather vague impression that fundraising organizations are subject to some form of monitoring, but may not know exactly which organizations are accredited.

The strongly positive effect of religious donations in 2001 indicates that religious giving is habit-like behavior: an additional €100 in 2001 is associated with an additional €86 four years later. Confidence, irritation, and perceptions of program spending are not related to religious donations.

The results in the second column reveal that learning about the accountability program increases giving to causes other than religion in 2005 by about €53 when sociodemographic characteristics and donations in 2001 are taken into account. Surprisingly, the effect of learning about the accountability program on giving to causes other than religion is smaller than the effect on religious giving.

The results in the second column also show that donations to causes other than religion in 2005 are less stable over time than religious giving. In addition, there is a "spill-over effect" of religious giving to nonreligious giving: donations to causes other than religion in 2005 are also correlated with donations to religion in 2001. An additional €100 to religion in 2001 is associated with an additional €42 to other causes four years later. Interestingly, such a spill-over effect did not appear in the analysis of religious giving. Involvement in religious organizations spills over into involvement in other organizations, but the reverse is not the case. Similar findings have been reported earlier for giving in the USA (Wilhelm *et al.*, 2008) and for volunteering in the Netherlands (Ruiter and Bekkers, 2008).

Finally, the second column shows that attitudes toward charitable organizations are related to nonreligious giving. Higher charitable confidence and more positive perceptions of the proportion of funds raised spent on programs are associated with higher donations.

The effects of learning about the accountability club on attitudes toward fundraising organizations

Table 11.3 tests the influence of learning about the CBF accountability program between 2002 and 2004 on confidence in fundraising organizations, beliefs about program spending, and irritation about fundraising organizations (all measured in 2006). The analyses include measures of the same variables in 2004, such that the effects of the other variables can be interpreted as the effects on changes in attitudes.

Although the analyses in Tables 11.1 and 11.2 show that most of the effect of learning about the CBF program is not a result of these attitudes, it is still possible that the accountability program does change them. If the accountability program works as intended, it should not only affect the magnitude of giving, but also improve the quality of decisionmaking about giving. Donors should obtain more accurate information about the costs

Table 11.3 *Regression analyses of confidence, irritation about fundraising campaigns, and beliefs about program spending in 2006 (n=692)*

	Confidence		Irritation		Program spending	
	Coeff.	p	Coeff.	p	Coeff.	p
2004 measure	.605	***	.345	***	.375	***
Aware already	.109	(*)	.050		−2.527	*
Learned about CBF	.131	(*)	.047		.140	
Education	.039	*	−.050	**	−.356	
Income (×10k)	.008		−.006		−.336	
Attendance	−.002		−.002		.007	
High trust	.174	**	−.166	*	−1.527	
Amount religion 2001 (×100)	.034		.091		−.030	
Amount other 2001 (×100)	.098		.147		−.023	
CBF* amount religion 2001	−.013		.150		−1.193	
CBF* amount other 2001	−.000		−.060		1.894	
Adj. R square	.381		.240		.201	

Notes: ***p<.001; **p<.01; *p<.05; (*) p<.10. Included in all regression models are controls for age, gender, marital status, working status, home ownership, town size, and religious affiliation.

of fundraising and program spending and may be less irritated by fund-raising campaigns when they know that an independent monitoring agency evaluates fundraising organizations.

However, learning about the accountability program between 2002 and 2006 has not changed the attitudes towards fundraising organizations much, controlling for confidence in 2004. There is a small and marginally significant positive effect of learning about the system on charitable confidence. This finding suggests that learning about the system increases confidence in charitable organizations a little. Learning about the system is not associated with irritation about the number of appeals or beliefs about program spending.[13]

[13] Additional analyses reveal an interesting interaction effect of learning about the accountability program with donations in 2001 on charitable confidence in 2004. Confidence in fundraising organizations in 2004 was higher among larger donors to causes other than religion after learning about the accountability program between 2002 and 2004. This effect does not occur among large donors to religious organizations, nor among small donors. There are no significant interaction effects of donations in 2001 with learning about accreditation on irritation or beliefs about program spending. These analyses are available from the author.

The results in Table 11.3 also reveal that persons with higher levels of education, lower incomes, and a high level of trust in fellow citizens have more positive attitudes toward fundraising organizations.

The effect of accreditation on fundraising income

The preceding analyses have shown how households change their giving and perceptions of fundraising organizations after learning about the CBF accountability club. Now I shift the perspective from donors to the receiving organizations. What are the benefits of accreditation for fundraising organizations in terms of fundraising income? Do fundraising organizations raise more funds when they are accredited? How much is the benefit of accreditation? Which types of nonprofit organizations benefit the most from accreditation?

To answer these questions, I analyze data from the Central Bureau of Fundraising on the income of 157 major fundraising nonprofit organizations in the period 1994–2004. Since 1994, these nonprofit organizations have submitted annual reports to the CBF each year.[14] Among other things, the database contains data on gross fundraising income and fundraising costs (in euros), the sector in which the organization is active, the work area of the organization (the Netherlands, abroad, or both), and whether the organization was accredited. These data were available for each year in the period 1994–2004 in which the organization submitted financial statements to CBF. Raw amounts reported in the database were deflated with the annual mutation in the consumer price index, taking 1994 as the base year. Total inflation in the 1994–2004 period was 25.8 percent, while average fundraising income grew by 32.1 percent. All amounts were log-transformed before analyses.

A fixed effects regression model is used to estimate the effect of accreditation on fundraising income. When studying effects of nonrandom changes using longitudinal data, this model is usually preferred over random effects regression models (Halaby, 2004).[15] Fixed effects models are more appropriate than random effects models when studying the effects of an intervention that is not randomly assigned to actors, but actors are selected into treatment. This is certainly the case for the accreditation of fundraising organizations. Whether or not – and if so,

[14] The original dataset contained data on a much larger number of fundraising organizations, increasing over time, from 345 in 1994 to 548 in 2004. In the analyses presented here, all organizations that had missing observations in one or more years were disregarded to rule out composition effects. Analyses on the full sample of organizations yield somewhat weaker effects for most variables.
[15] The Hausman test for model 1 is highly significant, $\chi^2=592.57$ (df=6), p<.000.

when – nonprofit organizations are accredited is not a randomly occurring event. The system started in 1997 with thirteen organizations.[16] In subsequent years, increasing numbers of organizations applied for the accreditation seal, also in other sectors than health. The fixed effects regression model rules out the possibility that stable, unobserved characteristics of nonprofit organizations, such as the sector in which the organization operates, confound the effects of accreditation (Allison, 1994).[17]

In order to evaluate the magnitude of the effects of accreditation, lagged fundraising income and fundraising costs in the current year, the preceding year, and two years before are included in the regression models. In addition, the analyses include a variable "year" to model the average annual growth in fundraising income.

Model 1 of Table 11.4 yields an estimate of the effect of accreditation of 6.7 percent, controlling for lagged fundraising income, fundraising costs in the current year, lagged fundraising costs, two-year fundraising costs, and year. This result supports hypothesis 1.

Model 1 of Table 11.4 also reveals an estimate of the effect of lagged fundraising income of 2.21 percent, indicating that fundraising income in the current year is weakly dependent on fundraising income in the past year.[18] The effect of fundraising costs of .337 indicates that a 10 percent increase in fundraising expenditure raises 3.4 percent more funds the next year. Fundraising costs in the preceding year have an unexpected negative effect. There is no effect of year, indicating that fundraising income grew along with inflation in the period 1994–2004.

Model 2 shows that the effect of accreditation is not constant in the period 1994–2004. The main effect of accreditation in this model represents the average effect of accreditation in the years 1994–2002. The

---

[16] The CBF announced its plan for an accreditation program in the early 1990s. It was tested among a group of three well-known fundraising organizations (NOVIB (currently Oxfam Netherlands), the Asthma Fund, and the World Wildlife Fund) that were approved in 1995 but were not allowed to use the seal until December 1996. Another group of ten organizations entered the procedure in 1996, and another four were accredited on July 1, 1997. The majority of these frontrunners were large health charities (e.g., Cancer Foundation, Diabetes Foundation, Kidney Foundation).

[17] I also ran "difference in difference" models using the generalized method of moments (GMM; Arellano and Bond, 1991) because the fixed effect specification may be biased as a result of autocorrelations among the residuals of the dependent variable and its lag. Estimates of a GMM model including the same variables produced very similar results as reported in Table 11.4, but without significant lagged fundraising income effects (results available upon request). However, in this model as well as a wide range of other model specifications, Sargan tests of overidentifying restrictions in GMM models were always significant, and autocovariance in residuals remained a problem. This implies that also the GMM specification may have produced biased estimates.

[18] This estimate is much lower than the estimate from an OLS (.968) or random effects GLS (.917).

Table 11.4 *Fixed effects regression of fundraising income on accreditation, lagged fundraising income, fundraising costs, and year*

	Model 1			Model 2			Model 3			Model 4		
	Coeff.	SE	p	Coeff.	SE	p	Coeff.	SE	p	Coeff.	SE	p
Income t_1	.221	.030	.000	.220	.030	.000	.215	.031	.000	.211	.030	.000
Fundraising costs t_0	.337	.029	.000	.339	.029	.000	.337	.029	.000	.338	.029	.000
Fundraising costs t_1	-.049	.033	.134	-.048	.033	.150	-.049	.033	.137	-.039	.033	.149
Fundraising costs t_2	.069	.028	.013	.068	.028	.013	.069	.028	.014	.068	.028	.014
Accredited	.067	.033	.046	.064	.033	.055	.073	.034	.030	.135	.046	.004
Year	.000	.005	.928	.007	.006	.239	.001	.005	.910	.001	.005	.904
Accredited, 2003/2004				-.067	.032	.037						
Accredited, <200k							-.112	.094	.234			
Accredited, health										-.051	.060	.399
Accredited, international										-.117	.056	.035
Accredited, religion										-.285	.117	.015
Constant	6.652	.453	.000	6.629	.453	.000	6.745	.460	.000	6.679	.453	.000
R2 within	.275			.278			.276			.281		
R2 between	.953			.953			.952			.950		
Observations	1142			1142			1142			1142		
Groups	137			137			137			137		

interaction term represents the effect of accreditation in 2003 and 2004. These years are considered separately because two organizations (Plan Netherlands and the Dutch Heart Association) received a great deal of attention in the media with the publication of managers' salaries. Fundraising income of these organizations declined in response to these media reports. The results of model 2 shows that fundraising organizations that were accredited in 2003 and 2004 reaped no benefits of accreditation in these years; the main effect of accreditation together with the interaction effect for the years 2003 and 2004 is about zero. In an analysis excluding the two organizations that suffered in the media (Plan Netherlands and the Dutch Heart Association) the same significantly negative effect of accreditation in the years 2003 and 2004 is observed. This suggests that the decrease in the effect of accreditation in these years is not due to the decrease in fundraising income for these two organizations resulting from negative media reports, but may reflect a decrease in the credibility of the accreditation seal across the whole philanthropic sector.[19] It is likely that the media reports in these years made the public aware that the accountability program has no standards regarding the salaries of employees of fundraising organizations. These media reports can be viewed as exogenous shocks that led to external pressure to create more stringent standards.

Who benefits most?

Models 3 and 4 of Table 11.4 test the effects of accreditation among specific groups of fundraising organizations. These analyses yield two conclusions. First, for organizations with low fundraising income (less than €200,000, n=6) accreditation yielded significantly smaller benefits than for other organizations. Second, religious organizations and international development organizations tended to benefit less than other organizations.

The first conclusion is discomforting for the group of small organizations that have submitted financial statements to the CBF since 1994. The cost of the accreditation procedure (about €4,500) is a substantial amount for small fundraising organizations, and it did not benefit them at all. Accreditation actually *reduced* fundraising income by almost 4 percent

---

[19] I ruled out the possibility that the benefit of accreditation for fundraising organizations is largest in its first year, and declines as organizations have the seal for a longer period of time. An analysis including interaction terms for all years shows a sudden drop in the effect of accreditation in 2003 and 2004, with 1997 and 1999 being better than the average years (2000–2001).

(.073–.112=−.039). Taking an organization with fundraising income of €500,000 as an example, the benefit of accreditation in the next year (€36,500) easily exceeded the costs. It should be noted, however, that the negative result for the small organizations does not emerge from the larger sample of organizations that submitted financial statements in at least two years. Among those organizations, the benefit of accreditation for the group of small organizations was equal to the benefit for larger organizations (results available upon request).

The second conclusion stands in contrast to hypothesis 6 that international development organizations would benefit more from accreditation. The results show that international development organizations hardly benefit at all from accreditation in the period 1994–2004. The net benefit for international development organizations is only 1.8 percent per year (.135–.117).[20]

Health organizations, which formed the majority of the organizations that were accredited at the start of the system, also reaped no additional benefits from accreditation. In fact, the benefit for health organizations is slightly smaller even than for organizations in other sectors (except international development and religious organizations). Remember that the initial group of organizations was dominated by health organizations. Combining the results of the present analysis with the earlier result that the benefit of accreditation was larger in 1997 and 1999, I infer that the initial group of organizations benefited more not because they were dominated by health organizations, but because they started in 1997, and that year and 1999 were particularly good years for fundraising.

Finally, I find that religious organizations that were accredited benefited less from accreditation than organizations in other sectors (except health and international development organizations). This result is surprising given the earlier result that religious organizations attracted donations from those who learned about the accreditation system. That result was driven by the increase in donations to churches that did not join the accreditation program. The present result is driven by religious organizations that did join the program.

---

[20] To some extent, this result is specific to those organizations that submitted financial statements throughout the entire period studied (1994–2004). In an analysis of all organizations that provided at least two years of data, the net benefit for international development organizations is 3 percent (details available upon request). The result is not due to changes in fundraising costs after accreditation because fundraising costs are included in the model. The result is also not a result of differences in size between international development organizations and other organizations because the effect is virtually the same when the interactions of model 1 are included.

Conclusion

The findings support the view that accountability clubs involving accreditation may help to solve the key accountability challenges for nonprofits: the fundraising problem faced by nonprofit organizations and the trust problem for donors. I found support for hypothesis 1 that accreditation increases the fundraising income of nonprofit organizations. I found an average 6.7 percent increase in fundraising income after accreditation in the period 1994–2004. I also found support for hypothesis 2 that individuals who learn about the accountability program increase their donations to charitable causes. The effect of accreditation is about €115 between 2002 and 2006. Only weak support was found for hypothesis 3, that learning about accreditation increases confidence in charitable organizations. No support was obtained for the hypothesis that learning about accreditation increases giving through enhanced confidence.

Among larger donors to causes other than religion, confidence did increase after learning about the accreditation, as did their giving. This finding supports the hypothesis that learning about accreditation affects large donors more strongly than small donors. However, a large part of the effect of accreditation remains unexplained. Perhaps accreditation merely justifies donations without improving confidence. When an independent monitoring agency accredits a fundraising organization that a donor is supporting, the donor may not necessarily feel more confidence in the organization, but will feel justified in giving. Further research is clearly needed to test this hypothesis.

Finally, the data suggest that the benefits of accreditation are smaller for international fundraising organizations. This finding stands in contrast to the hypothesis that international fundraising organizations are more strongly affected by accreditation than other organizations. It is unclear why this is the case. Because the trust problem is most pressing for international development organizations, one would expect them to benefit most strongly from the accountability program. With the present data it is difficult to explain this anomaly. Another unexpected finding that remains to be explained is that religious organizations failed to reap benefits from accreditation.

Discussion

The focus of this chapter has been on the benefits of participation in an accreditation club for fundraising organizations themselves in terms of fundraising income. But donors are also likely to gain from the accountability program when fundraising organizations comply with the standards of excellence required to bear the seal. It is likely that the quality of internal organization in general and accounting practices in particular, as well as transparency and accountability to donors, increases because of accreditation. However, these changes in nonprofit behavior are more difficult to measure and quantify and could not be studied in the present chapter.

Another area for future research is to study the decision to join an accreditation program. The CBF database only contains data on organizations that have joined and submitted financial statements to the CBF. It is natural to assume that this reflects a willingness to be transparent and an interest in accreditation. The development of fundraising income among organizations that did not submit financial statements remains unclear. It is even impossible to say how selective the sample of organizations is that is studied in the present chapter, because basic data on the universe of fundraising organizations are lacking in the Netherlands.

Despite its advantages, the CBF accountability club has some imperfections. The club is somewhat "leaky": churches have benefited from the system even though they did not join the program. While this can be viewed as "free-riding," it can also be viewed as a sign that the accreditation system is a public good benefiting the charitable sector as a whole, and not just its members.

As in for-profit markets (Bennett and McCrohan, 1993), the costs associated with accreditation may be too high for small fundraising organizations. For the first five years, the accreditation seal costs on average €3,872 (€3,439 in the next five years). Taking the 6.7 percent from Table 11.4 as an estimate of the average increase in fundraising income, fundraising income needs to be at least €57,791 a year for a minimum of five years to make the accreditation procedure worthwhile from an economic perspective. For organizations with fundraising income below this threshold the investment in the seal does not pay off.

In addition the club standards may limit participation. The maximum fundraising cost ratio of 25 percent may also be unfair to small organizations. This ceiling punishes new organizations, and organizations that are trying to raise funds for unpopular causes (Steinberg, 1986). The ceiling also punishes organizations that have no volunteers available for door-to-door fundraising. Fundraising nonprofit organizations receive a significant source of income at virtually no cost when they can use volunteer fundraisers. This is mainly the case for large, established health charities like the Dutch Heart Association and the Cancer Foundation (KWF). For a new organization, the ceiling of 25 percent may pose a problem, even when the organization has been active three years. The CBF acknowledges that the maximum of 25 percent may be exceeded in specific circumstances, and effectively uses a three-year average for fundraising costs in the evaluation procedure. This makes sense but may still be too stringent for specific types of nonprofit organizations.

A potential unintended side-effect of the increasing awareness of the accreditation seal and the 25 percent maximum for fundraising costs (the best-known standard) is that a competition for low fundraising costs may emerge. In order to present low fundraising costs to the public, fundraising organizations may be tempted to reduce fundraising costs administratively through violations of the principle of joint cost allocation or considering fundraising campaigns as programs when they contain educational material (Hager, 2003). At present, CBF accounting rules are not clear-cut on this issue. Although there are limits to the level of detail of standards that can be specified and the costs of enforcement of these standards, more specific guidelines are needed here in order to prevent misrepresentation of fundraising costs.

A final limitation of the accountability program is that it contains no standards regarding the salaries of managers. The Dutch public clearly desires more regulation and transparency here. Violations of (low) expectations on salaries caused a drop in fundraising income for two well-known fundraising organizations in 2003 and 2004. The analyses revealed that the accreditation seal lost its effect also for other organizations precisely in these years. A recent study shows that the Dutch public is increasingly concerned about the salaries of managers of fundraising organizations (WWAV, 2008). To keep the public's trust, it may be necessary to include rules on salaries for managers of fundraising organizations in the CBF standards of excellence. Also, enforcement of existing rules becomes more important if the program is to retain credibility among the public. Perhaps this is one of the reasons why the CBF has recently withheld accreditation from a few organizations. Adding standards on managers' salaries may also be a wise decision for the CBF. If members make rational decisions, they will leave a program without such rules if that does not pay off.

This chapter has provided a test of two key tenets of voluntary accountability clubs. First, the signals accountability clubs generate are received by key nonprofit donors and – if the club is strong enough – provide a credible signal. Second, principals are willing to reward nonprofits for credible signals. In the case of the CBF, many Dutch donors are aware of the accreditation program and those who are aware contribute more to organizations that participate in the program. Accredited organizations also see their donations rise.

What features of the CBF club account for these results? In comparison with many other clubs studied in this volume, the CBF is a relatively strong club. This in itself is a surprising fact. CBF shares similarities with the accreditation clubs in health and education in the USA studied by Bowman in this volume (chapter 3). Bowman argues that these clubs are strong because the nonprofits face a dominant principal, the US federal government, that essentially mandates participation in these clubs. That is not the case in the Netherlands. The CBF emerged from self-regulation efforts by fundraising organizations. Why such self-regulation efforts have not developed into strong clubs in other countries is a pressing issue for future research. To study this issue, cross-national comparative data on the emergence of accountability clubs are needed.

Without access to such data, I can only offer speculative hypotheses. One such hypothesis is that strong clubs emerge more easily in smaller philanthropic markets. Cooperation is much easier to organize in small groups (Olson, 1965). The Dutch philanthropic market is relatively small compared with that of the USA. It should come as no surprise that Dutch fundraising organizations are well-organized.[21]

Another hypothesis is that competition leads to weak clubs. In the US state associations studied by Tschirhart in chapter 4 of this volume, any given nonprofit might have more choices about different clubs to join. Fundraising organizations will favor joining a club that does not have strong standards to reduce costs. In addition, donors will find it harder to obtain good information about the club and to identify what is a credible club. Until recently, the CBF faced little competition from other clubs. In the absence of such competition, the CBF seal signals to the majority of donors that accredited organizations conform to the standards.

Appendix

Giving in the Netherlands Panel Survey

In the first wave of the GINPS, which was collected in May 2002, respondents reported about donations in the calendar year 2001. In the second wave, which was collected two years later, in May 2004, respondents reported about donations in the calendar year 2003. In the third wave (May 2006) donations in the calendar year 2005 were reported. The purpose of the analyses below is to see how giving to nonprofit organizations changes among respondents who learned about the CBF seal between 2002 and 2004 and among those who did not.

---

[21] Switzerland is another example of a relatively small country with a strong club (ZEWO). Group size cannot be the only factor. Despite its size, Germany also has a strong club (DZI). Also one wonders why a strong club has not emerged in the Czech Republic (see chapter 7 by Ortmann and Svítková in this volume). The Czech Republic is also a relatively small country. However, Ortmann suggests that the past decades of communist rule in the country do not seem to have created a fertile ground for cooperation among civil society organizations.

In all three waves, respondents reported whether they "knew the CBF seal for fundraising organizations" (no/yes). In 2002, 33.7 percent reported awareness of the CBF seal. In 2004, this proportion had grown to 42.9 percent; in 2006 it was back to 38.8 percent. Of those who were unaware of the existence of the CBF seal in May 2002 and also participated in the third wave of the survey (n=444), 25.7 percent had learned about it four years later. The major increase in awareness of the accountability program took place between 2002 and 2004, when 22.8 percent of the respondents who were unaware of the system in the first wave learned about it.

Most of the analyses are conducted among respondents who were unaware of the accountability program in 2002. Charitable donations were measured in waves with extensive survey modules (called "Method-Area" modules by Rooney *et al.*, 2004). I used reports on the amount donated to nonprofit organizations in nine different areas (religion, international affairs, health, arts and culture, public and social benefit, environment/wildlife and animal protection, education and research, sports and recreation, and "other") to construct three measures for both survey years: (1) total amount donated; (2) amount donated to religion; (3) amount donated to causes other than religion. I distinguish religious from nonreligious contributions because none of the churches in the Netherlands has the right to bear the accreditation seal. The mean for the total amount donated in 2001 among respondents who participated in all three waves (n=703) was €245; in 2003 it was €259; in 2005 it was €271.

In the analyses I regress donations in 2003 and 2005 on learning about the system, controlling for potential confounding variables to mitigate the concern that changes in giving between those who learned about the accountability program and those who did not are due not to learning about the system but to some other characteristics. It could be, for instance, that those who gave more to nonprofit organizations in 2001 are more likely to increase their giving in the 2001–2005 period and that they are also more likely to learn about the accountability program, but that the latter does not cause the former.[22]

As confounding variables I include the amount donated in 2001, generalized trust, the number of solicitations received (both measured in 2002), and a series of sociodemographic variables that are often found to be related to philanthropy: household income (log-transformed, originally measured in twenty-four categories ranging from €2,500 to

---

[22] Note that the measures of giving refer to 2003 and 2005, respectively, and awareness of the CBF system was measured in May 2004 and May 2006. For respondents who have learned about the CBF system after giving, awareness of the system could not have influenced giving. This time lag introduces a downward bias in the effect of accreditation.

€300,000, higher incomes truncated), marital status (dummy variable for being married), having children (1=yes), working status (dummy variables for working part-time or having no paid work; full-time paid work is the reference category), level of education (seven categories, ranging from primary education to post-doctoral degree), gender (female=1), age, town size (in thousands of inhabitants), and five dummy variables for religious affiliation (Catholic, Reformed Protestant, Rereformed Protestant, other Christian affiliation, nonChristian affiliation; no religious affiliation being the reference category). All these variables were measured in the 2002 survey.

Generalized social trust was also measured in 2002 with two items that are commonly used as two alternatives: "In general, most people can be trusted" and "You can't be too careful in dealing with other people." Responses to these questions were strongly correlated (r=.42). Because the effect of trust seems to be nonlinear (Bekkers, 2003) I did not use the original 1–5 scores, but recoded the average of the two items into a dichotomous "high trust" variable. Those with a trust score above the mean were considered as "high trusters."

Solicitations for contributions to charitable organizations were measured with a list of the ten different types of methods that nonprofit organizations use most frequently to raise funds. For each method, the respondent indicated whether she had been asked to donate to nonprofit organizations in the two weeks prior to the 2004 survey: 60.4 percent of the respondents reported at least one solicitation in the past two weeks. We distinguished between personal solicitations (42.2 percent) and impersonal solicitations (29.4 percent).

Charitable confidence was measured in 2004 with a single item asking "How much confidence do you have in 'charitable causes'?" on a scale from 1 ("none at all") to 5 ("very much"): 3.1 percent reported no confidence at all, 18.0 percent little confidence, 49.0 percent moderate, 29.5 percent much confidence, and 0.4 percent very much. A measure for irritation about fundraising campaigns ranging from 0 to 5 was constructed from two variables: whether people ever felt irritated by the number of solicitations for charitable contributions they received (0 if not, reported by 48.3 percent), and if yes, to what extent they felt irritated (1 "very little" to 4 "very much", reported by 5.6 percent).

CBF database

The sample of fundraising organizations in the CBF database does not represent a random sample of the population of fundraising organizations. "Bad apples" will be underrepresented because they are unlikely to have annual reports at all and if so, they will be unlikely to submit them to a monitoring agency. The mean amount raised grew from €3.9 million in 1997 to €4.7 million in 2004 (in concurrent euros). Fundraising costs increased too, and even more strongly in relative terms, from €559,000 in 1997 to €890,000 in 2004. In the first three years of the existence of the accountability program, 52 percent of the organizations that provided financial statements throughout the whole period were accredited (24 percent of all organizations in the sample that provided more than two years of data). The proportion grew at a slower pace in consecutive years, to about 65 percent in 2004 (42 percent of organizations that provided more than two years of data).

REFERENCES

Akerlof, G. 1970. The Market for "Lemons": Quality Uncertainty and the Market Mechanism. *Quarterly Journal of Economics* 84: 488–500.

Allison, P. D. 1994. Using Panel Data to Estimate the Effects of Events. *Sociological Methods and Research* 23(2): 174–199.

Arellano, M. and Bond, S. 1991. Some Tests of Specification for Panel Data: Monte Carlo Evidence and an Application to Employment Equations. *Review of Economic Studies* 58: 277–297.

Arumi, A. M., R. Wooden, J. Johnson, S. Farkas, A. Duffett, and A. Ott. 2005. *The Charitable Impulse*. New York: Public Agenda.

Bekkers, R. 2003. Trust, Accreditation, and Philanthropy in the Netherlands. *Nonprofit and Voluntary Sector Quarterly* 32: 596–615.

  2005. Geven van Tijd: Vrijwilligerswerk. In T. N. M. Schuyt and B. M. Gouwenberg, eds. *Geven in Nederland 2005: Giften, Legaten, Sponsoring en Vrijwilligerswerk*. Amsterdam: Elsevier Overheid, pp. 80–92.

Bennett, J. T. and K. F. McCrohan. 1993. Public Policy Issues in the Marketing of Seals of Approval for Food. *Journal of Consumer Affairs* 27(2): 397–415.

Bowman, W. 2004. Confidence in Charitable Institutions and Volunteering. *Nonprofit and Voluntary Sector Quarterly* 33: 247–270.

  2006. Should Donors Care about Overhead Costs? Do They Care? *Nonprofit and Voluntary Sector Quarterly* 35: 288–310.

Bowman, W. and A. Bies. 2005. Can the Charitable Sector Regulate Itself? *Nonprofit Quarterly* 12 (special issue): 39–43.

Hager, M. A. 2003. Current Practices in Allocation of Fundraising Expenditures. *New Directions for Philanthropic Fundraising* 41: 39–52.

Halaby, C. N. 2004. Panel Models in Sociological Research: Theory into Practice. *Annual Review of Sociology* 30: 507–544.

Lanzetta, John T. and James M. Driscoll. 1968. Effects of Uncertainty and Importance on Information Search in Decision Making. *Journal of Personality and Social Psychology* 10(4): 479–486.

Olson, M. 1965. *The Logic of Collective Action*. Cambridge, MA: Harvard University Press.

Parsons, L. M. 2003. Is Accounting Information from Nonprofit Organizations Useful to Donors? A Review of Charitable Giving and Value-relevance. *Journal of Accounting Literature* 22: 104–129.

Rooney, P. M., K. S. Steinberg, and P. G. Schervish. 2004. Methodology is Destiny: The Effect of Survey Prompts on Reported Levels of Giving and Volunteering. *Nonprofit and Voluntary Sector Quarterly* 33: 628–654.

Ruiter, S. and R. Bekkers. 2008. Religion and Voluntary Association Involvement over the Life Course: An Event History Analysis for the Netherlands. Manuscript, Department of Sociology, Radboud University, Nijmegen.

Sargeant, A. and J. Kähler. 1999. Returns on Fundraising Expenditures in the Voluntary Sector. *Nonprofit Management and Leadership* 10: 5–19.

Steinberg, R. S. 1986. Should Donors Care about Fundraising? in S. Rose-Ackerman, ed. *The Economics of Nonprofit Institutions*. New York: Oxford University Press, pp. 347–364.

Svítková, K. and A. Ortmann. 2006. *Certification as a Viable Quality Assurance Mechanism: Theory and Suggestive Evidence*. Charles University, Center for Economic Research and Graduate Education, Working Paper No. 288, February.

Terlaak, A. and A. A. King. 2006. The Effect of Certification with the ISO9000 Quality Management Standard: A Signalling Approach. *Journal of Economic Behavior and Organization* 60: 579–602.

Tinkelman, D. 1998. Differences in Sensitivity of Financial Statement Users to Joint Cost Allocations: The Case of Nonprofit Organizations. *Journal of Accounting, Auditing and Finance* 13(4): 377–393.

Wilhelm, M. O., E. Brown, P. M. Rooney, and R. Steinberg. 2008. The Intergenerational Transmission of Generosity. *Journal of Public Economics* 92: 2146–2156.

Wilke, B. 2003. Monitoring Charitable Organizations: Criteria and Assessment Methods. Contribution to the OECD/DAC Workshop "Development Partners in Evaluation," Paris, March 25–26, 2003.

Wing, K. and M. A. Hager. 2004. *The Quality of Financial Reporting by Nonprofits: Findings and Implications*. Brief No. 4 from the Nonprofit Overhead Cost Project. Washington, DC: Urban Institute.

WWAV. 2008. *Het Nederlandse donateurspanel: Onderzoeksrapportage September 2008*. Woerden: WWAV.

Zalpha van Berkel and WWAV. 2005. Publieksvertrouwen in de Goede Doelensector. Woerden: Zalpha van Berkel and WWAV.

Future research and conclusions

12   Conclusions: nonprofit accountability clubs

Aseem Prakash and Mary Kay Gugerty

Nonprofits and nongovernmental organizations (nonprofits, in short) have emerged as important actors across a wide range of policy areas. Along with their contribution to economic growth and democracy (Putnam, 1993), some view them as the key pillars of the emerging world society (Meyer *et al.*, 1997) and world culture. Given their policy potential and the policy hype that has often surrounded them, nonprofits have attracted significant levels of resources from governments, intergovernmental organizations, foundations, citizens, and corporations. The expectations for what nonprofits can accomplish are quite high, especially given the inadequate success of both market-based and government-based approaches in solving pressing policy problems.

This increased policy attention and the attendant rise in resource flows to the "third sector" have also led to increased scrutiny. Both practitioners and scholars have raised questions about the lack of appropriate accountability mechanisms to govern nonprofits: if nonprofits are showered with resources, how do we know whether nonprofits are delivering as promised? Nonprofits, as well as the donors that seek to fund them, have sought to address these accountability demands in several ways. This volume examined one important category of accountability mechanisms: voluntary accountability clubs. Theoretically and empirically, this volume explored issues such as how and why such clubs emerge, why nonprofits are willing to participate in voluntary programs that impose costly obligations, who sponsors these programs, and how participation in such clubs might reassure various principals about nonprofits' intentions regarding accountability and governance issues.

In examining accountability clubs, this volume contributes to an important debate on the emergence and sustenance of nonprofits. Hansmann (1980) identified two necessary conditions for the emergence of nonprofits. The first pertains to product characteristics (information asymmetries), the second to institutional features (the nondistribution constraint). Hansmann suggested that in product categories marked by information asymmetries (such as experience and post-experience goods), consumers fear opportunistic exploitation by profit-seeking firms. Because nonprofits are prohibited from distributing profits to owners, this institutional constraint provides credible assurance to consumers regarding the nonprofits' good intentions. Consumers may therefore assume that nonprofits are less likely to increase profits by engaging in opportunistic behavior, namely, providing a lower quality product while claiming (and charging for) a higher quality product. Thus, according to Hansmann, the nondistribution constraint helps assure consumers that nonprofits are trustworthy.[1] In Hansmann's (2003) view, this signal of trustworthiness is particularly important for "donative" nonprofits that derive a significant portion of their revenue from donations.[2]

Ortmann and Schlesinger (1997) suggest that the trust thesis rests on three assumptions. The first is that the nondistribution constraint sufficiently restrains opportunistic behavior among nonprofit managers. But the nondistribution constraint may not fully prevent opportunistic behavior since it provides only a "negative" protection against potential malfeasance, rather than providing positive incentives for managerial performance (Ben-Ner and Gui, 2003). And even if the nondistribution constraint could curb incentives for cheating, managers might also cheat in ways that do not require the ability to distribute profits. Nonprofit managers might have incentives to use surpluses for personal objectives such as high salaries, perks, or vanity projects such as expanding the organization beyond the optimal size.[3] Indeed, most scandals plaguing nonprofits pertain to the use of organizational resources for personal gain. Even in the absence of outright fraud, nonprofits may suffer from "goal displacement," "mission drift," or simply incompetence whereby nonprofits operate according to the preferences of managers and boards (themselves unelected), while paying less attention to the preferences of

---

[1] Given that one finds for-profits, nonprofits, and government-owned entities operating in the same sector, how might one interpret Hansmann's thesis in the context of mixed economies? We believe that the weaker version of Hansmann's argument offers a falsifiable hypothesis: the salience of nonprofits in a given sector is positively related to the levels of informational asymmetries between producers and consumers.

[2] Hansmann (2003) is particularly worried about trust issues in these donative sectors; he argues that in sectors now characterized by a mix of for-profit and nonprofit agencies, such as healthcare, the continued existence of many nonprofits may be the result of institutional "lag." Even organizations that might prefer to operate as for-profits adopt nonprofit status because governments tend to regulate nonprofits less.

[3] Hansmann's formulation has another problem: he implicitly assumed that managers and shareholders have identical preferences (or shareholders can monitor managers at low transaction costs). In reality, preference divergence is a major problem facing nonprofit actors as well. It is fair to say that agency conflicts are present with or without the nondistributional constraint. On this count, some lessons from this volume can be applied to understand agency issues in governmental as well as for-profit sectors.

funders, beneficiaries, or government authorizers (Steinberg and Gray, 1993; Ortmann and Schlesinger, 2003).

Second, the trust hypothesis also assumes that consumers recognize the implication of the nondistribution constraint. The evidence from the United States suggests that citizens have a limited understanding of what the nonprofit form entails (Schlesinger and Gray, 2006). Moreover, the way in which ownership form matters will vary across sectors. In particular, consumers may struggle to distinguish fee-based nonprofits from for-profits providing similar services in sectors where both institutional forms are common.

Finally, these internal adulteration problems posed by agency conflict are compounded by the potential for external adulteration: if consumers tend to trust nonprofits, crafty entrepreneurs might enter the sector to exploit this trust. It is possible that positive "selection effects" might help to temper agency conflict if nonprofits attract disproportionate numbers of ethical, "beyond temptation" managers who will not behave opportunistically. But empirical support for such selection effects is thin. Moreover these selection effects might also encourage adverse selection: unethical managers might seek to enter this sector given that the nonprofits that employ them cannot *ex ante* differentiate between unethical and ethical managers.[4]

The trust hypothesis might be defended in another way: increasing levels of professionalization might curb agency problems, especially if such problems are not willful but rooted in managerial ignorance. Indeed, if financial mismanagement can be attributed to managerial ignorance, it can be corrected. But professionalization is an industry-wide phenomenon that cannot help distinguish ethical agencies from unethical ones. If the potential for selection and adulteration effects is significant, professionalization will not allay principals' fears about agency conflict. In sum, agency problems affecting nonprofits range from outright fraud to managerial incompetence or ignorance. While the nondistribution constraint and selection effects might lower agency slippages, nonprofits are likely to continue to suffer from high levels of agency problems because of the lack of institutional oversight that compels nonprofits to disclose information and the potential for external adulteration. Eventually, these problems may erode the trustworthiness of nonprofits because they demonstrate that the nondistribution constraint by itself cannot curb agency slippages.

---

[4] Glaeser and Schleifer (2001) show how self-interested entrepreneurs might choose nonprofit status in order to weaken the incentives for *ex post* expropriation and thereby attract charitable donations.

How might ethical, unadulterated nonprofits respond to this concern and credibly differentiate themselves from adulterated organizations? This volume examines accountability clubs as a mechanism employed by nonprofits to respond to agency conflicts and adulteration concerns. The empirical chapters document club emergence across a range of settings and nonprofit sectors, from foundations in the United States (Frumkin, chapter 6) to NGOs in Africa (Gugerty, chapter 10). These widespread patterns of club emergence suggest that some nonprofits clearly recognize that the nondistribution constraint, even in combination with selection effects and professionalization, does not constitute a sufficiently credible accountability or signaling mechanism.

This volume suggested that nonprofits seek an institutional solution to the agency and adulteration challenges by participating in accountability programs. Drawing on Prakash and Potoski (2006) and Gugerty (2009), we conceptualize these accountability programs as voluntary clubs that impose accountability obligations on their participating members. In return, the participants can avail themselves of the club brand that helps the principals differentiate ethical and unethical nonprofits. Club participation can be viewed as another kind of selection effect whereby nonprofits voluntarily select themselves in for higher levels of accountability scrutiny. A key feature of voluntary clubs is that they help to separate the potentially adulterated agents from the unadulterated ones. Of course, after joining, participants can always shirk; that is why our framework emphasizes the role of monitoring to curb shirking.

We conceptualize accountability as an agency problem and model nonprofits as agents empowered to undertake particular tasks on behalf of certain principals, often according to an explicit contract or agreement. Because principals cannot be sure – for all the reasons enumerated above – that nonprofits are undertaking activities as agreed upon, nonprofits have incentives to join accountability clubs to assure their principals about their intentions. Otherwise they may face loss of funding, authorization, or support. Of course, all clubs are not alike in terms of the obligations they impose and the monitoring mechanisms they have in place to prevent shirking. Thus, the signaling ability and associated reputational value of the club brand is likely to vary with club design; Part II of the volume examines this issue. In particular we suggest that the identity of club sponsors has important effects on club design and the empirical chapters examine a variety of sponsors to examine these effects.

An important question is whether participation in accountability clubs is sufficient to allay the agency concerns of nonprofit principals. Part III of the volume examines the effectiveness of nonprofit clubs in this respect. Taken together, the ten empirical chapters in the volume examine the usefulness and limitations of our theoretical approach, and highlight the varying accountability challenges nonprofits face and the varying contexts in which they function. Below, we return to our original research questions and discuss the key lessons that emerge from the empirical chapters.

The empirics of club design

In the introductory chapter, we developed an analytic typology of nonprofit clubs, drawing on the two institutional features of clubs: standards and swords (the latter consisting of monitoring and enforcement). The framework suggested that reductions in agency losses would be greater in those clubs characterized by strong standards and stringent monitoring. Nonprofits incur higher costs to join these clubs because of the strong standards, and principals can be more certain of compliance because of rigorous monitoring. However, these are also high-cost clubs and some sponsoring actors may therefore shy away from creating them (Tschirhart, chapter 4).

This framework identifies the common institutional features of accountability clubs and permits analysis across multiple cases situated in a variety of contexts. An important goal of the volume is to ascertain the patterns of club emergence and the institutional structure they take, since there is virtually no previous systematic research in this area. To begin to answer these questions, we present Table 12.1, which integrates the clubs discussed in the empirical chapters into the analytic framework developed in the introduction. Several features stand out, which we explore in more detail below.

First, we note in the introduction that pitching club standards at an appropriate level for potential members is an important design issue. Strong standards create high entry costs, which only high-quality organizations will be willing and able to bear. Yet strong standards with little monitoring and enforcement will not be credible to principals, since it will be difficult to ascertain whether nonprofits are actually complying. On this dimension we find a fair amount of variance in the standards set by nonprofit clubs. For example the Council on Foundations standards (Frumkin, chapter 6) consist essentially of six words: mission, stewardship, accountability, diversity, governance, and respect. These "standards" are actually broad principles open to wide interpretation; given that foundations are subject to very little regulation, one might conceivably argue that these principles are indeed "beyond compliance," but it is unclear whether they can provide the basis for allaying the accountability concerns of foundations' main principal: the US government. In contrast, the Minnesota Council of Nonprofits standards are quite extensive,

Table 12.1 *Nonprofit clubs analytic framework and cases*

Club standards	Club "swords"	
	Weak monitoring and enforcement	Strong monitoring and enforcement
Lenient standards	Low cost Marginal branding benefits Minimal reduction in agency loss	Medium cost Moderate branding benefits Moderate reduction in agency loss
	Independent Sector (Young, chapter 5) *Nonprofit Academic Centers Council (Young, chapter 5)* *Council on Foundations (Frumkin, chapter 6)* *Most US state clubs (Tschirhart, chapter 4)* *Czech Donors Forum (Ortmann and Svítková, chapter 7)* *National Council of NGOs, Kenya (Gugerty, chapter 10)* *COMPAS Qualité (Zarnegar Deloffre, chapter 8)*	
Strong standards	Medium cost Moderate branding benefits Moderate reduction in agency loss	High cost High branding benefits Significant reduction in agency loss
	Minnesota Principles and Practices (Bies, chapter 9) *Sphere Humanitarian Principles (Zarnegar Deloffre, chapter 8)* *NGO Code, Ethiopia (Gugerty, chapter 10)*	*Minnesota Accountability Wizard (Bies, chapter 9)* *Joint Commission (Bowman, chapter 3)* *CBF, Netherlands (Bekkers, chapter 11)* *QuAM, Uganda (Gugerty, chapter 10)*

comprising 127 "practices" that quite clearly extend beyond extant reporting requirements for nonprofits (Bies, chapter 9). The observed variation in strength of standards must be understood, however, in relation to club decisions about swords. The Minnesota Council employs no swords, not even asking members to pledge to adhere to the practices upon joining. The Council relies instead on the idea of professionalization for enforcement. The Council on Foundations does ask members to pledge to uphold its standards and uses a "fire alarm" monitoring system in which complaints could be brought against a member and sanctions employed if the foundation is found to violate one or more principle. In contrast, some of the strongest clubs – the CBF in the Netherlands discussed by Bekkers (chapter 11) and the Joint Commission for health accreditation in the United States (Bowman, chapter 3) – set strong standards and rely on peer and third-party monitoring for enforcement. Interestingly, there is one empty area in the table. No clubs employed the combination of weak standards and strong enforcement. The small number of clubs with strong enforcement mechanisms suggests that the main challenge to developing effective voluntary clubs among nonprofits may lie in developing adequate monitoring and enforcement mechanisms and this is a key finding of the volume. As we discuss in detail below, this feature of club design is strongly related to the identity of club sponsors.

Research findings

In Part I of this volume, we pose a number of questions about voluntary club emergence. We ask what the potential is for nonprofit clubs to increase accountability in relation to current requirements, where voluntary initiatives arise (or do not arise), and how key features of nonprofit context affect the prospects for club emergence. Dana Brakman Reiser (chapter 2) addresses the issue of emergence by examining the potential for voluntary clubs to improve nonprofit accountability in the United States context and suggests that clubs may be more likely to emerge where the opportunities for signaling are greatest. Her chapter makes two important contributions to our understanding of nonprofit clubs. First she argues that arenas for accountability standards can usefully be disaggregated into three areas: financial, organizational/governance, and mission. The baseline standards for nonprofits (and the enforcement abilities of principals) vary widely across these three arenas. Existing standards for governance and mission, arguably key components of nonprofit trustworthiness that many principals care about, are the lowest, suggesting that even weak standards have the potential to create useful signals for principals. Standards for financial accountability in the USA, while weak, are further developed than in the other two arenas, and many nonprofit donors care less about the efficient use of funds than about usage according to their intended purpose, for which mission accountability might be a better measure. Moreover, Brakman Reiser argues, mission accountability is the least feasible area for government regulators to address.[5]

---

[5] As Brakman Reiser notes, her contribution is focused on the US context; in other contexts where existing nonprofit regulation is weaker, the development of standards regarding financial and governance accountability may be an important first step.

Brakman Reiser's second contribution is the articulation of conditions under which club standards have the potential to create branding benefits. In particular, she notes that existing standards may not be clear or may not be well understood by nonprofits. In this case, clubs that clearly articulate and promulgate standards, even if duplicative of those that exist, may have the potential to create branding benefits. By providing enforcement mechanisms, clubs create branding benefits even when their obligations mirror the existing standards. In such cases, we do not expect clubs to impose beyond-compliance obligations on their members. Once baseline standards can be enforced, clubs can be expected to incorporate beyond-compliance standards in their program design. The empirical chapters provide some support for this idea, which implies that in the early phases of club development and in arenas where nonprofit standards are not well articulated, weaker clubs will emerge. In the case of the Council on Foundations examined by Peter Frumkin in chapter 6, there are essentially no preexisting standards or oversight systems for foundations. Consequently, the standards that result from an attempt to establish a club are quite broad and weak. In the Minnesota case discussed by Angela Bies in chapter 9, the Minnesota Council of Nonprofits developed its club standards in an environment in which a charity watchdog agency had been setting standards for decades. As per our expectation, in this case the standards developed by the Council are relatively strong.

Woods Bowman's chapter on the emergence of nonprofit clubs in the USA over the past century (chapter 3) provides further support for the idea that club design will evolve over time and that the standards that clubs develop will respond to existing standards as well as the oversight and enforcement capabilities of principals. Bowman finds that health and education accreditation programs are the most common type of nonprofit club in the USA, but that the content of standards varies significantly between these two types. Healthcare clubs focus on standards for performance and quality assurance, while education clubs tend to focus on governance and financial accountability standards. Bowman links these differences to differences in information asymmetries related to industry structure: the financial well-being of healthcare institutions is particularly reliant on marginal patient revenue and this provides market incentives for good financial management so that accreditation clubs have less need of regulating these areas. Education institutions do not rely on marginal student revenue and are often run by academics rather than trained professional managers. Under these conditions, principals have greater concerns about financial accountability and education club standards reflect these concerns. Bowman also speculates that the maintenance of trust via accreditation clubs might be a reason why for-profit actors have not been able to establish a stronger presence in these sectors.

Clubs might also emerge at the state level in the USA in response to regulatory principals in this arena. Given that state governments in the United States independently set rules for the nonprofits operating in their states, as Brakman Reiser points out, nonprofits may seek collectively to influence their regulators via state-level nonprofit associations. It is logical that in addition to lobbying about mandatory regulation, these groups might also examine the possibilities of voluntary regulation. But among state-level clubs, emergence is surprisingly low. Mary Tschirhart (chapter 4) finds only five state nonprofit associations that sponsor accountability clubs among the thirty-five state associations she identifies. Club emergence among nonprofit associations is not associated with the density of nonprofits in a state, with associational capacity, or with membership in the National Council of Nonprofit Associations, which promotes accountability among state-level associations. Tschirhart hypothesizes that the diversity of members in most associations results in conflicting preferences over the desirability of accountability clubs and over the appropriate design of these institutions. This preference heterogeneity may stem from the fact that member nonprofits are beholden to multiple principals whose preferences regarding the stringency of club standards may not cohere. This may help to explain low levels of club emergence in the US states.

Gugerty (chapter 10) examines club emergence in a very different context, sub-Saharan Africa. She finds that nonprofit clubs are relatively prevalent in the region. Among the twenty-two countries she examines, nonprofit clubs have emerged in twelve. In all of the countries in which clubs emerged, nonprofits faced the threat of additional regulation, often repressive in nature. Among the eight countries that experienced no regulatory threat, only one club emerged. Several other chapters confirm that external threats, particularly regulatory threats to autonomy from government principals, play an important role in the emergence of clubs. Young (chapter 5) and Frumkin (chapter 6) both provide evidence that proposed increases in government regulation helped spur nonprofits to develop voluntary clubs with the intent of avoiding additional regulation. The threat of government regulation may increase the perceived benefits from club participation, making more nonprofits willing to bear the costs of club compliance. Significantly, many of the clubs that emerge from this threat are sponsored by broad-based nonprofit associations, such as the Independent Sector (Young, chapter 5), the Council on Foundations (Frumkin, chapter 6), and the Kenyan National Council of NGOs (Gugerty, chapter 10). When nonprofits seek to preempt government regulation, they may naturally wish to have the broadest protective umbrella available, but self-regulatory sponsorship has important implications for club design. Self-regulation tends to foster weaker standards and monitoring as a number of chapters in Part II illustrate.

Sponsorship and club design

Part II of the volume examines the relationship between club sponsorship and club design. A common theme in this section is the tension that exists in nonprofit membership associations between membership recruitment and club sponsorship. In the introductory chapter we suggested that when club sponsors are membership associations (a self-regulatory club), sponsors may find it difficult to restrict club entry, diluting the signaling capabilities of the club. The implication is that self-regulating organizations may therefore choose a more lax enforcement regime than principals would prefer. We find substantial confirmation of these ideas among the empirical chapters.

Self-regulatory clubs where participating members are themselves club sponsors will face a higher bar to gaining credibility because of potential conflict of interest issues. Clubs sponsored by independent actors (i.e., by nonparticipants) should face fewer credibility problems. Of course this is true only if independently sponsored clubs espouse stronger standards and establish more stringent monitoring and enforcement mechanisms. On this count, the volume chapters suggest that independent sponsorship is indeed associated with stronger club design. Table 12.2 arrays the clubs discussed in the chapters by sponsorship and the expected cost of joining the club, based on its standards and enforcement. The chapters show no evidence of a high-cost self-regulatory club. Principals appear to find the Netherlands' CBF seal of approval, sponsored by an independent agency, quite credible (Bekkers, chapter 11). In a similar vein, Bowman (chapter 3) argues that relatively high levels of public confidence in health and education organizations in the USA may be related to the strong third-party accreditation mechanisms there. Contrast this with accountability clubs discussed in Part II by Young (chapter 5), Frumkin (chapter 6), and Ortmann and Svítková (chapter 7), which are self-regulatory and quite weak. These clubs are susceptible to conflict of interest since they seek both to support and to monitor members. As a result, sponsoring actors in self-regulatory clubs should face a greater challenge in assuring principals that these clubs impose significant accountability obligations on participating nonprofits and have sufficient mechanisms in place to discourage shirking.

Table 12.2 *Club sponsorship and club cost*

	Self-regulatory sponsorship	Independent sponsorship
Low-cost clubs	*Nonprofit Academic Centers Council (Young, chapter 5)* *Most US state clubs (Tschirhart, chapter 4)* *Czech Donors Forum (Ortmann and Svítková, chapter 7)* *COMPAS Qualité (Zarnegar Deloffre, chapter 8)* *Independent Sector (Young, chapter 5)* *Council on Foundations (Frumkin, chapter 6)* *National Council of NGOs, Kenya (Gugerty, chapter 10)*	
Medium-cost clubs	*Minnesota Principles and Practices (Bies, chapter 9)* *Sphere Humanitarian Principles (Zarnegar Deloffre, chapter 8)* *NGO Code, Ethiopia (Gugerty, chapter 10)*	
High-cost clubs	*QuAM, Uganda (Gugerty, chapter 10)*	*Minnesota Accountability Wizard (Bies, chapter 9)* *Joint Commission (Bowman, chapter 3)* *CBF, Netherlands (Bekkers, chapter 11)*

In the for-profit sector, trade associations are in the forefront of lobbying the government on regulatory issues as well as establishing industry-level voluntary accountability clubs. On this count, our framework suggests that accountability clubs should be the natural outgrowth of activities of state associations. However, we find that the nonprofit experience is more varied than the for-profit experience in this regard. Tschirhart's chapter (chapter 4) showed that very few state nonprofit organizations have taken up accountability issues seriously, in part owing to a weak resource base and competing priorities. Gugerty (chapter 10) finds that in Africa, nonprofit associations do appear to be the most common sponsors of nonprofit clubs. But in both cases, the accountability clubs sponsored by nonprofit associations tend to be weak.

Echoing this point, Young (chapter 5) shows how the organizational incentives faced by nonprofit membership associations can conflict with the need to send strong signals of accountability. He examines the extent to which "industry trade associations" act as club sponsors, describing the evolution of two associations: Independent Sector (IS) and the Nonprofit Academic Centers Council (NACC). Similar to Tschirhart's state-level associations (chapter 4), IS and NACC were not originally established as accountability clubs. Thus, club sponsorship is a kind of mission-stretch for them. Unlike the majority of the associations studied by Tschirhart, however, both these associations (particularly IS) have sought to enhance the visibility and public image of their members and signal their emphasis on integrity to external principals. While almost all nonprofit associations studied in this volume have embraced accountability talk, their self-regulatory accountability programs continue to have weak swords, that is, they do not yet walk the walk. Young suggests this is because fostering accountability is not the overriding objective that participating members want their associations to pursue. The lesson is that while collective organizations such as trade associations appear to be ideal sites for establishing accountability clubs, they can anticipate push-back from their members as they expand their portfolio by taking on account-ability functions, since members may have joined the association for different reasons. Accountability-enhancing initiatives pursued by trade organizations might conflict with other objectives such as inclusiveness and diversity. This will be reflected in club design: the clubs they will sponsor are likely to impose modest accountability obligations and pro-vide weak monitoring mechanisms.

This sponsorship dilemma inherent in association-sponsored clubs is not limited to the US context, as shown by Ortmann and Svítková (chap-ter 7) as well as by Gugerty in Part III (chapter 10). Ortmann and Svítková present a case study of the Czech Donors Forum (CDF), a voluntary platform for cooperation between foundations and donors which can be viewed as an umbrella organization for philanthropic activities in the Czech Republic. In a transition economy such as the Czech Republic, with low extant regulation and the potential for many opportunistic actors, there may be strong incentives to promulgate a club with strong standards and swords because potential donors are in real need of credible signals about organizational activities. But the authors find that the CDF has established a club with weak monitoring and sanctioning mecha-nisms. Drawing on economic theory, Ortmann and Svítková show how self-regulating clubs may not have incentives to develop strong swords. Clubs signal trust via program design. In some contexts, clubs that iden-tify the "bad apples" among members may gain credibility. After all, this is a job clubs are expected to perform. This may be less true in transitional economies where overall level of trust in institutions is fragile. Strong

sword clubs that uncover fraud could in fact undermine their own reputation and that of their members if the identification of members that are
bad apples creates negative externalities for members who are good
apples. In this case outside principals may tend to believe that all apples
are bad. For them, club membership no longer distinguishes good apples
from bad. This suggests that the ability of a club to signal trustworthiness
via its swords is contingent on the broader institutional context in which it
functions.

Overall, the empirical cases presented in Part II of the volume suggest
that voluntary clubs established by participating actors (i.e., self-
regulatory clubs) appear to have lower credibility owing to the conflict of
interest issue, all else being equal. Compounding their credibility
problems, they also tend to have less stringent standards and almost all
have weaker swords in relation to clubs established by independent actors.
Part III of the volume examines the relationship between sponsorship,
design, and effectiveness, and suggests some conditions under which self-
regulating clubs might develop stronger standards and swords.

Club design and effectiveness

Part III of the volume returns to the issue of how clubs sponsored by
independent agencies differ from those run by nonprofits themselves and
examines the implications of these design features for club effectiveness
and the extent to which club principals reward members for participation.
In chapter 10, Mary Kay Gugerty examines the relationship between club
design and the expected effectiveness of nonprofit clubs in Africa. Her
chapter confirms the findings from other chapters that association clubs
that include all association members face large hurdles in developing
credible signals for principals, whether these principals are donors or
governments. When clubs have inclusive membership (as they often do
when threatened by additional regulation), the signaling power of club
membership is diluted, meaning that principals have no mechanism for
distinguishing adulterated from nonadulterated organizations.

The weakness of association-sponsored clubs, however, may stimulate
the emergence of parallel clubs with stronger signaling properties.
Gugerty finds that voluntary clubs in Africa tend to be stronger if they
emerge from previous efforts. In this case path dependency seeks to
enhance club quality instead of constraining it. Newer clubs in Africa
seek to establish detailed standards for participation and stronger certification mechanisms that can create a credible reputational signal. For
example, the Quality Assurance Mechanism (QuAM) under development in Uganda is sponsored by the two main NGO associations, which

realized that their existing passive codes of conduct were not sufficiently credible. Gugerty discusses two factors that motivated this club. First, the Ugandan government proposed quite restrictive NGO legislation which clearly showed that existing efforts at self-regulation were not perceived as credible by the government. Second, a number of high-profile scandals involving bogus NGOs gave legitimate organizations a strong incentive to develop a credible signaling mechanism. Thus voluntary clubs in Africa are emerging on the foundations of broad-based but weak association-sponsored clubs.

The development of the QuAM in an environment characterized by relatively weak institutionalization of nonprofit standards suggests that the development of strong standards in a self-regulatory club is not an impossible hurdle. Like Gugerty, Angela Bies (chapter 9) finds two forms of voluntary club that exist in a single context, the state of Minnesota. Unlike in the African cases, however, the first standard-setting program to emerge in Minnesota was a relatively strong donor-sponsored rating system. A statewide nonprofit association was subsequently established and eventually promulgated its own voluntary standards, partially in response to criticisms of the existing accountability regime. As the voluntary program grew, however, it bumped up against the accountability efforts of the charity rating program. As a result of the number of nonprofit professionals active in both organizations, however, a potential conflict resulted instead in a cooperative effort to divide up accountability efforts in the state. The nonprofit association continued with the development of strong voluntary standards (without swords) while the charity review transitioned from a rating system to an accountability club in which participation was voluntary. It remains to be seen whether this division of labor is an effective way to signal nonprofit accountability.

So far we have suggested that clubs emerge to signal nonprofit trustworthiness to principals. But clubs may evolve for additional reasons. While such clubs might be outlier cases, we need to examine such outliers to extend our understanding of nonprofit accountability. Maryam Zarnegar Deloffre (chapter 8) shows how the participation of humanitarian nonprofits in post-disaster evaluations of relief efforts influenced their definition of accountability and shaped the emergence of humanitarian accountability clubs. While important nonprofit principals, including the public, played a central role in calling for increased accountability, Deloffre argues that variation in humanitarian agencies' interpretation of their mission played the strongest role in shaping the clubs that emerged. Her chapter suggests that in nonprofit industries dominated by a relatively small number of large agencies, nonprofit clubs can play an important role in defining the parameters of accountability. In the case of the humanitarian sector, differing interpretations of the "humanitarian imperative" led groups of nonprofits to establish competing clubs based on differing ideas about the obligations inherent in humanitarian assistance.

In the process of shaping the behaviors of participating nonprofits, clubs might also influence the behavior of principals who are supposed to be receiving the club signal. René Bekkers' chapter on the accountability program of the Netherlands Central Bureau of Fundraising (CBF) provides some of the first systematic evidence available that club participation can create branding benefits for nonprofits and that principals are willing to reward club members for participation. In addition, he finds that learning about the CBF program changes the perceptions and behavior of donors. The CBF is a club with stringent standards and strong monitoring and enforcement that issues a "seal of approval" to those organizations that meet its standards. Bekkers finds that individuals in the Netherlands who know or learn about the CBF program increase their levels of donations to nonprofit organizations, in contrast to those who do not know about the club. His data also suggest that learning about the CBF program has positive effects on donors' confidence and trust in nonprofits more generally. This translates into club benefits for participants. Club participation results in higher fundraising income for nonprofits who participate. In combination these two results suggest that principals (donors) perceive CBF membership as a credible signal that the participating nonprofits are serious about dealing with agency issues. Consequently, club membership is associated with increases in fundraising income of nonprofit organizations. Club signals in the CBF case may be particularly strong because CBF has no competitors; it is the only accountability club active in the Netherlands and this may improve donors' ability to identify and make use of the signal it sends.

Future work

In addition to the questions about emergence, design, and effectiveness we pose in the introduction, the empirical chapters present a number of additional findings that suggest important areas for future research. Several chapters underscore that the development of voluntary clubs in the nonprofit sector should be viewed in historical and political context. Just as the fields of medicine and health developed licensing schemes as part of the professionalization of the field, the nonprofit sector in many settings may be at a stage in the development of the field in which the current debate and negotiation over standards will provide the basis for future club development. The chapters by Tschirhart, Young, Frumkin, and Bies all illustrate the ways in which nonprofit associations are working to define appropriate standards for the field. The parallels with other fields such as medicine or law, however, also suggest a cautionary note – the history of the professions suggests that accountability clubs can take on cartel-like behaviors, seeking deliberately to exclude some agencies to preserve the advantages of others. The Czech Donors Forum discussed by Ortmann and Svítková (chapter 7) appears to exhibit these tendencies.

The impact of the political and regulatory context on club emergence and development should also be more systematically explored. Bekkers (chapter 11) describes the relatively strong nonprofit club that has emerged in the Netherlands in the context of scant government regulation and strong public support for a private club: 40 percent of CBF revenue comes from public subsidies. Contrast these to the low levels of both public and private understanding and support for the nonprofit sector as described by Ortmann and Svítková in chapter 7 and the low level of financing available for nonprofit associations in Africa, as described by Gugerty in chapter 10.

Will public scandals encourage the establishment of clubs with stringent standards? Bekkers (chapter 11) provides strong evidence that the donations are quite sensitive to public scandal and that the negative reputational effects tend to have important externalities: he finds that donations to all CBF members are hurt by high-profile scandals among members. His findings show that incentives for disclosure of wrongdoing by club sponsors are indeed mixed. But his chapter also demonstrates how the revelation of high salaries for nonprofit executives spurred the development of new club standards around executive pay. Over the longer term, research on clubs should seek to examine the impact of revelation of potential misconduct on public perceptions of the club brand. Does revelation increase club credibility or lower public confidence in charities?

The chapters in this volume suggest that impending legislation or regulation has an important effect in encouraging the development of clubs. Does impending regulation have the same effect as scandals in spurring more stringent standards or enforcement? And how might this vary by sector? For example, this argument may not transfer as easily to foundations and grantmakers who have to satisfy the accountability demands of their own principals and enablers. Young (chapter 5) shows how the Independent Sector created its principles for nonprofits in response to increasing threats of additional government regulation. Gugerty (chapter 10) suggests that the threat of regulation is the major initial impetus to club formation in Africa. Frumkin (chapter 6) finds similar pressures in the foundation field, but notes that in spite of public outcry and Congressional hearings on foundation accountability, foundations do not perceive any compelling pressure to establish strong accountability clubs which can provide assurance to their various principals about their transparent and ethical grantmaking processes. While there have been moves toward self-regulation among foundation associations, these have been modest, as Frumkin traces through the evolution of self-regulation in the philanthropy sector. In response to the Tax Reform Act of 1969 (TRA 1969), the Council on Foundations led a national effort to improve public understanding of the work of foundations, to encourage professional management of these institutions, to expand evaluation practices, to ameliorate relations with recipient organizations, and to redefine private foundations as "public trusts" to be governed for public purposes. Subsequently, the Council promulgated a code of conduct, and similar to many for-profit trade associations, made acceptance of the code a condition of membership in the association. In the most recent phase of scrutiny, the impetus for renewed self-regulation came again from governmental regulations. While Sarbanes–Oxley was not intended to apply directly to foundations, its passage led some nonprofits and large foundations to debate whether they should adopt similar rules voluntarily to bolster public confidence in their financial integrity. In spite of Congressional hearings and scrutiny, however, not much progress has been made. Frumkin suggests that this is because foundations do not perceive any credible threat of new regulation. Consequently, they do not have compelling incentives to change their behavior in light of any outside standard or pressure. Most importantly, there is no vocal and well-resourced pressure group that is seeking to persuade foundations to adopt performance standards to which they can be held accountable. Thus, scandals alone will not create incentives for change; there need to be well-resourced and politically powerful actors who can convince nonprofits or foundations that they face a credible threat of intrusive governmental regulations unless they voluntarily adopt credible accountability systems.

The empirical chapters also suggest that variation in the identity, number, and nature of club principals plays an important role in club emergence and design that merits additional elaboration. Bowman (chapter 3) shows how accreditation standards in health have increased in stringency over time in response to the needs of a dominant principal, in this case the US federal government. The government has a strong public interest in having a reliable health accreditation mechanism and is willing and able to reward club participation with significant resources. Bowman's chapter supports the notion that club design may be more responsive to principals' demands when these demands come from a single principal. When accreditation is tied to large amounts of funding from this principal, nonprofits appear willing to participate in clubs even with relatively strong standards and enforcement.

The emergence of strong clubs may be further facilitated when those clubs are developed within a single sector or to address accountability dilemmas important to a specific set of principals. CBF, the accreditation club in the Netherlands studied by Bekkers in chapter 11, was developed to create standards for fundraising nonprofits, and donors constitute the main principal for this club. As Bekkers argues, CBF has developed a relatively strong set of standards accompanied by strong swords. Consequently, donors recognize the accreditation seal and are willing to reward nonprofits for having it. The presence of donors as key principals also motivates the relatively strong club developed by the Minnesota Charities Review Council, discussed by Bies in chapter 9. Yet, domination of accountability demands by a single principal by itself may not lead to the emergence of strong clubs. Both the Council on Foundations (Frumkin, chapter 6) and the Independent Sector (Young, chapter 5) face the threat of regulation from a dominant principal (the US government). Yet both have developed relatively weak clubs. Similarly, most clubs that emerge in Africa in response to regulatory threats are quite weak (Gugerty, chapter 10). This suggests that the stick of regulation may have different effects on club formation and design than the carrot of increased revenue generation from donations.

This volume also suggests that credibility challenges are likely to vary across nonprofits. Bekkers (chapter 11) found that the benefits of accreditation are smaller for international fundraising organizations, although the trust and adulteration problems are likely to be more pronounced for them. Arguably, the signal and assurance donors need from domestic organizations might be different from those expected from international organizations. More broadly, future work should investigate the extent to which Bekkers' findings are generalizable. Arguably, when principals have more difficulty evaluating the working and efficacy of nonprofits, they are likely to be more skeptical about nonprofit behavior. If so, nonprofits that operate in distant countries or work for less tangible causes like the environment and human rights will face higher levels of credibility challenges. Accordingly, a higher proportion of them can be expected to join accountability clubs. Further, clubs that emerge in these sectors are likely to impose higher levels of obligations and disclosure requirements on their members. However, nonprofits working overseas may face more resource constraints than nonprofits working in developed countries where key foundations are located. They may therefore have fewer resources to devote to establishing formal accountability systems. In this case the appropriate trade-off between cost effectiveness and club stringency is less clear. Future research should systematically examine these issues by engaging in comparative studies of clubs across issues sectors and continents, as well as by studying the propensities of nonprofits working in different contexts to join such clubs.

Future work should also examine other explanations as to why accountability clubs emerge. Our theoretical framework suggests that these voluntary clubs develop in response to the widespread perceptions of agency conflict and are tools employed by nonprofits to signal their accountability commitments to principals. But Zarnegar Deloffre's chapter on humanitarian agencies (chapter 8) argues that humanitarian NGOs created accountability clubs primarily because they believed they failed to meet their moral duty in the humanitarian response to Rwanda, not in response to agency dilemmas. While it is difficult to separate moral motivations clearly from instrumental ones, many scholars have suggested that some actors respond to the norms of appropriateness, rather than instrumentality (Keck and Sikkink, 1998; March and Olsen, 1984). Future research should carefully examine both the moral and instrumental bases for the emergence and sustenance of accountability clubs, as well as which category of nonprofits might be influenced more by one type of persuasion.

Overall, the theoretical framework and empirical chapters in this volume suggest that nonprofit accountability clubs will play an increasingly important role in nonprofit governance. Our volume has demonstrated the prevalence of these clubs and the important role they have played in mitigating information asymmetries and setting standards for nonprofit behavior. Understanding how and whether these clubs improve nonprofit governance and effectiveness is an important area for continued research. In many developing and transition economies, governments lack the capacity to engage in systematic oversight of the sector, yet significant portions of the public rely on nonprofits for the provision of important public services. This is true even in industrialized countries where the complexity of public–private–nonprofit interactions around public policy and service delivery continues to deepen. The chapters presented here suggest that there are at least two areas of great challenge for nonprofit clubs if they are to play a role in improving nonprofit governance and performance. The first is to develop a set of interorganizational standards for performance that are both reasonable and rigorous. The second is to develop monitoring and reporting systems that are effective enough to shape nonprofit behavior.

REFERENCES

Ben-Ner, A. and B. Gui. 2003. The Theory of Nonprofit Organizations Revisited. In H. Anheier and A. Ben-Ner, eds. *The Study of Nonprofit Enterprise: Theories and Approaches.* New York: Kluwer, pp. 3–26.

Ebrahim, A. 2005. Accountability Myopia: Losing Sight of Organizational Learning. *Nonprofit and Voluntary Sector Quarterly* 34(1): 56–87.

Glaeser, E. and A. Schleifer. 2001. Not-for-profit Entrepreneurs. *Journal of Public Economics* 81: 99–115.

Gugerty, Mary Kay, 2009. Signaling Virtue: Voluntary Accountability Programs among Nonprofit Organizations. *Policy Sciences* 42: 243–273.

Hansmann, H. 1980. The Role of Non-Profit Enterprise. *Yale Law Journal* 89(3): 835–901.

　2003. The Role of Trust in Nonprofit Enterprise. In Helmut Anheier and Avner Ben-Ner, eds. *The Study of Nonprofit Enterprise.* New York: Kluwer, pp. 115–120.

Keck, M. and K. Sikkink. 1998. *Activists beyond Borders: Advocacy Networks in International Politics.* Ithaca: Cornell University Press.

March, J. and J. Olsen. 1984. The New Institutionalism: Organizational Factors in Political Life. *American Political Science Review* 78: 734–749.

Mauser, E. 1993. Is Organizational Form Important to Consumers and Managers? An Application to the Daycare Industry. Ph.D. dissertation, Department of Economics, University of Washington.

Meyer, J., J. Boli, G. Thomas, and F. Ramirez. 1997. World Society and the Nation-State. *American Journal of Sociology* 103(1): 144–181.

Ortmann, A. and M. Schlesinger. 1997. Trust, Repute and the Role of Nonprofit Enterprise. *Voluntas* 8(2): 97–199.

Ortmann, Andreas and Mark Schlesinger. 2003. Trust, Repute and the Role of Nonprofit Enterprise. In Helmut Anheier and Avner Ben-Ner, eds. *The Study of Nonprofit Enterprise: Theories and Approaches.* New York: Kluwer.

Prakash, A. and M. Potoski. 2006. *The Voluntary Environmentalists.* Cambridge University Press.

Putnam, R., with R. Leonardi and R. Nannetti. 1993. *Making Democracy Work: Civic Traditions in Modern Italy.* Princeton University Press.

Schlesinger, M. and B. Gray. 2006. Nonprofit Organizations and Health Care. In W. W. Powell and R. Steinberg, eds. *The Nonprofit Sector: A Research Handbook.* New Haven, CT: Yale University Press, pp. 378–414.

Steinberg, R. and B. Gray. 1993. The Role of Nonprofit Enterprise in 1993: Hansmann Revisited. *Nonprofit and Voluntary Sector Quarterly* 22(4): 297–316.

Weisbrod, B. 1991. *The Nonprofit Economy.* Cambridge, MA: Harvard University Press.

Index